Ch. 11

285-288

255-257

"As one of those invited to present Matthew Fox at his receivement into the Episcopal priesthood at Grace Cathedral, I remember him standing humbly at the altar dressed in his plain white surplice. He wore a simple white rope girdle around his slender waist. Matthew's white hair and white skin made him seem just what he is, a man of more worlds than one. When the Bishop asked who brought this priest to the altar to be received, we replied according to the prewritten liturgy, but in my heart I felt these words: 'We present for your new embrace Dear God, one of your own special candles that a handful of powerful men has tried to extinguish. Here before you now is a man who refused to die, a man rising from the ashes, your beloved Matthew Timothy Fox.'"

CLARISSA PINKOLA ESTÉS, Ph.D., author of *Women Who Run with the Wolves,* and director of La Sociedad de Nuestra Señora Guadalupe

"There is a power in Matt Fox, something like primordial religion erupting within an organized, controlled, doctrinally defined church establishment trying to continue its course in a thoroughly civilized disciplined manner. He has raised religious issues at a level that neither ecclesiastical officials nor theologians nor moralists care to deal with. . . . His life and his writings are filled with learning and laughter, with loyalty and dissent, rationality and artistic sensitivity. . . . Those who judge him might also learn from him."

THOMAS BERRY, author of *The Dream of the Earth*

"'Hearing Matt Fox talk, I feel less lonely in the universe,' said a street priest fifteen years ago. We should *all* feel less lonely now with this exhilarating, deeply companionable book in our hands. The unfolding story of this irrepressible spiritual revolutionary enlivens the mind and emboldens the heart— 'must' reading for anyone interested in courage, creativity, and the future of religion."

JOANNA MACY, author of *World as Lover, World as Self*

CONFESSIONS

ALSO BY MATTHEW FOX

The Reinvention of Work:
 A New Vision of Livelihood for Our Time
Wrestling with the Prophets:
 Essays on Creation Spirituality and Everyday Life
Sheer Joy:
 Conversations with Thomas Aquinas on Creation Spirituality
Creation Spirituality:
 Liberating Gifts for the Peoples of the Earth
The Coming of the Cosmic Christ:
 The Healing of Mother Earth and the Birth of a Global
 Renaissance
Original Blessing:
 A Primer in Creation Spirituality
Illuminations of Hildegard of Bingen
Hildegard of Bingen's Book of Divine Works, with Letters and
 Songs (editor)
Meditations with Meister Eckhart
In the Beginning There Was Joy (a book for children)
Passion for Creation: Meister Eckhart's Creation Spirituality
Breakthrough:
 Meister Eckhart's Creation Spirituality in New Translation
A Spirituality Named Compassion (and the Healing of the
 Global Village, Humpty Dumpty and Us)
Western Spirituality:
 Historical Roots, Ecumenical Routes (editor)
Whee! We, wee All the Way Home:
 A Guide to Sensual, Prophetic Spirituality
On Becoming a Musical, Mystical Bear:
 Spirituality American Style
Manifesto for a Global Civilization (with Brian Swimme)
Religion USA:
 An Inquiry into Religion and Culture by Way of Time
 Magazine

CONFESSIONS

The Making of a Postdenominational Priest

M A T T H E W   F O X

HarperSanFrancisco
An Imprint of HarperCollins*Publishers*

Permissions begin on page 301 and constitute a con-
tinuation of this copyright page.

HarperSanFrancisco and the author, in association
with the Basic Foundation, a not-for-profit organization whose primary mission is reforestation, will
facilitate the planting of two trees for every one tree
used in the manufacture of this book.

A TREE CLAUSE BOOK

FIRST EDITION

Library of Congress Cataloging-in-Publication Data
Fox, Matthew
Confessions: The Making of a Postdenominational
Priest / Matthew Fox. — 1st ed.
p. cm.
ISBN 0–06–062865–0 (cloth)
ISBN 0–06–062965–7 (pbk.)
1. Fox, Matthew. 2. Spirituality. 3. Creation
Spirituality. 4. Biography. 5. Catholic Church—
United States—Clergy—Biography. I. Title.
BX5995.F65A3   1996
283'.092—dc20   95-38159
[B]   CIP

96 97 98 99 00 ❖ RRD/H 10 9 8 7 6 5 4 3 2 1

CONTENTS

Acknowledgments ix

Introduction: A Testimony 1

1. Becoming an Anglican:
   A Postdenominational Moment—January 1994 5

PART ONE

BEGINNINGS

2. The Dominicans: *The Training Years—1958–1967* 17
3. Family Influences: *Growing Up in the Fifties* 43
4. The Paris Years: *A Culture in Revolution—1967–1970* 61

PART TWO

TEACHING AND WRITING

5. The 1970s: *Early Teaching and Writing* 89
6. ICCS: *Training of Mystics and Prophets
   (with Assistance from Eckhart and Hildegard)—1977–1983* 113
7. The California Experience—*1983–1995* 133

PART THREE

CONFLICTS

8. "Taking on the Vatican Is Like Standing in Front of a Train" 163
9. A Year of Silence—*1989–1990* 179
10. Expulsion—*1993* 207

PART FOUR

QUESTIONS FOR OUR RELIGIOUS FUTURE

11. The End of the Roman Catholic Era? 227
12. A Postdenominational Priest Standing Outside the Rusty Gate 245
13. What Will Belief and Holiness Mean in a Postmodern Era? 271

Notes 291

To my brothers and sisters, Tom, Nat, Terry, Roberta, Michael, and Tricia, in gratitude for their solidarity and groundedness through many years of surprises

And to my parents, Beatrice and George Fox, for their many gifts of life

ACKNOWLEDGMENTS

How does one acknowledge those, living and dead, friend and enemy, who form one and help to delineate one? Acknowledgments for the stories in this book extend to all those mentioned herein and many not mentioned because of lack of space. My dedication of this book to family members is key, though I must include my aunts and uncles too, especially Doris and George Carland and Helen and Harry Bryans, and my grandparents. My many mentors mentioned and not mentioned in the text. Students, especially though not exclusively those at ICCS. Fellow faculty members, administrators where I have taught, monks, sisters, fellow activists. A special kudo to Marlene Denardo, Robert Rice and M. C. Richards, Adrianna Diaz and Jeremy Taylor, all of the ICCS faculty. All the artists and poets who have whetted my soul. And to Tom Grady of HarperSanFrancisco, who first proposed the idea of this book, and to Caroline Pincus with Sue White and Priscilla Stuckey, my editors. And to Dominican brothers and sisters in Holland who supported me and to those individual Dominicans in America who know who they are and who were not so threatened by Rome's attacks as to give up altogether on our solidarity, thank you! To my helpers Peter Farriday and Tom Barnes and Cliff Atkinson. To my Anglican brothers and sisters. And to Ben.

INTRODUCTION:
A Testimony

I was born on the winter solstice, 1940, at St. Mary's Hospital in Madison, Wisconsin. I am completing this book in Oakland, California, on the winter solstice, 1995. In between, over these fifty-five years that constitute my story, some telling events have occurred culturally, religiously, perhaps even spiritually. I write this book as a witness to those events—not under any pretext of being an impartial witness, just a witness with my own story and its perspective to share. Elie Wiesel has said that "Whoever survives a test, whatever it may be, must tell the story." It is under that rubric that I am telling my story, for the test I have survived may assist others today who find themselves either passing from religion to spirituality or trying to integrate spirituality back into religion.

I call this book a "confessions" in light of the original meaning of that word—"to bear witness," or as Jesuit theologian Karl Rahner put it, "the declaration of personal decisions and circumstances within the confines of a community."[1] I will try to tell my story *as witness* to the amazing events of my generation along with my personal decisions and circumstances vis-à-vis various communities of which I have been a part and as I experienced these events in society, in religion and church, and in my soul. Sixteen centuries ago, another theologian wrote a book also called *Confessions*. St. Augustine of Hippo was a psychological genius but a philosopher of dualism and a theologian of original sin. He is not my favorite theologian. I doubt that his and my book have an awful lot in common. For one thing, he was writing in the fourth century at a moment when Christianity was inheriting an empire, and I am writing at the end of the twentieth century at a time when we need to let go of empires. But maybe, for the discerning reader, Augustine and I do have something in common. At least a willingness to tell our stories. And to try to look for the role of spirit therein.

Like Henry Adams's autobiography, this book could have been called *The Education of Matthew Fox,* were that title not so prosaic and the subject so unimportant. But my own education has, I suspect, paralleled that of many of my contemporaries as we moved from *The Ed Sullivan Show* and Bishop Sheen to Elvis Presley and the Beatles, to JFK and Martin Luther King, Jr., to Vietnam and liberation theology and Watergate, and from Pope John XXIII and the Second Vatican Council to Pope John Paul II and his Opus Dei. In short, from the 1950s to the 1990s. For this reason I tell it.

I have never written anything like an autobiography before. I am shy about doing so. I made an entry in my journal a year and a half ago that I reproduce here.

August 3, 1993
An autobiography?
Why would anyone as shy and introverted as I am and as ordinary write an autobiography? Maybe because my story—and we all have a story—has become public in part and it might help people to hear the whole story insofar as I can tell it. Also, because the Spirit has worked in my life—as it works in everyone's life—but many people need others' stories to realize spirit in their own. Maybe I tell it too because my generation was bold enough to question many things and to seek spirituality over religion. We haven't succeeded in overthrowing the old order yet, and maybe there are some meanings to be found in my story about coming of age spiritually in the latter half of the twentieth century.

People I respect have encouraged me to do this book. My friend Joanna Macy, who is also writing an autobiography, tells me that at first she was intimidated: Who wants to hear about my story? Why am I doing this?—such questions went through her mind as through mine. But her answer is simple: each of us has only one story. It's our life story. If we don't tell it, maybe someone will miss something that might have assisted theirs. The whole attitude of an autobiography, Joanna insists, ought to be gratitude. I agree wholeheartedly. Thomas Aquinas says that "gratitude tries to return more than has been received."[2] I have received many gifts and graces in my lifetime, and I hope I have been able to offer something in return. I suspect this is what has driven me to be a writer. And, in this case, a writer of my story insofar as I see it at this time.

Mary Catherine Bateson says that what interested her the most in writing her book on five extraordinary women's lives "are the echoes from one life to another, the recurrent common themes."[3] Recurrent themes occur in my story too, and I trust that at least some are common to others, echoing as they do our shared experience of living through the tumult of the past fifty years and trying to fashion some kind of living wisdom, some kind of spirituality from those experiences.

I was asked to write an "intellectual autobiography." While my life and my passion have surely been about ideas—and so has the trouble I've gotten into—nevertheless I find that phrase a bit pretentious, so I prefer the term *cultural autobiography*. To me this means that all ideas are culturally based and that in writing my story, I am contextualizing it in the larger story of our cultural coming of age, with its achievements and mistakes along the way.

Joseph Campbell used to say that "None of us has lived the life we intended." This is surely the case with me. Left to my own imagination, I could never have composed a scenario that was anywhere as interesting as my life has been: starting out as an eager altar boy, a good Boy Scout, a relatively docile Dominican brother and priest, receiving an advanced degree in spirituality, teaching bishops and many others around the world about our Western spiritual tradition, and then ending up being expelled from the Dominican order.

A unique dimension to this book for introverted me is my sharing of dreams and journals and even my vision quest. I guess, as so often proves to be the case, I am being driven to practice what I preach, and having recently "preached" in my book on *The Reinvention of Work* of the need to pay more attention to our *inner work,* I am using this autobiography to share some of my inner life, its sources, its struggles, and its mystery. One of the great mysteries I hold dear is found in the questions, Where do our dreams, our visions, come from? Where does our creativity come from? All I know for sure is that I could not live without these mysterious breakthroughs and that I cannot take full responsibility for any of them. They come from a source more interesting than me. Let me give one example. After a recent lecture I gave in Hawaii, a young man from Boston approached me. He said that when he was diagnosed with AIDS I came to him in a dream wearing a white coat like a doctor and I said, "PWA does not mean People with AIDS. It means People Wanting Attention." He said that since that dream he is taking much better care of himself (including moving to Hawaii), and he is giving himself the emotional and spiritual attention he needs, and feeling stronger and fuller as a result. Yes, the universe is a very interesting place. And very connected.

A life is a complex and many-sided jewel, and it is a big thing, especially if lived on several continents as mine has been. Continents occupy each of our souls, of course, so I am speaking of both geographic and psychic continents. Thus many people and relationships and gifts and books and thinkers go unmentioned in this book—not from lack of gratitude but from lack of room. I was asked to keep it short—as short as a telling of fifty-some years of living will allow—sort of a "fractal autobiography." I've tried my best to do so.

1

Becoming an Anglican:
A Postdenominational Moment—
January 1994

It is January 8, 1994. I have just been received into the Episcopal church by Bishop Swing, bishop of California, in a ceremony in the side chapel of Grace Cathedral. It was a quiet ceremony on a rainy Saturday morning. I have walked down Taylor Street to a coffee shop where I pull out two sheets of paper—want ads photocopied from the *San Francisco Chronicle*. I scribble my thoughts on the back of them:

January 8
Mass with the bishop, my "reception-Confirmation." Two other persons at the mass—a middle-aged man who showed me around the cathedral, and a young man. I am moved to tears when the bishop asks me, "Are you here alone? Did you bring anyone with you?" Yes, I am alone. Alone again. I think during the mass of my thousands of hours of prayer with Dominican brothers; of the day of my ordination when I was moved so deeply by the Litany of Saints and former priests; of the advice from Abbot Winandy in my hermitage experience thirty years ago, "Someday you will be a hermit in a large city." So many years of being a hermit in so many large cities. They're playing Elvis—"I'm All Shook Up"—in the diner where I wait for my hot cocoa to be served. Is this the fifties or what? A '59 Edsel is sitting in this diner in downtown San Francisco with me, ten feet away—what is the universe telling me? I'm back in the fifties and starting my religious journey all over again. The fact is, as surprised as I am by my own story, I wouldn't change any of it, as far as I can tell.

My "Starting Over Day"—a "new Confirmation"; a "new" church tradition; a return to high school days and my passion to become a Dominican. Now I have a new passion: to be instrumental in seeing the young invigorate our Western liturgy—not for their generation alone but for the third millennium of Christianity. If I can play my modest role, I will. Confirmation Sacrament is after all our "rite of passage," our archetype to name the "spiritual warrior." Hopefully I received some "warrior grace" today to assist my rite of passage, and that of the church and our liturgy itself, to a new level of being in the world.

After the mass the bishop talks of the "revolution" we are going to pull off and of his Celtic roots and his many trips to Iona. Good. The die is cast. Something is afoot.

I also remember Thomas Merton's reception into the Catholic church in New York City and I wonder if it was as quiet as this.

"Epiphany" seems like the perfect day to be welcomed under these circumstances—to make more manifest the rich spiritual treasures of our Western spiritual tradition—our liturgy, our mystics, and our prophets.

Although two of my peers and closest advisers resisted my becoming Anglican, a letter from a twenty-seven-year-old artist figured large in supporting my decision. Mark Roth is a painter and writer who lives in the inner city of San Francisco. His family is longtime Roman Catholic, but his letter speaks to my own intuition that the generation in their twenties today are not concerned about denominations. They are postdenominational. Who can show me a twenty-year-old who is in touch with today's realities of ecological crisis, unemployment, addictions and who knows or cares about the differences between denominations?

In my journal I wrote of the growing commitment I feel toward youth.

December 5, 1993
At this time in my life, I have narrowed my vocation question to one: How can I serve the younger generation and those young ones to come, given my "powers," whatever they be?

I guess this is the question of an elder who is to undergo his fifty-third birthday this month.

A few days after my reception I invite Mark to dinner at his favorite Vietnamese restaurant downtown. The total bill for two is less than eight dollars. I ask him his goal in life. "To make revelry hip," he replies. It sounds good to me, so when I return home I look up *revelry* in the dictionary. It means to "make merry," from the French *réveiller*, to "wake up." *Revelation* comes from the same root word. This is what I call (and our mystical tradition calls) the *Via Positiva*. Mark gets it. Maybe his whole generation will get it. It would be a different world, a different church, if we all got it: if we all committed ourselves to making revelry hip. On the way back from the restaurant,

Mark shows me the place where a crazy street lady bashed him in the head with a board with a nail in it; the nail went fully into his skull; he bled like a bull as they took him to the emergency room. He likes the neighborhood and intends to stay there. I like the neighborhood too (though I have no intention of moving into it). His room, above a jewelry store, is clean and compact, with a bed in a loft and just enough room for him to paint the large canvases that lean against one wall. His paintings move me deeply. He is giving birth to his own style of color and story.

Herb Caen, the popular columnist for the *San Francisco Chronicle*, leads his column on January 9 with a statement about my becoming an Episcopalian at a ceremony on January 8. I am startled. Where did he get this news? Only two persons were present besides the bishop and two assisting priests. Then, too, Caen's brief comments were not accurate. He said that I "left the Catholic church," but I do not see it that way. The Roman Catholic church was never mentioned once in the ceremony; instead I was asked to recite the Nicene Creed—the creed I've been reciting since I was three years old. For years I have been saying that the lines "I believe in the one, holy, *catholic,* and apostolic church" do not mention the *Roman* church—they are a challenge to all churches to become more fully one, holy, catholic, and apostolic. I believe that the Anglican Episcopal church at this time in history is closer to being catholic than the Roman church is—it is catholic enough to include women in its leadership roles, for example.

Why Did I Become an Episcopal Priest?

If I "left" Roman Catholicism for the Anglican Episcopal tradition, it is not really a leave-taking but an embracing of a larger segment of the catholic tradition. And, given the realities of our time vis-à-vis Roman Catholicism, it is about including some Anglo-Saxon (and Celtic) *common sense* in twenty-first-century Catholicism. I am speaking, of course, about common sense regarding married *and* unmarried clergy; regarding ordaining women; regarding church structures that include genuine voice and participation of the laity as well as clergy (hints of democracy that so unnerve Rome); regarding birth control at a time when the human population explosion is threatening all life systems on this planet; regarding openly discussing homosexual clergy instead of pretending that a significant contribution to the spirituality of the greater community has not always been a gift of the clergy who are homosexual; regarding not granting to Rome itself too much power in church appointments, lawmaking, and so forth. The need to diffuse ecclesial power is paramount if we are to begin to imitate the early church at all and if we are to allow the Spirit to "blow where it will" from base groups in the diverse and wondersome cultures where authentic faith springs up and yearns to spring up. Also, there is common sense in the Anglican communion wherein liturgical rites are presented—*some* as prescribed in a book *but others as being a blank page whose forms need to come to birth in our time.* I have met bishops of the Anglican tradition who are truly leaders, who do not just say what some authority above them dictates as the appropriate thing but who actually have independent consciences and thoughts of their own; who write books and read them too.

Spirituality is required to wake people up and empower them to face the deep crises that earth is undergoing today, and the poor who constitute so much of humanity, and the young who are in despair, and the indigenous people who are being wiped out. At the same time, solidarity and community support are necessary to carry on the creative work that is needed, to critique one another gracefully, and to welcome one another. Hopefully, the Episcopal church will offer me some solidarity at this time. I believe the Holy Spirit is calling us to simplify our spiritual heritage as we move, more lightly, into the third millennium. As we move beyond denominational*ism* to a deep ecumenism. And as we listen to the Spirit working through young people, as it so often does.

Experiencing a Renewal of Western Worship in Northern England

In August 1993 our organization, Friends of Creation Spirituality, put on a five-day workshop in creation spirituality at Seattle, Washington. After my opening lecture I met four young persons who had flown to the workshop from Sheffield, England. They were from the rave subculture of England and informed me that they were busy re-creating the form of the Western mass in a community of three hundred people who called themselves the Nine O'clock Service (NOS). On the airplane returning to California, I read the literature that they had thrust into my hands and was astounded. Here was a committed, dedicated group of young people reinventing the form for the Western liturgy—exactly what I had called for in my *Coming of the Cosmic Christ* book five years earlier. I remembered their telling me that my theology had assisted them in their goals. I was particularly struck by one sentence in their literature: "This is not worship *for* young people; it is worship *by* young people." Yes, that would make all the difference, I surmised. How amazing that four young Britishers would fly all the way to Seattle to attend a five-day program in creation spirituality. They must be awfully hungry for spirituality. A very good sign.

The synchronicity of these NOS representatives approaching me in Seattle in August 1993 was stunning. The month before, I had submitted the final version of my manuscript on reinventing work to the publisher, and the last chapter of the book was titled "Ritual: Where the Great Work of the Universe and the Work of the People Come Together." In this chapter I discuss the need to reinvent work by rediscovering the power of ritual to reenchant our lives. And now this unusual group of young people, dedicated to exactly these tasks, was at my doorstep. Another synchronicity was that I discovered this community just five months after being expelled from my *religious* order, which was begun by St. Dominic in the thirteenth century because preaching was on the wane everywhere in the culture. It was dedicated to making preaching happen again, thus its name "Order of Preachers" or O.P. for short. Was this new order I was encountering a twenty-first-century version of the one I had known personally? This new one being dedicated to "ritual making" because in our time ritual is so on the wane?

A little over two months later, I made a pilgrimage to the north of Sheffield, England. Boarding the plane I told a friend, "If this mass is half as good as I think it will be, I want to spend the rest of my life getting it going in every city in the United States." The fact is, the mass was *twice* as good as I thought it would be!

About five hundred people attend the services and their average age is twenty-seven. One has to understand what a wonder it is that five hundred people of this age attend mass in the rotunda of Pond's Forge in Sheffield, England. I doubt whether in the whole United Kingdom there are five hundred people in their twenties attending mass on a Sunday.

The Planetary Mass I experienced at NOS went something like this: We enter a round, darkened room where there are forty-two television sets and twelve large video screens and projections around the walls—projections of dancing DNA, dancing planets and galaxies and atoms. The altar is a large round table that, being white, is also a projection screen. Throughout the service, slides are projected over it that vary in color and geometric form. Attached to the round or sun altar is an eclipsed-moon altar, thus bringing the balance of male and female archetypes into the center of the sacred space. The many pillars in the room remind one of ancient Stonehenge and serve as useful spots to place television sets and monitors and to project still more images.

I had two insights while worshiping at the NOS mass. The first was that this was a very friendly place for a generation raised on television and images. Projected on the screens and televisions are videos that the community has created during the week, as well as live images of events happening during the service. For example, the preacher is filmed live and thus appears, as do the celebrants, on all forty-two television sets and twelve video cameras. The reader of the epistle was shown from nose to chin as he read a rather sober passage from St. Paul on avoiding lust, adultery, and sorcerers. Following this reading, a video was shown that had been created that week: First the word *Lust* appeared, followed by footage of polluted waters pouring from a factory into a river and of cars polluting a neighborhood. Next came the word

Adultery and there were two scenes—one of John Major and Bill Clinton shaking hands and another, taken from a film, of Judas kissing Jesus. Next came the word *Sorcerer* and footage consisting of a televangelist preaching with a Visa card and a 1–800 number at the bottom of the screen. (I asked the community later whose idea the televangelist as sorcerer was and they pointed to a twenty-two-year-old woman in the community.)

I was stunned when, in the middle of the mass, a short youngster stood up and rapped my *Original Blessing* book. What an interesting way to do theology, I said to myself. And the message beats gangsta rap altogether. By employing the emerging urban folk language of rap and rave, this community is giving birth to a new language for worship, one that will serve well into the next millennium.

Another insight that struck me during the service was this: these people are taking television away from the "big guys"—the networks and government broadcasters and corporate sponsors—and are doing it themselves *and in the center of the city and in the center of their society: at worship itself.* No wonder they seem to have little trouble recruiting young people to their community, for they are offering *good,* that is to say, nontrivial, work to their contemporaries, so many of whom are out of work. It struck me that just as the Industrial Revolution had begun in Sheffield and has clearly died there, so today there is being launched a new revolution in northern England, one that is indispensable for an Environmental Revolution: that of making worship work for Westerners once again.

When I returned to the United States, I took my experience to Malidoma Some, a spiritual teacher from Africa, whose main interest is ritual making. We went walking in the redwood forest near Oakland where we both live. At the moment I told him about NOS, I could sense that his soul went running up a giant redwood tree. I had to wait awhile for him to retrieve it. He told me: "For several years living here in the States I have had a message recurring in my meditation. It said that America needs a great awakening. While my work in the men's movement is useful, it is not of the scale that is needed to wake up the West. But this Sheffield movement is. First, because it is made up of young people. Only the young can recover spirituality when it has been lost. Second, because it uses technology and that means it is *Western.* The West's gift to the world is technology, and the language of technology must be used for spirituality. Third, because the work is ritual and there is nothing more basic to regenerating a community than ritual." In a follow-up letter Malidoma spoke more of the NOS vision:

The rest of the world—including those who have checked themselves out of Christianity and those who dare not enter it or are pretending they are [Christian] because it makes them look good in certain quar-

ters—is waiting for NOS to happen in this country. . . . I see the radical-
ism in it as one aimed toward healing, reconciling, and restating people's identity. It is like a massive homecoming for the rest of the world
which the stultified religious conservatism has left out. . . .

Thank you for sharing this wonderful and most worthy project with
me. I would feel most blessed to be part of it. It is worth a life commitment.[1]

Having learned something about rave culture in England, I returned to
America and sat down with fourteen members of the rave community in San
Francisco for what was supposed to be an hourlong discussion. They ranged
in age from seventeen to thirty-four, and the discussion went on for nearly
four hours. Never in my life have I been with a group that was more articulate about its mystical experience. Indeed, this was the reason I had entered
the Dominican Order thirty-four years before—to explore spiritual experience. I had hoped to have many conversations like this. And now I had found
them with members of this community. This convinces me even more that this
first postmodern generation is gifted with a special grace for celebration,
community, and mysticism. But they need a prophetic tradition to put the
mystical energy into the struggle for justice and they need the contours that
worship can offer to keep mysticism from going the way of drugs. Drugs, I
believe, are inevitable if a culture fails to offer means of transcendence to the
young. And worship is the normal route for providing such experiences of
transcendence. What the young people are doing in northern England, in
reinventing the language and form of the Christian liturgy, moves me deeply.
The fact that the Anglican church is supporting this important movement
through the bishop of Sheffield and other bishops gives me hope that an analogous contribution can occur through that tradition here in America. When
the bishop of California also endorsed the idea, I knew I had found a new
home for my work. Thus, I joined the Episcopal church to make an "act of
solidarity" with the young people who are called to launch new Order of Ritual Makers. Ritual that heals, celebrates, revivifies, honors the gift of being in
all of us—this is the work of this new order. I hope to share solidarity with all
those today who are hungry for effective ritual and for community living, a
living that allows for conviviality, less compulsive economic needs, extended
families, and service to the larger community.

A New Vocation?

I was deeply moved and awakened by the liturgical renewal going on in
northern England. How can I help out? I asked. I learned that I could be useful by continuing to theologize and to do so in the context of their artistic
revolution. And also by becoming an Episcopal priest to help the process

along. Such a task seemed to me worthwhile and challenging. Why not? The pope doesn't need me any longer. Why not work with those who feel they can use whatever gifts I have to give? Thus I wrote in my journal the following entries:

January 8, 1994
My becoming Episcopalian is not about pleasing fifty- and sixty-year-old Catholics. It is about assisting the young people to reinvent forms of religion/spirituality praxis. Therefore it is about adultism. [Adultism is that sin whereby adults put down the young and horde the goods of the earth in doing so.] *I am growing in my awareness of adultism and its cures. Is this my vocation? To run interference for the next generation of priests and spiritual leaders to make creation spirituality come alive again, i.e., to recover healthy mysticism and prophecy?*

Undated, late January
Brian (Swimme) says my being a renegade priest already makes me exotic and glamorous as a Catholic theologian—so why be an Episcopalian priest? Maybe I can help more by not joining the Episcopal church.
   Maybe he's correct. I don't know. But still I believe our times call for some bold decision making, and if the Episcopal church is willing to sponsor rave worship and I can assist to pull it off, fine! In other words, I sense a reasonable chance for revolution of a nonviolent kind, revolution via ritual and a planetary mass. If I'm right, it's worth the effort. If I'm wrong, it's worth failing at.

Undated, late January
Hopefully my switch will be a wake-up call for other Roman Catholics to do something for the young vis-à-vis ecology, worship, education, spirituality, and something about the obviously sterile structures that are choking all forms of life in favor of a cult of papal personality in our times. Let us rescue what was beautiful and elegant and true of our tradition from its self-immolating structures and move on.

My Second Trip to Sheffield

In late January I made my second trip to Sheffield, this time to teach creation spirituality over a two-week period. Sometimes I taught groups of 220, sometimes a smaller group of 40 people. I was pleased to be *giving away* my teaching for a change instead of being part of institutions (such as universities) that charge a great deal for the privilege of being taught. (Isn't it part of adultism to make learning elitist for the young?) The students of NOS were free of something as well: they were palpably not there to get a degree or pass an exam or stroke their egos. They were there to test the truth of creation spirituality and, once testing it, to take it directly into their work and therefore into the culture at large. This made our encounters fresh and real. One evening the British biologist Rupert Sheldrake, with whom I have had several public dialogues, came north from his London home and we dialogued together on "The New Science and Creation Spirituality." These young people are passionate about the new science and equally curious about its relation to spirituality.

My traveling companion and co-worker was Russill Paul, a teacher of shabda yoga at ICCS (the Institute in Culture and Creation Spirituality) and a disciple of the late Benedictine monk Fr. Bede Griffith, in whose ashram in southern India Russill lived for seven years. Russill provided wonderfully practical spiritual praxis methods adapted from Hinduism for the members of NOS. My input included leading the group through the four paths of creation spirituality (the *Via Positiva, Via Negativa, Via Creativa,* and *Via Transformativa*); a day on Hildegard of Bingen (including her paintings); a day on Otto Rank's teachings about the artist and spirituality; and a day on the Cosmic Christ and the new findings from the Jesus Seminar on the historical Jesus.

The last event with the large group was a public dialogue between a biblical scholar and me. It proved to be a deep learning experience for us all, but it was painful as well. At the end of the evening, anger was expressed at a remark the scholar had made, "I experience God only in Jesus." This excludes all other religions, all art, all nature, all history of the universe, and the other two persons of the Trinity, the Creator and the Spirit. It upset many non-Westerners in the hall. My emotional instinct was to want to hug the speaker to protect him from the anger of the community. He was a gentleman and a scholar who had never in his life, he told me, dialogued publicly like this before. He was made vulnerable by the event. I loved his wit and his openness. But what occurred revealed the distance between one's work (even theological work) and one's spirituality. Yes, we must bring spirituality back to workplaces, beginning with theology schools.

While I was a bit embarrassed and hurt by the public anger at the end of the dialogue, because I felt the hurt in the speaker, still it was necessary. Truth is more important than manners at times. I learned how important creation *spirituality* is. Without spirituality we—all of us and especially rationalists—fall back on piety. The soul shrinks. The heart aches. We become cosmically lonely. Cosmically afraid.

Harnessing the Light

On my second trip to Sheffield I stopped in Holland to give a talk on Pentecost Sunday, 1994. The Pentecost story is bathed in light imagery—flames of fire are everywhere and so is cosmology and promises that the young shall lead in this spiritual rebirth. Light harnessing and light discovery characterize the twentieth century. Einstein's discovery of the speed of light early in the century led to a reinterpretation of physics and cosmology. In midcentury this knowledge was harnessed in the form of atomic power for atomic weapons. Now, at the conclusion of the century, we have a reharnessing of the light energy of media and television and a retelling of the Christ story promising the omnipresence of the divine light in our midst. Are there not intimations here of a new Pentecost? Pope John XXIII promised as much with the beginning of the Second Vatican Council, but the Catholic church has since failed to deliver. Can we, at the end of this century of light discovery, reharness light not for more efficient killing but for the melting of our hearts and souls, the warming of our imaginations, and the birthing of a true renaissance? Is this not the invitation that communities of worship can offer others at this historical moment?

My moving from the discipline of Roman Catholicism to that of the Anglican tradition is a small sacrifice to make to assist the midwifing of such a vision in my own culture. Besides, all indications are that postmodernism includes postdenominationalism. My lateral move from Roman to Anglican (and more Celtic perhaps) communion has a certain fit with postmodernism. The age of Pisces, the age of dualisms, of two fish swimming in opposite directions, and therefore the age of denominational*ism,* is finished. From now on denominationalism will be recognized to be as divisive a force as sexism or racism, as nationalism or militarism. This is not to say that traditions do not offer different insights, styles, theologies, and charisms. Only that we should demand spirituality from our various traditions at this time in history and not the idolatry of religious denominations themselves.

But still the question begs to be answered: How did I, a committed and practicing Roman Catholic for over fifty years, a priest in good standing for over twenty-five years, and a Dominican for thirty-four years, come to this place where I now find myself? How did a good Roman Catholic altar boy end up in Grace Cathedral in January 1994 being received as an Episcopalian?

PART ONE

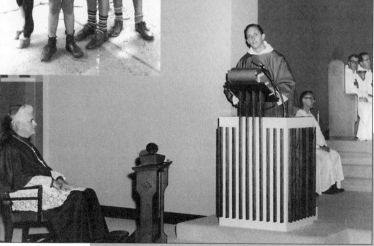

BEGINNINGS

This page: Matthew Fox giving communion to his parents, on the occasion of his first mass, May 1967.

Preceding page, from the top: Matthew Fox at the age of 8, 1948; with his sister Terry and brothers Nat and Tom, 1944; preaching his first mass, 1967, with Bishop Cletus O'Donnell of Madison, Wisconsin, in attendance.

2

The Dominicans:
The Training Years—1958–1967

In 1958 the requirements for becoming a Dominican included attending two years of college and then entering a novitiate program. The college that wannabe Dominicans attended was Loras College in Dubuque, Iowa. There we lived together in a dorm called Smyth Hall that held about forty students and three priest mentors. We led a quasi-Dominican life with group prayer three times a day; meditation; no dating or bar visiting allowed; a lot of study; quiet time; and sports. Other than that, we attended classes with the other students of the college and played intramural sports against them.

I loved my two years at Smyth Hall and Loras College. Though only ninety-five miles from home, I felt I was on my own, doing my thing. I loved the studies—lots of Latin and ancient history and English (where I could write). I enjoyed the prayer we did together and the picnics in the Dubuque parks. And I loved the sports. I was a good athlete, and being outdoors with the sun on my back and the earth under my feet and a team to work with was something of a mystical experience for me. Body awareness that came as part of sports was a big part of my coming to understand creation spirituality when it was named for me in the future. After all, isn't it our bodies that unite us to cosmic history? Are they not our link to the supernova explosion 5.5 billion years ago that birthed the elements in our and other creatures' bodies? I did not know this physics in my college days; I only knew that I relished playing sports as much as I enjoyed studying and praying.

In our chapel at Smyth Hall I had one experience in meditation time that was so profound I have never forgotten it: I saw myself suspended over a well of infinite depth and felt the gratuity and fragility of my existence. It was both exhilarating and liberating. It was an experience of trust, and a taste of how close to nothingness I am (we all are?). It was a reminder not to take existence for granted.

One of my most vivid memories from Smyth Hall is of the night Pope Pius XII died in 1958. He was the only pope I had ever known, since he had been consecrated pope in 1939, a year before my birth. The night he died there occurred as violent a thunderstorm as I, though raised in the thunderstorm-prone Midwest, had ever experienced. We were in the chapel saying our evening prayers, and suddenly water started rising all around us. It was getting hard to concentrate. The priests were not there that night. Suddenly we realized we were in a boatlike situation, only we had no boats! Then we rolled up our sleeves, found mops and buckets, and got to work. The fierce winds had driven the rain through windows and doors throughout the old building.

It was something of a metaphor. Pius XII stood for a kind of ascetic spirituality: he was thin, gaunt, gothic, aristocratic—indeed pious; his death was going to bring a flood of changes to church and society. More than any of us could imagine. An era had ended and was being swept away by the tides of change. Not only the church but society too was turning a corner. Two men named John—John XXIII and John Fitzgerald Kennedy—would usher in some of this tidal change.

Following two years of college in Dubuque, we entered the novitiate where our formal training as Dominicans was to begin. The novitiate for our province was a new building located high on the rolling hills overlooking the Mississippi River near Winona, Minnesota. It was a beautiful setting, with nature's glory all around. Lay brothers worked the farm, which included raising chickens and hogs. There was a cemetery for deceased Dominicans, a charming chapel, and individual "cells" or modest-sized rooms where the novices lived. Our novice master was new in the job, having just arrived from several years "down under." He spoke with an unusual accent and talked a lot about kangaroos and boomerangs.

Arriving with my classmates on a warm day in August, I was greeted with the name "Brother Matthew." New names were part of the rite of passage we underwent during that year. I had held back my tears only partially successfully as I said good-bye to my parents and brothers and sisters back home, for we had been warned that we would never return home (a more dire warning than was merited by the facts, especially as religious life evolved rather rapidly in the sixties). Nevertheless, the metaphorical meaning was real enough, as was made evident in a ritual that followed a few weeks after our arrival.

In that ritual, we took off our black suit coats and were frocked in a shiny new white Dominican habit that smelled of something so unique to itself that I have no words for it even today. At that same ceremony I was told, "In the world you were known as Timothy Fox; now you will be known as Brother Matthew." And a somber lesson was read about being as strong and guarded in our feelings as "stones and sticks." Our families, who were invited to attend, were quite sobered by this ceremony, as one can imagine. I found it all quite adventurous and possibly even romantic. It seemed like a great challenge lay ahead of us.

Today we have a name for such rituals; we call them "rites of passage." And it was that—a leave-taking from the "world" as we knew it and from our families as we knew them. It was a kind of growing up and a growing beyond, and to this day I give the Catholic church credit for possessing some rites of passage, even if they were perhaps unnecessarily dour-sounding in their language and theological bent. A rite of passage was a necessary part of this nineteen-year-old's experience, and I will always be grateful to the order for it.

Our year began with a retreat by Fr. Patrick Clancy, who had been our "superior" or "boss" at Smyth Hall for the two years I was there. I remember two things about that retreat: one was his citing Teresa of Ávila on why she became a nun—"because I want to see God"—and another was a personal conference we had. He spoke with the authority of a bishop and usually with sweat running down his face. I always liked him and still hold him in respect. One of my crises with my vocation at Smyth Hall had occurred when a very gifted, very glib classmate of mine, a Chicago boy who had attended the minor seminary there, began talking one day of "niggers and Jews." I was deeply upset by this language, told him so, and went to Fr. Clancy to talk about it. I said that if this is the way of the Catholic church and its seminarians, then I surely did not have a vocation (Loras College being my first experience of Catholic education since eighth grade). I told him I was instructed at home never to talk of other ethnic groups as this person was doing, and this person was a product of a lifetime of Catholic education. Fr. Clancy assured me that this wasn't appropriate language and that I was right to express my outrage. When we spoke in the novitiate he gave me a bit of advice: "Set your standards high," he said. "There will be moments in the order when you will be scandalized and disappointed. Don't go the way of everybody else if your conscience tells you otherwise." That advice has always remained with me.

The novitiate year was meant to be a kind of boot camp for entry into the Dominican order. For the most part, it lived up to its reputation. We rose about 5:00 A.M. in pitch darkness and made our way downstairs to the chapel, where we spent ninety minutes chanting the psalms, praying, and attending mass. Then we filed into the refectory where we ate our meals in silence with our capuches or hoods up, except for an occasional *gaudeamus* or break for conversation on rare feast days and holidays. Evening meals were also taken in silence, but there was reading by one of the novices, who was in turn corrected for any mispronounced words by the novice master whose job it was to be stern with us as much as he could. The readings included stories from the saints' lives (usually a martyr, it seemed, who died in some god-awful and picturesque way that did not fit too well with eating meals). The novice master also selected a more contemporary work for refectory reading. There was a small chapel on our side of the building where we gathered several times a day to recite the rosary and to pray from the *Little Office of the Blessed Virgin Mary.*

We had chores to do—cleaning the building, the toilets, working in the yard, planting flowers. There were also occasions for outdoor sports—football, volleyball, baseball, hockey, hiking—and handball indoors.

But most of all, we had time and space for reflection, reading, meditation. For me, it was a great treat not to have exam or classroom pressures to interfere with study itself. One spring day I was outdoors amid the newly budding trees. I went up to one of them and asked of the new bud as I held it in my hand, "What is life?" I felt a sense of the sacred in that new bud and of a mystery that had no answer. (When I had asked that question the previous year in my biology class at Loras College, the professor chastised me, saying, "Don't ask questions like that in science. Save them for philosophy class.") Here in the novitiate, I expected few answers; it was more a question of seeking a mystery rather than an answer.

My love of nature no doubt stemmed from my growing up in Madison, Wisconsin, where nature glistened everywhere and promised a full dose of *four real seasons* each year. Of these my favorite season was fall. The leaves of the elm, oak, maple, and poplar turned splendid colors everywhere one looked. The smell of leaves burning in the gutters alongside the streets; leaves to play in, roast potatoes in, play house in when we were little; and plenty of leaves to rake and make a few bucks. From the time I was three until I was in sixth grade, we lived in a white-frame rental house on Madison's west side. In the backyard were lilac bushes (to this day I am reminded of home every time I smell lilacs), pear, apple, and plum trees begging to be climbed and played in. The plum trees provided one of my older brothers, who was as enterprising then as he is today, with some business opportunities he could not resist. We would load up the family wagon with bags of plums and take them door to door to sell. My job was to put the decent-looking ones on top and cover up the soft and slowly rotting ones.

Madison had lakes everywhere. There were lakes for canoeing, lakes for fishing, lakes for swimming, lakes for ice-skating, lakes for ice-fishing and, for the very hearty, for iceboat racing. Eventually, after our family purchased a small boat with a fifteen-horsepower motor when I was in high school, there were lakes for waterskiing. Besides the lakes, the summer fruit trees, and the autumns, other awe-filled and mysterious experiences of nature for me were thunderstorms. Wisconsin has wonderfully memorable thunderstorms when one can smell the ozone in the air and see the magic of lightning and feel the roar of thunder. We kids loved experiencing them from the side porch of our house, where the rain would tickle our faces. I remember as a little boy being upstairs with the rest of the family during a great storm. My chin was resting on a windowsill taking in all the wonders. I turned to my parents and asked, "What causes lightning?" A few minutes later I was on the floor reading about lightning and thunder in the encyclopedia.

Winters in Madison were for real. Real snow, really deep, really cold. I remember toboggan runs in parks, on golf courses, on hills overlooking the frozen lakes—and the hot chocolate afterward; sledding down by the railroad tracks or out on Glenview golf course (across from which we buried my father's ashes seven years ago); snow forts and snowball fights; snowmen and snowwomen; the shoveling of snow to survive and to make money. A certain hardiness seemed to go along with marching to school and back in Wisconsin winters.

To Wisconsin I owe my love of nature and sense of the land—an experience that other nature lovers like John Muir and George Leopold also took with them from Wisconsin. It was in Wisconsin too that I first experienced an awareness of the Native American presence; and roots as only midwesterners can have them. Growing up in Wisconsin, I often felt a spirit presence in the outdoors, no matter what the season. Winona, Minnesota, like Dubuque, Iowa, was part of my feeling the roots of land and seasons.

During our novitiate year, we were allowed no television and no newsmagazines. However, as special concession to the fact that a Roman Catholic had been elected president that year, we were allowed to listen to John F. Kennedy's inaugural address on radio. I felt a certain pride in his election and in the elegance of his address as well as in the poem read by Robert Frost on that snow-bitten morning in Washington, D.C. I was reminded afterward by a wiser classmate whose political consciousness was better developed than mine how, as we huddled around the radio at the time of the Bay of Pigs attack, I was a bit of a warmonger, urging on the attackers to wipe out Castro's Communists.

One day the novice master called me in and gave me a "brand new book" on religious life to read. This incident proved to be what was probably my first conscious awakening about culture and spirituality. The book was written by an Italian cardinal, which in my naive opinion only added prestige to it. I took the book to my room and looked through it. Being a rather normal nineteen-year-old, I turned first to the chapter on celibacy. I began to read. The author set the question up this way: "Is it right for a celibate, on taking a shower, to wash all of his parts or not?" I did a double take. This was a "brand new book" on religious life? Showers were not my problem and never had been. I had been in plenty of them, since I played sports in high school and college. But washing your parts *was* a problem for Italian cardinals? Live and learn, I thought! I remember to this day holding the book over my wastebasket and saying something like, "My issues with celibacy are different from those of Italian cardinals." Thus, my first experience with what a difference culture makes!

After the snow-filled winter, spring was coming on in full force, and one warm April day I suggested to the community at large that we might want to meditate outdoors instead of in chapel, as was our constant habit. I received some strange stares from the "more grave" fathers of the house, and little support from anyone else. I tried to take time after that for meditation outdoors on my own, however, for I still found a special bond between nature and spirit.

For my meditations indoors I often began with a line from the Bible or a sentence that had struck me from a sermon or a talk we had heard or from a book I was reading. I would also try to translate the psalms that we chanted each day (for we chanted them in Latin) before coming to the office, and that way I would have more to meditate on during the community prayer. All these "techniques" were helpful in teaching me concentration and focus, which to this day are gifts for which I give credit to my years of meditation in the order. I remember one sentence, for example, from the Hebrew Bible where God is said to say, "Son, give me your heart," and that line kept me in a rich meditation place for many days.

When I think back on my Dominican years of training and how I was indeed nourished in a contemplative way, I am struck by poet Robert Bly's reflections about "garden work." He writes about the boy who is assigned to do *garden work*. "Garden," Bly points out, "suggests a place marked out, separated from farmyard, grain field, forest, or desert, in order that human beings can cultivate there precious plants or flowers."[1] It is a place set apart for inner work. The garden is a place to "develop introversion."

> In the walled garden, as in the alchemical vessel, new metals get formed as the old ones melt. The lead of depression melts and becomes grief. . . . The enclosed garden then suggests cultivation as opposed to rawness, boundaries as opposed to unbounded sociability, soul concerns as opposed to outer obsessions, passion as opposed to raw sexuality, growth of soul desire as opposed to obsession with a generalized greed for things. . . . The enclosed garden encourages true desire for the infinite more than the greed for objects; and we know that all true desire is dangerous.[2]

I cite Bly on the task of "entering the garden" because I think the garden as he describes it parallels much of what I experienced in the order's training.

Daily mass and meditation and study as well as separation from daily duties of earning a living—all this rendered garden work possible. And it was *dangerous*.

The novitiate year went by quickly. It was a kind of "sabbatical with a purpose" and I loved it. While we lost several of our classmates who decided to move on, those of us who remained seemed quite close and determined and eager for the next move. In August about sixteen of us took vows for three years, and our next stop was the Dominican House of Studies in River Forest, Illinois, just outside Chicago.

Dominican Studies in Chicago

The day after our vows in Winona, we donned our new Roman collars and black hats and rode the train from Winona to Chicago. As we arrived that night at the House of Studies, which was a large monastic edifice patterned after the European monasteries, a torrential downpour greeted us. I was shown around the rather dingy, meagerly lit building by an enthusiastic brother one year my senior who, oblivious of leaky pipes and water on the floor, even showed me the inner sanctums of the library where "forbidden books" were kept locked up. I wondered what books would be forbidden. Later, I learned that much of modern philosophy was included in the Index of Forbidden Books. That room too would be opened up and cleaned out by the Second Vatican Council.

Leaky pipes and dim lighting notwithstanding, this was my home for the next three years. About seventy-five young Dominicans were studying philosophy together in these halls. I was happy to be here, though a bit apprehensive as we listened to tales from upperclassmen of the courses that were held in Latin, of the grading system, of the demands and peculiarities of some of the faculty.

Here too the routine was quite stringent. We rose about 6:00 A.M. and went to the chapel for chanting of the Divine Office followed by mass. Then it was breakfast in silence a half hour before classes began. Classes lasted all morning, and after lunch we had free time, which usually consisted of sports: football and tennis and outdoor handball in the fall; hockey in the winter; softball and tennis in the spring. Plus plenty of walking around the spacious grounds. Sports seemed a rather healthy outlet for any pent-up frustrations brought about by communal living or academic pressures—one might say that we were free to beat each other up with hockey sticks, football tackling (though it was touch football), or baseball bats depending on the season. Evenings included a couple of hours of silence when we were in our rooms studying, followed by a low-key gathering in the recreation room for quiet conversation before final prayers or "compline" in the chapel. (We also chanted the office at noontime and before supper.)

It was a joy to be living and studying with so many young Dominicans and so many of them talented and committed. The rather serious routine was interrupted periodically with movies, which we would rent and show on sixteen-millimeter projectors. Our house chores included waiting on tables and keeping the buildings and grounds clean. There were rare forays to museums or outside lectures or ball games. I remember hearing Gabriel Marcel speak in the ballroom of a downtown Chicago hotel and Hans Küng at the Chicago McCormick Center. The theme of Küng's talk was: "Is there a difference between the modus operandi of the Vatican and that of the Kremlin?" It was a rather head-turning speech for a still-pious seminarian to hear. I was genuinely excited by his presentation and his question, which has obviously stayed with me all these years.

The dominant philosophers we studied were Aristotle and Thomas Aquinas. We read most of Aristotle's works and many of Aquinas's commentaries on them. (I did my B.A. thesis on the proof for God as found in Aristotle's *Physics* and Aquinas's commentary on Aristotle's *Physics*.) Our ethics class consisted exclusively of reading Aquinas's commentary on Aristotle's *Ethics* and *Politics*. While not always relevant to each and every pressing moral dilemmas of our time, this was an education that gave me leeway to think, reflect, critique, and look for answers. I remember, for example, the beautiful sections in Aquinas and Aristotle on friendship as the basis of society and morality. The existentialists were also part of our repertoire. I dived into Sartre with abandon, and Camus and Merleau-Ponty were also discussed.

One day in meditation I had an experience of my own *nothingness,* and I confided to a friend-adviser that I wanted that experience to be the cornerstone of my life. Years later when I would read in Meister Eckhart that "all creatures are a mere nothing" I found affirmation of what I had experienced. Knowing our nothingness makes letting go much simpler. Our nothingness is metaphysical and not psychological, however. By that I mean we come from nothing—thus our uniqueness—but our existence is not worth nothing. Indeed, we are all special because *we could be just nothing!*

Among my teachers, a few had a particularly profound effect on me—they encouraged me to think either by example or by interaction. One of these was a tall, lanky philosophy professor who confessed to having been both a fascist and a Hegelian at some time in his life. "Doc" Powell taught us sociology and spent the entire semester developing one thesis. On the last day of class he came into the classroom and said simply, "Please forget everything I said the whole semester. It was wrong. My thesis is wrong and unprovable." He erased the entire semester from our minds—or tried to—because he felt his inquiry wasn't truthful. Once I recovered from the humor of the situation, I have never forgotten the profundity of it. Here was a man living out the

Dominican vocation to "truth" who had the guts to admit to his students that his own search had been a mistake. Later he introduced me to Martin Heidegger's *Being and Time,* a book that had a deep mystical effect on me.

Fr. Athanasius Weisheipl was also a formative influence on me. Of the German school of study and learning technique, he was a stickler for detail, such as the proper form for footnotes, but he was also a very fine historian who held a doctorate from Oxford. I received a letter from him years later in which he told me that while I was one of his best students, he would never again read any of my books because in my most recent book I had connected spirituality and sensuality in one sentence. This statement was especially striking to me because his field was fourteenth-century science and religion, and it was at the end of that century that the great creation-centered English mystic Julian of Norwich wrote. She was one of the founders of the English language, and she wrote often and powerfully about sensuality and spirituality, for example: "God is the means whereby our Substance and our Sensuality are kept together so as to never be apart."[3] And, "both our Substance and Sensuality together may rightly be called our Soul. That is because they are both oned in God. Our Sensuality is the beautiful City in which our Lord Jesus sits and in which He is enclosed."[4] Clearly Fr. Weisheipl did not include the women mystics—even of his favorite century—in his repertoire. In all my studies with the Dominicans, from Loras College through the Dominican seminary and ordination (even including my three years in Paris), I never had a woman professor. One of my major papers for Fr. Weisheipl was on St. Augustine's concept of the immortality of the soul.

I was also affected by the work of Fr. Raymond Nogar, who was relating science and religion. And a very talented priest named Toni Schillacci was, in addition to being our metaphysics professor, a serious film buff who would sponsor film programs featuring the works of Fellini, Bergman, Antonioni, and other filmmakers understood as contemporary philosophers in their own right. He left the order and the last I heard was working for NBC television in New York City.

I was introduced to an exploration of the psyche by an older student who took me through a process of self-discovery by way of psychology and who invited me to read Freud's *Interpretation of Dreams* as well as the works of Jung, Rogers, Adler, Horney, and others. I would use this training to assist other brothers, and later as part of the counseling I was called to do in my various jobs.

Much was going on in the world around us. In the church, John XXIII was launching his revolution by way of the Second Vatican Council, and we saw signs of the effects of his vision all around us. We were allowed to cease our courses that were held in Latin and go into the vernacular. Theologians such as

Hans Küng and our own French Dominicans, M. D. Chenu and Yves Congar, were being rehabilitated. We were reading Teilhard de Chardin. And John XXIII's *Pacem in Terris* was published. Reading this document was a mystical and prophetic experience for me. Here was a vision of authentic ecumenism—he addressed it to *all* persons of good will, not just to clergy or Catholics or Christians or believers; here was a significant use of the powerful office he represented—calling the nations to disarmament and peace; here was a *vision* that challenged me as a young priest-to-be. It was to John XXIII and his vision that I gladly made solemn vows at the end of the year. He moved me as a human being—his sense of humor ("Here I am at the end of my life and the top of the heap," he told his first official visitor, the prime minister of Canada); his nonjudgmental attitude toward non-Catholics (a book has been written on his friendship with the artist Manzu, whom he hired to make the doors of St. Peter's basilica and who was an atheist); his strength (thanks to his peasant roots); and his spirituality (the idea for the Second Vatican Council came to him in prayer—he went through with it despite untold opposition within and around him).

I once met a priest who told me the following story. He was in Spain shortly before Pope Pius XII died and was staying overnight in a seminary. It happened that a certain portly cardinal named Roncalli (who was to be John XXIII) was also staying overnight there. At about two in the morning he heard a knock on his door. "Wake up, come downstairs," the visitor whispered. The surprised priest followed Cardinal Roncalli downstairs. There in the dining room was a complete dinner he had made himself. "I never like to eat alone," he said. "*Mangia, mangia.*" When a few months later this man was elected pope, the priest knew it would be a different kind of papacy.

The first picture I saw of him was when he was papal nuncio in Paris: He was at a party and he had a cigarette in one hand and a martini in the other. John XXIII enjoyed life; he even enjoyed—and was able to laugh at—his job, as for example the time he was asked how many people worked in the Vatican and replied, "About half."

In the country at large during my seminary years, Dr. Martin Luther King, Jr., and the civil rights movement were coming of age. The television news—which we were now allowed to see at night—showed police dogs attacking unarmed singers of freedom songs; there was protest in the air.

The war in Vietnam was also escalating and I had a personal experience with it early. We were having a Halloween party when I received a message of an urgent phone call. It was my brother; he had some bad news. A close friend of the family, a graduate of West Point whom my sister had dated back in Madison, had been captured by the Vietcong. The irony was that he had sent in his papers to be discharged from the army in order to return as a missionary with the Maryknoll Fathers because he, having learned the Vietnamese language, had fallen in love with the people and had wanted to be with them in ways other than war. A few years later he was to die at the hands of his captors. Questions began to be sown in my mind: Just why *are* we in Vietnam? I listened more carefully now to the assurances of our president and the reasons offered for our being there.

The Dominicans had a summer camp in the Marinette/Menominee region of northern Wisconsin and Michigan where we spent much of each summer. There were acres of lakefront for volleyball and for boating and swimming in the frigid waters of Lake Michigan. The food, which we cooked ourselves, was wonderful and plentiful, and the atmosphere of being outdoors, of having time to read and relax and play sports and cook outdoor fish fries on Friday nights, made this one of my favorite parts of growing up Dominican. I especially loved compline chanted at night just before bed in the wooded chapel in the wooded woods.

One summer afternoon in my third year of philosophy, shortly before my classmates and I were to make our final vows, I received an urgent phone call from Madison. It was my younger brother: "Mom has been in a grave car accident. If you want to see her alive, you'd better get here by this evening." Driving her little Corvair, she had been run into by another car. She was unconscious and stayed that way for days. I sat with her at the hospital during the odd hours and happened to be there when she woke from her coma. I remember her smile. As it turned out, she lost an eye, and her personality changed for years as she fought to get back her basic skills. Always an independent woman (she had traveled to Yugoslavia just a few months before the accident and thought nothing of getting in her Peugeot and driving to visit a daughter in college in Texas or a friend in Florida), she was now "grounded." She would never drive again. Such a radical change of roles was not easy for either her or my father to adjust to. But adjust they did.

A few weeks later about ten classmates and I took our solemn or final vows in the chapel at the House of Studies. It was a sober moment, not only because my father and brother were present and my mother was absent, but also because a serious commitment was involved. As mentioned earlier, I felt I was freely committing myself to John XXIII's spirit and vision for a church that reached out to others. The ceremony itself was simple and stark. It mirrored my feelings of being very focused. An image came to me during the ceremony; it was so vivid I have never forgotten it, but only in recent years, thirty years later, have I begun to feel that I understand it. What I saw was a bare foot, bloody and moving through mud and rain. For me it stands for the warrior side, the rigorous side, of the vocation I have come to know and to live. The promises I made that day, when deprivatized and extended to the culture at large around issues of relationship, power, and money (the traditional vows of celibacy, obedience, and poverty), have proved to be more demanding than I had anticipated as a youngster.

On taking my final vows and graduating with a B.A. and an M.A. in philosophy (I did my master's thesis on Immanuel Kant and the proof for God's existence), I was set for theology school, which meant a three-year stint and a master's degree in theology. Thus we moved to Dubuque, Iowa, and the Dominican House of Studies there.

Dubuque

I liked Dubuque. It was thoroughly Midwest, with four seasons and sturdy people, altogether unpretentious and unassuming. The Dominican priory, called St. Rose Priory, was a large red-brick edifice built in the 1950s, and its long hangarlike chapel contained a lot of cold pink marble. Light shone in everywhere, even on the cold winter days that somehow always included blue and sunny skies. The grounds of the priory building (since sold to the Southern Baptists) included tennis courts, football fields, and woods for walking and hiking. Adjacent was a golf course which, though we never used it, still offered a pleasant vista and landscape, a sense of space and sky that we had missed in the big-city atmosphere of Chicago.

Surprisingly, in the early 1960s Dubuque was a hotbed of ecumenism. The Dominicans at St. Rose Priory had linked up with the Lutheran seminary at Wartburg and the Presbyterian seminary at the University of Dubuque to pull off a uniquely ecumenical education for their students. We exchanged professors and classrooms, and we rubbed shoulders in some classes and in some outside social activities with these seminarians of other traditions. I had Presbyterian theologians as professors and traveled to the University of Iowa in Iowa City one night a week for classes—one taught by a Russian Orthodox theologian and another team-taught by a Protestant and a Catholic theologian from Germany. The ecumenical movement in Dubuque was led by a wonderful German woman, Eva Leo, an artist who worked as librarian at the Lutheran school of theology. She had fled Nazi Germany with her theologian husband and was widowed suddenly when, in the middle of a class lecture at the seminary, he had a fatal heart attack. Small in stature, she was greatly skilled at persuading and contacting and "networking," as we would call it today. (Several years later she led the anti–Vietnam War movement in Dubuque as well.)

I loved my theological studies. Things were coming together now. We were reading Aquinas's *Summa Theologiae* along with more contemporary theologians, and the excitement that the Vatican Council was engendering was palpable. But something else was happening to me as well; it came to a head as I read Martin Heidegger's *Being and Time*. The mystic in me was deepening, and I was yearning to spend more time with *being* and less on doing. I sought some understanding of it by asking questions of priests and confessors.

One of these priests said to me, "You should consider becoming a hermit." My first reaction was astonishment and laughter: "I, a hermit? I like sports and people and I want to teach or lecture." But this advice, given very seriously, began to haunt me during my first year in Dubuque. I began sneaking into a secret room upstairs behind the chapel where I could pray alone. Sometimes my prayer felt like it was five minutes long when it had in fact been two or three hours. And energy was always its result. I had a lot of energy for many endeavors. So drawn was I by the contemplative life at this time that I made a trip to the Trappist monastery outside Dubuque to visit an old friend from my childhood who was living there. The reason for my visit—which he surmised early on—was to check out that monastery as a possible vocation for me. It didn't seem quite my place, however. Still, the idea of the hermitage kept calling to me.

I could identify with the line from Rilke that says, "I want to be with those who know secret things or else alone."[5] I felt a great calling to be alone, to investigate solitude, to just be with being and be with God or the source of being.

Finally, I did research and learned of a hermit colony on Vancouver Island run by a former Belgian abbot named Winandy who was also a biblical scholar. When I approached my provincial about going there in the summer, he was not pleased. He said it was a crazy idea and listed all those Dominicans he had known who had run off to join the Trappists and had gone kind of crazy. But I insisted. Finally he said, "If you do this there is no guarantee you will ever be ordained." I said that that was okay with me. Reluctantly, he allowed me to go, but with a final admonition: "Don't ever tell anyone about this crazy scheme of yours. Tell no one." Many years after this trip I learned that my provincial, in corresponding with Abbot Winandy about my visit, had actually threatened him if he took Brother Matthew Fox away from the Dominicans. My naïveté being what it was back then about ecclesial politics, I would never have believed this threat could have been made.

When I look back on it, I think this was a very important moment in my development: I left the priesthood before I entered it. For that reason, I have always had a relationship with the priesthood that was nonpossessive and therefore somewhat playful. The priesthood was something I let go of early on. That summer I boarded the Empire Builder, which took me from Dubuque to the Far West for a wild and beautiful ride—literally and metaphorically.

When I returned, it was with more energy than ever, energy that I believe I ran on for twenty years. I was twenty-three years old and during my trip I kept a journal.

As I read over this journal for the first time in years, I am surprised by several themes that come up regularly in my later theological pursuits. Themes such as the relation of action to contemplation; panentheism; life as the ultimately sacred experience; work as a spiritual action; preaching as self/spirit revelation; blessing or goodness; trust; courage; rite of passage; listening; the meaning of holiness; grace; friendship; nature and the spiritual experience therein; conscience; criticism of "schizophrenic" spiritualities in a "sickened Christendom"; vocation; prayer and its meaning; freedom; awe; silence; nothingness; listening; seeking and finding God; beauty and the experience of God. Of course there is a dose of immaturity here as well, but I won't dwell on that with the hindsight of thirty years' experience.

The journal began on the train west with the question, "Why am I making this trip?"

Saturday, July 17, 1965
Now is the time. The moment of truth. I am alone and yet not alone. Going and yet not leaving. Happy and yet expectant of better things to come. The reason for the paradoxes: I am traveling seeking union—love. This is why I am not alone, because I seek the only resolution to loneliness, love. So many others in our country (indeed, world) are alone even though they be very much in the world of others, yes even though they be married. There is only one way not to be alone and that is to be deeply with others, i.e., to be with God.

How can I be going and yet not leaving? Because I am going, indeed running, to, not from. And what it takes to run to and to stick to it is, indeed, what I have and have been and have received. When one goes to he goes bringing. Bringing with, I run to increase what I am. It is not that I reject anything; but I want more.

More of what? Is it more happiness? Is it more of God? More of self? More of purity of intention, more unselfishness? More love?—more of all these things for others? Probably I seek all these things. Surely for others as well as for myself. But something is amiss in this explanation because I have already seen more. I have, in the souls of others, seen more goodness than I can take. How it has overwhelmed me! How it has reduced me to nothingness in its presence. To awe. To silence. This seems to be the first reason I am flying to be with God alone—I have seen too much good already and I must see . . . what? Its source? Its purpose? My role in it? Its authenticity?

I don't think so. I must see nothing. Rather I must be seen. Yes, that is it. To be seen in my dumb silence. In my worthlessness. In my unworthiness.

My nothingness. That is why I am fleeing: to be myself in the presence of God. That is, to be my nothingness and nakedly so in His Presence.

God help me to be so. How is it possible for me except by the goodness of the others who ask for me—that goodness which I've seen and therefore know exists. Oh God, pity my request.

I comment on the joy and eagerness of children I encounter on the train and on the beauty of the snow-touched mountains and the running river that we followed through the mountains.

Sunday, July 18
Since yesterday [on the train] *I have seen—again—God's two finest works. First, the human spirit, open and thirsty for the good, helpful and eager to share what is best. . . . The second finest of God's creatures is nature. And what I've seen today—those rugged, snow-touched mountains stretching for the heavens, masculine and indomitable yet creaturely and like hands held aloft in prayer. The rushing green river, cold and clear and tumbling, at times evolving into rapids.*

On the eve of my arrival I was experiencing what I would later write about as panentheism (God in us and us in God).

Monday, July 19
Tomorrow, tomorrow morning, is the time. Christ is near. No, better yet, as I learned in Communion this morning, Christ is not in me, but I am in Him. So too, He is not near, but I am nearer Him. I have two particular thoughts at this happy time of expectation: (1) Trust. Keep trusting Christ. Look how amazingly He has worked to draw you this far and to Him. Surely He will not fail me now. Whatever He has intended will be accomplished. (2) It is curious, but very meaningful to me, that, as I draw nearer to Christ and—in a sense—farther from others, I am drawing nearer to others. It's a funny thing, psychologically explained only partially by my happy observation of the friendship of these two priests, (whom I met on the trip) that my loved ones are close to me this evening. My family, my friends, my fellowmen.

Tuesday, July 20
I am writing this by candlelight. It is Tuesday, 9:20 P.M. My first day in a hermitage. What can I say? First I must confess that the physical setup impressed me neither one way nor the other. What privations there seem to be mean nothing to me one way or the other (at least so far as I can project). The first genuine impression I received was—I should have expected it, since this first brought me to the priesthood and to the Dominican vocation also— from a person. Brother Charles. I liked him. Brother Anthony too. I felt immediately that we had some important things in common. One important

thing: prayer and love of Christ. I sense already in the place (which is not, of course, true solitude but a via ad solitudinem) *the primacy and the power of friendship. How real it is that men must help one another to love Christ. And must love Christ in one another.*

I suppose I could describe my room. It's about ten feet by six feet. A mattress on the floor and the small desk I'm writing on. Walls that are insulated (with the insulation showing).

Surely this is a place where men seek God? But do they find Him? I am sure that He finds them. All He requires is the desire for Him and honesty. But there are many other places where men seek God—in marriages, in religious orders, etc. And I think the results could be the same, i.e., that men will be found by Christ insofar as they desire Him and are honest. Here, of course, the desire is evident.

Wednesday, July 21
It is not silence *we are bound to observe, but* listening. *Listening to God. In others, in ourselves, all about us. How many talks I have heard on silence which themselves betrayed the act of* listening. *For silence is for listening. And to listen is to love.*

Silence is a rule; but love is the law.

It seems to me that a true reformation of religious life must be principled on these two virtues, especially freedom. *A respected and a free individual is one who can "do whatever God tells him." He belongs to God, not to an immutable rule or a human institution or to pleasing men or to fulfilling extrinsic norms. Only by truly belonging to God can he be wholly authentic to self and to others and to Christ and to his vocation.*

In the practical order this would mean that, for many persons, schedules should be at a minimum. They should be encouraged to make their own— they should know when they sleep best, study best, recreate best, etc.

I go on to suggest that dispensations should be allowed in choral prayer so that the emphasis can be on contemplation rather than on "finishing" the office. In subsequent entries I am reflecting on and sorting out my own vocation.

The eremitical life, it seems, is not different from the contemplative nor the contemplative from the contemplative-apostolic. There is one vocation and that is living in God's presence. There are different ways of expressing this one life. Some can live in God's presence with others, some with much prayer and some contact with others, others in solitude.

Sometimes I think that what I'm looking for will occur only at death.

My first full day at the hermitage. What should I say? It is a beautiful life. With beautiful souls. Being loved much by God and returning much love. It has been a full day; I am tired. Who knows? Maybe my cooking will improve with the days of my visit.

I have done much praying about my vocation today. Clearly each hermit here feels his is God's finest calling. I believe they are correct . . . for them. It seems to me that every vocation is God's finest; provided we give everything to it, we shall be happy. This, of course, is the question awaiting me—which group is the finest . . . for me? In other words, In which group can I save the most souls? In which group can I love the most? In which group does God want me?

I have for a long time thought that to choose the hermits would be the more difficult choice for me, requiring harder things of me. Today I sense a change in this attitude. It occurs to me that this hermit life with its ever-present opportunity for contemplative prayer could be an easier way for my keeping close to God than the Dominican way with its apostolic demands.

Thursday, July 22
To do God's will, that is my only desire. That is my vocation.

If this means returning as a Dominican, it means returning as a better one. It means overcoming my timidity or shyness or pusillanimity with trust in Christ, whose will it is that He be known through me.

I must pray for courage. I need ever more courage to be either a good Dominican or a good hermit. Whether my vocation is to be a Dominican or a hermit I am not yet sure; but that it is to be a good one, that I am sure.

It occurs to me that Christ's life was nearer that of a contemplative-apostle than it was that of a hermit. The essence of His life, however, was not in contemplation nor in apostleship: it was in doing the will of the Father whom He loved.

My year and a half of weighing and measuring came to an end one evening when Fr. Winandy gave me a note, written after reading my notebook, advising me that my vocation was to be a Dominican priest and not a hermit. "Be a man of prayer, be fond of God's Word in the Bible, and above all look for Christ's love in everything," he wrote.

Friday, July 23
Fr. Winandy told me how he came to the decision by reading my notes: because it did not strike me immediately on seeing this life that it was my vocation. I must remember this as a sign for any true vocation. Psychologically speaking, I suppose it's a "conversion" phenomenon.

The Dominican vocation is to be in constant communion with God. This is what it is to preach and preach Christ. To be His constant companion so that whatever we do or are called upon to say is part of our prayer with

Christ. This is my vocation. It is my happiness. (Or rather, He is.) It is my holiness.

I look forward so much to returning to my Dominican family, all of whom I so love.

Sunday, July 25
Here's the answer to the contemplative-active dilemma. It was in Sunday Lauds all the time:

> Labia mea laudabunt te.
> Sic benedicam te *in vita mea.*
> Et in nomine tuo levabo manus meas. (Psalm 62)
> (My lips shall praise you.
> Thus I shall bless you *with my life.*
> And in your name I shall wash my hands.)

My life must be my prayer, my contemplation. God, give us—all of us—this grace!

A hermit (Brother John Baptist) said: "There is no question that you whose vocation it is to 'share the fruits of your contemplation,' to illumine rather than just shine, have the noblest calling. BUT . . . where is your contemplation? I have known so few contemplative religious. Without contemplation your vocation has sunk in its value and cannot be called the noblest of God's callings."

Monday, July 26
I am convinced that my greatest mistake all my life long has been in not trusting God enough. This trip, with its possibly portentous outcome, has taught me this trust. I now know *that Christ, who brought me here, loves each of us personally and watches all we do and hears all we wish for. Oh God! Give yourself to souls. It is all people wish for!*

I beg God's blessing in this regard in particular: that from here on, all the work I ever engage in—preaching, teaching, studying, counseling, writing—I may NOT measure as "hours worked," but may see for what they are: my life, i.e., the Trinity's way of being present in the world. For this constant vision I would give anything.

Isn't all the push on authenticity today what Christ meant by obedience—obedience to God, to the Father, to one's conscience! (Not to superiors, per se.)

On my final day in the hermitage I took a bar of soap, went down to the river that ran through the property, stripped, and took my first-ever bath in nature's own bathtub. It was a cold and exhilarating experience. Maybe a baptism in the river Jordan was like this. It was surely a new beginning for me. The freedom and energy I received in this visit and in the risks I took in following my heart here would keep me going for a long time to come.

Several things happened to me on my return from the hermitage to life in the priory. First was the amount of energy I had for my studies and daily responsibilities. One of these responsibilities was being made editor of a magazine the students published called *Reality* (I always felt the title lacked modesty). The magazine was rather stodgy, but it was an attempt to take our own work seriously and thus publish our better papers and research. After months of discussions we decided to bury this magazine and birth a new one, less stodgy and more fitting for our exciting theological times—1965, with the Second Vatican Council in full swing. So we started a new magazine and called it *Listening*, a title I chose from my own experiences. It has a quote from Martin Heidegger inside its front cover: "Being-with develops in Listening to one another." In the opening editorial I laid out the reason for the magazine.

> With us the touchstone to dialogue is not talking; it is listening. We are convinced that listening is the ground for genuine understanding. Only one who has first listened to his own being, and searched his own ignorance, and fathomed his own need is a fit participant for engagement with others.[6]

Listening published articles or interviews with the best thinkers behind the Vatican Council, including Hans Küng, Yves Congar, Karl Rahner, Edward Schillebeeckx, M. D. Chenu, and Bernard Haring. In addition, we published such thinkers as Martin Heidegger, Jürgen Moltmann, Barbara Ward, Albert Outler, Roger Schutz, Johannes Metz, and others. I was especially impressed with an article we translated by M. D. Chenu on "The End of the Constantinian Era," in which he spoke of the church cutting its ties with the privileges and worldview of the imperial ambitions of the Constantinian era. He had written the article before Vatican II; it had been published in France in 1961.

Cultural issues were addressed, such as film, and Flannery O'Connor's fiction; LSD and mysticism; science and theology; life in a ghetto; space travel; and youth culture. Dialogues between persons of different faiths were presented, and I exchanged opinions with G. Ledyard Stebbins, a professor of genetics at the University of California, Davis, in an article entitled, "Why I Gave Up Traditional Christianity."[7] Stebbins left the Episcopal church, frustrated by its dated liturgical language, by the theology of miracles, by the blood on the hands of Christian colonialists, and by a spirituality that no longer spoke to him as a scientist. This dialogue was my first foray into interacting with scientists around topics of spirituality.

In editorials, I wrote of Thomas Merton's hermitage experience and its invitation to the rest of us to respond to a "spiritual awakening. . . . The signs of such a movement will not be limited to a hermitage but will burgeon in a reawakening of the Christian conscience on today's critical issues: marriage and its meaning, politics as a service, civil justice, modern warfare."[8] In a subsequent editorial I talked about a "decisive Christianity—one founded on decisions that can rouse only insecurity." Risk marks today's Christian and especially the young, who must make decisions of depth about politics and the military, about business and religion.

> I was thirsty and you constructed a dam for me; I was starving and you brought me new farming techniques; I was oppressed by society's structures and you spent yourself in law, politics, economics to reconstruct society; I was ignorant and you strove to establish a school system; my culture was different from yours and you respected it; I was your enemy and you sought to understand me.[9]

Within the magazine's first two years, it had acquired over eight thousand paid subscribers. In addition to making some contemporary European theologians better known in America, *Listening* attempted to bring together culture and religious consciousness. When we published an article on Vietnam that was weak in its opposition to the war, my most trusted assistant on the magazine, Mike Duffy, quit in protest. It was a lesson for me in political consciousness. In subsequent issues we took a stronger stand against the war.

Editing *Listening* magazine was a great education for me. It plunged me into an ocean of exciting ideas in theology and culture at home and abroad. Not only soliciting articles and reading unsolicited manuscripts, translating articles and designing issues but also inspiring and organizing talent within the studentate, helping people overcome their self-doubts about being able to produce something from which others would benefit. In the process, I relearned the meaning of community, from the Latin *cum-munio,* to share a common task. (At one time we counted forty-four student brothers working on the magazine.) All work on the magazine was supplemental to our regular theological studies. But for myself and many others, it was a real enhancement of our theological education—a way to bring the new thought of Vatican II into our midst along with the responsibility that went with it.

There is an ironic story that has never been told about *Listening*'s financial survival. In our second issue we published a very fine critique of *Playboy* magazine by one of our more mature students, a psychology major. The critique was nuanced but clearly disapproving of Hugh Hefner's philosophy and exploitation of women. In the editorial to the issue I raise some questions about sexuality and Christianity.

The amazing reception accorded Hugh Hefner's PLAYBOY enterprise reveals more than a success tale, American-business style. Does the Playboy philosophy illustrate that Christianity has neglected a theology of sex that is real for our society with its prolonged adolescence, its leisure hours and its population concerns?[10]

One morning someone came into the theology classroom where I was sitting and announced that I had a long-distance call from Chicago. I could not imagine who it was. On the other end of the line was a Mr. Anson Mount, an assistant to Hugh Hefner in charge of "religious subjects" (in addition to the autumn football issue and other duties). He said Mr. Hefner loved our article, that it was the finest article ever done by a religious journal on his work. To make a long story short (one that included my visiting Mr. Mount at the Playboy offices in Chicago and his taking me to lunch at the Playboy Club, bunnies included), *Playboy* bought a large number of reprints of this article from *Listening* to distribute, I was told, to ministers and others who criticized Hugh Hefner unthinkingly. We at *Listening* saw that *Playboy* paid top dollar for the reprints and with the money we were able to promote our magazine more widely. The magazine marked my first foray into the secular world from my somewhat sheltered, monastic experience.

Though I had the provincial's approval and support for this venture from the start, other priests were not as pleased. It was not "normal" that student brothers not yet ordained should be busy "in the world" putting out a magazine and asserting themselves (though we did have three priests as "advisers" all along). Two incidents occurred that began to wake me from my political naïveté in the order.

The first was when the prior of the house, a very tall man who had always been friendly to me in the theology class he taught, stopped me in the corridor one day and said, "Brother Matthew, I will never forgive you for what you have done" (for starting the magazine). I was quite taken aback. As it turned out, a year later when the magazine was successful, this same priest was happy to tell people that he had been the prior when *Listening* was born. Lesson learned: Does anything succeed like success?

A second response was more sinister. My student master, the priest with overall responsibility for us students, called me in and said, "Congratulations. You made the Council vote for deaconate." Then his face froze: "By a vote of six to five." I was amazed. I only "snuck by."

"Why the close vote?" I asked.

"Well," he explained, "just before the vote was taken, a priest on the House Council pulled out a document that he said you had written and read from it."

I asked him more about this document and went upstairs and found my original. When I presented it to the student master, his Irish face turned a livid purple-red. "Why that son of a bitch," he said. "He left out words like *not* when he read this document to the Council."

"What do we do now?" I asked.

We decided to tell our side of the story. To do so, I interviewed everyone involved with the launching of *Listening* magazine, including young priests who were now stationed in Washington, D.C. We produced a lengthy document with over seventy-five footnotes, and the matter was laid to rest. Shortly afterward, the priest who had misrepresented my story on the Council was sent to Mexico City to work and I never saw him again. Lesson learned? Not all priests tell the truth. Not all Dominicans like one another or will be honest in dealing with dislike.

Several years later, one of the more perceptive professors at Aquinas Institute said to me, "Are you aware what a politician you are? The starting of *Listening* magazine was the biggest political coup ever pulled off in the history of the province. And students did it!" Actually, I did not see it as a political act. I just thought I was accepting my responsibility, but in a creative way, when I inherited an editorship position and reinvented the magazine we had been given.

Of course theology classes got me excited as well, and I read a lot for them, beyond what was required. I read the German Jesuit Karl Rahner's volumes of *Theological Investigations* diligently and was especially taken by an essay on "Priest and Poet" in which he says: "It would be a realization of that which as yet we glimpse from afar, if a priest were also to be a poet, if a poet were allowed to be a priest, if the life of a priest and that of a poet were to intermingle and be woven one into another."[11] One paragraph caught my attention so fully that I have never forgotten it.

> It is time that we asked: what has become of the times when great theologians also wrote hymns? When they could write like Ignatius of Antioch, compose poems like Methodius of Olympus, be carried away in hymnody like Adam of St. Victor, Bonaventure, and Thomas Aquinas? What has become of those times? Has theology become more perfect because theologians have become prosaic?[12]

As I retype Rahner's words thirty years after I first read them, I am moved by how important they were to me. How I chose a way to do theology that was not, in Rahner's words, "prosaic," or in the words of my generation, "exclusively left-brain." Yet I owe a lot to one of the headiest of them all, Karl Rahner. I believe this article entered my soul and memory more deeply than I knew at the time. It explains so many of the choices I have made over the years as a speaker, a writer, a theologian, and a priest.

Culture was also entering my (our) consciousness at St. Rose Priory by way of *music*. We would listen to Joan Baez and Peter, Paul, and Mary albums and were picking up on the more prophetic dimensions of music as our culture all around us was beginning to boil with discontent. (Several years earlier the Beatles had entered our lives, especially through the enthusiastic pushing of some Irish student brothers who had seen them live in Ireland shortly before coming to Dubuque to study.) One spring day an interesting stranger dropped in on us: he was a troubadour, about our age, and he was walking the country with his guitar. Several of us gathered around picnic tables in the backyard of the priory as he sang Bob Dylan's "The Times They Are A-Changin'." I was deeply moved. A stirring in my soul was beginning to tell me that work in the culture was just as important as work in the soul. Traditionally we had talked of contemplation and action; later I would call it mysticism and prophecy, but at this time all I knew consciously was that something deep was getting to my heart and passions.

Spirituality and Mysticism

I was high a lot of the time. The liturgy, the chanting of the office, friendships, the outdoors, studying theology, meditation—the silence and beauty of things and ideas all got me high. As my mystical experiences continued, I went looking among the priest-theologians at the priory for a spiritual director who could help me understand them. None of them could help me. Finally one of them said to me, "We priests haven't had the experiences you are speaking of. You are just going to have to deal with them yourself." I thought of what one brother had asked me in the hermitage: "Where are the contemplatives in your order?" And I became more and more aware of the lacuna in our education: in all my training as a Dominican we never had a course on spirituality or even a single *class* on the mystics. True, we studied Aquinas telling us that to illumine is better than to shine, but we never dealt with that ourselves. Nor in all my training did I hear Meister Eckhart's name used even once, despite the fact that he was a Dominican and the West's greatest mystic! I began to talk with our school officials about the need for such classes. I told them, "My generation is going to be more interested in spirituality than in religion." I urged them to send someone on to study spirituality. And I was more than happy to volunteer to be that someone.

"Where do you think one should go to study spirituality?" they asked. Their first suggestion was Spain.

"Oh, never!" I replied. "We don't need more sixteenth-century Carmelite spirituality from Spain." I was sure of what I spoke because, for my master's thesis in theology, I had received some very good advice from the faculty members I quizzed and they had urged me that, given my interest in spirituality, I should not begin with work on John of the Cross or Teresa of Ávila but on Jesus and the Gospels. This seemed to fit well with the urging of the Vatican Council to ground Catholic theology more in the Scriptures. Also, we were fortunate that a new faculty member had joined us after getting his advanced degree at the famous École Biblique in Jerusalem. As it turned out, he would be my adviser for my thesis on "The Prayer of Jesus in the New Testament and Its Significance for a Contemporary Theology of Prayer."

In the conclusion to that dissertation I made some points that I recognize today have been important to me ever since, such as that Jesus learned sensitivity and concern for others by immersing himself in their lives, and that culture and prayer go together, both for better and for worse. "The prayer of Jesus and the prayer of the early Church makes it clear that authentic prayer seeks to change the People of God in a particular time in history and in a particular culture. It is this time and this culture with its victories and its failures that must be the guiding norm for authentic prayer."[13] Jesus' culture was that of a Jew at a particular moment in the history of the Roman Empire. I learned the immense difference between Jesus who prayed and saw the world as a Jew, and the mystical tradition of the West that in great part saw the world through the dualistic philosophy of Hellenism. I reflect on how our mysticism must also reconnect to the Jewish spiritual consciousness even while we struggle for spiritual survival in the American empire. In my thesis I reflect on the necessary *tension* between prayer and culture.

> Those who wish to adapt prayer to contemporary culture, while they must be thoroughly familiar with that culture, must at the same time be aware of the new and startling dimension that prayer will bring to that culture. The Spirit working in men, while respective of and influenced by culture, is not limited to it.[14]

The next suggestion for a place to study, which came from the president of the school, was Rome. "Oh, no!" I replied. "Rome is the problem. I can't go there to study spirituality." He was clearly frustrated. The two places they had suggested, I wanted to veto. "Well, wise guy, where do you think you should go?" he asked. I said I didn't know but I would write Thomas Merton and ask him. The priest had a pained look on his face as though I was a bit mad, but he said I could go ahead and try.

I did write Thomas Merton and I told him something about myself, about my aspirations to study spirituality, about my desire to include psychology and world religions in my studies of the history of Christian spirituality, about my trip to the hermitage. It turned out he not only knew about the hermitage I had stayed in, but he himself had fought his abbot for six years in order to begin his own eremitical life. His first year in the hermitage was 1965—the same year I went to the hermitage. Interest in the eremitical life was becoming more widespread. I was amazed when only a few days after I posted my letter I received the following response.

January 23, 1967

Dear Matthew,

I'll do my best to answer your questions. Unfortunately, I am not too well informed as to what is available academically in this country. The first place that comes to mind is the Institut Catholique in Paris. Your general direction seems good: but where is Mystical and Ascetical Theology on your program? I don't think History of Spirituality covers it well enough. Maybe you include it in moral. If I can dig up a set of notes for the course I gave in "Mystical and Ascetical Theology," I'll send it along. [He did send me a package of his notes from teaching these classes and some articles he had not published.] Admittedly, one has to start all that from scratch. The Tanquerey approach just won't do. My own stuff is out of date after five or six years. . . .

I am glad you are going to work on spiritual theology. The prejudice in some Catholic quarters against mysticism is a bit strange, when outside the Church there is such an intense and ill-regulated hunger for and curiosity about spiritual experience (what with LSD and all that). I do think we are lying down on the job when we leave others to investigate mysticism while we concentrate on more "practical" things. What people want from us, after all, is the way to God.

I wish you luck in your search. Pray for me here in the woods. I feel very fortunate to have found what I was looking for. I keep you in my prayers. God be with you in everything.[15]

How perspicacious was the next-to-last paragraph! How relevant still today with the drug Ecstasy in the rave culture and psychedelics offering many people their only taste of transcendence because religion is preoccupied so often with itself instead of teaching spirituality or "ways to God."

Armed with this letter from Merton, I returned to my superiors and said, "Paris is the place. Send me to Paris." There was some resistance—it seemed that we never sent anyone to France who came back again, and the French Dominicans were still considered too theologically hot to handle by American Dominican standards.

Ordination came in late May 1967. It was an exciting day. The most mystical part of the ceremony for me occurred during the Litany of Saints when we ordinands were prostrate on the floor and the whole congregation was invoking this long list of saints. I felt the connection to a great line of spiritual leaders, of priests, trying to midwife the spirit in others. It was this sense of *ancestors,* of a connection with the past, with the communion of saints, with what today we would call a "morphic field" that moved me most about being ordained.

I preached at my first mass at Blessed Sacrament Church in Madison, scene of my entire religious upbringing previous to joining the Dominicans. Pope John XXIII featured prominently in my sermon, which was attended by many of my parents' Madison friends, Catholic and non-Catholic. Bishop Cletus O'Donnell of Madison came, as did friends of the family, former teachers at West High School, and a former girlfriend and her husband. Many of my Dominican brothers concelebrated the mass with me.

Shortly after returning to Aquinas Institute after the ten days we were allotted at home, I was called into the president's office. Good news! The provincial and his council had approved my going to Paris to get a doctorate in spirituality. Thanks to Merton, and some persistence on my part, I got the go-ahead. I had to finish my master's thesis during the summer and then move to France.

My last week in America I went to our Dominican summer camp to say good-bye to friends and, as it turned out, to make some new ones. I had a moving talk with a Dominican priest in his midthirties whom I had not met previously but whom I respected for the work he was doing with the poor and those on the edge. We talked about my upcoming French sojourn and I still remember his very serious words to me. "This will be the real test of who you are," he said. "You will have nothing to fall back on in Paris except yourself. Nothing you have learned previously about yourself or about any theological subject will matter compared to the challenges you will be facing probably all alone in Paris." It was hardy advice; a kind of warning that another rite of passage lay before me.

3

Family Influences:
Growing Up in the Fifties

My Dominican mentor was correct. In setting out for Paris at age twenty-six, I would be taking with me whatever the Dominicans had made of me the past nine years *and* whatever my family had made of me the previous seventeen years. Together they constituted my vocation as a young priest and Dominican wannabe theologian. As I look back on how my family influenced my vocation as a Dominican and theologian, I see as primal the following elements: love of nature (including sports); love of ideas; ecumenism; and lessons in letting go.

Nature and Sports in the Fox Family

I have already alluded to the natural beauty of Madison, Wisconsin, where I grew up. Sports were everywhere in Madison and among the Foxes; my mother and father were both excellent athletes, and my sisters excelled at sports as much as or at times better than their brothers. Sports were also a big part of our family's awareness because my father was assistant football coach at the University of Wisconsin from 1938 to 1948. The best years of that decade were before the war, when he coached players such as Elroy Hirsch and the team was highly successful. Football was more than a sport to my father; it had been, along with the Augustinian friars, his salvation.

Attending St. Rita's Augustinian high school in south Chicago as a teenager, my father excelled in sports. He was an angry kid and football was a sport in which anger could be rewarded. Being poor, with a father who could do little work because he was an invalid from polio, my father, George, as the oldest of three boys, had to take responsibility to keep the family going in hard Depression days. His success on the football field caught the attention of college scouts, and he got a scholarship first to a prep school in Pennsylvania and from there to Villanova University, on the main line outside Philadelphia.

Even as a student at Villanova he worked painting houses during the summers and sent money home. Thus football meant college for my father; it meant rescue from an otherwise unpromising future in poor, working-class Chicago. My father was the only one of his immediate family to go to college.

He gave great credit to the Augustinian priests who taught him morality and religion and offered models of male adulthood from high school through college. My father's anger no doubt stemmed from his deprived and difficult childhood. When I was ordained a priest, I received a letter from an old high school buddy of his named Red who said that my father was the "goddamn angriest young man I have ever known in my life." He expressed surprise that George had a son who was a priest and said, "He must have married a helluva woman" to have so tamed him.

Thus my father's third salvation, besides football and the Augustinians, was my mother, Beatrice Sill, whom he met in his junior year of college. She was a native of western Pennsylvania and was, as she liked to say, "as far away from being an Irish Roman Catholic as you can get." Her father was English through and through and an explicit "antipapist" who excelled at many things from banking to golfing to reciting Shakespeare. In the modest town of Warren, Pennsylvania, he had worked his way up from errand boy to president of the local bank. My mother's mother was Jewish—her maiden name was Jacoby—and from New York City. Her family never practiced any kind of Jewish faith, however, and when my grandmother married my grandfather she converted to the Episcopal church. My mother was raised as a rather strict Episcopalian. Her maternal grandmother was a concert pianist who had studied under Liszt and performed all over Europe.

The most formative moment in my mother's life was the sudden death of her father when she was eleven. On a visit to New York City with his wife, he became ill with what the doctor diagnosed as heartburn but in fact was appendicitis. He died within the day. His wife, accustomed to a sheltered life with servants, now had nothing to live on but an insurance policy that could not sustain their lifestyle. She and her three girls first moved to "the other side of the tracks" (where, incidentally, Roman Catholics lived) and eventually to Wayne, Pennsylvania, just down the road from Villanova University.

My mother's upbringing and my father's could hardly have been more different. She was a somewhat pampered child of a sheltered mother and banker father, Episcopalians in a small town in the East. He grew up in the tough neighborhoods of Chicago, helping provide for his struggling family because his father could barely work. His family was Roman Catholic and Irish when signs still read JOBS AVAILABLE. IRISH NEED NOT APPLY. My parents met and married secretly during my father's junior year of college—secretly because it was against the rules for him to be married while on the football team. Their marriage was not only verboten at Villanova University, it was a disappointment to both families when they heard of it, after the fact. My mother's family was not pleased that she had married a Roman Catholic, and my father's aunt told my mother on first meeting her, "We always hoped and prayed that George would marry a nice Irish Catholic girl." Judging from the number of times my mother repeated this story, there is evidence that she never quite got over it. An ethnic Catholic my mother was not.

Their first child arrived ten months later, and my mother took my brother Tom to my father's graduation ceremony. The Depression was in full swing at this time, but my father received a break. His coach at Villanova, Harry Stuhldreher, who had quarterbacked the famous Notre Dame "four horsemen" team, was hired as head coach at the University of Wisconsin and offered my father a job as one of his assistants. Thus in 1938 my parents set out for Madison with one son in their arms and another child on the way. A year later came my sister and a year after that, on the darkest day of the year, December 21, 1940, came me. Following a war respite, my three younger siblings were born in 1945, 1946, and 1947.

My mother had a rule that made her a liberated woman long before her time: no matter how many kids, diapers, or pregnancies (she gave birth to seven of us in eleven years), she took two hours every afternoon for herself. This might mean reading or bridge club or book club or sewing club (all the clubs contained interesting women, usually spouses of professors at the University of Wisconsin, and to this day my mother puts great emphasis on her friendships with women). Or it might mean hiking, bicycling, or tennis. For these outings, I was sometimes brought in tow. One of my earliest memories is of sitting in the leaves at the tennis courts at West High School (which I would attend twelve years hence) while my mother played tennis, screaming my lungs out at the loud noises the band made as it practiced.

I don't think my mother ever tamed my father; nor did he tame her. Both were strong personalities who seldom gave an inch when they disagreed. Their fights were real, and sometimes my father would remain sullen for a while. But there was always love there. We kids loved to see them dress up to go out dancing. They were a very handsome couple and, as my mother told me recently in her eightieth year, "I was as in love with him when he died [at age seventy-six] as when we first met." She also told me, in a surprise moment years ago, that "sex kept our marriage together."

Ideas and Religion at Home

I often tell my students that ideas liberate; ideas are nonelitist, that is, available to all who will entertain them. What did Karl Marx, whose influence on the twentieth century has been so great, do all his life except hang out in libraries and come up with a few significant ideas? The right ideas at the right time serve the people. I have always been excited about ideas. Perhaps this derives from my growing up in Madison, a capital city and a university town that had cultural advantages far beyond its size. It was full of people with ideas. My mother was one of them.

A few years into their marriage, my mother felt that it would not work to have a family that was half-Episcopalian and half-Catholic. She decided, on her own and without telling my father, to seek out instructions in Catholicism. She hunted around and found what she would call a "modern" priest. He played tennis with her and apparently had a head on his shoulders, so she took instructions from him, again unbeknownst to my father. When she had completed instructions she attended Sunday mass with my father as she often did and at communion time stepped into the aisle to go to communion. My father protested, saying she could not do that as a "non-Catholic." She insisted she was now a Catholic; a fight ensued in the side aisle of Blessed Sacrament Church. Both did end up at the communion rail, however. The argument over church rules, the independence of my mother, the fight resolved in communion—all tell something of our religious upbringing.

My father was quite a strict disciplinarian. He wanted us to behave in church, for example. One way he got us to do this was to quiz us after church on the sermon we had heard. Another way, which he applied to the four older ones when we were young, was if things really got out of hand he'd have us kneel after church with our hands folded on the card table for an hour. The only problem was that I, being the youngest and littlest, could barely reach the top of the table and invariably would fall underneath it. This would cause giggles from my siblings, and what was supposed to be tough, Augustinian penance for our sins often resulted in lighthearted merriment.

My father was a very good man. His moral conduct was strict and he was generous, contributing more money to the parish than wealthy people who had fewer mouths to feed. While his rather strict and literal idea of Catholicism was firmly implanted by his Catholic education by Augustinians, he did learn to loosen up over the years. Once, in his late forties, he had a stroke when alone at home. Thinking he was dying, he wrote a farewell letter to the family in which he said that he loved us all and whatever struggles there had been in our lives and mistakes in our upbringing, he was sure we all knew one thing: that love had been present in our home. He also said that he had never cheated on my mother. At the time, the late sixties, we children thought that was a bit "quaint" as a confession, but as I get older I admire his commitment not only to his marriage vows but to a morality in general. After he left coaching he went into business as a paint contractor, and he once told me late in his life that he was glad he was not in the painting contracting business any longer because he "could not stomach the cheating and under-the-table buy-ing of contracts" that was going on.

Besides his anger, I would say the second biggest shortcoming of my father was his naïveté. I think he trusted people and institutions more than they de-served. An example would be his trust of the church as an institution; another would be his trust of American capitalism and of a friend who steered him into the stock market when he retired (for the first time), with the result that my father lost all his savings and had to find new work in his sixties (which he did, managing a condominium in Winter Park, Florida). He also trusted Richard Nixon and the Republican party, and after Watergate he seemed rather mute about both subjects.

My father had an amazing streak of feminist consciousness—no doubt liv-ing with my mother helped to educate him in this regard. My sisters remem-ber how one day he called the family together when four of us were in high school and made this announcement: "I do not make enough money," he said, "to send you all to college, yet your mother and I want you all to go. Therefore, I expect the boys to work to get scholarships of one kind or other, and I promise I will pay to see the girls go to college." For a self-made man of the mid–1950s that was not a bad sense of values.

He never missed mass on Sundays or holy days, nor did any of the rest of us. At Lent he always gave up cigarettes and alcohol (he would drink a jigger of whiskey a night or two a week). He prayed sincerely at church, often with a rosary in his hand (though that was jettisoned after the Second Vatican Coun-cil). While he was more "religious" than my mother—more cognizant and caring about church laws and obligations—there was certainly a deep spiritu-ality to him as well. For example, I have already alluded to my mother's car accident when she was fifty years old. She was unconscious for days, she lost an eye, and her personality was severely affected for years afterward. Yet none of us ever heard him speak a word of self-pity or complaint about her in her altered condition. Instead, he was happy that she was still around. His faith kept him going in difficult circumstances.

I would call my mother more spiritual than religious. She read a lot (my fa-ther never read a book—not even any of mine—whereas my mother was and still is a constant reader even though she never went to college). She passed on exhortations that were more spiritual than moral, for example: "There's no such thing as boredom. Get outside and do something. Go to a museum or a park or get a book to read. No child of mine will ever be bored." Once, when I was fifteen years old, we were doing dishes together and she turned to me out of the blue and said, "Tim [that was my name then], whatever you do when you grow up, be a person with opinions." She had a sense of social jus-tice that came through on numerous occasions. She was always directing us to fix up boxes of clothes we had outgrown to give to the poor—provided the clothes were in decent condition. Earning money was a part of our growing up. We were instructed early that our family was large and we all had to "pitch in." Long before I knew what the word *college* meant, my mother informed me that I was making money from my paper routes and snow shoveling and selling peanuts and popcorn at the Wisconsin football games "to go to college."

My mother's greatest virtue is her zest for life. When she had her car accident in 1963, all the doctors on the scene and in the hospital said she could not survive. But weeks later she emerged from her coma and one doctor said, "She survived on willpower alone. Medically, she ought not to have survived." She herself told me later that she had what we call today a "near death experience" and that she decided to return to finish her work on earth. It is true that after her accident she was a calmer woman, and she did not fear death any longer (something she had feared ever since her father's sudden demise).

Mom always encouraged our interests and talents. For me, it was writing poetry and my love of Abraham Lincoln. During my childhood I must have received and read every book on Lincoln ever published. One treat she created when I was about eleven years old was to take a friend and me on a kind of Lincoln pilgrimage to Illinois—Springfield, New Salem, and his burial place. For me it was a great moment. In retrospect, I think she liked it as much as I did. One Christmas I not only got three books on Lincoln but Lincoln bookends as well—which I am still using.

One virtue I especially admire in my mother is that she knew how to let go of her kids. In fact, it was always my impression that she could hardly wait to let go of us so that she could get on with her many interests in addition to mothering: travel, reading, making friends, going to school, painting, and working. I cannot vouch for my siblings on this but for my part, when I left home at nineteen years of age for the Dominican novitiate, I was the one with tears, not my mother. When we had discussed my choice of vocation she had simply said, "I don't understand celibacy; but do whatever makes you happy."

My mother did her best to practice Catholicism as she was instructed, though she welcomed the Second Vatican Council with open arms, saying things like, "I told you that Latin is unimportant," "I knew that you can't go to hell for eating meat on Fridays," and "I never understood the rosary anyway." Probably the most problematic demand on her was cooking nonmeat meals on Fridays, Lenten days, and special holy days, which she sometimes failed to remember. One such Lenten Wednesday, when we all sat down to eat vegetarian and she brought on meatballs, there was a hush around the table. The kids in Catholic school told us we couldn't eat meat. She took her big wooden spoon, held it over the food and blessed it, and said, "It's a greater sin to waste food than to eat it. Eat the food and I'll confess the sin." We ate.

Ecumenism

I think it can be said that I grew up Catholic but not ethnic Catholic. To this day, unlike Andrew Greely, I refuse to identify Catholicism with south-side Chicago Irishisms. I believe the word *catholic* should be understood in theory and praxis for its true meaning: universal. Therefore, ecumenical. While we all have remnants of a tribal soul in us, our better angels are not always released by appeals to that soul.

Mom used to say that she anticipated the Second Vatican Council—and she did. Especially when it came to ecumenism, for my parents' friends were a diverse lot—Catholic, Jewish, Protestant. There was a respect for diversity but also a kind of pride (which emanated from my father rather than my mother) at being Catholic. We all went to public grade schools until the year of my fourth grade. There is a story that the then very Irish bishop of Madison once called my mother and complained that we were not in Catholic schools. Her reply was that (1) we couldn't afford it; (2) the public schools in Madison were of a very high standard; and (3) we received religious instruction at home and went to church schools for religious instruction as well. When he insisted that we would all go to hell if we weren't in Catholic schools, she replied, "Well, at least they'll be in hell with educated people." We never heard from the bishop again.

One of my parents' most far-reaching decisions was to rent a room in our house to a foreign graduate university student each time one of us went off to college. This meant I spent my high school years living on the third floor with an Indian Sikh (who would cook wheat germ at three o'clock in the morning); with a Venezuelan bullfighter manqué who would lift up his shirt to anyone interested to show his scars from bullfighting and who fell in love every time he left the house and would seek my mother's counsel after that; with an Australian who kept skis in the trunk of his car to escape to the Canadian Rockies should an atom bomb fall (given the state of his car, I don't think he would have made it as far as Minnesota); with a Yugoslavian Communist who was an engineering student; with a Scandinavian athlete and atheist; and so on. It was a tremendous education in ecumenism and in global awareness. I got the message that our world is not made up of Westerners, Catholics, or even Christians, and the message was delivered right in our home on a daily basis, at the dinner table.

Dinners were a serious ritual. All of us had to be home for dinner or call in and be excused. My father would lead discussions often, asking each member of the family for an opinion on the topic at hand. This was no doubt a bit of a trial for the younger ones as we older ones became more glib and facile at self-expression. Once, when I was in college, I brought a friend home for the weekend. After the first meal he said, "Eating with your family is like being at the United Nations. Not just the diversity of people but the topics you all talk about." I was surprised, for I presumed that what went on in our family went on in all families.

One day my parents sat us down at the round dining room table to explain something that was obviously very serious to them. I was a freshman in high school. Quite solemnly, they told us that we were one-quarter Jewish because Mom was half-Jewish. I was very touched by their presentation and I felt pride in this revelation. Imagine! We were Catholic, Protestant (at least Episcopalian—but I didn't make subtle theological distinctions at that time), *and* Jewish. We were, to use a phrase that would be common later, an ecumenical family. I had read a lot of stories about the Holocaust and would lie awake at night imagining how strong the survivors were. Of course I had Jewish friends at school, and we would point out the synagogues in neighborhoods we drove through, but to have Jewish blood in me—indeed enough to have been classified as eligible for the gas ovens myself—this was a moving moment of revelation.

I remember my father's chagrin and horror when a story appeared in the Madison paper about students from the local Catholic high school breaking into a synagogue and desecrating parts of it. My father went to apologize to the rabbi. Our family was sensitized to religious bigotry on a regular basis. My mother was especially sensitive to hypocrisy in religion, often saying that it would be better to be a good atheist than a hypocritical Catholic. There were Catholics in our parish who were famous for their piety—daily mass, for example—but they failed to impress my mother. Indeed, years later, I learned that the most visible of them—a married couple who went to mass every day but each at a different time—had been living in a loveless marriage, and I was struck anew by the wisdom of my mother's intuitions.

During my fourth grade (and my older brother's seventh grade), we all switched from public school to Blessed Sacrament grade school. I had wonderful Sinsinawa Dominican sisters teaching me from fourth to eighth grade. No "patent leather shoes" warnings; no beatings; no Jansenism. As it turned out, the public schools were advanced in reading, so I was often excused from reading exercises by my fourth-grade teacher and allowed to create my own reading in a back room.

As a youngster I found serving mass to be fun. It was a responsibility—you were expected to show up no matter what the time of day or night (the nights were for "Benediction" ceremonies) and, like the postal carriers, come rain or shine or sleet or snow. It was demanding—getting up in the dark; learning to recite Latin prayers that one only barely understood. It meant ringing bells at moments of mystery; hanging out in the sacristy with other nervous boys before the ceremonies began; being around the priests as they joked or prepared themselves for the service; sneaking an occasional fistful of unconsecrated hosts or a sip of unconsecrated wine; the smell of beeswax and incense and charcoal roasting; the compliments from lay brothers and others when we did well. Above all, serving mass as a youngster meant *entering the mysteries.* As a child, before I was old enough to serve at the altar, I was fascinated by church, especially the singing of the Latin Gregorian chant. Among the biggest mysteries for me as a boy was, What goes on before mass? What goes on behind the door and in that room from which priest and altar boys emerge? Needless to say, the day did arrive when I was able to answer that part of the mystery of the mass.

Polio: A Lesson in Letting Go and Not Taking for Granted

When I was twelve, a family vacation changed my life. First, there was the mystical side to it. I was struck by the wonder of seeing New York City for the first time. But the most moving mystical experience awaited me on our drive into Canada (my first foray onto foreign soil!) and the visit to Niagara Falls. I couldn't believe the power and majesty of it all as we stood, decked in yellow raincoats, underneath the falls and took in the colors and sounds and mist. My soul was radically opened up by that experience. On the way home we stopped at Indiana Dunes State Park for swimming and relaxation. A few months later the doctors who diagnosed my polio traced the infection to the swimming at that park.

Polio altered my life, especially my inner life. The year before, a playmate who lived up the block from me had died of polio. So I knew something of the effect of polio. Yet when I learned I had it, I felt no fear. In fact, I felt a certain secret pleasure at the attention I was getting while living for months in the hospital. Classmates and relatives and family friends sent stacks of get-well cards that we strung up around the hospital room. The doctors, fearing that other children in our family could contract the virus from me, forbade direct contact; instead, my brothers and sisters were allowed to visit outside my window. The only real pain was the spinal tap when I first entered the hospital; a few days later, when out of curiosity I reached back to touch what I imagined to be a gigantic hole in my back where they had done the spinal tap, a shudder that I will never forget went through my entire body. I rather liked the nurses who fussed over me, and I eagerly awaited the grape juice that was brought on a cart every night. All in all, my memories of being in the hospital are not painful. If anything, a kind of joy entered my heart at that time. A joy and a trust.

No doubt the real event of polio for me was the letting go of my father's—or my culture's?—unspoken agenda for me. I was twelve years old; my brothers in high school were playing a lot of serious football, and I imagined that that was my destiny as well, since I was the son of a football star and coach and a boy growing up in the 1950s. But now that was not to be. I had polio. I could not walk. They could not tell me if I would ever walk again. I let go and became very open to other possibilities of growing up.

And that was when Brother Martin entered my life. This soft-spoken Dominican brother, with a special accent all the way from Louisiana, who spoke so quietly and had crystal-clear eyes and a puckish smile, visited me regularly in the hospital. We would talk and laugh, and I was genuinely moved by his presence. He was harboring a secret at the time: a vocation growing in him to be a contemplative monk. Shortly he would act on that vocation and leave the Dominicans to become a Trappist monk. But his joy was contagious and he gave me, subtly, another way to see the world. One that was softer and more heart-oriented. One where sensitivity counted and was okay. His contemplative nature invoked my own.

Having polio taught me something about solitude: that it was okay to be alone and to not be in control. Trust is important. And waiting is part of life.

As things turned out, I had the best of both worlds. Though I had polio and my legs were affected, I gradually, with therapy, got my leg movements back. Within a year I was playing sports again. Only this time there was a difference inside me: first, I felt deeply grateful, not to anyone in particular—not even to a God-in-the-sky—but to the universe itself. I was well. I could walk and run and play. I felt an exuberance and I said to myself, "I will never take my legs for granted again." My eighth-grade teacher, a stern principal of Blessed Sacrament grade school, admonished me that I should play less vigorously at recess. But I was just exercising my joy at being able to run again. Today I like to tell people that mysticism is about "not taking for granted." An ecological awareness is therefore a mystical awareness—not taking health or healthy air, water, forests, soil for granted. Clearly, my polio experience baptized me into a mystical awareness.

My second feeling on emerging from my sickness was one of having let go of a burden. I was no longer just my father's son; I could make my own way. As it was, I did indeed play sports in high school but with more detachment (and less strength) than my brothers, and that was fine with me. There were other men to emulate—my uncle George, for example, and especially Brother Martin. My vocation began with my polio experience. I became a more serious person, a more conscious one as we would say today. And more sensitized.

Years later, my mother told me my parents' side of my polio story, a side I had never known. When she and my father came to me after the spinal tap to tell me I had polio, and did so in the most solemn of ways (after all, my father's father had been crippled most of his adult life by polio and our neighbors had lost their son to the virus the year before), I simply responded: "I know." My father was flabbergasted. "How did you know?" he asked. "I overheard you discussing the possibility on the phone a month ago," I said. My father's attitude toward me shifted at that moment, and Mother explained it this way: All his life Dad had admired *physical courage*—that was what football was all about and it got Dad where he was in life. But I, a twelve-year-old boy, had shown a *moral courage* that totally amazed him. She explained that Dad was never the same after that, either in his relationship to me or in his attitude toward life.

All I remember is simply facing sickness and death as children often do: without a big agenda around it.

In retrospect, I can see that my having polio was a kind of rite of passage or coming of age. I left home—not out of anger or disappointment, but out of necessity—when I had polio, and I matriculated into another home, a larger one—call it church, spirit, community.

After my polio and during my high school years my father was, as my mother later pointed out to me, very different in his relationship to me. I frankly do not remember having a single argument with him as a teenager. He trusted me, would lend me the car whenever I asked and it didn't interfere with his needs. We were not really close, but we were friends. One evidence of this is the moment when I decided to try out for the priesthood. I made the decision myself, telling no one except a priest at Blessed Sacrament with whom I was having regular talks. When it came time to break the news to my family, I chose to tell my mother, who in turn told my father. I remember the only conversation he and I had about my choice. He said simply, "Do what you feel called to do. Remember what Jesus said, 'You have not chosen me but I have chosen you.'" He was, of course, more than pleased with my decision. On the day of my first mass ten years later he told me, "This is the happiest day of my life." But he never pushed and never interfered, and during all the years of my training he kept a quiet support of my vocation. I never felt any pressure from him other than to always try to do my best, a value he and my mother instilled early in all of us.

When I became the kind of priest I did, he was less than enthusiastic about my work. I know he never read any of my books, but he knew a lot of my positions on the Vietnam War, for example, or on corporate power in America, and did not agree with them. Yet we always maintained a polite discourse (often I avoided political subjects). All family members agree that it is a kind of blessing that he died before my year of enforced silence by the Vatican and before my expulsion from the Dominican order. He was the conservative in the family—he even voted for Barry Goldwater—but he was a conservative with a conscience and a conservative married to a woman who was anything but conservative. And in many ways he was much more nuanced than conservatism would have it.

The finest talk we ever had as adults occurred in the midseventies when I confided to him some of the struggle I was undergoing in the Dominican order. I was startled at his response. First, he talked at length about *envy* and how envious men had driven him out of coaching at the University of Wisconsin and had done their best to smear his character in the process. And then he posed a question to me that was so radical, coming from him, that I am surprised by it still. He asked simply, "Why do you stay? Most of your friends have left. Why not leave?" I don't think he was subtly attempting to get me to rethink my vocation by this question; my father was not subtle in his psychological approach. I think it was an honest, man-to-man question. I felt a great deal of newly found freedom in my vocation after that conversation. By the midseventies even my father, lifelong Catholic that he was, found a lot of church goings-on difficult to stomach. And his wisdom in attributing my troubles essentially to envy was something to ponder. Though he was a conservative Catholic, he had outgrown and transcended any ethnic or even punitive attitudes in his faith.

High School: The Beginnings of an Intellectual Life

Though I was granted a scholarship to attend the Catholic high school in town, I chose instead to follow my older siblings to the public school. In retrospect, going to West High was a very important step in my journey of love of ideas and pursuit of ecumenical religion. I made good friends there, persons who went into the Peace Corps and beyond; who have worked for the governor of Wisconsin; who teach feminist courses in universities on the East Coast. Some friends were Jewish; some agnostic; some Protestant. This variety challenged me intellectually. Philosophical debates abounded during my time at West High, and when I was challenged I would turn to my parish priest, who was a Dominican, for answers. He had me read G. K. Chesterton's *The Everlasting Man* (which took up evolution in a way that only Chesterton could take it up) and his *The Dumb Ox* and *St. Francis of Assisi*, books that dealt with Thomas Aquinas and Francis and first woke me up to the idea of a Middle Ages that might not have been all a dark ages. I was made quite conscious of my Catholicism in this public-school milieu. I remember my first semester in an English class when we were reading *A Midsummer Night's Dream* and there was a line about "nuns in the nunnery." I objected to that phrase, comparing it to "cans in a cannery" and pointing out that I had been taught by nuns and none of them described their home as a "nunnery." I remember the stares I got from other students, and from then on I was pretty much the token Catholic in my class. I didn't flinch from the designation, and I suspect I rather liked the responsibility.

Throughout high school my favorite classes were English and history. I had some wonderful teachers (most of them women) in these fields who inspired and encouraged me and whose senses of humor made it all worthwhile. I most liked English because I could write and get ideas across, and of course I loved the readings, especially Shakespeare. Reading Shakespeare always engendered mystical experiences for me. My mystical life, my soul, was enlarging as I read literature, and I looked forward to these times with delight.

I think history moved me for the same reason that reading about Abraham Lincoln during my childhood had moved me: history was like a stage on which greatness strode. I was filled with respect and awe for many historical figures, most of whom I desired to emulate in some way. The first time I visited my mother's family in Pennsylvania, I kept a journal of the trip (and eventually wrote a long poem about Wayne, Pennsylvania, the town where my grandmother lived). While in Pennsylvania, we made an excursion to Independence Hall, the Liberty Bell, and other historical sites. As a child I was fascinated to see where the Declaration of Independence had been written and argued over, and to see the balcony where President George Washington had launched the experiment in democracy.

Religion was not the only fascination I had as a boy, even after my polio. Politics also interested me and in 1954, shortly after we obtained our first television set, a drama unfolded that so mesmerized me that I would skip school or run home during the lunch break just to watch it. I am speaking of course of the Army-McCarthy hearings.

Joe McCarthy was *our* senator. My father had voted for him; he represented our state; *and* he was a Roman Catholic who, as we were all instructed to be, was anticommunist with a vengeance. I would ask myself, Must I like him because he is Catholic too? I remember the moment in the Army-McCarthy hearings when Walsh nailed McCarthy—not on a legal point or a parliamentary maneuver but on a moral, even spiritual, point. I can hear Mr. Walsh asking the question even to this day, "At long last, sir, have you no decency?" I think McCarthy lost everything at that moment, but of course we hardly knew it at the time.

My interest in politics stemmed from my interest in Abraham Lincoln. The more I read of his life and speeches, the more enamored I was with the man. I wanted to be like him. Maybe I should become a lawyer and a politician and run for office someday. These two main interests drew my attention: law (that leads to politics) and religion. I had to decide which direction to go in life before too long.

In high school I graduated from a daily paper route to a newspaper stand at a strategic location—in front of my local church. It was quite a hot little business. Sales increased considerably, the stand was less an eyesore than the previous one, the customers were friendly (after all they *were* buying on their way out of mass), and now I had to get up early only one day a week. The Dominican brothers would stop by regularly to chat and exchange stories, and it put me in a milieu of parish goings-on. Today we might say it was a kind of "ministry."

In retrospect, I can see that what the newsstand did for me *most* was to put me in a position to critique sermons. Since there were seven masses each Sunday, and since my work mainly consisted of being there when mass ended to catch the crowd wanting its Sunday paper, I had a lot of time between acts. I would spend much of that time taking in the various masses—*especially* when it was fifteen or twenty degrees below zero outside. Most winters I attended about six masses (I would sneak home for a quick breakfast during the seventh one); and that meant six sermons; and that meant a lot of thinking about what did and did not constitute good preaching. My Sundays became a kind of theological/preaching workshop for me and raised my consciousness about theology and about communication—the good communicators and preachers and the bad ones.

In addition to scoring this kind of "Olympics" of mass and preachers on Sundays, I got into another habit. Since I no longer had to peddle daily papers before dawn, I was free in the mornings before breakfast and I started going to daily mass. I liked daily mass. The quiet, the silence, the mystery (it was still in Latin), the attention the heart got, the Scripture readings, the saints' lives to meditate on (each saint had a day of the year to be remembered), the ecstasy of God becoming bread (a more radical notion and less anthropocentric than God becoming just human!), the communion time, the masses for the dead (the priest wore all black) when the organist would sing the requiem mass in Gregorian chant—all this moved me deeply. My favorite mass day was Saturday because at that time Saturdays were dedicated to Mary if they weren't filled up by some saint's feast day. For Mary's feast days the readings were from the wisdom literature of the Hebrew Bible—Proverbs and Song of Songs and Sirach. Wonderful images strode threw my heart during those masses—images for which at that time I had no names at all. They were just something sacred and useful and good nourishment for the heart. Following are a few such texts:

> Alone I encircled the vault of the sky,
> and I walked on the bottom of the deeps.
> Over the waves of the sea and over the whole earth,

and over every people and nation I have held sway. . . .
From eternity, in the beginning, he created me,
and for eternity I shall remain. . . .
Approach me, you who desire me,
and take your fill of my fruits.

SIRACH 24:5–6, 9, 26

From everlasting I was firmly set,
from the beginning, before earth came into being.
The deep was not, when I was born,
there were no springs to gush with water.
Before the mountains were settled,
before the hills, I came to birth:
before he made the earth, the countryside,
or the first grains of the world's dust.
When he fixed the heavens firm, I was there.

PROVERBS 8:22–26

Here was a world removed from football and cars and the anticommunist ideas in the air. Perhaps a better one; certainly a deep and memorable one. A world of mystery and what I can call today "cosmology." A world that today we recognize as the world of the goddess.

Another religious exercise I engaged in was to read the Bible every day. I set as a goal for myself to read the entire Bible, and I figured to do so I would have to read fifteen to thirty minutes a day. I did indeed finish the whole Bible—how much of it I understood or even found interesting would be another story. But I felt I was doing something worthwhile, and there were times that a kind of truth or insight broke through with some force. I kept this practice a secret and until this day I have never told anyone about these Bible readings.

At home my education continued along the lines of my parents'—and especially my mother's—values. Reading was important to her and therefore to the whole family. We subscribed to as many as thirteen magazines at one time. Among them were *Time, Life, Saturday Evening Post, Reader's Digest, National Geographic, Boy's Life, Popular Mechanics, Mechanics Illustrated, Ladies' Home Journal, Quick,* and *Sign* (the one Catholic magazine). I read *Time* religiously and all the others as well (with the exception of *Ladies' Home Journal*). Bishop Sheen was a hero in the household (we watched him on television every Tuesday evening), and I was struck by his oratory and impressed by his audience, which included non-Catholics as well as Catholics. To this day, I remember Bishop Sheen mocking Karl Marx and Sigmund Freud in his programs. While I went along with his sarcasm at the time, it has struck me since that it rings strange for a person with a doctorate in philosophy, as Sheen had, to hold Marx or Freud up to ridicule. No doubt the sponsors of his program (Admiral was one, as I recall) were pleased with Sheen's ecclesial support of capitalism. With McCarthy *and* Bishop Sheen preaching anticommunism, Catholics were becoming more and more mainstream in America.

My dating life was pretty normal and fairly uneventful. In my four years of school I had three girlfriends, the third having remained a friend to this day. The first girl's desires didn't match the moral warnings I got from my parish priest so we split up, though cordially. The second girl and I got along fine, but after a while I became restless and told her I wanted to play the field as I was thinking of becoming a priest and wanted to get more experience with a variety of girls. She broke down and cried—whether because we were breaking up or because I was becoming a priest I don't know—but that left me free to date someone else. That someone else became important to me for the rest of high school and my two years of college. She was smart, assertive, funny, and serious—a very serious Lutheran girl. We had plenty of theological and other discussions. She married a radical Jewish historian and recently surprised me when she said she never felt comfortable with my efforts at playing football in high school because I was "so sensitive a person." This strikes me today because it feels like so much of my adult work has been more like playing football, that is, struggle, than it has been nourishing my sensitivity. Whereas my years of training as a Dominican and the long hours of prayer and meditation did indeed feed the sensitive side of my soul.

I worked several jobs during summer vacations, one of them at a pop factory well outside the city limits. I would bicycle the ten miles or so to work, work all day in the sweaty factory, bicycle home (sometimes stopping in a church for a few minutes of prayer), and then suit up for my summer softball game. I loved being out in the grass, underneath the sun, hitting the ball or someone. There was mysticism in all that too: a union with the earth, the sky, the sun, my body, and the camaraderie of a team at struggle.

The most important thing I learned at my summer job was *what I did not want to do with the rest of my life.* One man, a refugee from Russia, had been labeling bottles and packing them for forty-some years. I said to myself, Education is important. It's college for me. I could never do this kind of work for the rest of my life.

Between my junior and senior years in high school, I read two books that affected me profoundly. One was Leo Tolstoy's *War and Peace.* For me it was a panoply of life; it was life put to words; it was all of life—politics and war and love and death; and it was all sacred. I told a friend that the experience of reading that book "blew my soul wide open." I will always believe that I owe my decision to enter the Dominican order more to Tolstoy than to any other single person. On reading that book, I was desirous of pursuing "soul work." I wanted to go someplace where Life and the Sacred could be explored. Perhaps I owe my long-held belief that spirituality and art go together to the influence that Tolstoy's art had on my journey.

Then I made a retreat (each year our religion class, sponsored by our local parish, made a retreat to a local seminary on the other side of Lake Menona). I loved those retreats—the silence and sense of depth; the time to think, write down questions, and have them answered. On that retreat I picked up a book called *Seven Storey Mountain* by Thomas Merton. That book also moved me and gave me more insight into where one goes to explore the soul more fully. It promised me spiritual experience, an experience of God that I believed I was already imbibing in some small way. But I wanted more, like the man (the monk) who had written this book. I thought of becoming a monk like Merton, and I read about the monastic life and studied books about other religious orders. When I began gingerly to talk about these matters with my parish priest, however, he recommended the Dominicans, the order to which my parish priests and lay brother friends all belonged.

I was drawn to the order by these people. They seemed happy and serious and about something important. To hear them tell it, they combined the best of both worlds: they experienced meditation like the monks but they worked "in the world" by teaching and preaching. I had a secret desire to bring "faith" to the University of Wisconsin crowd—to lecture and preach in universities. The Dominicans, with their story of beginning when universities came into existence and being there with the best of them—the University of Paris, for example—seemed to offer some possibility of fulfilling this secret wish. My parish priest gave me a book called *The Priest* and I read it carefully, hiding it in a desk drawer on the third floor of our house.

My senior year of high school, I made a retreat to the Dominican House of Studies in Dubuque, Iowa, where Dominicans studied to become priests. It was a shiny, new building smelling of incense and fresh paint. It was large and sunny and above all filled with Dominicans or wannabe Dominicans. During the retreat I was struck deeply by the chanting of the Divine Office that they did in choir stalls several times a day. It was a profoundly aesthetic experience to hear this beautiful music. Meeting with them in their recreation room, I was struck by their alertness and joy. I decided, on my way home from Dubuque, that this was what I wanted to try after graduation from high school. I would put law and politics on hold; I would follow my heart; I would choose to join the Dominicans.

From the Languid Fifties to the Stirring Sixties

I had grown up in the fifties amidst Bishop Sheen and Wisconsin's own Senator McCarthy and "I Like Ike" politics. But something deeper lay below the surface, a kind of spiritual stretching that would change the way we saw the world. The taking-for-granted sameness of the fifties was destined to unravel in the sixties. The modern age was beginning to yield to the postmodern one. As David Halberstam sees it, the fifties were quiet on the surface, "almost languid," but below, passions were beginning to boil. The rock-and-roll scene as symbolized by Elvis Presley, the development of the birth control pill, the coming of age of television, the civil rights movement in the deep south—all would exert a profound influence on society in the next decade. And progressive theologians in the French Catholic church especially—Teilhard de Chardin, Yves Congar, and M. D. Chenu were offering ideas so radical that their books could not be published. Yet, in the sixties, they would emerge as leaders of the Second Vatican Council.

> The era was a much more interesting one than it appeared on the surface. Exciting new technologies were being developed that would soon enable a vast and surprisingly broad degree of dissidence, and many people were already beginning to question the purpose of their lives and whether that purpose had indeed become, almost involuntarily, too much about material things.[1]

Perhaps I and my generation of spiritual-seekers were aptly described by Halberstam. Below the surface we were beginning to pose fundamental questions—about spirituality, about the purpose and allegiances of our lives—that would encourage dissidence to flourish in both society and religion. And what more interesting place than Paris, France, to witness the modern world falling apart and a new spirit emerging?

4

The Paris Years:
A Culture in Revolution—
1967–1970

What did I know about France or the French? I had had one year of French in college and had kept a reading knowledge of it alive, reading as I did the French theologians such as Yves Congar and his mentor, M. D. Chenu. My speaking and listening grasp of French was practically nonexistent. Fortunately, our province had a priest, Dan Morrissey, studying in Paris at the time. Dan, who was also from Wisconsin, became a wonderful friend and guide, introducing me to the Champs-Elysées (where we stopped my first night in Paris for a sundae served at the rear of an auto dealership) and the Dominicans at the Éditions du Cerf on boulevard du Latour Maubourg, who were kind enough to welcome me for liturgy and for dinner once a week. They even did my laundry and allowed me a small chapel in which to say mass. Dan also got me a room to let with a French family.

Paris and the Parisians

My lodgings was a story in itself, since the family with whom I lived turned out to be Integriste, the extreme right-wing Catholics of France. Their violence was matched only by their anti-Semitism. Their solution to the Vietnam War, then raging at full force, was for America to drop the atomic bomb first on Hanoi and then on Moscow. One group beat up the priest-psychologist Marc Oraison (fundamentalists don't *like* psychologists) and over his brutalized body poured red paint and wrote *Credo* (which means "I believe" in Latin, their religious language of preference). My landlady once said to me, "Jesus was not a Jew." I asked how she knew that. "Because his father wasn't Jewish—it was the Holy Spirit."

"But Jews trace their lineage through their mothers," I advised her.
"Well, Mary wasn't Jewish either."
"Why not?"
"Because she wasn't circumcised."

Their logic was very special.

My landlady was a widow with three unmarried sons in their twenties who lived at home. One day she said to me, "Since the Second Vatican Council all faith has gone out the window in the church."

"What is faith?" I asked.

"Faith is the pope and my catechism," she answered.

"Well, are you aware that the pope called the council and signed all the decrees of the council?"

"Then," she said, "my faith is just my catechism."

I remarked to myself what short shrift the pope got. "Well, please show me a copy of your catechism," I asked her.

"I can't. It went out of print in 1926."

Each member of our five-person mélange was responsible for his or her own cooking. The problem was there was no stove, only a burner, and the smallest of refrigerators. Thus a lot of juggling occurred around mealtime. But on those occasions when we did share a common meal, conversation got very lively. Hands would fly and gestures would dance, the result being that glasses would fall crashing from the table; no one would notice—the conversation came first. The sound of broken glass crunching under our feet accompanied our eating and arguing. It was at gatherings such as these that I learned how seriously the French take their most cherished sport of conversation.

Fortunately, this same family had a run-down chateau in the countryside to which it retired for long weekends, and I was often left by myself in the house to study and run my own affairs. Perhaps my finest moment with this family came during the *"evénements,"* the student-led protests that brought down the de Gaulle government. One day at the height of the crisis, when everything had shut down in Paris, the workers and youths were marching right down our street chanting their slogans and demands. (Usually they marched in the Latin Quarter, and we lived in the seventh arrondissement.) At the head of the parade was a large red flag. As the chants became louder and louder, closer and closer, my landlady came to me in near panic. "They are coming, they are coming," she shouted. "They are going to behead us all. It is just like the Revolution all over again!" (The Integristes have yet to get over the French Revolution. One day this woman said to me, "In the Revolution they took away our king; now, with the vernacular in the mass they want to take away *our church!*" This is the reason they attended *only* masses in Latin.) With the marchers minutes away from the house, the madame pleaded with me, "Will you hear my confession? Will you hear my confession?"

Now here was a dilemma indeed. No good priest turns down a request to hear someone's confession and *certainly not* in a moment of potential martyrdom such as this woman was fantasizing for herself and her family. I had to think fast. "One moment, Madame," I said. I walked to the window, threw it open, stuck my head out, and shouted to the marchers below, "*Vive la révolution!*" Turning to the woman, I said, "And now your confession, Madame?" She demurred. "Not now," she said. I was relieved. And the priestly office had not been altogether compromised. It was perhaps the quickest thinking I have ever had to do on my feet.

I loved Paris. I could walk forever the streets of the Latin Quarter. There were Saint-Séverin; Saint-Julien-le-Pauvre; Notre Dame (even if Thomas Aquinas once said, during the construction of it, that he would give the entire cathedral for just one lost book by theologian Gregory of Nyssa); the monument at the end of the Ile de la Cité to the deported ones of the Holocaust; Shakespeare and Company, where T. S. Eliot, Hemingway, Joyce, and so many other great writers had hung out; the cafés, the restaurants, the smells (especially that of garlic) everywhere, particularly in small elevators in apartment buildings; the ghosts and memories and history of it all. I used to walk the Latin Quarter imagining what it must have been like in Aquinas's day or Abélard and Héloïse's day, when the university was just coming into existence and ferment was everywhere. The museums drew me regularly, especially the Rodin museum, which was within walking distance of where I lived my first year in Paris, and the Jeu de Paume, where the impressionists were displayed. I reveled in the Seine, the Champs-Elysées, and the numerous *quartiers* that were off the tourist track; the architecture, the flowers, the open markets, the *charcuteries;* the good, reliable, and cheap *vin ordinaire.* The movies too. How the French loved the cinema! I learned to love the cinema also, and when my money ran out at the end of the month, as it always did (I was living on $150 per month that included everything—room, board, books, and tuition), I had to choose whether to eat or go to the movies. I invariably chose the latter as it was a way to experience some community in a big city as well as to improve my French. The result, however, was that I lost some weight.

In addition to a sense of history, Paris gave me a sense of the artist. Little children accompanied their parents to art museums and appeared just as curious and enthralled with the paintings as the adults were—this was new to me. When my mentor Père M. D. Chenu would one day say to me, "Remember, the greatest tragedy in theology in the last three hundred years has been the separation of the theologian from the poet, the dancer, the painter, the dramatist, the potter, the filmmaker," I knew what he was talking about. I too had ceased writing poetry the moment I entered higher education. Now, in Paris, the poet began to return to my soul. There was permission in the air to be an artist. Here I learned that art is not about getting a degree or even being a genius. Art is about the way we see the world, and let it see us. I had to leave my own country to learn this lesson, but it was a lesson I have never forgotten.

Paris also gave me a deeper sense of culture and its power in our lives. Learning a new language means letting go of one's own. This did not come easily for me. I remember sitting on a bus one day and noticing a three-year-old child chattering away to her mother. What are these feelings arising in me? I wondered. They were feelings of envy! Imagine that—envying a three-year-old! Any American who has visited Paris knows that the Parisians are not famous for befriending Americans fumbling with their language. I was such an American. And this during the Vietnam War when few French or other Europeans respected the United States anyway. I knew I was getting some French when I began to dream in French (bad French I am sure); that was a sign that I was starting to leave America and the American language behind. But it was a long time coming.

Being immersed in an ancient, fascinating, rich culture and seeing things in a whole new way with a new language and new customs and new food and new values were all part of my awakening in Paris. They were all part of learning about culture and religion, culture and spirituality—an awareness that was deepened considerably by my master's thesis in theology on Jesus' prayer in the New Testament. As an American in Paris, I was learning about the relativity of my own culture: its language, its history, its interpretation of history (someone in America had taught me that we had invented cars and cinema and all kinds of things that Europeans would have other opinions about), its global politics, its war in Vietnam, its racism, its mythologies. The low point of my being in Paris must have occurred when I sat in a restaurant and heard a loud American woman say, "Look, they have bread too!" (Someone had taught this woman that we Americans invented bread.) Of course this cultural relativism had another side to it too: as an outsider I had something to teach the Europeans as well—about wilderness and spirituality, for example, and about lack of cynicism. But this would have to wait.

Institut catholique de Paris

With Dan's help I made my way to the school of my choice, the Institut catholique de Paris, or the "Catho" for short. The Institut was begun in the nineteenth century, but the theology faculty, where I enrolled, traces its history back to the original University of Paris in the twelfth century. I loved the French system of education at the doctoral level, since it emphasizes *thinking* and is only minimally concerned with exams, pleasing the faculty, memorizing. (I couldn't help comparing this to the German system where several American Dominicans of my generation were sent. One had a complete nervous breakdown and never returned; the other two never finished their degrees and did not seem to enjoy their studies very much. Had I entered the German system I don't think I would have been able to accomplish what I did during my days in

France.) The French system presumes that by the time you arrive at the doctoral level you know your field substantially, and now is the time to buckle down and do your own serious work. At least that is how I interpreted it. The permission given to think and to be creative was exactly my cup of tea. I thanked Thomas Merton many times over for his advice to come here.

I did not have all the prerequisite degrees that the French require for the doctorate. However, the head of the department, Père de Lavallette, a strong and sturdy French Jesuit, waived my requirements when he saw the degrees in philosophy and theology that I did have (including the licentiate in theology granted by the Dominican Aquinas Institute). When he saw *Listening* magazine, I was in. That was interesting to me: that the French so respect publishing that they will give you credit in effect for writing, editing, and publishing a magazine.

Registration day at the university was a bit of a shock. We filled out several pages of questionnaires and then were told to line up in the next room. The "next room" was a huge hall with one light bulb hanging down on a frayed wire above a card table that had one broken leg. A young woman sitting at this shaky table was taking our papers. The process was very slow as she was working all alone. As I got nearer the table, I noticed that piles of our papers were on her desk and when a pile got too large, she simply pushed it with her elbow off the table and onto the floor. Around her feet were stacks and clusters of documents from students wanting to enroll at the Institut catholique. Clearly French priorities in education did not include Anglo-Saxon orderliness and efficiency at the bureaucratic level of registration.

Don't get me wrong. I loved going to school at the Catho. Now I was getting what I had sought for so long: some solid history, theology, and methodology about our Western spiritual tradition. My professors were impressive; the courses were interesting. After choosing four doctoral seminars, I was free to take whatever other lecture courses I chose. I had plenty of time to read and study on my own, learning the history of spirituality that way as well.

I came to Paris with one pressing, urgent question that superseded all other concerns for me: what is the relationship—if any—between prayer and social justice? I felt that was the most foundational issue for me and possibly for my generation. In the midst of social revolutions such as the civil rights movement and the anti–Vietnam War protests, this question kept haunting me. It seemed to be the nexus where culture and spirituality or culture and healthy religion met. But there was very little that I could find in the traditional literature that answered that question for me. I remember how excited I was to see a book by Père Danielou with the wonderful title *Prayer as a Political Problem*. My heart sank as I read it, however. Unfortunately, the title was the only worthwhile part of the book. His politics were rightist and his grasp of prayer was anything but magnificent. I began reading Bouyer's four-volume series on the history of Christian spirituality from the Bible to the twentieth century, taking copious notes and following the leads in his footnotes to other books. I realized that it would be a process, wrestling with my fundamental question about prayer and justice, spirituality and culture.

My classes at the Catho were a big help in and a large part of that process, though sometimes I felt like we were taking two steps forward and one back; or two back and one forward. From Père Michel de Certeau—a young and vibrant though slightly nervous Jesuit who came to class in dark glasses, having recently been in a serious automobile accident—I took a seminar on the seventeenth-century Jesuit Père Surin, who was a chaplain sent to the infamous convent in Loudon where possession was said to have seized the nuns. Surin went quite crazy himself, it seems, and I wrote a paper for the course discussing whether Surin was altogether *mentis capax*. From Abbé Louis Cognet, the director of the spirituality program at the Catho, I took a course also on seventeenth-century French spirituality and did a paper on Charles Bernier's experience and theology of nothingness. While I respected both professors, neither of these seminars was what I was looking for: I was keen on relating spirituality to politics, and seventeenth-century France would be the last place to look for such a connection. On the other hand, by becoming so steeped in the spiritual pathology of that period (Madame Guyon, one of the Parisian gurus of the period, had the name "Jesus Christ" carved on her breasts—for whom to see, I was never sure!), I was seeing the *via negativa* of modern spirituality: how *not* to do spirituality.

The lecture courses I chose to attend included a course on spirituality and world religions taught by a Belgian Dominican named Cornelius who looked like Yul Brynner with his bald pate, and a course on mysticism and culture taught by Henri de Lubac. Paul Ricoeur offered a course on language and structural analysis, but he lectured to a large hall of eager students with a toothpick in his mouth and did not speak particularly clearly. After the third class, I turned to a French student and said that I was not very good at French and was having trouble following him. "Well," he said, "I'm having trouble understanding him also." There was some comfort in this. In my first year there, Louis Cognet offered a course on Bach's spirituality, and though my French was too lean to understand much of the technical language, I would sit in the back of the room taking in by osmosis what I felt was an important subject. I remember saying to myself that there was *no theology school in all of North America* where one could listen to someone lecturing on the spirituality of Bach. Even though I wasn't getting the details, I was truly in a good space just being there.

Cognet himself offered a three-year lecture course on the entire history of Western spirituality. These classes were especially valuable to me. His knowledge plus his sense of humor made the time pass swiftly, even when it was deep winter and he had to compete with the one radiator that kept singing out of tune and releasing enough heat to overheat the entire school. In his final year of lectures, he covered the pressing theological issues of the sixties: the role of Karl Marx, who was "far more influential on religion than Père Lacordaire" in the nineteenth century; the role of Freud and psychology—the analyst is often the priest in our society; subjectivism of seventeenth-century Protestant and Catholic spirituality as passé today; secularization; atheism. He said that the "death of God" theologians were asking the basic spiritual questions of our time, including those of language itself. He urged us to go beyond the *pessimistic* theology of Augustine and its Neoplatonic suppositions. Cognet cited Dietrich Bonhoeffer for his emphasis on the essential role of justice in our spirituality, thus putting an end to pietistic religion. God becomes engaged *by creation*—not just by the incarnation. This would prove a dominant theme in my development of a creation spirituality.

After I left the Catho, Cognet, who published ten books on Christian spirituality and was an accomplished organist and photographer as well as a scholar, died suddenly of a heart attack in his early fifties a year. I will never forget his final lecture, in which he laid out the principles that must guide a new spirituality for our times. He said that we need a spirituality that includes the body, justice making, a sense of history and evolution, therefore a spirituality of matter that is cognizant of science. In that final lecture Cognet challenged me deeply when he said that

> all we know is that there's a real drama going on and we're in it and so is God—we don't know how it will turn out. The reign of God is already here since salvation is not somewhere else. Terrestrial values are real values—justice, generosity, kindness are already salvation. The Beatitudes are right now; justice has to be reached on this earth. To work for it is the church's duty. There must be a vertical as well as a horizontal relationship to God for these things to happen, say what you will. The task can fail—evolution can contradict itself. The risk is real.[1]

In retrospect, I can see that much of my work has indeed been a response to Cognet's challenge in that lecture.

I attended a course on the philosophy of religions in which the professor spent the better part of one class mocking the English theologian John Robinson's book *Honest to God* before about one hundred French students. This offended me deeply, as I liked Robinson's book a lot and even if I hadn't, I respected his fine biblical study in *The Body*. So I approached the professor after class and objected to his treatment of Robinson and his failure to mention Robinson's other works. To his credit, this professor began the next class apologizing to the students and then discussed Robinson's work with more balance. Still, I had learned another lesson about culture and religion: the French and the Anglo-Saxons have no love lost between them. Indeed, in general, in Europe I found a lot of nationalistic jingoism mixing in with theological agreements and disagreements.

A valuable lesson in culture and religion occurred when I took a brief excursion inside the chapel church attached to the Catho. This church had housed a large seminary at the time of the French Revolution. A guide took us from room to room, pointing out where the Revolution's kangaroo court was held, where the heads of the two hundred priests and seminarians were cut off in the backyard, where the blood flowed. At the end of the tour, he led us to the basement where the bones of the seminary "martyrs" were stacked along the walls from floor to ceiling behind glass. A veritable wallpaper of bones! During the tour the guide had often referred to these chaps whose bones were now behind glass as "our martyrs." At the end of the tour I asked him, "Tell me, sir, at the time of the Revolution, how much property did this seminary own?" He was eager in his response. "Oh," he said, "we owned [notice the "we"] all the property from here to the Bon Marché [a mile of choice property in the Latin Quarter], and the Benedictines owned from there to the Seine [two more miles of choice property in the Latin Quarter]." Well, there you have it. Two hundred years after the French Revolution, some French Catholics have yet to get the point of it all: these people weren't martyrs; they were privileged ecclesiastics who were sucking the poor dry, while they lived in religious splendor and took fanciful vows of poverty. I imagined a young seminarian asking his superior for a sous to take a ride downtown while his *order* owned enough property to feed and house half the starving souls of Paris. Culture and spirituality, indeed!

The best friends I made at the Catho were American sisters who were working on various kinds of doctorates abroad. They were fun, alive, critical in their thinking, and experiencing the winds of freedom that they had not felt for years in the convent. We would often have group meals together or go to shows and other events, and my respect for them never waned. Several of them later left the convent. But during my sojourn they were soul mates and true sisters on joint spiritual journeys in every sense of the word.

The two most influential doctoral seminars I took were from Abbé Marchasson and Père M. D. Chenu. Marchasson was an older priest, a scholar whose expertise was nineteenth-century French history. He had devised a method (the French were very big on *methods*) for examining nineteenth-century French newspapers to derive from them the philosophy behind the culture. There were only five of us in the class, and except for a friend from Sri Lanka whom I talked into taking the class with me, all were scholars of French history (at least two were museum curators). The museum curators would be shouting out dates and arguing with each other about them while I was just hanging on trying to get the numbers straight, knowing little more of French history than 1789, Napoleon, and the First World War. After several weeks of this, I began to ask myself: What am I doing here? Why did I take this class? Then the great French word hit me: *la méthode!* Method. Yes, the methodology was interesting and it held promise, if I was serious about studying culture and spirituality. Why not take the method used here and apply it to contemporary America?

With this in mind, I asked for a meeting with Marchasson and made my proposal to him: I would do my doctoral study on some influential American publication, employing his methodology to discern the ongoing suppositions in that culture toward religion/spirituality. "Ah, yes," he said, "you can take this method to the New World." *The New World,* I thought. I had never looked at America that way before. For me it had been my *only* world, and currently, with the riots and rebellions and the bloody mess in Vietnam, it appeared anything but new.

Then there was my encounter with Père Chenu. Seventy-six years old, big, bushy eyebrows, excited, dynamic, funny, political, warm, affectionate—he became my mentor. He was the reason I remained a Dominican. He had what I hoped to see in all Dominicans: life, passion, political consciousness, wisdom. And above all, the French *passion for ideas*, an intellectual life, an intellectual history, that served a greater cause. It was Père Chenu who kept me in the order—not because we ever talked about it but because of his example. From the French, and from Père Chenu in particular, I learned respect for the power of ideas and for those who carry them.

While I owed to Abbé Marchasson a methodology that gave me access to a critical appraisal of religion in my culture, I owed to Père Chenu the answer to my question of questions: how do I relate spirituality to culture, prayer to social justice, politics to mysticism? He named the creation spirituality tradition for me. In encountering this tradition, my entire life would gain a focus and a direction that it never had before. It would also gain a notoriety that I never, in my ecclesial naïveté, could have predicted.

I remember as if it were today that moment in our seminar, in the dimly lit upper room at the Catho with the green velvet cloth on the table, when Chenu named the two spiritual traditions: that of "fall/redemption" and that of "creation-centered spirituality." Scales fell from my eyes; I was bumped

from my horse! The most pressing question I had brought with me to Paris—
how do mysticism and social justice relate (if at all)?—now had a context! So
did the issues of dualism and the demeaning of body and matter. Creation
spirituality would bring it all together for me: the scriptural and Jewish spirituality (for it was the oldest tradition in the Bible, that of the Yahwist author
of the ninth or tenth century before Christ); science and spirituality; politics
and prayer; body and spirit; science and religion; Christianity and other
world religions. It would be my task to study creation spirituality more
deeply and to begin a cultural translation of it. This task would prove to be a
process in its own right with unforeseen consequences.

In Chenu's seminar, three-quarters of the students were from Latin America. It was in his work in the worker-priest movement in the forties and fifties
that Chenu developed the methodology of praxis preceding theory. He used to
say, "I did not do theology in an armchair. I tested it in the field." He would
attend meetings of the worker-priests and workers just to listen to their dialogues. He was not there to give speeches, but to listen and offer feedback if
asked. It is little wonder that liberation theology's base-community movement
found such support in his person and in his methodology. That is one reason
why Gustavo Gutiérrez cited Chenu so often in his classic work A Theology of
Liberation and why students from Latin America were so drawn to him.

Chenu had been a peritus or theological adviser at the Vatican Council and
was largely responsible for the "Church in the Modern World" document,
though he complained later that what he had proposed as a text had come
out "sounding so clerical, so scholastic. They'd taken that little brat of mine
and drowned him in holy water." Time and again he reminded us that movements of the laity had sparked the church renewal in the twelfth century, "the
only renaissance that succeeded in the West" because it came from below and
not from above. Laity would lead today's renewal of church life too, he was
convinced.

We met when I was a student in his seminar on twelfth-century spirituality.
He would bring huge picture books to class, volumes on the twelfth-century
cathedrals. "You can't do theology without art," he would say, and "you can't
understand twelfth-century spirituality without appreciating the architecture
and the artisans and engineers behind it." In addition to appreciating the artist,
Chenu also welcomed youth. He never talked down to students when he
taught. I never heard him do anything but encourage young thinkers, exuding
enthusiasm and excitement about their questions and ideas. His approach to
thinking was one of "Yes, and . . ." not "Yes, but." He had a deeply youthful
soul himself; no trace of complacency or cynicism was visible in him. He was a
deeply joyful and humorous man. Once, when he was discussing Nicholas of

Cusa in class, he gave the basic information about him: a theologian, a scientist, a mathematician, a diplomat, and "a cardinal in the Roman Catholic church." Immediately his eyes began to twinkle and he looked up swiftly to say, "Not necessarily a good reference, you understand." Though Chenu was silenced and forbidden to publish for years under Pope Pius XII, there was no bitterness in the man. The artist Frederick Franck went to the Second Vatican Council uninvited because he felt it was appropriate that an artist be present. He spent three years there, sketching the faces of all the participants. He told me one time that Père Chenu "had the most interesting visage of anyone at the council."

Sometimes when I wonder what my role is as theologian I think of an interview Chenu gave when he was eighty-six years old. Asked "What do you think of the crisis in the Church today?" Chenu replied:

> It's a godsend. A theologian has to be immersed in the movement of history. You might say that when something new is beginning, when things start to fall asunder, that's when he's most deeply happy, because then he's given a unique opportunity to observe the Word of God at work in history. The *nowness* of the Word of God, shaking up the world—that's where true theology springs from!. . .
>
> Christians fear change, and so does the Church, insofar as it is a society of Christians. Afraid of being blamed by the future, it prefers security to freedom. I prefer freedom.[2]

During our seminar with Chenu in the spring of 1968, all of Paris was paralyzed by student riots and strikes of civil workers. The Sorbonne was closed, as were most schools and businesses, though the Catho was still in session. At the end of one class, Chenu shut his notebook and said, "We have been talking about twelfth-century history—here is your chance to make some history. Go out and join the revolution! Don't come back next week; come back in two weeks and tell me what you have contributed!" He was seventy-three at the time.

Cultural Turmoil: The Modern Era in Collapse

Chenu was right, of course. The sixties were reaching a crescendo. The modern age was crumbling all around us and something new was yearning to be born. It was a confusing and demanding and exhilarating passage. The Catholic church and all of Christianity was being awakened by John XXIII and the Council, and the society was being awakened by youth revolts in Europe and at home. The Vietnam War, the civil rights movement, assassinations, Stonewall—all this was searing our hearts and souls, pitting father against son and brother against brother and daughter against mother. I met a young American soldier who told me that when President Nixon ordered the invasion of Cambodia in late April 1970, many of the American soldiers in Germany, where he was stationed, were as irate as American students across the country (at Kent State, four students were killed by National Guard soldiers and eleven others were seriously wounded). The officers in his army unit called a gathering to explain why America had invaded Cambodia. "It was to stop the Communists," the officer in charge explained.

The soldier telling the story, an Iowa boy, asked the commander, "What is a Communist?"

"Why, everybody knows what a Communist is," replied the officer.

"Then tell us. Since this is the reason we have invaded Cambodia."

"A Communist is, a Communist is," he stuttered, "a Communist is . . . someone who invades someone else's country." This was the kind of eldership that our generation was experiencing in army, government, and church. It was laughable; but also tragic.

It is difficult to exaggerate the cultural turmoil that was everywhere in 1968. At Grant Park in Chicago, during the Democratic Convention, my closest Dominican friend, Dan Turner, now a young priest, was attacked by the police while demonstrating against the Vietnam War. At the time the police were attacking him and others with tear gas and clubs, my provincial was sitting in Mayor Daly's box at the convention. This is how estranged the Dominican family, like many families, was becoming over the cultural upheavals of the day. Dan wrote me a powerful letter about the conversion he underwent by putting his body on the line in Grant Park. He had been working with poor black families on the west side of Chicago; within two years he would leave the order and get married and continue his work with the disadvantaged for years to come.

In France, I was learning that the gods that were tumbling in America were also tumbling in Europe. The cultural revolution was by no means an exclusively American happening. Daniel Cohn Bendit and other youth leaders were awakening the students of Paris, Bonn, and beyond. Students in Paris took on the police night after night with cobblestones ripped from the streets of the Latin Quarter and trees felled on the boulevard Saint-Michel. My sympathies were with the young in Paris as they certainly were with the anti–Vietnam War protesters at home. And I felt then as I do today that this season of the death of God was indeed the death of something. A culture perhaps. A worldview. A religion. A certain way of defining the human soul. The stakes were high, and we were all involved whether we chose to be or not. I supported those choosing to be involved. That was where life was happening. And life, I would gradually come to learn, is the biblical word for *spirit*.

One night during a seeming lull in the battle between young Parisians and the police, a friend and I went down to the Latin Quarter to check things out. When someone threw a smoke bomb down the narrow street just off boulevard Saint-Germain where we were having dinner, we knew the events were not yet settled. Heading into the boulevard, we saw a phalanx of riot police spreading itself along the width of the street and marching our way, batons drawn and riot helmets in place. Turning in the other direction, we saw the same: another phalanx headed our way. We tried first one door along the street, then another; they all seemed locked, and the police were getting closer. Then a door swung open and we rushed inside and were met by a crowd of *voyous* or rebellious youth with stones in hand who had obviously been at the barricades for days. We went to the back of the group and held our breath as the police passed the front door. Then we snuck out the door behind the police and made our way to the métro station, covering our noses against the tear gas everywhere in the air.

The next morning I read in the newspaper the reason for the police sweep of the Latin Quarter. Their goal was to enforce a law just passed by de Gaulle's government: any foreigner caught by these police would be immediately deported, no questions asked. My career as a spiritual theologian might have come to an early end had we not found one open door on the boulevard Saint-Germain.

Something was indeed punctured and collapsing in the late 1960s, and from my vantage point in Europe I knew it was not just an American thing, though in America children were bombed in a Birmingham church; civil rights activists such as Chaney, Schwerner, and Goodman were murdered; Medgar Evers was murdered; black students were killed at Jackson State and white students at Kent State; Malcolm X was assassinated, as were John F. Kennedy, Robert Kennedy, and Martin Luther King, Jr. I was in Paris when King was murdered, and I had left the city, which for all practical purposes was completely shut down, to get a week of freedom in Zurich when I heard the news of Robert Kennedy's murder. I dropped to my knees; something had died, I felt, in the American political soul that night in a pantry in a Los Angeles hotel. King was murdered, and I saw no political figure on the horizon who could bring black and white together in American politics, after Robert Kennedy.

Misuse of power was everywhere, not just in Vietnam. Chicago police murdered Black Panther leader Fred Hampton while he slept. "The FBI schemed at Dr. King's death. The CIA murdered abroad. The FBI repressed at home with its massive COINTELPRO program," as cultural critic Gary Wills writes.[3] I believe today that among those assassinated at this time was Thomas Merton, the Trappist author and mystic. One person who had met him described him as being "like a New York taxi driver." He was not the absent-minded professor type. Yet we are asked to believe that he stepped out of a shower soaking wet in Bangkok and plugged in a wall fan that electrocuted him. Dutch television film of his final talk reveals that he was in a brand-new, sturdily built retreat center made of concrete blocks. There is little likelihood that the electricity was flawed. Furthermore, there was motivation to murder him. He was the first American religious figure to come out against the Vietnam War. This caused controversy within his own church and among some of those in power. He was going around Southeast Asia for months before his final speech asking people *in English* for their ideas on his theme of "Karl Marx and Monasticism." When his monks back in Gethsemani heard of his sudden death, their response was "assassination" as well, for they knew of the threatening mail he, like Dr. King, had been getting for years. I once asked a CIA agent who was in Southeast Asia at the time whether they killed Merton. "I will neither affirm it nor deny it," he said.

"Could you have?" I asked.

"A piece of cake," he replied. There was no security whatsoever at the retreat center. The irony for this deep pacifist was that his body was flown home on a CIA plane.

It was not only in the streets of Paris, Chicago, and elsewhere that a revolution was afoot. The Dominican order too was being challenged by its younger set, and I am proud to say that I was part of that movement. It happened like this. Some German and Belgian Dominicans who were students of Johannes Metz at Münster University invited us to a meeting for young Dominicans from all over the world to be held near Trier, Germany. Metz was the architect of "political theology" and his students lived up to that billing. They were an impressive and engaging lot of Spaniards, Germans, Dutch, Belgians. Also at the meeting were young Dominicans from Yugoslavia, England, and France. We Americans—of which there were now six in Europe from our province—headed for the event. Fifty-five Dominicans from ten countries and fourteen provinces were in attendance.

During several days of negotiations and meetings, there was an atmosphere of excitement, revolution, concern, promise. We finally agreed on a "working document" that we published that called for some radical reconstructing of the Dominican order. We spoke to the crisis of the relationship of church and world. Noting that our society is "in the throes of revolutionary change," the accord calls for the church being more in the world—not in the sense of conforming to it but, "on the contrary, the Church stands out as *critical* of the world: from her faith in the promises of God, she denies that the injustice, hatred, misery and oppression which mark the human situation must have the last word."[4] Calling for "institutional criticism" after the prophets of old, including Jesus of Nazareth, the declaration speaks to the situation in the church and the Dominican order, which "have come to hinder the tasks which they should be taking up, and to enforce this stagnation by repeated appeals to the loyalty of the subject." Sounding a methodology from liberation theology, the document speaks of a need to change our ways of thinking and theologizing.

Theology must take the form of a theory of the Church in action: only in this way can theology and praxis mutually influence each other. The starting point of theology ought to be the scandals of our present society. A truly critical theology would at the same time act as a critique of the sort of theology which acts as a superstructure, an immobilising and inhibiting factor in the life of the Church.[5]

The document calls for forms of community life that "are not necessarily within the limits of the traditional forms" and that go beyond adapting "classical forms" of religious life. While endorsing "the possibility of engaging oneself to celibacy by a free personal choice," it takes a stand on the misuse of celibacy.

We reject the misuse of celibacy as a means of exercising power in behalf of the institution. All too often in the celibate life the aggressive instincts of the personality are channelled into the search for power—the arbitrary domination which can be exercised by any juridical power, by priest over people, by major superior or Roman authority over its subjects.[6]

The final statement of the declaration refers to the document that we American Dominicans brought with us to the gathering. "We endorse the document entitled 'What World?' submitted by the American participants, and accept it as an instance of the pragmatic application of the principles on which we are agreed."[7] Topics treated range from Vietnam to joblessness to women's rights to homosexual oppression to oppression of the young. I had presented that document in a somewhat impassioned speech during the conference. When it came time to elect leaders to keep the movement going, I was elected head of the secretariat on a secret ballot. A fellow American Dominican who was counting ballots said, "Matt, this is your finest hour." Fortunately, other members of the secretariat, far more versed in the languages and politics of European Dominicanism, did the work in the future for the organization. But my visibility at that conference did not sit well with my provincial back in Chicago, who wrote me that I should either quit the organization or quit my studies and return to America immediately.

We four Paris Dominicans responded to the provincial's criticisms in a public letter to the province that challenged his caricature of the event as a "group of dissidents" by pointing out that studium professors of theology, priors, missionaries, and others delegated by provincials and local communities had been present. In response to his request to quit the movement, we wrote:

> We have found in this movement persons of quality, an international perspective, a theological awareness and an evangelical purpose—ideals encouraged in us by our province. We all feel that our concern and participation in this movement is part of the original assignment given us to explore the fields of pastoral, spiritual and anthropological theology. This *is* the direction that theology is taking at the present time, and this direction can only be studied and known from within.[8]

As it turned out, a provincial assembly was held in Chicago at which many of our progressive-thinking Dominicans pushed for changes on the American side of the ocean as well; their support of us Dominicans who attended the Trier meeting diffused the political cloud hanging over the movement, and I stayed in Paris without leaving the organization.

Religion, Culture, and *Time* Magazine

I have already mentioned how I was taken by Marchesson's methodology and its potential for a serious cultural critique and how my awareness of spirituality's interaction with culture was becoming more and more manifest to me. After much back-and-forth about which American journal to pick for study, I decided on *Time* magazine. It was a kind of lifeboat to many Americans abroad, it represented some quintessential American values, and it had been a staple on our coffee table at home during my high school years. Here would be a chance to critique American middle-class values "from the inside." I went to England to interview Henry Luce III, the son of Time founder Henry Luce and the head of Time Incorporated's London office. (I remember handing my coat to his butler and saying "Thank you" and learning later that one does not say thank you to a butler. But, after all, this was my first experience with a butler.) I made several trips to New York City to use the archives at Time Incorporated, staying each time with the Dominicans at St. Vincent Ferrer Priory on Lexington Avenue. Remembering how someone had said that the older and richer Mr. Luce got the more pious he got, I donned my Roman collar and, telling some of the head people at Time about my desire to do a doctoral thesis in theology on their founder and their work, I managed to tap into whatever piety still lurked around the Avenue of the Americas and did indeed gain access to the inner sanctum of their archives. They told me that I was the only outsider ever allowed into those archives.

Working on *Time* magazine was truly a baptism into my *intellectual* radicalization. Learning the ideology and jingoism that lay behind the weekly "news" that *Time* packaged so glibly for middle-class Americans was an eye-opener. Henry Luce, the genius founder of Time Incorporated, called America "the principal instrument of [God's] will on earth" and said, "The future of the Western tradition is first of all and primarily a question as to the future of America. . . . No nation in history, except ancient Israel, was so obviously designed for some special phase of God's eternal purpose."[9]

I selected the year 1958 and read every word printed that year in the magazine, from advertisements to National Affairs, from Religion to Art. One conclusion I came to was that there was far more of "authentic religion" in the film reviews and art section than in the religion section, which was invariably preoccupied with institutional religion—buildings, bishops, and so on. If one wanted spirituality, it would be better to go to the book reviews, for example. Another finding was the realization of how glibly American industry and advertisers were using religious language to carry out their ideological convictions.

The newsmagazines were the precursors of television news. Both have their editorial biases built into them. The chancellor of the University of Chicago, Robert Hutchins, was not deceiving us when he declared that *Time* has more effect on American culture than the entire university system put together. My skills at political/cultural criticism were being honed in working on my dissertation. The head of the theology department, Père de Lavallet, said on hearing of my topic: "At last! An American doing an interesting doctoral thesis!" I appreciate to this day the elasticity and creativity that the Catho allowed me and other students.

Among other American students there, I think I was considered something of an oddball, doing my thesis on *Time* magazine. Others working in the area of spirituality were writing theses on seventeenth-century French mystics or fourth-century prayer books. Among the latter were many students getting doctoral degrees in liturgy. One day I asked a group of liturgy majors what I thought was a fundamental question. "What is prayer?" I asked. "How would you define prayer?"

They looked at me as if I were from another planet. "We don't ask questions like that," one of them replied.

"Well," I said, "I think it's presumptuous of us to think that prayer is necessarily going on at liturgy. We ought to examine what prayer means."

To write my thesis I had to leave Paris. I had observed American priests who had been in Paris as long as eight years and had still not completed their doctorates. I wanted none of that. As much as I loved France, I had no doubts that my work was in America, and especially so given the profound events of those years. I was determined to finish my degree in three years and get home. At that time friends took me for a visit to the Basque country in southwestern France, near the small town of Saint-Jean-de-Luz and the Spanish border. I fell in love with the area and the culture. Here was a place I could get my work done. I was able to rent a room on a Basque farm. The young family (he Spanish; she French) included two little children. Turkeys outside my room awakened me each morning. It was an idyllic place in which to work. Renting a 1948 Renault from a local farmer for sixty dollars for the summer, I was able to write all morning and drive down to the beach for a long lunch break and work again into the afternoons, as well as hike along the maternal hills, mixing in with the many local shepherds. I ate my evening meals in a local Basque inn run by a large and energetic family. One day in the middle of my writing I said to myself, "I am a writer. This is the happiest I have ever been."

The Basque people were a big part of my coming to consciousness about culture, since they still had theirs. Language (I loved their music at the local mass and would sing along with them after a fashion), dances, costumes, food, music—it was all still intact from centuries ago and mysterious origins. One Sunday mass the priest, who preached in French, attacked Americans for destroying the Basque culture. I tried not to take it personally, but I did sneak out more shyly than ever.

One afternoon while I was at my typewriter a woman came to my door. "There is a phone call for you," she said hurriedly. Who could be calling me here? I thought, for I had never seen this woman before. Following her, I trudged over farmland and dale until we arrived at her home. There I picked up the phone and heard these lines, "I am madly in love with you. We must meet right away." I had no idea who this was, and meanwhile the woman who had fetched me was listening in the adjacent room with her ear against the curtain.

I said, "Who are you?"

The caller responded, "I can't tell you. We must meet."

I consented to meet her the next day, and when I drove to the designated place a woman wearing a white blouse was there. She jumped into the car hurriedly and said, "Go, get away from here fast." She was obviously known in this small town and didn't want her story told.

She explained that we had conversed one day while standing in line at the local post office (one spends a lot of time in lines in France) and I had made her laugh. From that time on she had been in love, had often watched me at the beach, and so forth. I quickly laid down some ground rules. First of all, my French was not nuanced; second, I was not in love with her for I didn't even know who she was; third, I was busy working this summer and had to complete my work; and fourth, I was a priest. With that, she shouted, "A priest! Is it a sin to fall in love with a priest?" Assuring her that was not the issue, I proposed that we be friends and let it go at that. So we became friends, and she told me after a while that our friendship allowed her to let go of a relationship with a sailor that was not to her liking. We corresponded for some time after I returned to Paris. I learned a lesson from this experience: that celibacy can be a helpful and positive life force to people, for it can help them let go of relationships that do not serve them well.

Today as I read over the introduction to the dissertation, I sense some of the passion I was feeling living through the events of the late 1960s and trying to relate them to my vocation as a Dominican priest. The very first sentence talks about "the disciples of Jesus and the disciples of Karl Marx" and how "today religion troubles the believer and the atheist alike." I talk of secularization, religionless Christianity, atheistic religion, and the death of God. I call for moving from the "Cartesian dichotomy of truth vs. doubt, reason vs. imagination, of body vs. soul, constructed to save faith's mysteries in a period of rational science." I allude to the liberation movements in South America, of atheists meeting priests in guerrilla movements, of the place of *prophecy* within religion. And I emphasize how we must grasp more deeply the "world where religion intermixes with a culture." I ask questions about the exploitation of nature and the dehumanizing by technocracy and other "problems of post-industrial and late capitalist society." I felt permission to approach religion in the inductive fashion of analyzing the media itself from my mentor Père Chenu, who had written that theology ought not to work "from an abstract and extra-temporal analysis, as we have long done, but 'to scrutinize, to discern, to interpret' in history, in the Church in act, the 'multiple languages of our time.'"[10] I hint at a distinction between spirituality and religion when I speak of the role of a hypocrisy

> that searchers of true religion will no longer find the depths to forgive
> and that will send them to wander the earth in lonely search of religion
> where there is genuine prayer of honesty and courageous stands of
> prophecy. It is this sense of disenchantment that will feed the cry to
> "damn the institutions" of religion.[11]

I recognize secularization as a process of moving from one cultural stage to another, "deculturizing religion and reculturizing it."

In returning to this dissertation in the context of my European experience of 1967–1970, I am amazed at how fundamental it was to all my subsequent writing, to all my agendas, hidden and not so hidden, of the subsequent twenty-four years. The passion for justice, for relating Marx to Jesus; the interest in prayer as both celebration and honest critique of evil; the revolt against psychologizing and privatizing religion; the faith in artists to be our spiritual leaders; the labeling of living versus dying religion and the ambiguous role that ethnic religion plays in all that; the hypocrisy and decadence of which religion is capable; the false religions of American culture from consumerism to nationalism and anticommunism—all these set the pace for my interests that were to develop both theoretically and practically in subsequent years. They also amount to a kind of "tying up" of loose ends from the religious journey as a Catholic growing up in an ecumenical family setting in the fifties. I conclude by acknowledging how close spirituality is to many people.

> The most fundamental and far-reaching conclusion we can make regarding the spiritual in American culture today is simply that people very often *are* leading lives of living religion . . . without knowing it. . . . Living religion . . . is saying Yes from the heart but it is also preparing the way for uttering Yes by saying No. For this latter task in particular talent and commitment is called for today for modern man is swamped in ideologies posing as religion. . . . How about the chasm between law and justice? between education and thinking? between liturgy and prayer? between philanthropy and justice? between prophetic help for the oppressed and ideological support for vested interests? One can sense from the nature of these questions that the task at hand is not speculative but is demanding as much action as thinking.[12]

This latter point seems to mirror the liberation theology mode of reflection based on praxis. I predict that artists will prove to be the "staunchest allies" of a critically understood living religion, and I point out that my study shows that 19 percent of the articles in the Books section of *Time* are about ethnic religion while 60.5 percent are about religion as a response to deep human need or as prophecy. In contrast, in the Religion section, 53 percent of the articles are taken up with ethnic religion. "Thus, in a word, one will find more authentic religion in reading the Books section than in reading the Religion section. This reveals what we have seen elsewhere, that religion is disassociating itself from former cultural patterns—even those of religion."[13]

More Awakenings in Culture and Spirituality

The cultural/spiritual education I sought was coming at me from many sides and from many places beyond the classroom or my formal studies. On one of my research excursions to London I met on the boat ride across the English Channel an American about my age who was on vacation from a strenuous job he had just finished as Dick Gregory's presidential campaign manager. He was a rich man's son, having been taken to school in a chauffeur-driven limousine as a child, and was obviously angry and rebellious about the privileges of wealthy, white society, which had wounded him so deeply. We visited the

British Museum together, and I will never forget going from exhibit to exhibit with this bright and radical young activist (who dressed smartly, complete with pointed umbrella)—and then we came upon the great Magna Carta, a primal document in democracy (or at least democracy for the middle-class landowners). There was another document right next to it. I was stunned and surprised when I saw it. No one in any of my years of Catholic education had told me it existed, much less that one could visit it at the British Museum: the Papal Condemnation of the Magna Carta! What a companion to be with as I read the papal condemnation. My religious/cultural education was indeed broadening.

Another memorable encounter occurred when I was living in the south of France and visited Carcassonne. As the sun was setting I walked down the hill from the walled medieval city toward the modern city and found a simple café. When I entered the crowded bar and sat down to order my dinner, a hush took over. The patrons stopped their animated conversations and looked at me. The waiter came and asked where I was from. "America," I confessed. He went and spoke with others at the bar, came back, and said he could not serve me until his "leader" came. I waited, somewhat curious about this kind of courteous refusal to serve a customer. Finally, a young man appeared, about my age. My waiter and several others consulted with him at the bar; he nodded his head and came over to my table. "What are your views on the Vietnam War?" he asked. "Why are you in France? What are your views on President Johnson?" I had opinions on all these subjects and voiced them, aware now that the entire restaurant was silent and all ears tuned in to our conversation.

After about twenty-five minutes of interrogation, he smiled, stood up, and said to the barman, "Serve this man; he is one of us." The bar broke into applause and conversation resumed. The leader sat at my table and told me the following story: The bar was a Communist bar owned by the workers of the town. He himself was the leader of the Communist party in town (he was only twenty-six) because he was well educated but his heart was with the workers. He had a Ph.D. in chemistry from a university in Paris but could find no work. That was what the cultural revolution going on in France and Europe was all about, he explained. He returned to Carcassonne, his hometown, and found no work there except organizing the workers to struggle for their rights. My being an American was a shock to the partisans in the bar, but I had answered all the questions put to me in a manner that very much satisfied them. They too were against the Vietnam War and what the American empire was doing in the world.

My mother visited me in Paris as I was finishing my dissertation. One day she suggested that we invite a young German to dinner; he was the brother of a German exchange student who had lived with our family a few years previously. It turned out that Jorgen was a nineteen-year-old gay man, and he came to dinner with his lover, a thirty-four-year-old French Canadian. This was my first experience with a gay couple. They held hands at times and they kissed unselfconsciously. The irony of all this occurring within my mother's eyesight was not lost on me, as she had never pronounced the word *homosexual* in her life, as far as I knew. Jorgen was a troubled young man whose father was a tyrant and still a Nazi and whose mother had committed suicide when he was a young teenager. I became a kind of counselor to him, and from that relationship my own feelings about homosexuality matured from curiosity to letting go of fear to trust. Sadly, his life ended in suicide six years after I left Europe.

An incident that raised my consciousness about adultism (though it would be years before I heard that word for the phenomenon) occurred in one of my visits to New York City to research my dissertation. I was eating in the refectory of a large Dominican community in Manhattan. Next to me was an older priest, a very large man, who went on and on about how awful the young Dominicans were today, how evil Woodstock was—he had numerous complaints. I didn't argue; I just listened. Then as he left the room, which was empty except for us, he stopped at the door, turned around, and bellowed in his most sonorous preacher's voice: "Let the young do whatever they want. *We've got the money.*" And with that revelation, he stormed out.

Back in Paris, in February, I had the privilege of chaperoning seventy American college students on a visit to Russia. When our group was scheduled to meet with seventy-five Russian college students, we entered a large gymnasium and gravitated to one end. The Russians stood at the other end. Nothing happened. Separating us in the room was a wall of ice representing all the myths, shibboleths, and hatreds that our respective governments had fed us about each other for decades. Then someone in our group struck up a song, Peter, Paul, and Mary's hit song "Leaving on a Jet Plane" (this was the first time I had heard it), and all the Americans joined in. The Russians responded with a song of their own, the "Volga Boatmen," which I recognized. Then another song from our side; then from theirs. Then the Russians started to dance a Cossack dance; then with each other. Then the Americans began to dance. And finally, the two groups meshed in their dancing.

It was a profound experience for me of the *power of art to melt ideologies and hearts.* It was concrete proof of the importance of art and prophecy that has always stayed with me.

I also made the acquaintance of the American ambassador to Paris, Sargent Shriver, and his wife, Eunice, who was John F. Kennedy's sister. The Shrivers were committed Catholics who liked to attend mass regularly, and they would invite my friend Dan Morrissey to say mass in their home at the ambassador's residence. I was invited as a sort of pinch hitter on occasion. Meeting guests in their home such as Arthur Ashe and Rose Kennedy and James Jones, author of *From Here to Eternity*, and his wife, who was a recovering Catholic, was a nice addition to my education. When his son Timothy turned fourteen or so, Sargent Shriver took me aside and said he wanted him exposed to the "other side" of life from that of well-to-do ambassadors. Could I help? I knew a restaurant in Pigalle sponsored by a local parish that was a drop-in place for down-and-out *"petites artistes."* A priest operated the tiny place, which offered simple food in a clean atmosphere; upstairs was a tiny chapel. Some American sisters and I had volunteered to do dishes there. So the ambassador's son got an alias—"Timothy Sterling"—and took the métro each week to wash dishes in Pigalle.

One night, following a party at the residence, and feeling quite mellow with good wine inside me, I walked up to the Trocadero and was enjoying the moon, stars, and darkened Paris when I heard a voice behind me say in strongly accented English: "Why doesn't anyone love me?" The question was repeated, and turning around I saw a young, unshaven man with tears coming down his cheeks saying again, "Why doesn't anyone love me?" We got to talking and then went to a bistro, where I listened to his story.

He had a gun in his pocket—which he was only too eager to show me—and was going to commit suicide that night. He was Lebanese and years ago, at sixteen years of age, had killed a Muslim man in Beirut. The result was that he became a marked man and had to leave the country, for the relatives of his victim were out to kill him. His father ushered him out of the country, and he had been wandering ever since: Greece, Germany, Scandinavia, now France. He was lonely and wanted to die. I took him to the apartment where I was living that year with two other American Dominicans (fortunately one was away that week). I put him up with us, gave him some clothes, and together we tried to get him some work. We became friends and he visited me for a spell in the Basque country, where, among other revelations, I learned that in his visiting prostitutes in Paris (his father had told him never to pass up an opportunity to have sex with a woman), he had left behind the underwear I had given him with my name on it: "Matthew, O.P." (Could I ever have explained this to the Vatican police!) The last word I had from him was this: he was planning on smuggling himself into America by stowing away on a ship inside the life raft and, when he spotted the Statue of Liberty, swimming ashore. (He had no valid passport.) I hope he made it.

While in Paris, I wrote an article entitled "What Is Prayer?" that was published in *Listening* magazine. In it I make the point that "the classic formulas" for defining prayer, such as dialogue with God,

no longer seem to answer the question of prayer for modern man. . . .
The real problem in prayer is not that God is effecting no changes in
the world; nor that he is distant; nor even that he is silent. The prob-
lem is that, being so close and so broadly diffused, men still miss him.
That is why the process of prayer is the process of man changing, not
God.[14]

I emphasize what I call the *horizontal* side of prayer as distinct from the
more familiar *vertical* side, and I talk about "the field of prayer." I offer my
own definition of prayer: swimming.

Describing prayer as swimming implies immediately the indispensable
reality of the field of God's love. . . . A fish in water evidences a certain
passivity in its natural habitat, a seemingly utter dependence and relaxation in the medium. . . . To talk of prayer as swimming removes any
quid pro quo connotations. . . . Prayer is thus removed from the category of means and reinstated as an end. . . . The fish does not call for
water; it is there already. So the praying person does not call forth
God. God is already here. Prayer calls forth the person, in ever deeper
levels of his personality, to break loose, to see and behold.[15]

Graduation and Last Days in Paris

Defending my thesis upon my return from Russia in March 1970 was a rich
experience. I had been to dissertation defenses at the Catho wherein there
was, figuratively speaking, blood on the walls. (One American's *thesis adviser*
told him that his thesis was so weak that he didn't know why he bothered to
write it; another American had a member of his thesis jury hold up a historical text, only one of three existent in the world, and ask why he hadn't asked
him for it.) My jury was genuinely engaged in the topics I outlined, and they
gave me a surprising *maxima* (the French equivalent of *summa*) *cum laude*
grade for my efforts. Someone told me that the last person to graduate from
this faculty summa cum laude did so fifteen years before me and his name
was Hans Küng. We had a party featuring plenty of sangria and gâteaux
basques (a pastry unique to the Basque), both items I had enjoyed among the
Basque people. The party was a very joyful occasion. I felt relieved and that I
had accomplished what I had set out to do in Europe.

That night I called home and spoke to my father about the events. He was
genuinely proud of my accomplishment, thrilled to hear of the grade I had received in my doctorate. Later, when I wrote our provincial newsletter the
same news, they changed "summa cum laude" to "magna cum laude." I always thought that was telling: that my first family took pride in my accom-

plishment but my second (Dominican) family felt compelled to water it down.

The day after my thesis defense, three American friends and I headed for Spain and sunshine and a vacation. As we left Paris, I heard on the car radio for the first time a new Beatles song, "Let It Be." With that song—as so often happens to me with music—it all came together. The struggle with Parisian weather and the French language, the doubts of whether I could get what I needed from the French and complete my work in time, the wondering about the strangeness of my dissertation and whether a cultural study could be done amid so much cultural turmoil, made sense: in short, my love-hate relationship with Paris had come to an end. There was no love-hate anymore; there was only love. Hemingway had it right: "If you are lucky enough to have lived in Paris as a young man, then wherever you go for the rest of your life, it stays with you, for Paris is a moveable feast."[16]

On leaving the Catho I scarcely knew what a gift I had been given, for Père Chenu retired from teaching that year and Louis Cognet died suddenly the next year. I had been blessed to be among the last of their students. In my writings up to this point, modest as they were, I was wrestling with similar themes about mysticism and politics, prayer and social justice, culture and religion. I was trying to understand this cultural/spiritual revolution that was unfolding around me and inside me throughout the sixties. I was a citizen of two continents, a theology student keen on two separate, though complementary, interests: spirituality *and* justice movements. Gary Wills gives credit to the sixties for some significant moral advancement in our culture.

> Some of the moral anguish of our time is based on moral alertness, an awareness of others' rights. Insofar as the '60s are still a force in our present, we need more of them, not less—more civil rights, more women's rights, more gay rights, more citizens' say in government, less censorship and less hypocrisy. The '60s, too, were not the good old days—there are no good old days. But much of what is good around us took its origin from that troubled and troubling period.[17]

After completing my degree, I still had one more task ahead of me: a semester in Münster, Germany, to learn more German and to study with the political theologian Johannes Metz. The Catho was wonderful for history and methodology, but Metz was asking the more pressing political issues of theology, and the proof of it was the kind of committed and politically conscious students gathered around him. (I am still in touch with some of them, such as Karl Dirksen of the Dutch Dominican province.) As it turned out, when I arrived in Münster I learned that Metz had been in an automobile accident and had turned his course over to his students. In class we spent the entire semester going over one brief paragraph by the sociologist Jürgen Habermas—quite a different story from American universities, where one is often asked to read a book a week.

My last night in Europe was most memorable. A Dutch doctoral student had completed his dissertation on Marx and religion, and everyone was talking about it as the most important doctorate done in years at Münster University. He and I stayed up all night arguing about Marx, religion, and what Marx had left out. I insisted that while much of Marx's sociological critique was right, he neglected the role of symbol, metaphor, art, and beauty in a political as well as a religious mindset. To my amazement, along about 4:00 A.M. he said to me, "You are right. This aspect of religion is missing for the most part in Marx and in my treatment of Marx." I was moved at this man's humility, but also by the strength of the thesis I had been putting together about the balance of justice and mysticism. The first attempt to apply this thesis had been passed and was successful.

With his encouragement humming in my ears, I made my way to the Cologne airport and home. My Paris days were ended; my European foray was complete. I would never be the same person again. But our culture had changed irrevocably as well. A critical understanding of culture and spirituality was coming together for me. However, some bumpy times lay ahead in my return to our studium in Dubuque, Iowa. Even in Dubuque the cultural earthquake was being felt, among the young in particular.

PART TWO

TEACHING
AND WRITING

This page: At Holy Names College, 1993.

Preceding page, from top: At Mundelein College,
Chicago, first year of the Institute (1977); lectur-
ing outdoors at ICCS, Chicago (1981); above
Holy Name College among Redwoods of Oak-
land with companion, Tristan (1989).

5

The 1970s:
Early Teaching and Writing

I began the sixties as a curious but mostly docile Dominican novice, eager to experience God and to apply myself diligently to learning our tradition of prayer, study, philosophy, and theology. I ended the decade an ordained Catholic priest with a doctoral degree in spirituality, and with many experiences under my belt from living abroad during the cultural collapse of the sixties. I had experienced up close how culture influences prayer and theology. I had also made a commitment at Trier in favor of a new relationship of the Dominican order to the youth and to social transformation. Like many of my generation I was angry at my government for carrying on a war in Vietnam that seemed morally indefensible. These passions would make me some friends, but they would make me some enemies as well.

Back to Dubuque

In the late summer of 1970, I was genuinely looking forward to returning to the Dominican community at our Aquinas Institute in Dubuque, Iowa. The feeling that the community there was supporting me and was looking forward to my return had kept me going during some lonely times in Paris. On returning to Dubuque, I resolved to keep a low profile. I had plenty of work to do: I was asked to return early to take up the editing of *Listening* magazine again; I had entirely new classes to teach and therefore prepare for, and I was ecstatic about being able to teach eager young theology students for the first time, to share the exciting ideas that had come my way in Europe. I was determined to put my doctoral thesis into shape and publish it. (Doubleday turned it down so I decided to publish it myself as *Religion USA*.) As it turned out, however, my efforts at "low profile" were not low enough.

The trouble began sometime in October, about six weeks after school began. The prior of the house came to me and said it was my turn to celebrate the community mass. It was my first chance to preach to the Dominican community, about sixty of whom were students in training. I gave a homily on "What Celibacy Is Not," in which I emphasized that celibates were not to be sexually repressed or neutered folk. That night about twenty students lined up at the door to my room, eager to talk. They came in one by one; many of them cried, not a few of them mature persons in their late twenties. They were crying out of joy and pain. They said I had really spoken their language and they had felt themselves understood "for the first time" in the order. This was the generation of young people who had had a very difficult time trying to grow up in the late sixties: their contemporaries were off in Vietnam killing and being killed; the Vatican Council had unleashed a freedom in the church and in religious life for which few elders were prepared; the very building they had been trained in at River Forest, Illinois, was undergoing repairs and they had to move out for a year; and they had been in Chicago for the events of the Democratic Convention in 1968. In Europe, there were many instances in the order of young persons moving away from giant priories and into small communities, so I told students about this and listened as they discussed it.

This did not sit well with those priests whose job it was to oversee the training of these students, however. While my classes were interesting and the students were responding and doing good work, life at the priory was getting less and less cheerful. There was an election for "subprior" or the second-in-charge of the house. I had urged at a public meeting that we elect a student since there seemed to be a real lack of communication between the students and the priests in charge. That idea was not considered, however, since the Dominican laws required that a priest be subprior. Weeks after the election, we had still not heard the results. I went to the prior and asked him who won the election. "Oh, didn't we tell you?" he said. "You won the election but the house council felt you were too dangerous and castigated the vote." Apparently I had received almost every student's vote and almost no priests' votes. He asked me to keep quiet about this action by the council. I pointed out that there was no such requirement in the constitution of the order and that "adults who make decisions about other adults' lives ought to take responsibility for their actions."

When the students heard about the goings-on, there was upset. For many it was the "last straw" in the pinch they were experiencing—as so many of their generation—between inherited authority and their own needs and expectations. Many left the order around that time. I moved out of the priory at the end of the semester and relocated with two Dominican priests in Chicago, from where I commuted to Dubuque one day a week to keep my teaching commitments for the second term. A rupture existed in terms of a different consciousness in the order. As I look back on those days, I sense that the breaks that occurred—which were painful, I am sure, to all—were almost inevitable. My being a bit more "low profile" or a bit more dialogic with the prior and others would, I believe in retrospect, have changed nothing. The rupture that was splitting our culture was splitting its religious foundations as well. As Gary Wills points out, "the cultural '60s, as opposed to the calendar '60s, ran into 1973."[1] Religious institutions were as affected by this cultural upheaval in the early seventies as all our other cultural institutions. By this time, 1971, nearly all my closest Dominican friends had left the order, as had many of the priests and sisters I had studied with in Paris, and my student masters and many professors from my Dominican years of training. This exodus was a sign of the times: all orders were experiencing it; indeed, most families were experiencing it.

That summer I taught in the Institute of Pastoral Studies at Loyola University in Chicago, thanks to the invitation of Fr. Jerry O'Leary, a Dominican who had studied with Margaret Mead at Columbia Graduate School of Education and was director of this most creative pastoral program. One of my students was a Catholic sister from Emmanuel College in Boston, and she invited me out to her school to teach one course there in the fall. I felt it was a special opportunity to get some distance from things in the Midwest and to finish the book on prayer that I had researched extensively while in Paris. After meeting with my provincial, I accepted the invitation and drove to Boston with Brendan Doyle, a friend and Dominican brother. We packed all our belongings in a 1963 Rambler that we had bought for $225. We stopped in Steubenville, Ohio, on the way to perform what we called a "concert-commentary," which was Brendan singing the music he had composed and the lyrics I had written and my commenting between the songs on their meaning. It was our effort to reinvent a methodology for teaching spirituality, one that spoke to the heart via song and not just to the head. The concert-commentary was received with absolutely no enthusiasm; as it turned out, Steubenville was a deeply depressed place.

Boston and Marshfield

Arriving in Boston, we had some hustling to do to survive. The thousand dollars I had been promised for the semester (four months) was the extent of our income. Brendan eventually found a two-nights-a-week job singing in a local piano bar on the ocean near where we lived. We got a cheap rate for our little house since it was in Marshfield (pronounced, I learned, "Maaashfield"), a summer resort town, and winter was coming on. But the universe provided through the good graces of a "base community" (the name at that time was "underground church"), which had heard about our coming and was looking to hire a priest. The Emmaus community was a special group of Catholics with a conscience who could not stomach the church's silence regarding the Vietnam War and other atrocities they felt were happening in our culture. (One of the members was a retired nuclear submarine captain turned peacenik.) The unofficial "pope" of the group was a vital, busy, Italian Mother of all Mothers named Emma Sansone. Her daughter, Grace, mother of two sons, was one of many go-getters in the group. It seemed that they had had a falling out with the monsignor of their suburban parish for his lack of social conscience, and they and the other sixty or so persons were determined to remain Catholic but creatively so.

Becoming allied with this group of lively, question-asking, fun-loving, but socially committed people and their families was a real joy. Our masses brought forth the artists and musicians from the group, and meals together were part of our shared communion. At Christmastime they gathered their canned goods together to give to the poor and decided that Brendan and I were the poorest persons they knew, so we were inundated with canned foods that lasted for months and got us out of our financial hole. In the spring, I conducted a six-week seminar for them based on my prayer book, and the final day of the class I left open to their questions and discussion. One of the women, whose husband was also there, raised the following question: "My neighbor is a widower," she said, "and I feel sorry for his loneliness. I wonder if it would be a moral act on my part to sleep with him occasionally." The entire group took up the discussion at that point, and at the end of the evening a visiting priest from Maine came up to me, staggered and obviously shaken, his eyes as big as grapefruits. "In our parish," he said, "the hot question has been whether to have communion in the hand or not!"

I wrestled that year with whether to stay in the order or leave. As I have mentioned, most of my friends had left; I was clearly not well received by the powers that be in the priory to which I had returned. Where does one go with a doctorate in spirituality? As I pondered these questions while marching up and down the cold-swept beach of Marshfield in winter, the ocean gave me the answer I was seeking. "Do what I do," the ocean seemed to be telling me. "Create. Create your work. Create a lifestyle outside a large priory that feeds the work. Stay and create." It seemed like good advice. I stayed. I created.

An exciting moment for me occurred that fall. Following my class at Emmanuel College one evening, the administrator came into the classroom and said there was a letter for me from Harper and Row publishers in New York. I sat down at a student desk and opened the letter. It was from a Harper editor who said that they wanted to publish my book on prayer, and that I should come to New York as soon as possible to talk with him. It was a breakthrough moment in my life. Maybe I was a writer after all! Rejected by a Catholic publishing house, my manuscript was well received by this "secular" publisher in New York. My editor was a lay Presbyterian deacon from Arkansas named H. Davis Yeuell, a gentleman who spoke with a broad southern accent. He told me that he had stayed up all night reading my book and could not put it down until he finished it. He was so excited about it that he gave it to his sixteen-year-old son, who also stayed up all night to read it. "Any book that I and my son can both get so much out of," he told me, "is going to be a classic someday."

Although I had researched substantial portions of the book while in Paris, I had begun the actual writing during the winter break in the Midwest. During the writing of the book, which I had intended to call "Spirituality American Style," I had a memorable dream of a dancing, musical, mystical bear. By that time I had learned to trust my dreams more than institutions and other literal structures, and so I changed the title of the book to the unlikely one of *On Becoming a Musical, Mystical Bear: Spirituality American Style.* Just before the book went to press I ran across a couplet from T. S. Eliot that struck home to me:

> Perhaps it is not too late . . .
> and I must borrow every changing shape
> To find expression . . . dance, dance
> like a dancing bear.[2]

I am still moved by how these words of Eliot struck my soul then and continue to do so today: "Perhaps it is not too late"—at that time I and many others in our culture felt it *was* becoming too late to come alive and change our ways. What method does Eliot offer for acting before it is too late? "I must borrow every changing shape." Forms must change; metaphors must be born anew.

It was only after the "bear book" appeared that I learned that worship of the bear was the oldest form of worship in North America, that our ancestors on this land honored the bear as human because it stood on two legs, and as divine because it was so powerful and awesome, and that it was redemptive and healing in its powers. What a perfect Christ-image for a North American spirituality! Clarissa Pinkola Estes, in her book *Women Who Run with the Wolves,* relates a story from Japan about "The Crescent Moon Bear" in which the bear represents "the great compassionate Self" whom the heroine of the story feeds. The bear metaphor reminds us of the side of the compassionate psyche that is not tame but wild. To encounter the bear is to wake up. "We lose our illusions when we take the risk to meet the aspect of our nature that is truly wild."[3] In addition, the bear symbolizes resurrection because the bear hibernates and comes back to life. In a poem I wrote that accompanies the book I describe the bear as "popping marshmallows all day and all night dipping honey." That is to say, this bear knows how to enjoy life (mysticism); on the other hand, he is also "getting ready to stick out his chin" for justice's sake (prophecy).

As it was, of course, my choice of this book title was a mixed blessing. Intuitives and artists *got* the title; more literal types, such as many academicians and theologians, self-appointed heralds of social justice, and somber students of spirituality (to say nothing of book salesmen), did not get it. Calling my first few books after dreams and nursery rhymes also served a useful function; it kept the inquisitorial minds off my trail for many years. Wouldn't the Vatican thought police look silly raiding a bookstore for the dangers inherent in a book called *On Becoming a Musical, Mystical Bear* or *Whee! We, wee All the Way Home: A Guide to Sensual, Prophetic Spirituality*? At least for a while, it gave me some latitude in which to roam in search of a viable spirituality.

In the bear book, I treated what I considered to be the nexus of the spirituality question: what is prayer? I offer my definition of prayer as "a radical response to life." Being radical, it is about *roots* (*radix* means "root" in Latin) or depth forces that bring nourishment and life. I note two basic roots that prayer is about: first is celebration or our Yes to life—I call this "mysticism" or our "becoming rooted," prayer as radical psychologically. The second response to life that is radical is our No to life's enemies such as injustices—I call this "prophecy" or our "uprooting." This is prayer as radical socially.

In that book I was clearly bringing together the elements of culture and religion, mysticism and social justice, that had been burning in my soul for so long. I consciously move beyond what I saw as a kind of "standoff" in the language of "action versus contemplation" and by recovering more ancient language, that of mysticism and prophecy, present them not as a dualistic competition but as a both/and dialectic. We are prayerful when we undergo mystical experiences *and* when we march in the streets or struggle to resist shadow forces through reinventing work, education, or religion. A Trinitarian consciousness helps us to see that this intercourse between mysticism and prophecy gives birth to more Life, that is, more Spirit in the world.

I deliberately avoided the word *God* and substituted the word *Life* in my definition of prayer. The term *God* is too subject to projections and carries so much baggage from our religious woundedness that it seldom conjures up the great mystery that divinity is and that prayer is meant to tap into. "Breath of Life," which after all is the meaning of the Jewish word for "Spirit," is what draws us to pray whether in celebration and gratitude or in struggle, wrestling with demonic spirits of racism, militarism, and so on. (Only recently did I come across Thomas Aquinas's statement in the thirteenth century, "God is Life, per se Life.") I am explicit in the bear book about moving from a Greek or Hellenistic mysticism (on which the fall/redemption school bases itself) to a Jewish one (which is creation-centered and forms the basis of Jesus' mysticism). I present panentheism (God in us and we in God) as a theological category for the first time in my writings. It represents a liberation from the "God in the sky" theism that still reigns in most theologians' heads and in most attempts at ritual and public worship.

An important part of the bear book was the invocation of the artist as an instructor in life and therefore in spirituality. I cite Leo Tolstoy on how the mission of the artist is clear: it is "to compel us to love life in all its countless and inexhaustible manifestations." And I cite French critic Charles Du Bos's judgment of a favorite book from my adolescence that helped drive me to my vocation, Tolstoy's *War and Peace*. Said Du Bos: "Life would speak thus if life could speak."[4] One of the major breakthroughs for me in preparing this book was reading Malcolm X's autobiography. He was a contemporary figure of our sixties culture who I felt incarnated the conversion and transformative aspect of prayer after his pilgrimage to Mecca. This made him truly radical.

One of the more difficult decisions I made with the bear book was to stick with the word *spirituality*. I did not like its overly introspective and navel-gazing connotations, its "God and me" privatized connotations. But I also felt that there was no other word in our language to describe the core quality of healthy religion and that *spirituality was a word worth redeeming*. A Lutheran pastor, on reading my bear book, said to me, "Spirituality is where the action is in American religion today; and we Lutherans have never even used the word!"

When the bear book appeared in 1972 it brought me a lot of mail and many invitations to speak and conduct workshops. I welcomed these opportunities to travel the country and learn what people were thinking and how my thoughts might influence their own. I returned to Chicago, found a part-time job in Loyola University's theology department, and continued to teach and lecture. After one of my lectures a woman said, "You must write a practical book that outlines the how-to of prayer more than the bear book does."

I put myself to that task and wrote *Whee! We, wee All the Way Home: A Guide to Prophetic, Sensual Spirituality*. In that book I distinguished between what I called *natural* and *tactical* ecstasies—differences between, for example, experiences in nature, art, friendship, sexuality, work, and suffering (what I call "natural ecstasies") and rosaries, celibacy, fasting, and the like, which are tactics for bringing about an altered consciousness (what I call "tactical ecstasies"). People found this distinction very helpful—I remember lecturing on the distinction at a Catholic church in western Chicago and getting a standing ovation. This reception convinced me of the power and practicality of this distinction. In addition, in this book I was wrestling for the first time with a different way of naming the spiritual journey. *Whee!* stood for our experiences of ecstasy; *We,* for our symbolic consciousness which develops when we move from I to We; and *wee,* for our prophetic struggle wherein we are reminded of how small an individual is, taking on large powers and institutional "dragons," in the struggle for justice.

About this time, while I was teaching at Loyola in the summer of 1972, a student of mine, Sister Anne Madden, who was a Sacred Heart sister from Barat College, told me of a job opening at her school, which was located in Lake Forest in the northern suburbs of Chicago. She drove me up to visit the campus and the president. I was hired as full-time chair of the religious studies department. The starting salary seemed impressive to me: twelve thousand dollars for the year. After being hired I bought a new Ford Maverick, and the first day of school someone called me out of the library to tell me that a giant Pepsi-Cola truck had smashed into it in front of school and folded it up like an accordion. That is about the only negative memory I carry from the place.

Barat College

The Sacred Heart sisters I got to know were intelligent, fun, and committed to their work, which was to educate women of all ages. There were Sister Martha Curry of the English department, Sister Sophie Cooney, the brilliant and well-traveled head of the humanities department, and many others I counted among my friends on and off campus. At this time many middle-aged women were beginning to return to school. We began the year with three students majoring in our department of religious studies, but by the time I left four years later, there were twenty-nine. We did many creative things, including sponsoring a mass in Latin complete with a Gregorian chant sung by students of my medieval class. I enjoyed teaching interdisciplinary courses with other departments, including sociology of religion, and literature and spirituality, where I was introduced to Adrienne Rich's poetry. Rich has been a tremendous gift to me ever since. I employed Albert Einstein as reading material for my basic course on religion in America, for I was moved by his conscience and his sensitivity to mystery and mysticism. I also used Norman O. Brown's *Love's Body* and *Life Against Death* and Sam Keen's work on Dionysian versus Apollonian thinking. Being the only full-time teacher in the department, I taught subjects ranging from the Scriptures to the mystics, to liberation theology, and psychology and religion. It was great fun teaching these women. They were eager to learn and just getting their wings, thanks to the emerging feminist movement.

Feminist Catholic theologian Rosemary Ruether agreed to teach a course with us, and I invited Mary Daly to speak at a school-sponsored symposium.

I had been deeply affected reading Mary Daly's *Beyond God the Father*. I felt that here was a theology doing more or less what I was trying to do: leaving behind symbols, names, and metaphors that were not working for us. In my enthusiasm, I telephoned her at Boston College where she was teaching, introduced myself, and thanked her for her book. I told her that her book "made Karl Marx look like a wimp." There was a long pause and she said, "Thank you very much." Later, when she came to campus and I met her, I realized I had said just the right thing in praising her over Marx. I remember her Irish wit and dancing eyes over dinner, but I also remember the commotion she caused when, at question-and-answer time following her presentation, she refused to let men ask any questions; it was time for men to listen to women for a change, she explained. Half the Barat faculty walked out at that point. Her visit raised the roof at Barat, and for months afterward they were talking about it.

Of course, the biggest single gift granted me at Barat College was a deepening of feminist awareness. Sitting day after day and hearing women's stories in class and out of class was an eye-opener. It was not unlike visiting a third-world country for the first time. One's own privileges came into focus. I remember telling a friend one day that, based just on stories I had listened to at college, the statistics we had been given in America about rape were all off. It was my experience that one out of three women had stories of rape to tell.

Middle-aged women would come in and tell me stories of how they had to fight with their husbands (who had M.B.A.'s and were running things in the city of Chicago) just to return to college and finish their B.A.'s. One woman had to move out of her house. I felt a solidarity with their struggle. Together we read women philosophers and theologians, and I was able to enter into the awakening of many of these women. I remember one day a young woman, who was fulfilling a class requirement by leading the group, came in with red tea. We sat around drinking it as she expounded on what it was like going through her menstrual period. It was as if I was making up for those years of training in the order and in Paris without women instructors, and I was being given a crash course in women's studies.

Jewish students at Barat taught me many things. I remember the day in class that the students, most of whom were Christian, got into a discussion of original sin. At the next class meeting, a Jewish student came up to me and said, "What is this original sin that the students were discussing?"

"Surely you know about original sin in Genesis, don't you?" I replied.

"No," she said. "I've been a practicing Jew for forty-one years and have never heard a rabbi or anyone else talk about original sin." That was an eye-opener for me. The distinction between the Fall and original sin deepened my realization of how un-Jewish much of Christianity is. This same student had worked hand in hand with Rabbi Abraham Joshua Heschel over the years and she introduced me to his work. That was a tremendous gift, as I grew to love him, his theology, and his witness (he marched with Martin Luther King, Jr., at Selma, for example). He was a leader in Jewish-Christian ecumenical dialogue. The older I get the more I appreciate returning to his spirituality of awe, wonder, grace, and prophecy—a creation-centered spirituality indeed. If I were on a desert island and allowed only one theologian to read, it would be Rabbi Heschel. Somehow when I read him I feel I am reading the kind of mentors read by Jesus, who was, after all, Jewish.

One evening in 1976 we had an autograph party in the wood-paneled library for my new book, *Whee! We, wee All the Way Home*. We had hors d'oeuvres and champagne and plenty of people—the only problem was the book never arrived! Sister Anne Madden, who was always a delight and whose wig was always just a bit askew (we took bets on whether this was intentional, for she loved to make people laugh), came up to me and said, "An autograph party without a book is like a wedding without a bride. Or a funeral without a corpse." She was right, and I've always been a bit paranoid of autograph parties since that one fiasco.

In the preface to the paperback version of my *Musical, Mystical Bear* book, which appeared in 1975, I looked forward to a possible men's movement someday, since "an alteration in a woman's view of herself will eventually result in an alteration of a man's view of women and of himself." I pointed out that creation spirituality is feminist "insofar as it equates the artistic quest with the spiritual quest, as it insists on a mystery-oriented, participatory relationship to creation, as it questions drastically the phallic definitions of prayer that most of us have inherited, and as it opts for the yeses as well as the nos in life."[5]

One day I received an invitation to be on a panel at an Episcopal church to discuss women's ordination. Although the organizers had assured me that the pro and con factions would be equally represented, those representing the pro faction were far outnumbered. Only a woman deaconess and I (a non-Episcopalian) were pro, and three or four male priests were con. The worst part—though the most educational—was the spirit in the room. The sexism was palpable. A meanness in the visage of persons whose body language told you that nothing would ever move them gave this away. I recognized the symptoms, for I had been in enough situations about racism or homophobia to have a nose for such things. The debate went on for some time, but I will always remember the undercurrent of sexism that formed the true substratum for the opposing arguments. There was an ugliness to it that stays with me today when I read about Anglican priests becoming Roman Catholic because of the ordination of women. I lost at least one Episcopalian priest's friendship because of my stand on women's ordination.

When three bishops of the Episcopal church dared to ordain eleven women priests in 1974, I felt a keen responsibility to invite one of these woman priests to Barat College to say mass. Rev. Alison Cheek, a native Australian working in Philadelphia, came and celebrated mass for us. It was a powerful and archetypal event, and I remember a counselor at Barat, who was a mature and strong woman, with tears coming down her cheeks during the mass. This event gave birth to another happening.

Eight months later I received a letter from Cardinal Cody, the archbishop of Chicago. It began quite personably, saying that he had never had the pleasure of meeting me and would I please come to his residence to see him. (He was a near neighbor to the Playboy mansion in Chicago's Gold Coast Lincoln Park area.) No agenda was offered. I arrived at his mansion and was let in by two women workers who ushered me to a waiting room. One woman was tall; she said that her back was killing her, and then she got down on the floor to work on papers there. I asked her why she worked on the floor if she had a bad back. "Because the cardinal likes to work on the floor," she replied. I waited and waited and noticed large photographic picture books of *The Police* stacked on the coffee table. I did not know that such books existed.

Finally the cardinal arrived and I was ushered into a red velvet room the likes of which I had not seen since the museums of Europe. In extending his hand and on greeting me the cardinal said, "I am writing to the Congregation for the Doctrine of the Faith, your master general, and the pope to put you on trial and remove you from the priesthood!" We sat down, and I was silent. I had no idea what his agenda was; what skeleton in my closet he was rattling. We waited in silence. Finally he said, "I have photographs of you concelebrating mass with an Anglican priestess at Barat College." I asked if I could please see the photographs, and he replied that he hadn't been able to find them before our meeting. I said that *if* there were such photographs I would personally pay out of my own pocket to prove that they were doctored, for I did *not* concelebrate with an Anglican "*woman priest*" because that would have been "the height of chauvinism, my saying move over, woman, I'm going to do this right."

At that point his entire demeanor changed; it was as if air had been let out of him. He calmed down, and his little legs whose feet did not touch the floor started to swing like a small boy's. "Well," he said, "I have saved you. I have waited six months from getting this evidence to hear your side of the story."

"Thank you for saving me, Cardinal," I replied rather coldly.

"Yes," he said, "Cardinal Suenens saved priests of his diocese who had enemies who doctored evidence against them." Then he took out a two-inch-thick folder on me and thumbed through it. "What is this about a 'sensual spirituality'?" he asked.

"Well, you know how Thomas Aquinas says that all knowledge comes through the senses," I replied.

"Well, do you have an imprimatur?" he asked.

"No," I said. "Since the Second Vatican Council we don't need imprimaturs. Critical reviews in Catholic journals will do."

And he shouted, "But how will I control theologians without an imprimatur?"

"Control theologians?"

"Yes, how will I control theologians in my diocese without an imprimatur?"

"Good news! Cardinal," I replied. "The book is not being published in your diocese but in Wilmington, North Carolina."

During the course of the conversation, he confessed to not being able to control his theologians, his sisters, his priests—all of them. I had this picture of a man who had fought all his life to climb to the top of a hierarchical ladder, and now that he was up there he was saying the game is over, there is nothing there. I left the meeting deeply encouraged: it had not been a radical theologian a la Hans Küng but a conservative cardinal and protector of the status quo who had revealed to me that the control game was dying. As I emerged from the cardinal's mansion I learned that my new puppy, Tristan, who had accompanied me, had been doing *his* business on the cardinal's lawn while we were conducting *ours* inside. I did not punish him.

Several years later my provincial was meeting with the cardinal and my name came up (Cody was famous for never forgetting a name). "Matthew Fox," he said, "he's an interesting person and boy is he tough." I took this to be about as fine a compliment as one could ever receive from a bully—being called "tough."

The best test of any teaching experience is what students do on graduating. I have been very proud of those graduates of Barat College's religious studies department whom I have run into over the years. One is a lawyer working with women's groups and oppressed peoples in Chicago. Another (whose consciousness opened up in high school under the influence of drugs) became a Sacred Heart sister and has been deeply involved in social justice struggles for years. Another started her own magazine.

My quest for inventing methodologies as well as finding material for courses was put to the test one day. A parent in the Highland Park area where I lived informed me that his ten-year-old son and some of his friends were bored in their religion classes. Would I teach them religion? We met, six ten-year-olds and I, on Sunday mornings for religion class. The first semester I took them to my basement, and with loads of two-by-fours and chicken wire and wallpaper paste, we constructed catacombs complete with hanging skeletons and other details that boys love. I had them read articles on the catacombs, and we would sit in there and tell stories and occasionally have mass. The parents would call me and say, "We don't know what this has to do with religion, but keep doing whatever you are doing. Our sons talk all week about this experience and look forward to coming."

I enjoyed this experiment in educational methodology, and the next semester we made an eight-millimeter movie (this was before videos) of the *Musical, Mystical Bear*. In each instance, the students were *doing something* with their hands. This hands-on education I would later call "extrovert meditation" or "art as meditation." I owe much of this insight to my oldest brother, Tom, who has been a pioneer in innovative education for some time.

Two years ago, a young man came up to me after a lecture I gave in Chicago. "Do you remember me?" he asked. I did not. "I was in your catacomb class nineteen years ago, and it was the beginning of my life's work. You handed out stones and had us make up stories about them while we sat in the catacombs. Now I hunt stones for a living and carve them. I travel all over—I've been in avalanches in the Himalayas hunting for stones." He then presented me with a large, beautiful stone with carvings of all the continents—his "earth stone." He later sent me a booklet on the rituals he has conducted with these stones. I was stunned by this encounter. But just a few days later, in giving a talk at the Chicago Art Institute, I was approached by another young man. Again, he asked if I remembered him. I did not. "I was in your catacomb class nineteen years ago and you had us paint. Now I am a painter, a graduate of this institute." Once again, I was moved by how influential *the right method of teaching* can be in a person's life when it comes at the right time.

I received an invitation to preach on Buddha's birthday at the Buddhist Temple of Chicago, and I chose the occasion to preach on the "middle way" of both Buddha and St. Dominic. They gifted me with copies of the Zen poet Kenji Miyazawa's poetry and invited me back several times to preach and also to work with their teenagers. I was touched by these experiences and found them a practical exercise in what I would later call deep ecumenism.

My years at Barat College corresponded with the Watergate capers and all the connecting issues of constitutional illegalities, fourteen high government officials going to prison, and so on. I volunteered to work for McGovern in 1972, distributing leaflets and doing other campaign jobs in the suburbs of Chicago (one co-worker was an intense fellow named Jim Wallis who would shortly move to Washington, D.C., and begin the famous Sojourners community), and I was deeply discouraged by McGovern's loss and the immensity of it. It turned out that our Emmaus community was also working hard on McGovern's behalf back in Massachusetts and that the headquarters for his campaign was in the basement of my old friend Emma Sansone. It was depressing, watching the state of American politics and the media's slow pickup on the subject. Part of my depression was almost beyond naming: it had to do with the manipulation, not just of religion, but now of spirituality as well. In the 1975 preface to the bear book I cite Jeb Stuart Magruder, one of Nixon's helpers who went to jail, as confessing that "we had private morality but no public morality," and I comment on how

> the privatized spirituality of the Watergate White House (complete with its well-publicized prayer breakfasts, religious sycophants and winning-is-all mentality) has been stripped naked. . . . Watergate then has become an archetype of the privatized spirituality that, lacking any concept of prophecy or moral outrage at social sin, wraps itself publicly in pious platitudes and flights of mystical feeling [I should have said pseudo-mystical feelings of power]. . . . Prayer as a cover-up for injustice is dead.[6]

About this time I was invited to do a study on "Spirituality and Education" based on a poll conducted by the National Conference of Diocesan Directors, who by then were quite familiar with my bear and pig (*Whee!*) books. As part of my study I chose to visit the most promising-looking programs in spirituality around the country. I found that they were all lacking in feminism, art, social justice, and a biblically based or Jewish-based understanding of spirituality. The best of the lot was at the Institute in Spirituality and Worship at the Graduate Theological Union in Berkeley, California. While I was visiting, a young man in the program took me aside and said, "We study *about* John of the Cross's mysticism but we don't study how to be mystics ourselves. It's still a head trip." Those words ring in my mind even today, twenty years later. Studying *about* instead of *how*; education as a "head trip."

I wrote my study as a three-part article that appeared in *The Living Light*, a religious educational journal that was the official publication of the Department of Education of the United States Catholic Conference. In the study, I urge religious educators to "teach religion less and spirituality more" and say that people are bored with talk "*about* God (much less about church, sacraments or ecclesiastical politics), they want to know God; not about God."[7] In our times, attitudes are in flux around such subjects as "sexuality, guilt, injustice, racism, womanhood, technology, institutions (including institutional churches): global destruction vs. global survival. A God dedicated to incarnation that was not also re-experienced in such a period would be no incarnate God at all."[8] I talk of how spirituality differs from theology because, among other things, spirituality is a skill and an art; it is a practice and the key to it is simply: "Does it work? Is it working? Are we experiencing God? All spirituality is about experiences. Our faith is in the God of experience, the experienced God." I make a point that was being driven more and more home to me as I listened and spoke around the country: that "I have seldom met a person who never experienced God; though most people I have met are not aware that they have experienced God."[9]

Speaking of the Hellenistic, Jansenistic, and Roman influences on American Catholicism, I find three elements common to all that afflict our spiritual awareness: that body and soul are in conflict, that is, that the spiritual is what is immaterial; that spirituality has nothing to do with politics; and that asceticism is more pleasing to God than discipline.

I speak of the "tremendous craving for spirituality" that I had observed while lecturing around the country. I warn that it will take some "serious and substantial un-learning and re-learning of spirituality" if we are to make the required transformation happen. To assist that reeducation I laid out a basic blueprint for a spirituality institute that would "teach the spirituality of Jesus in our time." Six categories of courses were included: *Mystical Traditions* (including Catholic, Protestant, Jewish, Hindu, Buddhist, and Islamic); *Artist as Spiritual Voyager,* wherein dramatists, musicians, writers, dancers, painters would lead us in their experiences of "prayer, wrestling with devils and demons, ecstasy and hell, through their struggle with their vocation";[10] *Professions as Spiritualities,* in which we subject our work experiences in teaching, medicine, law, business, science, and journalism to a critical spiritual analysis; and *seminars* on topics such as women as spiritual leaders, North American Indian spirituality, black spirituality, sexuality as a spirituality, and liturgical worship and spirituality.

Workshops would pass on *skills* that are so necessary for spiritual practice such as creating religious symbols; Zen, yoga, transcendental meditation; Gregorian chant; biofeedback; filmmaking; painting; dancing; pot throwing; celebration skills and practice; starting and operating community co-ops; and pacifism as a spiritual and political discipline. Finally, *Special Events* such as circuses and clowns, an opera, ethnic dances, notable speakers, and camping trips.

These ideas were really the seeds for what was to become the Institute in Culture and Creation Spirituality (ICCS): seminars, art-as-meditation classes, weekly "forums" (what I called "Special Events"), ecumenical and culture-based spiritual education that included heart and mind education. We announced in the magazine that we planned a spirituality institute like the one I was describing at Barat College. That was indeed our intention, as a committee appointed by the school had spent months planning it. However, the idea was then vetoed by the president. I decided it was time for me to leave Barat College; I had been there four good years and learned much, but it was time for me to implement the vision for an institute in spirituality.

A Broader Spirituality

Before my vision for a spirituality institute became a reality, three other events happened that changed my life forever. One was that I moved. I had been giving a retreat at the Benedictine retreat center in Madison, Wisconsin, on a weekend. At the end of the retreat a woman took me aside, saying she had something important to tell me. "Listen to me," she said, "I'm sixty-five and older than you. I was with Fr. Cooke in Milwaukee several years ago when he was teaching us laypeople with energy and skills of communication comparable to yours, and we were so hungry that we drove him out of the priesthood. You are tired; you need to take better care of yourself. Your message and your way of presenting it are dynamite. But if you don't take care of yourself, we laypeople *will eat you up and spit you out and drive you from the priesthood* as we did Fr. Cooke." I was struck by her comments and her passion; she had hit a note. I was tired. On the way home, thinking about how to take better care of myself, I remembered my list of natural ecstasies from the pig book. The first one I had mentioned was "nature." It was time to move from Highland Park closer to nature.

Brendan and I found a wonderful place in a small village in the Fox Lakes area north of Chicago. It stood on two lakes—one at the front door, one at the back—with a woods next to it. It was made to order for calming the soul: the land, the water, the woods, the sky, the quiet. Now I had a way to protect myself. Creation would do it.

A month or two after I moved into this contemplative place, three friends arrived from Germany eager to see the United States in this bicentennial year of 1976. The five of us piled into my sister's Dodge camper and headed west. It was a beautiful trip, through the South Dakota badlands, along the Missouri River, to Yosemite and Yellowstone, and then back home through the Grand Canyon, the Painted Desert, Colorado. There, a few miles out of Denver and just two days from home, a pickup truck pulled out from a stop sign on our left and smashed into the driver's seat where I was sitting. The other passengers seemed okay, but I was seriously injured. They put me in an ambulance and I passed out in the examination room.

I was now to learn what physical pain meant. I was in constant pain for two years, pain so great that I never had one full night's sleep in that time. I would lie on my bed and shut my eyes, and my head felt so gigantic in its pain that the only image I could come up with was a map of the United States. My head was as big as the United States—and as full of pain. I learned to live with the pain— I learned you *can* live with pain—but it takes a lot out of you. Life becomes just living with the pain, and little energy is left for other things. I managed to teach that year, which was my final year at Barat College, but it was very difficult from a physical standpoint. I went to neurosurgeons, who were unable to relieve the pain. They would give me drugs but I never took a single one.

I was fortunate to have the support of Brendan Doyle, and of our new puppy, Tristan. Though I did not heal physically, I learned to enter into my pain and be with it. From that experience I was, without knowing it, preparing my next book, *A Spirituality Named Compassion*. I was learning compassion the surest way to learn it: through my own suffering.

During this period another friend entered my life who has been with me ever since. I was reading the Hindu scholar Coomaraswamy's book on art and spirituality and came across an essay on Meister Eckhart. As I started to read it, I was startled to see entire sentences in Eckhart that were in my *Whee! We, wee* book. Unnerved, I put the book back on the shelf. A few months later I tiptoed back to it, continued the essay, and found still more sentences that I had published that year in an article on sacred space and sacred time. Now I let go of my fear and said to myself: Here I might have a brother! I got my first book on Meister Eckhart and had not yet opened it when my doctors persuaded me that they could relieve my pain through an operation. They would do a fusion on my vertebra, connecting some hipbone to my neck bone; it was somewhat risky, they explained, for if the spinal cord was damaged during the procedure, I would be a paraplegic. But that did not seem so different from my limited state of being at the time, so I gave my go-ahead.

During the operation, while I was under anesthesia, Meister Eckhart came to me; we didn't talk, we just walked together on a beach. It was the most transcendent dream of my life. From that time on, I knew he and I had a rendezvous together. After I left the hospital I found a library where they had a lot of Eckhart's works in Latin. We were indeed becoming fast friends. One thing I found in him that I could find nowhere else was a rich treatment of the theological concept of *compassion*. Since Jesus had said in Luke's version of the Sermon on the Mount, "Be you compassionate as your Creator in heaven is compassionate," one would think that compassion would be a rather operative category in Christian spirituality. But it was not and has not been. Instead, *contemplation*—a word that never crossed Jesus' lips, for it is not Jewish—and *perfection*—a word mistranslated from Matthew's version of the Sermon on the Mount but truly defined by Luke as compassion—have dominated Western spiritual theology. Here was one more instance—and a deeply egregious one at that—of Hellenistic spirituality swamping Jesus' spirituality. Eckhart has an entire sermon in which he exegetes at length this phrase, "Be you compassionate as your Creator is compassionate," and he develops a theology of compassion throughout his work.

Examining the meaning of compassion, I found that while our English language has sentimentalized it, equating it with pity and feeling sorry for and dropping crumbs from the table—*Webster's* dictionary actually says that the meaning of compassion as a relation between equals is obsolete—the biblical tradition is much more to the point. "Compassion means justice," says Eckhart, teaching from the Jewish tradition. But it also means celebration. Compassion is about our shared interdependence; thus we are compassionate when we struggle for justice and other forms of healing *and* we are compassionate when we celebrate. As Eckhart puts it, "What happens to another, whether it be a joy or a sorrow, happens to you." I was amazed to learn how little the category of compassion had been developed by Christian theologians. Albert Schweitzer had of course done the best job in our century, and a Japanese theologian, Kazoh Kitamori, who was a convert from Buddhism, had written a fine book on compassion in which he called for substituting a "Theology of the Pain of God" for a "Theology of the Word of God." Compassion names God's pain as well as ours. Jewish theologians such as Rabbi Heschel and Rabbi Samuel Dressner also developed a rich theology of compassion. Liberation theologians like José Miranda, who wrote that the word *hatred* in the Bible means "a simple lack of compassion," were also recovering this rich theological category. Miranda also underscored the necessary connection between *justice* and compassion, noting that it was Hellenistic philosophy and not the Bible that separated love from justice.

In compassion I found another way to name and deepen that basic theme that I had been wrestling with continually since before my days in Paris: the relation of justice and mysticism. As the psalmist puts it, "In compassion, peace and justice kiss." But to recover compassion we would have to dismantle the preoccupation with contemplation as a basic spiritual category.

I was assisted in examining this problem when I co-led a retreat for college students on the side of Mount St. Helens in the state of Washington. (This was a few years before the volcano blew its top and this retreat center and all else on the mountainside disintegrated.) We met for the weekend at a YMCA camp on the mountain, and my co-leader was a woman who had us doing circle dances and singing "We are dancing Sara's circle" to the tune of the overly familiar hymn "We Are Climbing Jacob's Ladder." I was very moved by the experience; I remember watching these big, heavyset young men in their mountain boots dancing a minuet, and I realized once again how radical art is. Their spirit itself was transformed by the demands of the dance; they became gentle and light in spite of their clothing and demeanor just by the requirements of doing a minuet. And then those contrasting words, *dancing* versus *climbing*, kept coming back to me. So I went home and further pondered the rich meaning of "dancing Sara's circle" and how different an energy that was from "climbing Jacob's ladder." Again, I tried out these ideas on people in lectures and workshops and got an overwhelming acknowledgment of their power. I showed how our male ancestors had far too often equated spiritual attainment with "climbing up," as if God were away from the earth (and from *mater* and *materia*, "mother" and "matter") and that the word *compassion* only came at the end of a long descent: at the top is God and Contemplation; only on the way down the ladder is there compassion—but who lives so long as to experience it?

The circle, on the other hand, already contains the divine energy; it is panentheism (God around), not theism (God as up). In the circle are laughter, earthiness, equality, and partnership, for we look one another in the eye. There is always room for more; competition is not built into this form as it is in ladder-climbing, where only a few make it to the top. A ladder mentality as a spiritual archetype legitimizes power-over relationships and hierarchies of all kinds. Compassion is passion *with* and requires a different kind of energy. Once after I had presented this teaching in a lecture, a woman told me, "I am the wife of a corporate vice-president; we have been in the corporation over twenty years. And I will tell you the truth: I do not know anyone in the corporation who is happy. We are all so busy staying on the precarious ladder, so afraid of falling, that it occupies all our attention. There is no joy."

The recovery of compassion as *the* most operative category in a Christian spirituality is an outcome of our letting go of patriarchy. After all, in Hebrew the words for compassion and womb are from the same root (*rehem* and *rahamim*). Furthermore, for the Jew, compassion is *the* most appropriate name for God—it is the unique divine attribute. Which is certainly why Jesus could say, "Be you compassionate as your Creator in heaven is compassionate" and in doing so is calling us to our divinity. Eckhart has a brilliant sermon that I call "Compassion Is an Ocean: The Mystical Side of Compassion" in which he says: ". . . the highest work of God is compassion."[11] The repression of compassion as a theological category in Christianity is a major scandal. It is evidence of how far the church and its theologians have wandered from Jesus' message. It is evidence of how patriarchy, more than Jesus' Jewish spirituality, has ruled Christian history.

The Jewish and feminist poet Adrienne Rich offers the finest summary of the meaning of compassion that I have ever come across. She calls compassion "the most that we can do for one another" and defines it as knowing we're "not unique." In other words, compassion constitutes our interconnectivity: it is the joy *and* the sorrow we share.

I had a personal bodily experience of the earth's compassion in its way of absorbing our pain. My knees had been sorely affected by my car accident (a doctor on the scene of the accident thought I had two broken knees). Walking the hard terrazzo floor at O'Hare airport, which I did every time I caught a plane to lecture someplace, was an excruciating experience with every single step. I learned to concentrate on each step I took, thereby entering into the pain. Yet when I came home and walked the fields near my house with Tristan, the act of walking was totally different: with every step there was a firm but gentle connection with the earth. The earth, I learned, was strong and firm (after all, all the elements of terrazzo came from the earth), yet it was gentle and just soft enough to absorb the pain of wounded knees.

The next summer my doctors scheduled a second surgery. I was still in great pain in my knees, wrists, and back. The surgeons said they would operate on the knees. When I asked, "What will you do?" they said, "We'll go in and look around." This did not give me much confidence. I told my sister Terry about it a week before the scheduled operation, and a day later I received a call from her employer, a holistic chiropractor in Phoenix, Arizona. I felt he asked me better questions than the neurospecialists had in two years of turning my body over to them. I canceled the surgery and flew out to Phoenix. In one weekend with that man, I received more relief from my pain than I had in two years and over ten thousand dollars of bills from the neurosurgeons. (He charged me forty dollars!) He gave me exercises, some of which I could do alone and some with another person, that relieved the pain and got my body healing itself again. I was deeply affected by this evidence of alternative ways to heal, and it occurred to me that the hierarchy of the medical establishment may be as out of sync with our bodily needs as the ecclesial hierarchy gives evidence of being with our spiritual needs. It was thanks to this holistic doctor that I had the health to carry on my work.

Since that experience I have found other doctors willing to go beyond literal Western medicine who have helped me profoundly. Something they all had in common was that they *taught me about my body*—a very neglected part of my, and I dare say almost *everyone's,* education in the West. My own relationship to my body was not unlike that of many Westerners I have known. As a child, I was not too pleased with my body.

Polio altered my relationship to my body. I think it made me more appreciative of and grateful for my body just as it was. I learned not to take it for granted. My automobile accident at thirty-five also made me more aware of my body and appreciative of its daily gifts to the larger me. My body has come through for me on so many occasions. (I guess this relationship to my body makes me different from Francis of Assisi, who saw his body as "brother ass.") I like my body. We have done what we have done together. In spite of jet lag from international travel, strange beds or lack thereof, accidents, sickness and exhaustion, whatever I have accomplished in life I owe to a body-soul friendship. Body is, after all, where we all undergo our relationship to the cosmos. For the elements that make up our bodies were birthed in supernova explosions in space 5.5 billion years ago.

In *A Spirituality Named Compassion*, I took up the theme of cosmology explicitly, struck as I was by the psalmist's poem that says, "God's compassion is over all that he/she has made" (Psalm 145:9). This sense of the all, of our relationship to *all* things, was a healthy antidote to the overly psychologized and personalized morality that most religious teachers were feeding us. It also leads to issues of our relationship with animals and issues of what we know today as animal liberation. In this book, I confessed for the first time that Tristan was my "spiritual director" and that in saying this "I am only being partly facetious." While I was in pain for two years, Tristan, as so many animals do, sensed my pain and would lie under my chair when I sat outdoors. He was wonderful company—playful, rambunctious, smart, and sassy. Where we lived was a dream world for a puppy, a Rousseauistic paradise with acres of fields and trees to explore and lakes to jump in on hot August afternoons.

Tristan was an amazing judge of human character. Once when a carpenter friend was doing some work on our house, he brought a buddy with him as a helper. But for the many weeks that it took to complete the work Tristan *never* let this friend's buddy pet him; he always growled under his breath when this fellow came near him. Months after the job was completed, my friend learned that his buddy had skipped town with the money I had paid them for the work. He was a thief. How do animals know such things? After that experience, I always made a point of having Tristan greet or at least check out every worker I hired in the house.

Tristan kept my life and work in perspective and was a companion in writing twelve of my fourteen books. For example, when I was writing books on my typewriter and would pile papers on the floor around my desk he would, after a few hours of being with me in my work, get up and deliberately walk on my stacks of notes and chapters. He was reminding me that, as exciting as ideas can be, life contains other realities as well. It was time for a walk in the woods, a time for leaving the work of the mind behind. And walk in the woods we would, with him leading the way, turning back to see if I was coming along and not dragging my feet, and surging on ahead sniffing, smelling, chasing, barking, seeing and hearing what my senses could only imagine was out there.

Based on lessons I was learning from Tristan's and my friendship, I outlined in the compassion book "Spiritual Lessons Animals Teach Us." Among these are that it is good to be an animal; ecstasy without guilt; play; nonverbal communication and its power; openness and sensitivity; beauty; sensuousness; that climbing Jacob's ladder is unnatural; humor; and silent dignity. Under the last-named category I anticipated my *Original Blessing* book when I wrote: "Animals have a sense of their own worth and dignity—a pride at their own unique existence that subtly suggests that no one ever preached to them about original sin."[12] Clearly, one cause of my dissatisfaction with the theology of original sin came from my experience with animals other than human ones.

Along with cosmology, in the compassion book I discuss compassion and science, including physics and biology, and I talk of moving "from a mechanistic and piecemeal universe to an organic and interdependent one."[13] If compassion is interdependence and the new paradigm in science is about interdependence, then science is lining up to be an ally with a healthy, compassion-oriented spirituality. I was very excited about the implications of this reality, and science would fully enter our ICCS curriculum before long. In speaking of creativity and compassion, I urged moving from a "fetish with the cross to an exploration of the empty tomb," employing ideas from two newly found friends, the potter-poet M. C. Richards and the psychologist Otto Rank. Richards says: "We have to realize that a creative being lives within ourselves whether we like it or not. And we have to get out of its way, for it will give us no peace until we do."[14] I found in her book, *Centering,* a powerful affirmation of the spiritual linchpin that was the praxis upon which ICCS was based: art as meditation. She presents the case for the spiritual experience that making pots is. Whenever I had doubts about what we were doing with art-as-meditation classes at ICCS—and I did have doubts for it seemed too incongruous in our academic system—I would go back to her book, my "bible" in art as meditation. Years later she joined our faculty in Oakland.

I discovered Otto Rank's work through reading Ernest Becker's *Denial of Death,* in which he says that Rank's *Art and Artist* was the most important book of his life. I interacted with that book in an article on "Otto Rank on the Artistic Journey as a Spiritual Journey and the Spiritual Journey as an Artistic Journey." I still go back to that article regularly for the wisdom contained in Rank's analysis of who the artist is: "one who wants to leave behind a gift"; the principal obstacle to his/her creativity: fear of death, which is based on a fear of life; and the artist's principal challenge: to balance one's work with one's living. In the compassion book, I take up Rank's analysis of the need for forgiveness—forgiveness that we must all bless ourselves with if we are to overcome the guilt of creativity and get on with being the artists we were meant to be. His message is all about resurrection—although he was a Jew, he felt that Jesus' and Paul's message about resurrection was the most "revolutionary idea" in human history because it frees every individual to create by freeing us from our fear of death.

After I left Barat College I received a call from Sister Mary de Cooke, B.V.M., of the Mundelein College religious studies department on the north side of Chicago inviting me to teach in their graduate division. I asked if they would take my program as well as me. After some discussion they agreed, and ICCS, called the Institute in Creation-Centered Spirituality (later to be the Institute in Culture and Creation Spirituality), was born.

6

ICCS:
Training of Mystics and Prophets (with Assistance from Eckhart and Hildegard)—1977–1983

Above all else, the Institute in Culture and Creation Spirituality (ICCS) was a conscious, deliberate effort to reinvent our forms of education so that learning spirituality would be possible. I started it because spirituality was not being taught in our schools or seminaries or theologates. And it was not being taught because it *could not be taught,* since we continued to rely on Descartes, Kant, and other modern European thinkers who equated truth with "clear and distinct ideas," located our souls in the pineal gland in our heads, and ignored both body and creativity. The idea of mysticism that prevailed during the Enlightenment—that it could be taught as *technique,* a kind of engineering of the soul (e.g., Ignatius's *Spiritual Exercises*)—ignored the aesthetic dimension to education. We had to change our methods of learning if we were to educate for compassion.

Educating for Spirituality

The goal of creation-spiritual education is to train mystics and prophets. In terms of education, we were trying to develop intuition *and* intellect; right *and* left brain; mind, heart, and body. Accordingly, the first faculty member I hired in setting up ICCS at Mundelein College in 1977 was Tria Thompson, a dancer who could teach circle dances and who could get everyone involved in movement. It was my way of doing something concrete about the body-soul dichotomy that I had felt for years was at the core of misbegotten fall/redemption spirituality. (Did Augustine ever dance once he became a Christian, I wonder.) Others joined us from the Mundelein College faculty, most of whom were successful teaching in our program. A few were not. A member of the music department spent the course dissecting Beethoven's Fifth. I learned about this when a young male student in the program said at the end of the term, "I guess I'll never get music." I asked what he meant, and he told me of his despair at sitting in that music class. I had to relieve that teacher of her job, and I gave it to Brendan Doyle, who I knew loved music as meditation and could invite others into that same sacred space with ease. It was a hard lesson learned, that graduates of our music conservatories and art institutes, like seminarians, often enter such schools because of their soul-experience with music or art, but by the time they graduate they are all technique and no soul. Being able to connect the two again can take a long, long time. Especially if one is in academia.

Our program met with stiff resistance from some faculty from other departments and from the administration. I think only the early support of the religious studies faculty and the department head, Sister Carol Frances Jegen, saved us from being expelled at Mundelein. That plus the success of the program, which brought in solid graduate students in sufficient numbers to pay for our program and to contribute to the support of the rest of the department. The members of the department were all fine people and doing good things. I never felt anything but support from them. One B.V.M. sister, Blanche Marie Gallagher, who was a painter long committed to the vision of Teilhard de Chardin, came on board to teach Painting as Art as Meditation, and her contribution was warmly received.

One way I have of understanding the ICCS experience is to say that our form of education seems to awaken the chakras, the seven energy centers of our bodies according to Eastern philosophy. The throat chakra, especially, seems to open up at ICCS. Students often report that they "find their voice" there. I remember a tiny Catholic sister from Houston who was in our program a few years ago. She did a vision quest and came back to tell me that an eagle had come to her, pointing to her throat. We discussed the metaphor, and its meaning was clear to both of us: the eagle is often a prophetic symbol, and the throat chakra energizes the voice. Was she being heard? Had she spoken out? Where is the trumpet in her? A few years after she returned to her work, I received a letter from the hospital staff: "What happened to our sister at ICCS?" they inquired. "She's got so much energy and strength that she's running the hospital here."

A phenomenon that confused me during the program's first year was this: I was my own administrator and chief "listener," and I remember remarking to a friend that I would have to put Kleenex in next year's budget—so many students came in and cried. I was not at all prepared for this reaction to the program. But I came to realize that once you reintroduce art as a major part of education, the truth of people's lives starts emerging. All the truth: that which is denied, that which has been kept down for years and hidden. Thus, all the tears. Art as meditation is a kind of truth serum. You take it at the risk of letting some long-held-down genies out of the bottle. It releases secrets long kept underground. Tears are a sign that things are melting; water is flowing; and our pain is coming unstuck, unjammed.

But of late among ICCS students I would say there is less crying and more shouting; less stuck pain and more anger. There has to be room in our education and our worship for this venting and letting go so that breathing (Spirit blowing) can happen again. It does not make for easy going in all classroom scenarios, but it is part of the process of healing and coming alive, therefore becoming spiritual again. And there are ways—premodern ways such as drumming and chanting and dancing and getting into the body by whatever means—that assist the process, that channel the energy, that provide a safe ritual space for our letting go. When grieving occurs, creativity flows and wisdom happens again. Some wonderful people enrolled in our first-year class at ICCS—several of whom I am in touch with still, eighteen years later. I remember one student, a forty-year-old Franciscan sister, a fine, lively person who came to me in April and said, "This is the first spring of my life. I've never been so alive. The painting class has me aware of the colors and smells and forms of spring all around me." We had found a new—and very ancient—way to convert people, to awaken their senses. The secret was art as meditation. Art is the missing link between spirituality and social justice.

One proof of this is what happened in one of our compassion practicum classes. Each spring the students do a compassion practicum that takes them into some group at the edge of our culture. One group of students chose to go to Cook County Jail and do a day of art as meditation there. A few days later I received a call from the woman in charge of out-events at the jail. She said that she had been directing such projects for nine years and had *never* had a response as powerful as she had from our students' visit. I quizzed the students on what they had done: just a day of poetry, dance, storytelling—a chance for prisoners to tell their stories. One prisoner said, "This is the first time in my life that I have had a chance to express myself." The poor are deprived not only of money but just as often of the *skills* and of the *encouragement* to express themselves. Art as meditation is for everybody—especially the most oppressed.

ICCS's first year was not easy (I don't remember a single year that was). In the middle of the year two angry women stalked out of the program, leaving only a note behind. Another woman frowned the entire year, in class and out. Five years after she graduated I received a letter from her in which she apologized. She now had a doctorate in theology and understood what it was we were trying to do, how different it was from regular theological education, and how needed it was. I took this lesson to heart: Don't judge students harshly. They might "get it" down the road.

Actually, Fr. Jerry O'Leary, who was a very experienced educator, had advised me when I first laid out my plans for ICCS: "Remember, even your best student will only get 10 percent of what you are trying to teach." That advice has stayed with me over the years.

Building a Learning Community

One of the features I had built into the ICCS program to enliven the educational experience and to prevent a hothouse atmosphere was a weekly "Wednesday forum" to which we invited some outside person or group who was doing lively things in art, mysticism, politics, or spirituality. We were treated to many fine experiences on those Wednesdays, when we gathered together in the wonderful living room of the mansion on the shores of Lake Michigan that housed Mundelein's religious studies department. A sister who had known Thomas Merton well and had picnicked with him on occasion came and read his Zen poetry. (On hearing his "I am a bell" image for the first time, I was hit hard by Merton's feminine side. I realized how the male mystic must find his feminine soul and the female her masculine soul if we are to bring genders and holiness together.) Ken Feit, a spiritual fool of whom I will tell more later, came to lead us in foolishness; Sister Terisita Weind, who years later would be fired from a parish in the Chicago diocese because her leadership was a threat to the male structure, spoke on black spiritual experience, as did theologian Nathan Jones; Walter Brueggemann spoke with passion on the prophets, and during his talk a woman student, a Celtic poet with a sharp wit, leaned over to me and said, "This man wears his testicles on his tongue." One visitor was a Taoist man from China who had worked with Dag Hammarskjöld at the United Nations. I had met him when lecturing in California and he told me I was "the only Taoist theologian" he had ever heard speak in the West, although he had visited many churches and temples looking for a theology that connected to his own. At ICCS he spoke to us about Hammarskjöld's spirituality. Among all these wonderful encounters, perhaps the favorite was the yearly visit from Robert Bly.

At that time Bly was not a men's guru but a guru of the Eastern mystics. He would sit with his mandolin on his lap. A musician told me it was always off-tune, and he played it very badly, but it *did* settle the left brain and provide a mystic atmosphere. He would recite from heart-memory the words of Kabir or Rumi. It was always an event of deep meaning to me, the faculty and students, and as it turned out, to Robert himself. On one of his visits, he told me that while on the road doing his poetry and readings at other colleges around the country, he would dream of ICCS. "Why?" I asked. "Because your people here are on a spiritual journey, and they understand what I am doing. In most colleges, everyone is busy giving me grades on my poetry."

Dr. Helen Kenik made a significant contribution to our work when she joined our faculty in its second year, bringing with her a deep understanding of creation theology in the Scriptures. She had done her doctorate under Walter Brueggemann on a theology of kingship based on the Book of Kings (1 Kings 3:4–15) and, being a former Dominican herself, *got* what we were trying to do. It was she who introduced me to the theology of the royal person. Later, when we had moved ICCS to California, she and her husband came out to join us.

One Wednesday afternoon when Bly was visiting, another visitor sat in on the event. He was a tall, lanky mathematical physicist from Tacoma, Washington, named Brian Swimme who had just come from a scientific conference in Milwaukee. He told me later how going from the heady experience he had had in Milwaukee to being at our institute, sitting around a living room with an off-key poet reciting Kabir's mysticism with political asides thrown in, was just a jump to another level of being. Later I was to do a workshop in Seattle that Brian attended, and I remember how touched I was to see a physicist dancing Sara's circle like the rest of us. After the workshop, he took me to his home and pulled my *Breakthrough* book down from the shelf. He had completely annotated all 545 pages! No theologian I know has ever done that.

Brian and I began to carry on a rather lively correspondence. Our collaboration would have a deep effect on ICCS and our subsequent work. He felt that the "DNA" for altering the face of Christianity was happening at ICCS and that by grounding theology and education in the aesthetic we were transcending "the dominant stream of philosophy and theology since Aristotle." He felt the coming together of my work with the mystical patterns emerging from today's science. With meditation at the core of the ICCS curriculum, the conceptual can become deepened by the student's taste of experience and the experience can be deepened by the conceptual. Yet experience comes first and precedes the purely intellectual. A theology based on concepts will see a chasm as the principal reality—thus the need for redemption. But a theology founded on the aesthetic and on feeling (meaning an experience of beauty) begins with relationship as an ontological first principle. Thus compassion becomes the fundamental truth of the universe. In this context the cosmos itself becomes non-other and alive, and each and every being in the universe relates to it. Brian liked that ICCS was rooted in tradition and that the Jewish understanding of compassionate love-justice was the culmination of our educational effort. This was another way by which we were escaping the Hellenistic, substance-based metaphysics of the West. Now the real dialogue with Buddhism could begin.

Brian told me how he had studied Christian theologians for years, including Rahner, Lonergan, the Dutch Catechism, Charismatics, Schillebeeckx, Barth, Teilhard de Chardin. "And then I happened across Matthew Fox and I knew instantly that this was it. This was the sourcepoint for the future revisioning of

Christianity into the restructured global cultural order." On June 11, 1981, I wrote the following to Brian:

> If things keep evolving favorably, we may well have as core team in a year: a professional fool; a husband-wife drama team; a dancer; a Jungian analyst with ten years' experience in group work with ex-prisoners; a physicist-mathematician-mystic; a spiritual theologian; a biblical theologian; a musician. Sound crazy? I hope so!

Brian expressed a passion for history and philosophy that could not be denied. So much of my work at this point was either intellectual (writing, lecturing, teaching) or administrative and practical (recruiting students by lecturing around the country, raising money to pay the faculty, finding the right faculty, and so on). Brian kept a "balance" in the sense of seeing ICCS and its potential from the point of view of the history of Western philosophy and culture. Rarely have I been so encouraged to keep going on the path I was on.

Brian and I led a workshop together for the first time in 1981 at a summer program at Dominican College in San Rafael, California. Its title was "The Universe Is My Body: The Emergence of Meister Eckhart's Vision of Cosmic Interpenetration in the Theoretical Physics of the Twentieth Century." I felt then—as I always did in our subsequent dialogues—that half the accomplishment was simply our showing up on stage together: how long had it been since a physicist and a theologian had thought out loud together, and not just about *methodology* but about the moral and spiritual passions of our culture? I remember when we did a dialogue in Seattle, a woman came up afterward and said she had brought her sixteen-year-old daughter with her "kicking and screaming." Her daughter was very bright and had dropped out of school. In the middle of our dialogue she turned to her mother and said, "Mom, now I know what I want to do with the rest of my life." The power of cosmology—of the coming together of science, mysticism, and art—ought not be ignored.

Among faculty members at the San Rafael summer program were the street priest from Harlem, Bob Fox; the spiritual fool Ken Feit; and the Seneca Indian and Franciscan sister Jose Hobday. My first encounter with Bob Fox illustrates how creation spirituality contributes to social change. Bob and I were both scheduled to speak on an ecumenical program in Portland, Oregon. I spoke about our divinity, our creativity, compassion, and art as meditation. Then Bob stood up, all six-feet-two-inches of him, and his opening line was, "Hearing Matt Fox talk, I feel less lonely in the universe." Then he began to cry. Until then, I had never seen a grown man cry before an audience of a thousand people. He went on to say, "Matt has learned his spirituality—what did he call it? creation spirituality—his way. I have learned my spirituality on the streets of Harlem, but I will tell you this: we are talking about the same spirituality. All you can really do for the very poor is to awaken their creativity by whatever means possible so that they can liberate themselves. Matt does it his way. We do it by doing rubbings of manhole covers and other ways."

Bob and I worked together frequently after that; sometimes we did workshops in various cities, especially on the East Coast. I loved the man; he had the gift of Celtic oral excellence and he had the large heart to go with it. Attending the celebration of his twenty-fifth anniversary as a priest was a high point in my life. I sat between two prostitutes during the mass, and I remember the party in the church basement with two images: the first was the Hispanic policewoman joining the dances after a couple of hours; and the second was my going to bed at 3:00 A.M. and turning and seeing Bob leading a Zorba the Greek dance. Bob was one-of-a-kind; he was as much at home with his friends in Harlem as with farmers or with business executives or doctors. He challenged people and saved many people's "souls," as I was told at this anniversary party. He died too young. But he was tired and needed a rest. Many of us felt he failed to take care of himself; but more likely he had so identified with the people of Harlem that he chose not to live a lifestyle beyond their means—including a lifestyle of privileged medical attention.

At the memorial mass we held for Bob at ICCS, Luisah Teish, who teaches African dance on our faculty and who knew Bob from summer programs we did together, told this story. The day he died, she had written him a letter about a powerful dream she had had. In it she was in Africa surrounded by many elders (Teish is an ordained Yoruba priestess). But there was one white man there too—it was Bob Fox. "What's he doing here?" one of the elders asked her. "He stays; he's one of us," Teish replied. Teish remembered attending a class of Bob's during the summer program. "I don't remember what he said, but I remember that he spoke in the cadence of an African drum." I can never forget this eulogy to Bob Fox: he, a New York Irishman and a monsignor ("a mistake in the archdiocesan computer," he used to say), had by the end of his life become so much like his people that he spoke in the cadence of their drum. It's evidence of a life fully lived.

Another teacher of ICCS students and myself in Chicago was the itinerant fool, Ken Feit. Ken had started life, one might say, as a Jesuit working in the inner city of Milwaukee and had been told by his provincial that he must give up his foolishness and start teaching high school like other obedient Jesuits. "But Paul and Ignatius urge us to be fools for Christ," Ken argued. "Not that kind!" shouted his provincial. So, given the two options, Ken had to resign from the Jesuits and follow his fool's vocation. He got himself educated as a fool by attending clown college; by attending a school for the hearing impaired to learn sign language; by studying with Native American storytellers; by going to Africa to learn from African storytellers. He took his rituals, his fool's mass, and his stories around the world—he took the Trans-Siberian Railroad, for example, getting out at stops in Siberia and miming on the platform; he spent time with Mother Teresa's dying ones in Calcutta; and he journeyed throughout the West. When Ken and I talked about his working with us on a magazine, he came up with the idea of doing a column for each issue that would be (1) upside down and (2) edible. Yes, he wanted his readers to *eat* his column, eucharistlike, each issue. Ken worked with us during our five-week summer session in San Rafael. His course, entitled "Clowning and the Art of Failure," was described as:

> An exploration into the literary and historical motifs of the priestly clown and fool with emphasis on mask, makeup (whiteface), and pantomime. Students will discover their own clown character and interact with the off-campus community. Students will be joined the last two weeks of the workshop by a bevy of clowns including jugglers, unicyclists, etc.

Ken and I had talked at length about his joining our faculty at ICCS because he was now ready to get "off the road" and do more teaching of the next generation. But he had one more trip to make before settling down—to Central and South America. He would be back by January so he could join our faculty for the second semester.

As it turned out, Ken did indeed have one more trip to make, but it was not to Central and South America. After our summer session ended, on driving back to Chicago from California, he had a car accident and was killed. He was forty years old. His last words, uttered to his traveling companion, were, "Shut up, can't you see I'm dying." Ken wanted to experience everything, and he was conscious and curious in entering into his own death experience. When I received the news of Ken's death, I was at home at the lake. Putting the phone down after getting the news from his sister, I walked, stunned, into the backyard and down to the waterfront. There, on a cattail, was a yellow bird singing away. I had never seen the bird before, nor did I ever see it again. I felt it was Ken's soul. He had fooled us all this time. And he was chirping beautifully.

I called Brian Swimme and asked him if he would join our faculty to take Ken Feit's place. Brian had met Ken only a few months earlier and had written me his response to the encounter: "I met the Foolish Feit! He is truly one-in-a-cosmos. We have seventy million lawyers and one Fool. . . . Feit gave expression to the same yearning that we have both experienced from sources stretching from Marxists to Mystics."

Brian was deeply affected by Ken's death, but he said he would think the invitation over. Later he told me he went to a favorite rock near the sea, lay down on the rock, and felt Ken's spirit enter his body. He called me and said yes, he and his wife and two children would head out to Chicago soon. So Ken's early death brought a physicist more swiftly into the work of ICCS. I like to remind Brian, whenever we have differences, that he is a substitute for a professional fool. As it turned out, Brian spent one year in Chicago, during which he displayed his considerable charisma as a teacher and taught a course on Whitehead and creativity. That same year (1992) we also coauthored our brief *Manifesto for a Global Civilization.*

Jose Hobday has a gift of teaching the heart ways of her indigenous ancestors. She joined our faculty in California in 1990 as an act of solidarity with me when my troubles arose with the Dominican order. Shortly afterward, she was canceled from speaking at an archdiocesan event in New Orleans because a radical right-wing Catholic group objected to her work with us. "I've been speaking for twenty-eight years and no one has ever questioned my Catholicism until now," she declared. She decried "this group of right-wing wackos trying to hurt my reputation—these kind of people are the skinheads of the Catholic church."

John Giannini, a Jungian analyst who worked with ex-prisoners in the Safer Foundation, was a man of great heart. We did some workshops together jointly sponsored by ICCS and the Jung Institute, and he joined our faculty, as did Errol and Rochelle Strider for a year. They did powerful work in awakening consciousness through mime and dramatic pieces that they created. Another person who joined our ranks was the political scientist and activist Dick Simpson. Dick has written a number of books on politics and was an elected alderman in Chicago. He represented the independent opposition during Mayor Richard Daly's tenure. Dick and I taught a course together on politics and compassion in which we dealt with the likes of Mahatma Gandhi, Dorothy Day, Daniel Berrigan, and others. Later he was ordained a United Church of Christ minister, and the last I heard he was running a very active parish in downtown Chicago. He was one of those prophets in his own field who recognized the need for a link between spirituality and politics and was actively working to bridge the two worlds.

A school is only as good as its faculty and the vision that inspires it, but the test of its mettle is in the work and being of the students after they leave. Given that test, I had to be proud of what was going on at ICCS. To mention just a few of our graduates from the Chicago years: Camille Campbell, a Carmelite sister, is principal of a girls' high school in New Orleans that has a waiting list of several years to get into; she has employed a creation-centered philosophy in that school for years. Joe Kilikevice, a Dominican brother, has taken his considerable gifts as an artist and steered them into a profession of giving retreats and spirituality workshops, especially in the areas of men's liberation and of the Aramaic Our Father and circle dances. (I remember when he came to ICCS, accomplished as he was in photography, painting, and clay, and was deciding what courses to take; I asked him what most made him afraid. "Dance," he said. "I have two left feet." Dance he took and dances he now leads.) Imelda Smyth, from Ireland, returned there twelve years ago and started a women's center in Tallaght. There was 80 percent unemployment, drugs, alcohol, and much family abuse. Today, even though their center was burned down three times by raging neighbors, the women of the district, though formally uneducated, run three hundred programs a year. Hope and healing have returned for women, men, and children alike. Barbara Clow, together with her husband, Gerry, took a failing publishing house in Santa Fe, New Mexico, called Bear and Company and turned it into a thriving enterprise bridging the gap between New Age and Christian mysticism. Sister Alexandra Kovats, a refugee from Hungary and a sister of St. Joseph of Peace in Seattle, showed exceptional skills as a down-to-earth feminist who loved dance and spirituality and life itself. She, along with Jean Lanier, joined our faculty. Jean was a gestalt therapist who had studied with Fritz Perls at Esalen; she knew how to handle groups and was enthusiastic about creation spirituality since she and her husband had run a retreat center patterned after Esalen for six years in Spain. These are just a few of the graduates of Mundelein College and ICCS who have honored us by the quality of their work.

Getting Eckhart Known and Naming the Four Paths

The first talk I ever gave on Meister Eckhart was at the Quaker House in Highland Park, Illinois, in August 1977, a month before ICCS opened its doors. I remember it well for two reasons. First, there was a young man there, a mystic-farmer from Nebraska who, though raised evangelical, had discovered Eckhart on his own and who, on hearing me speak, canceled his scholarship to Yale Divinity School and joined ICCS. Marvin Anderson has been a good friend ever since. He introduced me to the idea of the farmer as mystic. (He said to me, "Every small farmer is a mystic, but this is never alluded to in the churches where rural people pray.") He also introduced me to the writings of Wendell Berry, among others. Second, the head woman of Quaker House, after I had spoken on Eckhart for an hour, shouted from the back of the hall, "My God! He sounds just like George Fox!" (the founder of the Quaker religion). She was right—Eckhart represented that marriage of mysticism and political-social consciousness and justice that had gone underground with his condemnation but resurfaced in the seventeenth century with George Fox, and with radical Protestants such as Hans Hut, Sebastian Franck, and Hans Denk in the sixteenth century. These theologians, unlike Luther, stayed with the poor and peasants and saw in Eckhart's theology of the word of God—for example, "that every creature is a word of God"—a theology that supported the wisdom of the poor.

I edited a book at this time (1981) called *Western Spirituality: Historical Roots, Ecumenical Routes,* in which I wrote for the first time about Eckhart and for the first time about the Four Paths of Creation Spirituality. This represented a big step for me—for years I had been trying to extricate myself and Western spirituality from the quagmire of the three paths of Plotinus and Pseudo-Denys, namely those of Purgation, Illumination, and Union. I felt this way of naming the spiritual journey was putting a stranglehold on our spiritual lives—why no mention of delight and pleasure? of creativity? of social justice?

Now, having begun my plunge into Eckhart's works, I had a new way to tell the story of our spiritual journeys. At first I was confused, for my professor of spirituality in Paris, Louis Cognet, had written of Eckhart's brilliance in naming the *Via Negativa;* but he made no allusion to the importance of Eckhart's *Via Positiva.*[1] This was by no means my experience in reading Eckhart. I found him saying such things as "Isness is God" and "God is voluptuous and delicious" and "God enjoys himself/herself." I found that Eckhart was as deep and rich in the *Via Positiva* as in the *Via Negativa* and that when one acknowledges this and puts them together, a third concept results! I called that the *Via Creativa,* a term I invented but a concept that is everywhere in Eckhart—the path of creativity, of giving birth. "What does God do all day long? She lies on a maternity bed giving birth," Eckhart declares. But creativity is not where Eckhart stops—nor does our spiritual journey. What, after all, is it we are giving birth to? Men of great evil, such as Hitler and Mussolini, can give birth to their devious visions. No, there must be still another path, that which tests our creativity by way of *justice:* the *Via Transformativa,* the way of compassion and social justice and celebration. Eckhart, while lacking this term too, certainly had the *concept,* as when he says that "God is justice" and "for the just person as such to act justly is to live; indeed, justice is her life, her being alive, her being, insofar as she is just."[2]

Furthermore, and most important, Eckhart *lived* this prophetic path, supporting the women's or Beguine movement of his day, even after Pope John XXII threatened excommunication to priests who worked with the Beguines, and supporting the peasants of his day, preaching to them in their new "German" dialect. At his trial, he was accused of "confusing the simple people" by telling them in their language that they were "all aristocrats, noble people" and meant to "soar like eagles."

I remember lecturing on the Four Paths at the Graduate Theological Union's Lutheran School of Theology in Berkeley. Afterward, a man introduced himself as a visiting professor of Jewish spirituality from Switzerland who had done his work under Professor Gersham Scholem. He was highly animated, saying that I was the first Christian theologian he knew who had consciously thrown out the three paths of Plotinus and company (who did not know Biblical thought) and that my four paths "were deeply Jewish." Furthermore, my emphasis on wisdom and Christ as Wisdom was the "bridge we Jews and Christians have yet to walk down together." He said, "Now—with these four paths and with wisdom returned—a Jewish-Christian spirituality can happen!" Years later I met a rabbi who said to me, "If you Christians truly believe that Jesus is wisdom, then I as a Jew must call him 'son of God,' for we believe all persons who imbibe wisdom truly are sons and daughters of God."

My major work on Meister Eckhart, *Breakthrough: Meister Eckhart's Creation Spirituality in New Translation*, appeared in 1980. *Breakthrough* contains thirty-seven of Eckhart's major sermons or treatises, arranged according to the four paths and with commentaries after each. It was the first volume of Eckhart's writings based on the critical German and Latin texts—the previous translation, that of William Blakney (1941), was not based on critical texts. Some time after the book came out I met with a professor at Villanova University who had published some articles on Eckhart that I had respected. He said to me, "If you are right about Eckhart, then the rest of us are all wrong."

I asked him why.

"Because I have never seen justice or compassion as an important category in Eckhart," he replied.

"Maybe that is because you weren't looking for it," I said. "The three paths of Plotinus and the anti-Semitism of Western philosophy have you philosophers crippled. You don't consider the Bible a philosophical text, and you don't look for terms like *justice* and *compassion* because you're out of touch with Jewish thought. Eckhart was not a philosopher as philosophy has evolved in the West. He was a preacher and theologian who knew the Bible and especially wisdom literature inside and out."

I never heard from this man again. Dr. Helen Kenik told me that reading Eckhart's sermons was like reading the Gospel writers. He was so steeped in the Gospel theology that he actually wrote out of it as did the Gospel writers in writing about Jesus.

Several years ago a woman told me this story, which she swore was absolutely true. She had been in a depression for two years and one day had an inspiration to go to a bookstore, hoping to find a book that would help her. As she was perusing the bookshelves at eye level, a book fell down from a higher shelf and hit her on the head! It was *Breakthrough*. She had never heard of either Eckhart or me, but she took the book home, drank from it deeply, and it turned her life around. Since then she has read everything she can find on creation spirituality.

Discovering Hildegard

After exploring Eckhart's thought more deeply, I began asking myself: Where does he get all this good stuff? Who besides Aquinas is an important influence on him? Over the years, commentators had given much credit to Neoplatonists and others, though most of these commentators knew nothing of the Bible (which, after all, Eckhart chanted daily as a Dominican); nor did they know anything about the women mystics, it seemed. Eckhart led me to Hildegard of Bingen, the twelfth-century Benedictine abbess who was a true renaissance woman and genius at music, art, healing, and intuition. As I began to read her, I saw deep resonances with Eckhart's work, especially her sense of cosmology and earthiness and body. And so I plunged into her work and began lecturing on her, and reproduced her paintings and my commentaries on them in *Illuminations of Hildegard of Bingen*. Later I put out a book that contained fifty of her most exciting letters to popes, bishops, and politicians, plus ten of her songs and her last and most mature work, *The Book of Divine Works*. We began an arts-as-meditation class in which our students learned to sing her music, which was so erotic and demanding—a true musical *yoga*—that students were guaranteed a mystical experience in class. This was getting high on breath, which, as Hildegard taught, is nothing other than *ruah* or spirit. I was so excited when the great geologian Thomas Berry visited ICCS for the first time and, sloshing through the January snow together to supper, we discussed Hildegard of Bingen. He was the first person I had met who knew of her and, of course, admired her.

At a "Women and Ritual" conference in Oregon I showed slides of Hildegard's illuminations and commented on them. Afterward, a woman came up excited and said, "I can hardly wait to run home and tell my teenaged daughters about Hildegard. I'm Catholic and up to now I have only been able to talk about Mary. Now Mary was a good person, but she didn't *do* all that much. But this Hildegard—a dramatist, a poet, a musician, a painter, a prophetic critic of the church, a healer—now *there's* a role model for my daughters." Not having daughters of my own I had not faced this challenge, and I was struck by how women have been deprived of good role models by our silence and put-down and misunderstanding of our great women such as Hildegard.

I had another experience with Hildegard on the occasion of the fifteen-hundredth anniversary of St. Benedict and his great achievement in launching the monastic order that bears his name. I was invited by women and men Benedictines at Lisle, Illinois, to conduct a daylong workshop. I decided to spend it on Hildegard, since they needn't listen to me but they ought to listen to one of their own. When we began the day I asked, "How many of you here know of Hildegard of Bingen?" Only about 15 of the 150 persons present raised their hands. At the end of the day an old nun, blind and in full habit, came up to me wagging her finger: "Isn't it a scandal that a Dominican had to come and tell us about Hildegard? I heard of her sixty-three years ago in the novitiate and nobody has spoken of her since." I turned to a young sister and asked, "Surely you learned of her?" "No," she replied, "we only studied the male saints of the order."

In 1982 I published a little volume called *Meditations with Meister Eckhart* that I hoped would provide a right-brain introduction to his wonderful thought. It was the first of a series in which I planned to make our Western mystics available to a wider audience in a poetic, right-brain format. Volumes that followed included meditations with Mechtild of Magdeburg, Julian of Norwich, Hildegard of Bingen, Nicholas of Cusa, Teilhard de Chardin, the Hopi, and others. Gabrielle Uhlein, who wrote *Meditations with Hildegard of Bingen*, was a German woman who had grown up near the Rhine but had never heard of Hildegard until she came to ICCS in Chicago. It was telling to me that we at ICCS were "bringing back" the Rhineland mystics to the Rhineland people, but there was logic to this: creation theology had been so run out of town by the fall/redemption tradition in Europe that it took the Americans, imbued with memories of Native American spirituality, and with some wilderness still intact, to recover our lost creation mystical tradition in the West.

Ominous Clouds from the West Coast

The first lecture trip I ever made to the San Francisco Bay Area was at the invitation of some lively Dominican students at the Graduate Theological Union who had invited me to speak on the subject of my new book, *A Spirituality Named Compassion*. This was in 1979. I stayed at the Dominican House of Studies, a beautiful pink building nestled on a cul-de-sac in north Oakland that brought back memories of my days in the River Forest priory. On the evening of my presentation, my hosts took me to the Dominican School of Philosophy and Theology, across the street from the Pacific School of Religion, which was the venue for my lecture. I spent an hour or two chatting with Dominican philosophers in their building and was then led across the street for my talk. It was an exciting event, and the place was packed. Afterward, the student organizers were ecstatic. "Everyone was there," one of them said, "the Jesuits, the Franciscans, all the Protestant groups. Except, of course, there was not a single Dominican professor there." I wondered why, but subsequent history would point to this observation by a Dominican student as being ominous indeed. Why would Dominicans not be interested in one of their own lecturing on compassion? Since my visit preceded any attacks by Cardinal Ratzinger, "heresy" could not have been the source of their displeasure. Nor could wild rumors about my residence, since I lived in the Midwest. Years later when I learned that some Dominicans of the western province were a big part of the push to expel me from the order, I was reminded of their conspicuous absence that night. And when a new president of their school, who was from the southern province, hired me to teach a course there and the Dominican faculty vetoed the choice, I was reminded once again of that night of the Dominican absence at GTU.

Another invitation that drew me to the West Coast also proved to be the beginning of something ominous. Dignity, the organization of gay and lesbian Catholics (yes, dear, there *are* gay and lesbian Catholics), invited me to give a keynote address at its convention in Seattle. This was the convention that became notorious for initiating Rome's attack on Archbishop Hunthausen, both for his hospitality in welcoming Dignity to Seattle and to mass in the cathedral and for his stand against the military in America. (He refused to pay that portion of his income tax that went to the military. He told me once that reading my book on compassion helped him make up his mind to take the stand he did against America's militarism, even in an area where the economy was highly dependent on the military.) Now that investigative reporter Carl Bernstein has revealed the "deal" that the CIA and the Vatican arranged about Solidarity in Poland, and about liberation theologians in South America and peace bishops in North America, Hunthausen's struggle becomes all the more noble.

I was pleased to accept this invitation to speak, and in preparation I spent considerable time talking to gay and lesbian groups in the Chicago area such as MCC (the Metropolitan Community Church), Dignity, and Integrity (the Episcopalian group) to get their ideas and feedback on my own ideas. I gave a talk that was later published as "The Spiritual Journey of the Homosexual and Just About Everybody Else" in Fr. Robert Nugent's *A Challenge to Love: Gay and Lesbian Catholics in the Church*. My talk was the beginning of my trouble with Rome, as there was a gang of disgruntled Catholics (Catholics United for the Faith, or CUFF) who kept track of all comings and goings at the conference and who mailed a thick batch of materials about me to Rome following my presentation. I was then on Rome's hit list. CUFF is an ideological group of thugs who attack by lies and innuendo anyone to the left of Attila.

In my talk I outlined the four paths of creation spirituality and suggested that they help name the homosexual's journey in a special way—for example, the *Via Negativa* is known earlier to gays than to most people because they must "let go" earlier of society's definition of "normal" sexuality and must often let go of family and others who expel them. As a result of this deep letting go, a disproportionate percentage of homosexuals are in the arts—creativity is more opened up and becomes almost a necessary path to survival. But how important the *Via Transformativa* is—to relate one's own suffering to a large picture of solidarity with others who suffer, so that one's world and *the* world grow into a state of compassion.

I began my talk with a story from Sister Jose Hobday, the Seneca spiritual teacher who took me aside at our conference at San Rafael and said, "Matt, I've been wanting to ask a white man this question for years. What is it with you white people about homosexuals? We don't even have a word for homosexuality in our language; we don't care who someone sleeps with as long as they get up in the morning and contribute heartily to the tribe. In fact, it is well known that homosexuals were spiritual directors to our greatest chiefs; the homosexual brings special spiritual power to the community." I said to Jose, "Haven't you heard of homophobia? The West is deeply invested in it."

Since that conversation I have had the opportunity to research some other native peoples and have found that the same situation obtains in Celtic tradition and in some African traditions, namely, that the homosexual has often played the role of spiritual leader or spiritual director to tribal chiefs. Imagine how much spiritual leadership a community is missing, then, by being stuck in homophobia and forcing gays and lesbians into ghettos where so often they, having internalized their own oppression, play out the worst-case scenarios of addiction (whether to drugs, alcohol, or sex) that a heterosexist society has projected onto them. Everyone loses when homophobia reigns.

Little did I know, in giving this talk, the reverberations from Rome to Chicago to California that would eventually be felt in my life. But were I asked to do it all over again, knowing what I know today, I would surely jump at the chance. I will always share solidarity with my gay and lesbian brothers and sisters, and I believe that our culture's ability to purify its soul of homophobia remains as one of the litmus tests of holiness in our time. Holiness and homophobia are incompatible.

Sister Jose Hobday was a teacher to me on this occasion and on many others. The native wisdom she incarnates is so simple, so profound, so real. And it comes out of much suffering and oppression—it has been paid for at a great price. She herself is an immensely gifted speaker. We once shared a podium at a large spirituality conference and she was the first to speak. Following a break, as I was making my way to the podium, she approached me and said, "I left my notes on the lectern. Please gather them up for me." Expecting to find a thick sheaf of pages (she had spoken eloquently for an hour), I instead found a single three-by-four-inch card with four words on it! I liked her earthiness and her ability to speak about everything from sexuality to running noses with depth and honesty. Her essay in the *Western Spirituality* volume was on "Seeking a Moist Heart: Native American Ways for Helping the Spirit."

A Native American priest from New Mexico, Fr. Ed Savilla, had been a student at ICCS its very first year. With his and Jose's encouragement I went to several Tekekwitha conferences of native peoples the following summer. At one in Minnesota, I attended my first sweat lodge. It was an eye-opening, heart-opening experience. I went in quite exhausted and with my back injury hurting me from the long journey that day. When I left the lodge, my back was fine and my spirits were soaring. My first twenty minutes in the sweat lodge, sitting in the complete dark and with the heat of the hot rocks and sweat beginning to rise, I thought I was going to die. I began looking for a fire exit or a fire extinguisher, and when I discovered that neither was available, I realized I *was* going to die. With that, I yielded to the experience and that is when it became prayer for me. I also remember being behind a young Indian holding his newborn baby in his arms as we all danced to the drum in circle dances that evening. I was deeply moved by the beauty of that father-baby relationship and by the meaning of its being blessed in the context of the tribal dance. The experience of sweat lodges and native dancing has played a deep and essential part in my spiritual practice ever since.

One lesson I have learned from native people and from feminists is the recovery of power, healthy and authentic power. I remember Jose speaking of "power objects" of native peoples at our summer workshop in San Rafael, and I was alerted to a positive side of the word *power*. Certainly my generation has lived through deep abuses of power in Vietnam and Watergate. But women and native peoples were offering us a different insight: power isn't bad; it's what we do with power and what kind of power we are dealing with that is the danger.

The West Calls

Our seven years at Mundelein were challenging and rewarding. But something else was developing. My brainstorming sessions with Brian Swimme all pointed toward an expansion of the ICCS program, and Mundelein was a city school with no physical room for expansion. Art-as-meditation labs were hard to come by (we had to periodically bail water from the photography lab located in a basement space that flooded regularly). There was also the call of the west that Brian articulated so strongly: Science and Mysticism were dialoging *there* and not *here* (in Chicago), and they needed the Western tradition, namely creation spirituality, to enter the dialogue. After all, science itself was a Western invention and Einstein was a Jew, not a Buddhist. The president of Holy Names College in Oakland, Sister Lois MacGillivray, heard of our continued interest in coming west and flew out to talk to us. She stayed in Chicago talking with the ICCS faculty and staff for three whole days. Clowns and all (for I had hired a clown who had graduated from our program after Ken Feit's death), musicians, physicists, Jungian analysts were part of her conversations. She returned home and said she would work on convincing her board of regents to hire us.

Brian and I flew to California in January to look at the Holy Names College campus and meet with its dean and others. When we boarded the plane in Chicago it was sixty degrees below zero with wind chill; when we got off in Oakland it was sixty-five degrees above zero. I stood on the beautiful Holy Names campus, surrounded by flowers and sunshine, and said to Brian, "This is the easiest decision of my life." Everything seemed to be coming together to bring us out west.

I worked to design flyers and programs and faculty for the eventuality of moving the program to the West Coast. I remember the moment that summer when I received a phone call from Sister Lois. "You have been approved," she said. "Come on out." I was thrilled. My fourteen years in Chicago had been rich ones, but I was ready to leave the winters behind and have new beginnings in the Bay Area, where one out of four American scientists live and where so much was heating up around art and culture and spirituality.

It was another year before we would move the program out west, and during that year (1983) I wrote *Original Blessing*. That book was really a summary of what I had learned in trying to probe, poke, ponder, and push the limits of this hidden, often condemned, usually ignored tradition of creation spirituality. In it I made something of a synthesis of the many poets and feminists, psychologists and social changers, scientists and biblical texts that make up this rich spiritual tradition. I subtitled it "A Primer in Creation Spirituality." In many ways *Original Blessing* was the culmination of all I had learned in teaching at ICCS in Chicago. It was my thank-you to the many persons at Mundelein College who had supported me and ICCS in those good years. The book would appear in the fall of 1983, just as we were launching our first semester of ICCS at Holy Names College in Oakland. The popularity of *Original Blessing* would fuel some interesting fires, including one under the Congregation for the Doctrine of the Faith in the Vatican (whose former title was the Holy Office of the Sacred Inquisition). But that conflagration was still a little time away.

Shortly after receiving the phone call from the president of Holy Names College inviting us out to Oakland, I had a remarkable dream. I was riding a roller coaster–like train with my mother at my side. It was exhilarating and joyful, and we went down, down, down into ancient places and amid ancient sites: we went into Egypt (a flight into Egypt?) among temples and pyramids and ancient gods and goddesses (Isis, the black Madonna?). Yet I knew it was also a journey to California that was depicted. In the dream my mother lost one of her red shoes and I had to go looking for it. Intimations of the "yellow brick road" journey that I felt was ahead of me out west. But also a deeper exploration into what Frederick Turner calls the "aboriginal mother love" that characterizes native religions. Freedom, exhilaration, and the exploration of new but ancient underworld places—all this was in the dream and all this awaited me in California and beyond. My horizons regarding culture and religion were sure to expand.

7

The California Experience—
1983–1995

The dream I had before leaving for California promised a *deepening* of the spiritual journey, a deeper dive into the underground, into the cave, into the ancient mysteries of goddess and Gaia lore. Several dimensions lured us to California: the dialogue between science and mysticism; the East–West connection; the flexibility of Holy Names College; but also the sacred wilderness that still lived in the west.

The Sacred Wilderness

Few people have understood the spiritual call of California as deeply as its own native poet (and former Dominican Brother Antoninus), Bill Everson. In his rich study entitled *Archetype West: The Pacific Coast as a Literary Region,* Everson talks about how the wilderness actually marks the demarcation between American and European philosophy and how this experience constitutes *"the* characteristic American religious and aesthetic feeling."[1] In the west, Everson feels, one "experienced Nature not as refuge, as Thoreau experienced it at Walden, but as *encounter* . . . mystic encounter."[2] This certainly corresponded to my experience. The ocean, the redwoods, the mountains, the *edge* of Western civilization where California stands—all this conjures up something deep for me, a kind of "root-force in the human soul," as Everson names it. Without being jingoistic, I might add that *spiritual encounter* named my experience of nature in Wisconsin and Illinois as well. But the drama is more stark in California. The sense of mystic encounter in nature Everson recognizes as the essential genius of American spirituality. It was John Muir, a Celtic refugee from Scotland and from profound abuse by his Calvinist minister father, who stood up as a prophet on behalf of the sacred wilderness.

Muir was bringing into comprehension the awesome scale of Western landscape as the focal point of the underlying American intuition: the vision of God in Nature. For . . . in the heart of the American, despite his credal adhesions, the two terms, God and Nature, were covertly interchangeable. Nature *is* divine, the American soul was saying.[3]

But the forces of utilitarian expansion were colliding with this mystical sense of awe and divinity in wilderness when Muir came on the scene—just as they are doing all around the world today as we destroy rain forests and seas, fisheries and coral reefs, soil and indigenous peoples in the name of multinational profit seeking. Everson comments:

Because of the national religion of formal Christianity, which had been utility-oriented following Protestantism's revival of the Old Testament injunction to "subdue the earth," the actual pantheistic base had been largely unconscious, delineated by Emerson and Thoreau and Whitman, but not thoroughly articulated by the public at large.[4]

Here in California, Muir woke up the American conscience, fighting for Hetch Hetchy with such statements as these published in 1912: "Dam Hetch Hetchy? As well dam for watertanks the people's cathedrals and churches, for no holier temple has ever been consecrated by the heart of man." Everson sees Muir's struggle to defend the land as "perhaps the chief turning point in the spiritual life of the nation," for it marked the end of the ideology of unlimited expansion, and instead called on human restraint: "man was going to have to think of depriving himself rather than abusing his environment."[5] An ecological consciousness emerged from the west thanks to Muir's struggle. The spiritual power of the west is not just about the lack of cities. It is something else, something more positive, as Everson observes: "Already at Walden Thoreau felt hemmed in. . . . the West was not just unpopulated, it was, and remains, geographically vast. Quite apart from the civilization factor the prospective Western situation differs in scale, is essentially panoramic."[6] There is a *vastness*, a sense of cosmic wilderness, that awakens the human soul in the panoramic scale of the western landscape and thus elicits mystical encounters. All this was more than theory to me, as it has been to many visitors to the west. The vastness of nature here touched my heart and soul and gave deeper meaning to the terms *creation-centered spirituality* and *panentheism*.

Everson cites two European philosophers—Spanish-born George Santayana and the Frenchman Alexis de Tocqueville—to buttress his point that the American west turns European philosophy around. In 1911 George Santayana gave a lecture at Berkeley in which he said, "When you [Americans] escape, as you love to do, to your forests and your Sierras, I am sure again that you do not feel you made them, or that they were made for you. They have grown, as you have grown, only more massively and more slowly."[7] When I stand before eighteen-hundred-year-old sequoias, I know what Santayana was talking about. Santayana proposed that if European philosophers had lived among the mountains of the American west, all of Western philosophy would have been different from the tradition handed down since Socrates.

> For these systems are egotistical; directly or indirectly they are anthropocentric, and inspired by the conceited notion that man, or human reason, or the human distinction between good and evil, is the center and pivot of the universe. That is what the mountains and the woods should make you at last ashamed to assert.[8]

Tocqueville, as Everson emphasizes, pointed to a political basis for America's panentheism. He identified it with the idea of democracy.

> In the democracies the idea of unity so possesses man and is sought by him so generally that if he thinks he has found it, he readily yields himself to that belief. Not content with the discovery that there is nothing in the world but a creation and a Creator, he is still embarrassed by this primary division of things and seeks to expand and simplify his conception by including God and the universe in one great whole.[9]

Thus, cosmology and politics come together in the psyche of the American west. Here ecology and the moral issues it brings forth cannot be ignored. In this kind of culture, ICCS would no doubt find a rich soil.

Setting Up Shop

In 1983 six faculty members made the journey out west: Brian Swimme, Brendan Doyle, Jean Lanier, Alexandra Kovats, Joe Kilikevice, and myself. We formed a core staff for ICCS; the other faculty would be "native talent" drawn from the Bay Area. Among this native talent was Luisah Teish, who taught African dance and rituals with us and who is an ordained priestess of Oshun in the Yoruba Lucumi (African) tradition.

Setting up shop at Holy Names College was wonderful in many respects. The college had excellent space for our art-as-meditation classes, with an entire center dedicated to clay and painting and photography labs. The setting was beautiful and peaceful, yet only fifteen minutes from the library resources at the Graduate Theological Union in Berkeley. The administration was very welcoming and knowledgeable about what we were doing and why. The chair of the religious studies department, Sister Delores Rashford, was a major supporter, as was Sister Louise Bond. The president, Sister Lois MacGillivray, stood by us through thick and thin. The academic dean of Holy Names

College, Dr. Velma Richmond, herself an English professor married to an English professor (and Englishman) who taught at the University of California, Berkeley, was especially welcoming to us. I remember the day we met, we had a fine talk on Julian of Norwich, and when she and I met Starhawk and Teish for the first time and this Chaucerian scholar asked Starhawk in her most professorial tone, "Now tell me, Starhawk, what does a witch do all day long in addition to doing rituals?" I knew we would have a good and fruitful relationship at Holy Names College.

The college saw ICCS as part of its mission to be "committed to the humanistic and spiritual values of Catholicism hop[ing] to further in its students a deep appreciation of Christian responsibility and respect for self and for others and a dedication to the institution's idea of service." This commitment helped Holy Names College to be strong when opposition and attacks came—which they did very soon. Even before we arrived, a right-wing Catholic paper went after us, with Starhawk at the center of the story. I came to hire Starhawk because I went to Rosemary Ruether, who had taught each year with us at ICCS in Chicago, and asked her if she would join our faculty out west. She explained that she couldn't move, but she recommended a young feminist thinker whom she had worked with in Kentucky that summer. "Starhawk is very bright," she told me, "and she already lives in the Bay Area." That is how a witch joined our faculty.

Based on the scurrilous reportage in the Catholic newspaper, I received a hate letter telling me that I should "burn in hell with Starhawk and all your other pagan friends!" The letter was signed "an ecumenical Christian." I have to admit I was taken aback by the venom of the attacks. It had never occurred to me that Christians had not had enough of witch burnings and paganphobia: somehow I thought Salem and witch hysteria were out of our system. I soon learned otherwise and so did the college, as alumni and others were whipped up to complain about our presence on campus. But to the credit and honor of Holy Names, it never backed down, and still has not to this day, when greater powers in the Catholic arsenal aimed their guns at it.

My dream about descending with my mother into ancient and wonderful chambers of goddess lore and Egyptian mythologies, while it was a delightful dream as I experienced it, was also a warning: one does not leave topside and go down under without paying a price. Those on the top, in the bright daylight of their own power, are not always hospitable to those traveling on the underside. To seek the goddess below is seen as a threat to those honoring the God above exclusively. Meister Eckhart said that "God is a great underground river that no one can damn up and no one can stop." But those above ground condemned him as a heretic. To explore the premodern spiritualities in a culture or subculture that is ill at ease in the modern world itself is to court a certain kind of opposition whether one wishes it or not. It is to raise long-dormant images that people (and sometimes their institutions) would prefer to keep hidden.

I hired Starhawk not because she was a witch but because she was an articulate spokesperson for the women's movement. But with her fine books, *Spiral Dance* and then *Dreaming the Dark*, she proved to be more than that. I admired her stand on social justice and her willingness to demonstrate for nonviolence and pay the price, which she often did, going to jail in protest. In jail she would often hold rituals with the inmates that attracted the envy of the guards; so eventually she was able to bring both together. Ritual holds that kind of ironic power within it. I admired Starhawk's lucid mind and gentle manner and also her willingness to lead chants—a bit off-tune. This gave me permission to do the same, and I have incorporated several of her chants and dances into my various workshops over the years. I also like the response she gave the *National Catholic Reporter* when asked about the church: "I don't know why church authorities are threatened by me, since we didn't burn any of them at the stake over the centuries." Of course I respect her work in attempting to recover the native peasant tradition of Europe for the wisdom it can bring us today. Our species needs all the wisdom it can muster at this time of history, and Starhawk is making a generous contribution in that regard. What has always struck me most about her courses with us on ritual is how *playful* are the spirit and the tone of what she teaches. Surely the elements of play and unselfconsciousness constitute one of the biggest lacunae in Western ritual as it now stands. I consider Starhawk to be very much in the line of her Jewish, prophetic ancestors.

Jeremy Taylor, a Unitarian minister and part-time anarchist who is a genius at dream interpretation, joined us in 1986. He has taken Jung's dream analysis to whole new thresholds of wisdom, including political-social interpretations of our dreams. (His work with dreams began when he was a leading mixed-race workshop and found insurmountable tensions between blacks and whites. He told them to go home that night and listen to their dreams. The next day the dreams helped heal the group and get the energy moving again.)

Dr. Robert Frager, founder of the Institute of Transpersonal Psychology, also joined our faculty. He felt we were less tied to the need to turn out therapists with their shingles and could thus work more fully in the area of spirituality as such. Robert, who is an ordained dream interpreter in the Sufi order of Halveti-Jerrahi Order, is also by birth a Jew and by education holds a doctorate in psychology from Harvard and a black belt in aikido from Japan. Among the new and charismatic faculty that arrived at our front door was Robert Rice, a dancer, painter, and physical therapist. When he told me he visits old-folks homes and gets them all to dance, even those in wheelchairs and those who can move no limbs at all—"I get their eyes to dance," he said—I hired him on the spot. A few years later, at a workshop we conducted in North Carolina, Robert choreographed a dance between himself and a paraplegic in a wheelchair. I was one of many who shed tears at the beauty of the experience.

From within ICCS itself, more talent emerged. Dr. Jim Conlon had attended our first summer workshop in Toronto when he was managing internships and fieldwork for students at the theological school there. He attended a full year at ICCS and is now the director of the program. Sister Marlene Denardo came to us from Rome, where she had been working in her order's headquarters, but also from four years' experience in Africa and fifteen years' experience in Brazil. She was involved in the founding of Christian base communities in Latin America in the days when the members would gather in the evening for meetings and some would be tortured and killed on the way home from the meetings. This was during the military dictatorship in Brazil, while American gunboats hovered offshore giving a strong signal of support for what was going on. Marlene went through the ICCS program as a student and is now an assistant director and valued faculty member teaching courses on feminist awakening, ecofeminism, Judy Chicago's *Dinner Party,* and creation-centered spiritual direction.

Other talented staff were Paula Koepke in massage, Betty McAffee in photography, Ted Feldman in music and administration, Dr. Mary Schmidt in the new cosmology and the new physiology, and Dr. Dody Donnelly on the medieval mystics. We have been honored the past few years to welcome M. C. Richards to our faculty to teach "Word, Color, and Clay" as arts as meditation. A few years ago, we sponsored a celebration on the august occasion of the twenty-fifth anniversary of her book *Centering,* which was a veritable "bible" for me and sustained me for years. Her old friends from Black Mountain days, Merce Cunningham and John Cage, were part of that celebration. Since it took place during my year of silence, I could not speak; however, I did write a letter and Jose Hobday read it to the assembly. In it I praise M. C. for being a "weaver of pots, a painter of words, a harvester of colors, a befriender of heretics, a champion of the earth, a sister to the mentally handicapped, an artist who never abandoned poetry for power, and the only one I know who, on her seventieth birthday, went out and got her ears pierced!"

Tom Hayden, the California legislator and social activist, also joined our faculty. He told me in 1992: "The only interesting thing happening in politics is spirituality and ecology, and you people are doing both, so I would like to join you." That was enough for me, especially given his impressive track record all the way back to his involvement in the civil rights struggles in the

1960s, during which he was frequently arrested, plus his work with SDS and against the Vietnam War. In class one day he was talking of Al Gore's getting a soul experience when, in his forties, he held his dying son's body after he was struck by a car. As it turned out, the son lived but the father was moved by a connection between that moment and the tragedy the earth is also undergoing in its wounds and travail today.

I asked Tom when he got his soul. At nineteen, he said, he fell in love and followed his girlfriend to the South, where the civil rights movement was going on. He got arrested twenty-three times in the next two years. That was his first soul awakening. There are two sure ways to find soul: through tragedy, as in the case of Al Gore; and by falling in love. Of course, they are deeply related.

Another faculty member who deeply influenced all of us at ICCS was Buck Ghosthorse, a Lakota spiritual teacher. He, along with his wife, Donna, worked with us for three rich years. Buck told me that he didn't want to teach white folks but that he had a dream that told him he ought to for the earth's sake, since the earth was in such peril and white folks were running so many things. He heard about ICCS through a student of ours, and so he joined up. Buck set up a sweat lodge on campus, and it was customary for the ICCS faculty to sweat together at the beginning of each semester. He taught courses on Native American ritual, and his wisdom came through in many dimensions. His office was the coffee shop—he never wanted to be too far from the source of all coffee—and he would hang out there for hours, being available to our students for discussions, rapping, and laughter. Buck honored me beyond words when he called me down to his class on the playing field one day and, in a simple ceremony, bestowed on me the gift of his sacred pipe, with which he had prayed in sweat lodges for twenty-six years. This is more powerful than being ordained a bishop, I said to myself. On the way back to my car with the pipe I ran into Luisah Teish, who exclaimed, "Honey, that's powerful medicine! Anything you pray for with that will come true." I have relied on that pipe often for prayer and centering in my life.

The presence of Buck was a great gift to us all. He was in a real sense the *host* faculty member—after all, it was his people who welcomed all comers to the Americas centuries before. Once when we faculty were disrobing for the sweat, a Jewish faculty member, Elan Shapiro, who teaches an excellent course called "Touch the Earth" wherein students get to know the various bioregions of the Bay Area, turned to me and said, "I must be the only Jew in the world stripping naked on a Catholic college campus to do a sweat with Catholics, Protestants, Hindus, Buddhists, Sufis, and Indians!"

Other talented teachers who have joined us include Neil Douglas-Klotz, one of the leaders in the worldwide "Dances of Universal Peace" movement, which is recovering ancient circle dances from all cultures and all religions and is also birthing new ones, including some based on the mystics we have been translating from the West such as Hildegard, Eckhart, and Mechtild. Neil has taken his dances to the Middle East and to Russia as well, where as many as seven hundred people have gathered for an entire week of spiritual dancing. Neil also translated from the Aramaic, Jesus' language, overly familiar sayings from the Gospels such as the Lord's Prayer. His translations reveal how much more cosmic and mystical the Gospels are than we would have imagined.

Adrianna Diaz, a richly talented and hardworking painter and writer, was a student at ICCS the first year we were in Oakland. Her classes on clay and on painting as meditation have deepened the journey for many students, and her recent book, *Freeing the Creative Spirit,* is a superb naming of that journey and how to get in touch with it. Shanja Kirstann, who has developed her own work as shaman and wild woman since, also contributed deeply to our work at ICCS. Onye Onyemaechi is an African tribal man who leads persons in drumming and finding that power within. Betsy Rose, the folksinger, spent a year with us as a student and has returned often as a teacher. Russill Paul, a young man from southern India who spent seven years in Fr. Bede Griffith's ashram before making his way to the West with his wife, Asha, brings the power of Shabda Yoga, music as sound, to our students from the ancient practices of Mother India. When I asked him to teach the course in singing Hildegard of Bingen's music, he was stunned to find how "Indian" she was in her modes and tones. Hildegard was raised and trained in a Celtic monastery along the Rhine. There has always been a rich connection between the Indians of India and the Celts. (Indeed, some scholars believe that the Celts originated in India.) Ana Matt, who spent years living in Tibet, Japan, and Israel to learn spiritual traditions in practice and with practitioners, brings a deep dimension of living-world spiritualities to her teaching of the same.

I feel that the microcosm that ICCS is represents the authentic macrocosm of our shrinking, global culture. If diversity cannot get along in a learning situation, then where can it get along? If spirituality and cosmology cannot welcome diversity, then where will it be welcomed and by whom? Once we let go of education as an exclusively left-brain exercise, then diversity, creativity, new life, and new ideas can flourish again. Egos melt in the presence of the cosmos. They are dwarfed by it. Our faculty works well together because we are all *on a search* and have learned that valuable lesson of respect for each other's journeys and awe in the presence of the search, a cosmic invitation that is mysterious and bigger than any one of us or any of our ideologies. In that sense, we might call ours a postmodern faculty. We all have "et cetera" after our names; none of us feels locked in to any particular mask or role that we are duty-bound to play. There is respect for diversity, a lot of laughter, and a cosmological matrix that holds so much diversity. Also, the Four Paths allow us to agree on a common language for our respective journeys. Many of our faculty have published books over the years and many are involved in numerous spiritual witnesses, ranging from going to jail in nonviolent protest of militarism or nuclear power (Marlene tells me that some of her deepest spiritual experiences have occurred in being carted off to jail for making such protests); to helping in the reclaiming projects after the disastrous fire in the Oakland hills (Elan Shapiro was hired by the city to do this); to working with the Oakland Men's Project on healing men and ridding them of their violence (Victor Lewis, a graduate of ICCS who teaches a course on "Healing the Heart of Justice," works full-time with the much respected Oakland Men's Project); to working with men's liberation groups and women's liberation groups; and more.

I am very proud of our faculty. Some have moved on, such as Dr. Beverly Rubick, who heads the Center for Frontier Sciences at Temple University in Philadelphia, which encourages scientists to pay heed to the connections of body, mind, and spirit; and Buck Ghosthorse, who runs a spiritual center in the mountains near Seattle where he trains Indians and white people in ancient practices of sweat, sun dance, and vision quests. I have a feeling that the universe provides us with the faculty we and the students need, pretty much at the right time.

We started Friends of Creation Spirituality (FCS), a nonprofit organization that sponsored numerous five-day summer workshops all around the United States and in countries such as Australia, New Zealand, and Ireland. Invitations to speak and lead workshops continued to pour in from around the world. Students came in larger and larger numbers to ICCS, culminating in one year's enrollment of ninety-five students. Such numbers forced us to split the program into three "tracks" in order to keep the educational experience intimate, and this we did with emphases on Ecojustice, Spiritual Psychology, and Culture and Creation Spirituality. FCS also sponsored a series of public lectures called "Viriditas" or "Greening Power" (a term coined by Hildegard of Bingen). Among the featured speakers were poet Gary Snyder, feminist philosopher Susan Griffin, economists Hazel Henderson and Frances Moore Lappe, the founder of Food First, monk Fr. Bede Griffith, Native American teacher Jose Hobday, visionary Joanna Macy, and feminist Charlene Spretnak.

Our Wednesday forums proved to be as rich in Oakland as they had been in Chicago. Penny Lernoux, author of *People of God: The Struggle for World Catholicism,* spoke to us a few months before she died a premature death of cancer. In her book, she lays out the shadowy dealings of the present papacy, facts that were seconded a few years later by Carl Bernstein. She and her husband had lived over twenty years in Colombia until they returned to the

States shortly before she died and after she received threats from the cardinal of Colombia, who has since moved to the Vatican.

Thomas Berry has been a yearly visitor, and his power and stature grow as his prophetic voice of outrage at the killing of the planet is finally being widely heard today. I am always inspired anew by his message and his person. I especially appreciate his point that "ecology is functional cosmology"; thus he brings together the sense of wonder that the cosmos gives us with the sense of responsibility we need toward the earth as it suffers today. Fran Peavy came on several occasions to delight us with her political satire and outrageous humor. Sam Keen, Rollo May, Satish Kumar, Charlene Spretnak, Joanna Macy, Elinor Gadon, David Whyte, John Robbins, astronaut Rusty Schwiekert, Melidoma Somé, and Brother David Steindl-Rast have also been our teachers at these enlightening forums.

What about our students? They continue to be a diverse lot. We have had students in their twenties and students in their seventies (whose souls were very young indeed). One graduate ran for a judgeship in Houston on a green ticket in November 1993, and won; another was the first publicly gay seminarian to be ordained in the United Church of Canada; others have returned to their respective countries to teach or lead in some capacity in New Zealand, Australia, South Africa, Peru, Holland, England, Ireland, and Canada. We have had graduates elected provincials of their congregations; Catholic sisters who have started their own rural parishes; artists who have recovered or discovered their gifts in our program and truly done things with them after graduation; musicians who have cut records and become prophetic folksingers; writers who have published books; students of television who have pursued careers there; scientists who have gone on to get Ph.D.'s in environmental science; husband-wife teams who have gone to work on Indian reservations; workers in prison who have returned to that important work; newly retired persons who brag about "starting life all over" thanks to ICCS; priests who have quit the priesthood (and some who have stayed with new vigor and commitment); ministers who have renewed their ministries; seminarians who have reentered seminary and some who have quit; a rancher who quit ranching when one of her calves was paralyzed by an effort to brand it and who is now working with youth gangs using methods of creation spirituality.

At least five students have come knowingly or unknowingly on their final journey of preparation in their dying of AIDS. I think of Michael, for example, a young-looking forty-year-old from Indiana who had worked in inner-city churches in Detroit as a musician and liturgist, who had hosted a gay radio show in Indianapolis (and received death threats for it daily), who at the age of seventeen was a conscientious objector to the Vietnam War and was subsequently thrown out of the house by his father, who said, "Either come back in a uniform or come back in a casket." After Michael's death his father wept as he acknowledged, "His morality was more right than mine." The last time I visited Michael in the hospital, he said to me, "Tell the people that AIDS is a blessing. It is a blessing to the individual because the journey is so deep; and it is a blessing for society because it will teach us to be more honest about sexuality." He died quite suddenly and I was out of town. Those who were present tell me that, because he was a nurse, he knew that he would have forty-five minutes to live once his oxygen mask was removed. He gave the orders on when to remove his mask. In those forty-five minutes he wrote on a pad of paper, "There is no death, there is only life." He embraced all the members of his large, catholic family. And then he waved good-bye as he died.

That night I had an unforgettable dream about Michael. We were walking with my dog, Tristan (something the three of us did a lot during Michael's last summer), in a midwestern town. The dog ran across the street and jumped into a large puddle. Michael and I ran after him and suddenly there rose from the puddle a huge bubble. And in the midst of the bubble was Michael as a young boy, smiling and beaming. I have never worried again about Michael since that dream.

Tony was a therapist, an astrologer, and a feminist archaeologist who worked with Marija Gimbutas in Crete. An Italian who had left the Catholic church in his adolescence because of the message he received about being gay, he came to my medieval mystics class and fell in love with Hildegard of Bingen just as he also was diagnosed as having AIDS. When he died he was in the hospital and on the phone with a close friend in New York, who said, "Remember what Hildegard says: 'You are embraced by the arms of the mystery of God.'" With those words in his ear he died. He had told me that discovering Hildegard was such a return for him to his Catholic roots, that he had known there was some wisdom there, but with Hildegard he could finally experience it.

Matt was a heterosexual semiprofessional baseball player who was living life on a fast track with unlimited amounts of beer and girlfriends. From one of the latter he contracted AIDS. He found in the mystics of creation spirituality a language that corresponded to his own mysticism as he traveled his new journey with his sickness. He dedicated himself to visiting high schools and speaking in frank language to the young people about safe sex and, above all, about self-esteem. He told me several times before he died that AIDS was a blessing for him: it shortened his life, yes; but it deepened it immeasurably. His wisdom was hard-won and very real. He derived great joy in sharing the lessons he learned with the young.

ICCS and the Eighties

In 1985, in order to reach out to the broader culture with the ideas and movement that creation spirituality represents, we launched a magazine. We called it *Creation,* with the subtitle *Earthy Wisdom for an Evolving Planet.* We hoped that this magazine would offer opportunities to get creation spirituality and the new science more fully into our culture and elicit a "cutting-edge" dialogue with persons interacting on subjects such as ecology, spirituality, ritual, art, and justice-making. Over the years the magazine has sponsored interviews with such persons as Sister Thea Bowman, Ernesto Cardinale, Hazel Henderson, Howard Rheingold, Leonardo Boff, gang chaplain Fr. Greg Boyle, liberation theologian Ivone Genara, Jean Houston, urban ecologist Elan Shapiro, Fritjof Capra, Paula Gunn Allen, Charles Birch, feminist filmmaker Donna Read, Wingari Maathai, Celtic singer Noirin ni Riain, Edward Schillebeeckx, T. S. Ananthu, William Everson, John and Nancy Jack Todd, Patricia Mische, Herman Daly, Jan Minkiewicz, Jamake Highwater, Thomas Berry, Joanna Macy, Frances Moore Lappe, Gary Snyder, Jerry Mander, and others. And many writers equally diverse have published in the magazine on a range of issues connecting cultural events to a creation spirituality. The magazine has evolved considerably during the ten years of its existence, including a name change to *Creation Spirituality.* No doubt it will continue to do so.

For me, one of the high points of the magazine was publishing an issue on Howard Thurman, the creation-centered African American mystic and theologian who was an important influence on Dr. Martin Luther King, Jr., and who learned Meister Eckhart as a young college student sitting at the feet of the Quaker writer Rufus Jones. This connection between Meister Eckhart's spirituality and Dr. King via Howard Thurman (who was the one person King requested to see from his hospital bed in New York when he was stabbed in 1958) deserves to be explored more deeply. As part of the celebration of the Thurman issue, we held an event at Oakland's Allen Temple Baptist Church. Rev. J. Alfred Smith, the prophetic pastor there, and Dr. Howard Thurman's widow were part of the event. My article on Thurman in that issue demonstrated how his thought covered fully and in depth the four paths of creation spirituality.

Much has been made of how Ronald Reagan never acknowledged that his father was an alcoholic, so he was the perfect political mouthpiece to preach "good news" over a blanket of denial to Americans: who had lost their first war; who had undergone the national trauma of Watergate, watching their president quit under threat of prison along with the fourteen members of his staff and cabinet who did go to jail; who waited in line at 3:30 A.M. to fill up their cars with gas after Middle Eastern sheiks decided to pull the plug on our oil addiction; who watched American hostages paraded daily on television ("Day Thirty-one of the Hostage Taking"); whose military trained torturers so that they could return to El Salvador and torture their own people; whose government supported the very thugs who had kept the violent Somoza in office for forty years in Nicaragua; who saw their life savings lost, to the tune of hundreds of billions of dollars, by savings and loan institutions that our taxpayers have to bail out; and who saw HUD, the Housing and Urban Development Department that was presumably in business to help the homeless and downtrodden, cough up its money and loans and privileges to the already well heeled. Denial was indeed a mechanism that kept America going in the eighties. Spirituality is one way to cut through denial. Meister Eckhart teaches that "God is the denial of denial." If God is the denial of denial, then the decade of denial that the eighties was, certainly was a decade of deicide. Never was God deader than at that time!

Meanwhile, back at ICCS, we were trying to do our small part in denying denial. We tried to do something, for example, about the boredom created in most liturgical situations in our time. Might liturgy, instead of contributing to denial, actually help to cut through it? We must have been doing something right when extreme right-wing Catholics made their way to Holy Names College on the occasion of the second of our three "cosmic masses" in the gymnasium of the college. For these masses, we met in a gymnasium to allow the body its proper space for moving and dancing. The first one was dedicated to Healing the Earth; the second was a Thanksgiving for the Body (in November); and the third was for the Wounded and Divine Child (in December).

For the body ritual Dr. Beverly Rubick, a biophysicist on our faculty, and I created a ritual using slides from photographs now available of twenty-six organs of our bodies. The participants stand before a large screen, see each of these organs projected there, hear Dr. Rubick intone two sentences of how the organ blesses us daily, and then bow in respect, chanting a "Te Laudamus Domine" or thank-you to God and the organ and the universe. It is a very reverent ritual that I have since led in numerous places from Australia to Pennsylvania. But these terrified Catholics would hear nothing of it as they shouted and screamed at us from outside the gym. Fortunately for us, Buck Ghosthorse had come that evening with several large Indian friends to bless people with smoke as they entered for the mass. The Native Americans were smart enough and imposing enough to keep the angry protesters at bay for the duration of the service. They stayed outside, angrily shouting the rosary at us during the course of the mass. Afterward they sent letters to Cardinal Ratzinger, telling him that we were worshiping body parts and extolling genitals at mass! Since, for some perverse reason, the Vatican tends to believe reports like that, I am sure their protests had the desired effect. I remember

Buck coming up to me after the event and saying, "I have never met a group of persons who would attack others at worship." "Welcome to the white world and to present-day Catholicism in particular," I replied.

For our third and final cosmic mass, we hired security guards to protect us from our fellow Catholics. (I told the students that we might have to revert to catacombs to worship in like the early Christians, this time to protect us from our fellow Christians as we pray.) A woman from San Francisco came up to me and told me that she had attended all three cosmic masses and was thankful for this form of worship, which "we will all be praying in, forty-five years from now." She understood; it's too bad the Vatican did not.

We put on one mass to which no protesters came. It was a Hildegard of Bingen mass held in Holy Names College chapel. Brendan Doyle led the choir in singing several of Hildegard's songs; we erected a large screen behind the altar on which we projected images of her paintings; the entire mass was in Gregorian chant and Latin; and readings and commentaries were from her writings. It was, I believe, the first introduction of Hildegard to the Bay Area *and* to America at large. Feminist author Charlene Spretnak was among those who attended that night; she said afterward that if she had known about Hildegard she might not have had to leave the Catholic church for Buddhism.

Perhaps our most ambitious undertaking was the Vietnam Ritual to Mourn and Grieve War that we cosponsored with the Swords to Plowshares organization of Vietnam veterans. Robert Bly, Michael Meade, and I were asked to lead this ritual, for which about fourteen hundred people showed up at the Fort Mason Conference Center in San Francisco. Over one hundred vets, men and women, American and Vietnamese, were involved in producing the event, which included altars made to honor the three stages of grief (red for rage, black for sorrow, white for transcendence). Tunnels provided the veiled entrance from the street into the sacred space; "campfires" were erected where storytellers stood to tell their tales of the war in somber darkness; giant puppets of war roamed the stage evoking outcries of anger from the audience encouraged by Robert Bly. Finally the group, with candles in hand and chanting an African dirge, moved in procession over military property to the water's edge, where we placed our candles on an altar. At the exact moment that the last candle was placed on the altar, the sky opened up with a deluge of rain (this in the driest winter San Francisco had experienced in years). The skies were crying; it was a good sign that our ritual bore some power and that now our tears over Vietnam could and ought to be shed. Sue Espinoza, our executive director at FCS, deserves a lot of credit for bringing together the diverse coalitions that made this ritual possible.

Another phenomenon of the culture of the eighties was fundamentalism. Apart from the pathos in the Tammy and Jim Bakker show; apart from the scandals of Jimmy Swaggart swaggering about on stage by day condemning all believers other than his own kind while by night he visited prostitutes; apart from the sad ripping off of the aged and the poor to build silly theme parks (go water-sliding for Jesus and eat a hamburger for the Lord); apart from the racism and anti-Semitism and fraud and anti-intellectualism and hypocrisy that mark so much fundamentalism in America, what else is afoot there? In one word, I see fundamentalism as the opposite of creation spirituality. Fundamentalists do not want to be bothered with mysticism *or* cosmology. Why not? Because Jesus has all the answers, and by Jesus they mean their projections onto Jesus. Theologian Edward Schillebeeckx has warned that faith without an understanding of creation is "a pure projection."[10] They want *nothing* interfering with their projections—not even dinosaurs. (I heard a fundamentalist on English television explain that God put dinosaur fossils and dinosaur eggs on earth "to test my faith," so that while he might be *tempted* to imagine the earth was older than the biblical forty-five hundred years, he would not waver!)

Fundamentalism makes a religion of fear and serves right-wing politics. St. Augustine was right-wing in his politics—in struggling with the Donatists in North Africa, Augustine gave orders that have poured from the mouth of every dictator since then: "Coerce them to come in." This political method of coercion, adopted by the theologian of the Roman church and its Roman Empire, has been repeated by secular and religious powers alike over the centuries. Inquisitions, witch burnings, gay burnings, Crusades, slavery, religious wars, have they not all carried this mode of "coerce them to come in"? Shooting a doctor at an abortion clinic is an act of coercion indeed, covered with religious legitimization. Fascism and fundamentalism go hand in hand, for fascism is, in Susan Sontag's definition, "institutionalized violence." *No one* could ever accuse fascism of being about justice or compassion or celebration. Fundamentalists develop a christo-fascism, yet everything we know about the historical Jesus points to the fact that coercive powers crucified him *because* he was preaching about the nearness of God and the reign of God to *every* person, especially the poor, the outcast, the ones different from the others. Fundamentalism and fascism pray to a *theistic* God, a God who is *above* and *over* us and who is in no way God-with-us, God-among-us. Panentheism is an affront to fascism and fundamentalism for it implies democracy, the very heart of Jesus' teaching that the reign of God is among us all. Especially those without power.

I found politics in America very frustrating in the seventies and eighties. The Democratic party ran George McGovern, Jimmy Carter, Fritz Mondale, and Michael Dukakis during these years. (I voted for each of them because that was the only choice I had.) What do they all have in common? Lack of fire in the belly. Lack of sensuousness. Lack of lower chakras. This is something Robert Kennedy, for example, had in spades. It's kind of a Catholic thing; it comes from being out in the cold, from being wounded and in touch with those wounds; with Robert Kennedy it came especially after his brother's death, and this is why he had a rapport with the black community. They have been out in the cold (or the blazing sun as slaves) for so long that they know when another is or is not in touch with their grief, pain, lower chakras, call it what you will. It is a soul thing. Catholics used to have it because they were oppressed and because they were angry and because they believed in something. But as they have risen to middle-classdom, they too rarely show it anymore. Film critic Pauline Kael asked the question in the midseventies, "Why are all the best movie directors Catholic?" (She had in mind Scorcese, Coppola, Fellini, among others.) She answered it this way: "Because they experience more sensuality in their childhoods." This is what is missing in the plastic, clean-as-Disneyland ethos of so much white Protestantism. It lacks the power to arouse and to move. It only has a Kantian ethic of duty and responsibility. It lacks eros. It lacks the goddess energy.

How absurd that phrases like "family values" were taken up by right-wingers when it is their policies that so often break up families. I can't imagine a more basic family value than ecology—isn't tearing down rain forests an affront to family survival, supposing that healthy air is useful to children and adults alike? Isn't a widening gap between haves and have-nots very hard on the family's survival? Is accumulating money and stock and power in the hands of a few good for values of any kind? But the "left wing" avoids value-oriented language, preferring to stick with the strictly modern ideology that paints the sciences as "value free." When progressive thinkers and doers stay as far away from religion as they can, they *turn over religious language and religious values to the very fundamentalists whom they oppose as political right-wingers.*

There is only one way out of this dilemma of turning religious language and values over to the right wing: progressive thinkers and doers must go back and deal with their wounded religious child, must heal it, let it go. They must substitute grown-up religion, that is, spirituality, for that wounded religious child that they are in denial about and consequently must shut out of their hearing. There can be no authentic political coalitions built in America that do not heed the religious dimension—that do not put fire in the belly about justice and compassion, for instance.

There was a thirty-nine-year-old woman in the ICCS program a few years ago who had grown up Southern Baptist. She left it all when she was seventeen years old, slamming the door as she exited. She went about her life, became a therapist and a feminist, and was a very strong-minded individual when she came to ICCS. But she was blocked up and couldn't create as she wanted. I told her to write a paper on what was good about growing up fundamentalist. Her paper praised her religious experience as a child for several specific things: the assumption that one can and does experience God in this lifetime; good music that created a community experience; the demand for a commitment or response to a call. With gratitude for what was good in her otherwise toxic religion, she was able to leave it behind less out of anger than just of having outgrown it. Then she was free to create.

Learning by Traveling

Over the eighteen years of its existence ICCS has graduated some eight hundred people, and workshop participants have numbered about eight thousand in the United States and other countries. We have been sowing some seeds, and often they have fallen on ground that encourages their nurturance and growth. The work of awakening religious and other institutions to spirituality goes on in many and varied forms. Over the years I have probably given more than a thousand talks, workshops, and retreats. I have spoken in every state except two (Alaska and Mississippi) and in numerous countries around the world. I have always considered these lecture tours to be part of my education—to learn how other areas of the country and the world are living out their spiritualities and how creation spirituality is useful to them.

What is speaking like for me? One friend who accompanied me on an international trip said that when I speak, after about seven minutes of warm-up, I go into a kind of overdrive gear and start communicating directly and deeply with the audience. For my part, I only know that sometimes (not always) there is indeed a communion reached between myself and the listeners in which I feel buoyed and communicated to, so that I become a listener even while talking. Once, when I was speaking on compassion to Catholic teachers in a Washington, D.C., ballroom that was filled to its eighteen-hundred-people capacity, in the middle of my talk I found myself on the ceiling, at the chandelier, looking down on the room and on myself talking. After a brief time I returned to the podium (where I had been all along). It was a very peaceful out-of-the-body experience. After the talk, several people commented on the communication they had felt. I had felt it too. In these instances my own philosophy comes home to me: our work is meant to be—and can be—our prayer. If it is a radical response to life, it is prayer. Thus I find that my work, whether it is lecturing or studying, writing or researching or teaching, is often a prayer. Prophecy leads to mysticism just as mysticism leads to prophecy. Of course, work is also a drudgery for me at times and a burden and an exasperation. But who isn't beset by drudgery at work?

One surprise came my way after I gave a weekend retreat in Kirkridge, Pennsylvania, a wonderful alternative retreat center run by two fine people, Bob Ranier and his wife, Cynthia. Approaching one man in his thirties who had seemed especially attentive the entire weekend, I asked him who he was and what had brought him to the retreat. He said he was a Southern Baptist preacher who had been—*literally*—reading my book *Original Blessing* in the closet with a flashlight and had begun preaching from it. He felt he would probably be defrocked, but he so believed in what the book said that he was not afraid. Furthermore, he said, he had found another "closeted creation-centered Southern Baptist minister" at this very retreat!

After a workshop I conducted at an Earth/Spirit conference in Portland, Oregon, a young man came up to me and said, "I've been an environmental zealot for fifteen years, but this workshop and its circle dancing is more radical than my chaining myself to trees and going to jail. I want to take this back to my co-workers." A few months later I ran into him again. He said that taking the dancing to his co-workers had awakened their imaginations so that they were now less into an us-versus-them mentality and were building a broader constituency for their struggle. An example was their recruiting hunters, since hunters were sensing the loss of game as the forests got mowed down.

One evening in Cardiff, Wales, after I had lectured on "Creation Spirituality and the Celtic Tradition" at a Presbyterian church, a man in his early twenties approached me to say that he was a member of this congregation and was thrilled to see the church full for the very first time in his life. Thirty-five people was the usual number for Sunday services. "How can we fill this church?" he asked. I told him the first thing the congregation must do is remove the pews so that circle dancing, the body, and cosmology can return. "Oh!" he replied, "we could never do that. This parish is 150 years old."

"One hundred fifty years is a tradition to be honored," I replied. "But someday Christians are going to have to choose between their anthropocentric traditions and those of the universe, which is, after all, fourteen billion years old. Besides, if you remove the pews you might lose half of your congregation—say about seventeen people—but you would gain hundreds more: artists, dancers, scientists, young people, and bored older people who are being excluded from worship by the headiness of it all."

"Now I get it," he remarked. "You're talking about a revolution." I guess I was. For some time I have felt that worship is the nonviolent revolution that no one has tried yet.

I did a workshop for Protestants and Catholics in Corrymeela, a peace center in northern Ireland. A northerner had warned me beforehand, "Don't do it. People are killing each other there; they don't want to hear about creation." When people arrived they were weighed down with years of war on their shoulders. But by the end of the day, after a lot of imaging and discussion and circle dancing out on the lawn overlooking the coast, people left energized and walking upright. A Catholic sister came up to me and said, "This workshop has put the last thirteen years of our history into a totally different context." Cosmology has that kind of power.

Once on a long flight home from a lecture tour in Europe, I asked myself, What am I doing? Why all this travel, all this work? And a very vivid image came to me. I saw the planet with longitude and latitude grids on it and little fires at the corners of the grids. I remarked to myself, I'm starting little fires around the earth. I'm a spiritual pyromaniac. This fit well with the aboriginal teaching I learned from Eddie Kneebone Down Under: the stars are really the campfires of our ancestors, who are looking down at earth for our campfires to see if we are burning or not, alive or not. It also fits with the Pentecost fire imagery.

About the year 1987 I felt a definite and perceptible shift in attitude when I was on the road. For the sixteen years I had done such work, the basic response of the audience (with some exceptions) had been "Yes, but. . . ." Always the buts, always the rational objections, always the rationalizations. (I find that intellectualizing is one of the surest ways of staying in denial. One can "Yes, but . . ." an infinite number of times. Indeed, right up to one's death. Or that of the earth. Or that of our young ones.) But about 1987, a decided shift occurred. People were raising fewer and fewer objections to my issues of earth crisis, youth crisis, the need for cosmology and spirituality, the boredom that religion and education engender. Instead, people were responding with: "More, more. Tell us more about spirituality. More about grief. More about the dark night of the soul. More about creativity. More about transformation. More about awe and wonder and joy." Something was shifting in the American soul—even that word, *soul,* was becoming a topic for discussion again and within a few years would make the *New York Times* bestseller lists. It was as if our culture at large was discovering it had a soul for the first time in a long while. We were going deeper. We weren't buying all the lies of our government and its politicians. Many were; but many were not. A men's movement was emerging to help men cut through their denials *as men* and begin the journey of descent into their own vast wildernesses. And a cultural phenomenon called Joseph Campbell came along at just the right time, and with just the right interviewer, a Texan minister turned media wizard, Bill Moyers, to assist that downward and outward journey. *The Power of Myth* was a benchmark in American spiritual awareness not only because it was Campbell's swan song (he died shortly after its final episode was taped), but because it was a swan song for something else: our running from our own depths—what Campbell acutely named our "bliss," our "generativity," our wisdom, our stories. The success of that program demonstrated that we had not altogether sold our souls. We were still hunting for them.

The Cosmic Christ

When I made a retreat at Lake Tahoe with the Joe Campbell/Bill Moyers videotapes, I was stunned to hear Campbell say, "The closest thing I know to a planetary mythology is Buddhism, which sees all beings as Buddha beings."[11] I had just published my book on *The Coming of the Cosmic Christ,* and though Campbell did not use the term *Cosmic Christ,* the concept was everywhere evident in his discussions. Christ saying, "I am the light of the world"—all of this is no longer left to the domain of theologians to comment on. It is part of our new cosmology. There is light or photons in us, in our food and the matter with which we interact, indeed in every atom in the universe, as physicist Fritz Papp of Germany has demonstrated. It belongs to us all. It is part of our medieval heritage from Hildegard of Bingen, Francis of Assisi, Aquinas, Mechthild, Eckhart, Julian, Nicholas of Cusa—all were impressed by the Christ in all things. Why is it that Francis's most famous poem, his "Canticle to the Sun," never mentions the name "Jesus" once? It talks about brother sun and sister moon and stars, brother wind and air, sister water and sister earth our mother—his mysticism was a Cosmic Christ mysticism, and that is why it was not sentimental. Yet his interpreters have been far less cosmological—and consequently far more sentimental. Indeed, we have accomplished true denial of Francis's radical vision by locking him up in birdbaths and the other superficial ways we have of taming him.

The Cosmic Christ is an affront to adultism because it is always young—the "cosmic *lamb*" (not sheep) was slain on the cross according to the Book of Revelation. The fundamentalists have had free rein with this book for decades because our liberal, text-oriented, academic, modern theologians had no mysticism: they had, in Jaroslav Pelikan's words, "deposed the Cosmic Christ" and made the quest for the historical Jesus necessary.[12] But to depose the Cosmic Christ and its mystical archetypal power is to leave ourselves without a way of reading our apocalyptic or wisdom or even prophetic literature. And that is why Enlightenment theologians turned Revelation over to the fundamentalists, who have done strange things indeed with such Scriptures—for example, declaring that Jesus was coming on a *nuclear cloud* to save the 144,000 who alone would be saved. Without a cosmology, one cannot deal with angels, demons, dragons, goddesses, cosmic lambs, or lords who are rulers of the universe—all the players who make up the drama of Revelation. That book, which is in my opinion clearly the most *political* of any in the Bible, needs to be reappropriated. The Cosmic Christ theology makes that possible.

Often when I have done workshops on liberating the Cosmic Christ within us, I have felt how the recovery of cosmology liberates lives through personal as well as communal stories. A perspective on the Cosmic Christ also allows us to liberate the Scriptures themselves. They come alive in all new ways when we can read them through this tradition—in which, incidentally they were written, since the loss of cosmology is a *modern* problem, *not* part of the first-century Mediterranean world in which the Christian Scriptures were put together.

To rediscover the Cosmic Christ does not mean we ignore or throw out the historical Jesus. Quite the opposite. At the same time that I have been working with scientists, artists, and native peoples to reintroduce cosmology to our Western faith heritage, the Jesus Seminar and like groups of biblical scholars have been working to find out what we do and do not know about the historical Jesus, his teachings, and his words. That accomplishment has just about reached its crescendo and can be found in the work of people such as Dominic Crossan, whose books *The Historical Jesus* and *Jesus: A Revolutionary Biography* summarize what has been learned. We can say that Jesus was a "peasant, Jewish Cynic." The cynic part involved a practice and lifestyle among the peasants that opposed the mores of cultural honor and shame, and of patronage and clientage, that dominated Mediterranean culture in Jesus' day. "They were hippies in a world of Augustan yuppies." The historical Jesus developed a strategy for liberating persons that included "free healing and common eating, a religious and economic egalitarianism that negated alike and at once the hierarchical and patronal normalcies of Jewish religion and Roman power." He announced the "brokerless kingdom of God" by insisting to those with whom he spoke that there existed an "unmediated physical and spiritual contact with God and unmediated physical and spiritual contact with one another." Indeed, this contact constituted the presence of the kingdom of God.[13]

How does this relate to my findings regarding the coming of the Cosmic Christ? First of all, we learn that the vast majority (about 85 percent) of the Christian Scriptures are about the Christ rather than about Jesus. Moreover, the early Christians *so trusted their own experience of the Christ that was awakened directly or indirectly by Jesus that they did not hesitate to put words into Jesus' mouth*—words that they felt he ought to have said, might have said, or would have said had he known what they had experienced. Amazing! Such trust in one's mystical experience! Such trust in the Cosmic Christ. Would that we had as much trust today.

The wonderful Celtic poem, below, from seventh-century Wales carries the same message. It is an "I am" poem and therefore a Cosmic Christ poem, for the Christ is the divine in every being, and one name for the divine that Scriptures give us is "I am" (Exodus 3:14).

GOD

I am the wind that breathes upon the sea,
I am the wave on the ocean,
I am the murmur of leaves rustling,
I am the rays of the sun,
I am the beam of the moon and stars,
I am the power of trees growing,
I am the bud breaking into blossom,
I am the movement of the salmon swimming,
I am the courage of the wild boar fighting,
I am the speed of the stag running,
I am the strength of the ox pulling the plough,
I am the size of the mighty oak tree,
And I am the thoughts of all people
Who praise my beauty and grace.[14]

So much creativity and trust of the local, cultural, experience of the Christ lies behind this poem! The believers were not content, as fundamentalists always are, in just reiterating what was known, in playing parrot or tape recorder to scriptural passages. They read the "I am" poetry in John's Gospel, "I am the good shepherd; I am the light; I am the door; I am the living bread," and got the message and went on to speak *out of their experience*— many experiences of which the historical Jesus had no inkling. There are no wild boar fighting in Israel; nor salmon swimming; nor oak trees growing. What a lesson there is here, as there is in the findings of the Jesus Seminar: Christian faith is *not* just about the historical Jesus. It is also about the Cosmic Christ. It is about creation *and the divine presence in it* and about the spirit *and divine presence in it*. Thank God for the Trinitarian Christians, who represent this kind of analogous way of speaking of divinity and refuse to lock God up behind our projections. The implications of recovering a Cosmic Christ theology are vast, both at the level of personal esteem *and* at the level of relating the political and the ecological.

Recently I gave a weeklong seminar in the Philippines. The first several days, a group of Marxists was resisting the message quite strongly. On the sixth day I shared the Celtic "I am" poem and invited each person to create a Philippine "I am" poem. The energy in the hall was palpable as each person and team rushed to get the microphone to share its poem. At this point the strongest of the Marxists, a woman who had resisted for days, turned to me with a large smile on her face, a face that had lost twenty years in six days. "Look what you have done," she said. "You have turned us all into poets." I replied, "No, I haven't. You are all poets. Cosmology just let the poet in you come out."

Several years ago I was invited to speak at Yale University by the dean of students of Yale Divinity School. (Student deans more than academic deans extend invitations for me to speak at theology schools.) I spoke on mysticism and the mystics, and afterward a woman came up to me and said, "I am so angry I can hardly talk." I asked why. "Because," she said, "we invited the faculty and not a single faculty member was here and what you talked about is *exactly* what they have to hear about."

"But that young black man who spoke up, surely he is a professor?" I queried.

"Oh, he teaches in the Yale undergraduate school; he teaches courses on mysticism there. But we don't have a single course on mysticism."

I was thunderstruck that *undergraduates* could study mysticism at Yale but not seminarians and divinity students. "Well, tell me," I said, "what did they say when you invited the faculty to hear me speak?"

"Mysticism is a fad."

I went away dizzy, absolutely dizzy, that one of our most prestigious divinity schools had no courses on mystics and mysticism and considered mysticism a fad. So I wrote an article for *Creation* magazine entitled, "Is Yale Divinity School a Fad?" in which I pointed out that mysticism was *far more ancient* than Yale Divinity School and would be around *many centuries longer,* long after the buildings of Yale had turned to dust—provided our schools and religions and their centers for training spiritual leaders allowed mysticism to flourish again. Several months later I received a letter from a Yale alumnus who had passed my article on to the academic dean of the divinity school. He included a copy of a letter he had received back from the dean that was *blue* in its outrage at my article. However, it was a valid issue and still is: how many of our seminaries are offering or even can offer courses on healthy mysticism? I have heard from the grapevine that Yale Divinity School has such a course now.

Part of a Cosmic Christ theology is experiencing the Christ nature in all beings. I was gifted with such a friendship for seventeen years in the person of my dog, Tristan. He it was who brought ecology and cosmology together for me in everyday practice, as he would require regular hikes in the Illinois woods and, later, in the redwood forests of California. His name was apt, for Tristan was a Celtic prince and a passionate lover, and the Tristan I knew was a being of princely dignity with an indomitable zest for life. Though not standing over ten inches high, he never backed down from a potentially trying encounter, no matter how big the other dog. His soul was magnanimous and I frankly don't think he ever knew how small his body was. Entering a room, he would fill it by his presence. When he was fifteen years old he was attacked on the street by a pit bull. I was out of town at the time, but I am told that he bled profusely and was very near death. The veterinarian who treated him said, "Any other dog his age and size would have died. He had an immense spirit to live." His spirit was great; his love of life, his eros, was indomitable right up to the end.

He was my spirit-guide for seventeen years, and after his death he has appeared in my dreams and those of others who knew him. I include him among a pantheon of spirits that have assisted me over the years. What realms did he come from? What realms did he know? What realms did he return to? That is where his dignity and ability to keep his own counsel and his own secrets take over. Living with an animal like Tristan reinforces one's capacity for living in mystery and letting mystery be mystery.

Now he has returned to what Aquinas calls "the Source without a Source," the source of his Beauty and ours. I miss him and I dedicated my book on the spirituality of work to him. He companioned me for half of it before he died. It is appropriately dedicated, for he never shrank from his work. He completed it with bountiful integrity. His work was mystery. But it had something to do with my work and with what Rilke calls the "great work" of the universe itself. Rilke says:

> Somewhere there is an ancient enmity
> between our daily life and the great work.[15]

With Tristan—and perhaps with all animals—there was no enmity between his daily life and the great work. There are lessons for us human beings to learn from this. I will always be grateful to Tristan for his work and to the universe for lending me such a special co-worker. "All wisdom," Thomas Aquinas says, "is given to us on loan." Knowing a being like Tristan steels one against all temptations to anthropocentrism.

Now that many of my books are being translated into foreign languages, the dissemination of creation spirituality is reaching wider and oftentimes more appreciative audiences. For example, in a welcome turn of events, six of my books have been translated into German, and the Germans seem to understand what I am doing much more than do American academicians. German reviewers have said that my work is "a whole new way of doing theology," a way that is needed. On a recent trip to Germany I was interviewed by a journalist with a Ph.D. in theology (a common occurrence in Europe and a very rare one in America). I noted the occasion in my journal.

June 6, 1994
A moving experience when . . . a Lutheran priest and editor of Religionem im Gesprach *came to interview me. He put my five books in German on the floor and explained them to me.*

1. Cosmic Christ = *the big vision*
2 and 3. Creation Spirituality *and* Original Blessing = *the* ways *to the vision, Creation Spirituality is necessary to free first-world peoples*
4. Compassion = *the* goal *of the human race*
5. *Aquinas book* = proof *that what I'm doing* is *in our tradition and proof that our tradition has often been misinterpreted and misused*

I was especially moved by the last reference to the Aquinas book—he gets it! Of course my Eckhart books and Hildegard books demonstrate the same truths. However, they are not in German and Aquinas after all is main-stream, i.e., a declared saint of the church.

Another development abroad has been the number of base-community groups that have sprung up with sound leadership in countries such as England, Ireland, Wales, Australia, New Zealand, Holland, Sweden, Switzerland, and Germany. This seems to be a reverberation of the base-community process started in Latin America.

A dark side to being in California is the accusation of "New Age" or "flaky." I have yet to hear that accusation from anyone who has read my books or studied the tradition. And creation spirituality *is* a tradition. Was Père Chenu New Age? Does a New Ager write a 560-page book with over twenty-four hundred footnotes on a medieval saint-philosopher who has been dead for seven hundred years? Or a 500-page book on a Dominican preacher dead for six hundred years? Or two books on a Benedictine abbess dead for eight hundred years? What's New Age about that? Recently I received a letter from a doctoral student doing his studies on creation spirituality. He wrote: "Having studied in depth your first book, *Musical, Mystical Bear,* 1972, I *know* you aren't New Age. The basis of your ideas is in the book and it preceded New Age by years!" People forget that ICCS began in the Midwest—in blue-collar Chicago—and not on the West Coast. There is a kind of intellectual laziness in the American media that wants to ascribe all mysticism to being New Age—more evidence of how uninterested religion and education have been in disseminating the news that mysticism existed in the West long before New Age. In response to one such lazy journalist writing in the *Baltimore Sun* about my work being "lightweight," intended for "bored middle-class consumers," a person wrote a letter to the editor that said in part: "Hardly the case! My encounter with Creation Spirituality has led me to go to school for five years to get a graduate degree in theology, quit my nice government job, and devote the rest of my life to helping people on an authentic spiritual path. It most assuredly has been a threat to my lifestyle. And I am not alone." The biggest difference between Creation Spirituality and New Age is the recognition of darkness, shadow, and injustice in the former and the too-often quest for light in the latter. Just as I can be critical of one-sided education that is all left-brain, so too there is such a thing as "right-brain excess," and some New Agers suffer from this.

New Agers are themselves maturing, and now one hears talk of an "old New Age" and a "new New Age" or New Age II—the latter being represented by those who do include a social-justice agenda in their worldview.

Earth Tremblings

On October 17, 1989, an event occurred that brought together nature, culture, and a kind of spiritual awakening. The Bay Area suffered a severe earthquake, 7.1 on the Richter scale. Sixty people lost their lives; 600,000 commuters had to find alternate ways to get to work; telephones were out; ordinary citizens emerged as heroes and heroines overnight. I offer here a shortened version of a poem I wrote in my journal at that time.

> It was Descartes, the philosopher of the modern era,
>   who said
> "I think therefore I am"
> and who added "we will master and control nature."
> Lies, Lies, anthropocentrism, selfish, egotistical lies!
> Earthquakes teach me otherwise.
> Nature is bigger than the humans.
> The We is bigger than the I.
> Cosmology will return. Even if it must break open the
>   earth, bring down our bridges and highways,
> set fire to our anthropocentric hearts
> to do so. Set consumerism to conflagration.
>
> Earth says: "Creation exists, therefore you are."
> On this plank
> Let new political parties rise.
> Let new economic systems emerge. . . .
> And what about religion?
> Can it awaken us also?
> Can it quake with new visions, letting ravens loose and
> reclaiming new birds of Spirit?

It occurs to me that if one is to ride deeply into the earth, as my California dream promised, one is going to encounter earthquakes and other disturbances. There is a risk in every journey we take, especially the deepest ones. One pays a price to live near the wilderness of California. Beauty includes terror.

But another earthquake was trembling beneath my feet as well: an ecclesial one. From the very first days of my stay in California, its rumblings could be heard and felt.

PART THREE

CONFLICTS

This page: At Stations of the Cross event, in Find-horn, Scotland, during Holy Week, 1992.

Preceding page, from top: Walking the ruins of Hildegarde of Bingen's monastery in Diesebodenburg, Germany. Meeting with Leonardo Boff in Petropolis, Brazil, 1990 (David Gentry Akin, then editor of Creation Spirituality *magazine, is on the left). Drumming with two wannabe Swedish shamans in the woods outside Stock-holm, Sweden, 1992.*

8

"Taking on the Vatican Is Like
Standing in Front of a Train"

I don't believe in inquisitions. I never have. I was embarrassed by inquisitions when they were brought up to me in high-school debates with non-Catholic classmates ("Of course they are a thing of the past," I explained); and I am even more embarrassed that they have returned in our time. I don't believe in banning books or in threatening thinkers. Arguing freely about ideas and attempting to put ideas into practice are the surest ways to let truth emerge and falsehoods settle out. I thought the Second Vatican Council did away with the spirit as well as the letter of book-banning—the Index of Forbidden Books, and the inquisitorial mode that had hung around the Vatican for centuries. I was wrong. The papacy of John Paul II brought it back.

The pope appointed Cardinal Joseph Ratzinger to spearhead the Congregation for the Doctrine of the Faith (CDF), which until 1908 was called the Holy Office of the Sacred Inquisition and from 1908–1968 was called simply the Holy Office. Ratzinger was a theologian in Germany in the 1960s and was present at the Second Vatican Council, where he made some interventions on behalf of the more progressive forces. Since that time he has had a considerable change of face. Fr. Bernard Haring, a distinguished moral theologian whose work is respected the world over, was called in for a session at the CDF. Later he compared it to an interrogation he underwent at the hands of the Nazis during the Second World War and said that the Vatican experience was more frightening.

Dominicans in Defense of My Work

Shortly after arriving in California I had received a letter from my provincial in Chicago explaining that the Vatican had received complaints about three of my books and that the master general of the Dominican order had requested that our province set up a commission to review these three books.

They were *On Becoming a Musical, Mystical Bear; Whee! We, wee all the Way Home;* and *Original Blessing.* The complaints had come from Seattle, where I had delivered the keynote address for the gay and lesbian Catholic group Dignity and where I had more recently conducted a workshop on Hildegard of Bingen in Archbishop Hunthausen's parish. They came from CUFF (Catholics United for the Faith) and from followers of Constance Cumbey, who was giving talks saying that "Matthew Fox and [Brazilian Bishop] Helda Camera are the anti-Christ."

The commission set up to review my work consisted of three theologians, two of whom had been professors of mine in Dubuque and none of whom was considered radical or far-out in any way. The commission's cover report summarized their findings. I cite from that summary.

> The enduring question that must be addressed to any spiritual theology is its fidelity to the Scriptures, the tradition of the Church and the present magisterium. One must distinguish between the intention of the author to be faithful to Catholic teaching and the degree to which other theologians can perceive evidence of that fidelity. Fr. Fox's literary works indicate that he does not see himself as formulating a totally new spirituality, but rather rediscovering a traditional spiritual insight that has been lost, or at least obscured, within the historical life of the Church especially in the post-Tridentine period. He understands himself as applying the insights of the tradition of Creation-Centered spirituality to contemporary problems. One can certainly question the extent to which an author has correctly or incorrectly interpreted his sources. But Fr. Fox's manifest intention is to rediscover a vision of Christian spirituality which he believes has deep roots in the tradition of the Church and which will be of pastoral assistance in an American cultural context. . . .
>
> We believe that there should be no condemnation of Fr. Fox's work issued as a result of this commission's study, but rather an invitation to our brother to an on-going dialogue with his peers in the various disciplines of theology in which they assist him in clarifying his own theological thinking and indicate areas in which his theology seems to be at variance with the commonly held teaching of the Church.[1]

In the original letter about this matter, dated October 19, 1984, the provincial said that if the commission found any substance to the questions raised about my work, they would submit questions to me in writing. Since I never received any questions from the commission, I conclude today as I did then that no heresy was found. I received a personal note from one member of the commission after the commission had submitted its report. It said, in part:

May 6, 1985

Dear Matt,

I hope that you don't feel that we were too critical or harsh. We tried to express support and respect for your work while being sufficiently critical that the Congregation for the Doctrine of the Faith would be satisfied and not pursue the matter further.

You have made a fine contribution to the life of the Order and the Church, Matt, and I hope you will be left in peace by Rome so that you can continue your ministry knowing that you are appreciated and respected by your brothers.

All the best!

Fraternally,

[name withheld]

Returning to this letter today I am quite touched, since the priest who wrote it was part of the group that urged my dismissal six years later and since the documents sent to Rome at that time implied that I was *always* a troublemaker and an embarrassment to the province.

Now we had a new provincial, Fr. Don Goergen, who was himself a published theologian. When he came to visit me in November, we discussed the seriousness of Rome's position and on December 2, 1985, he wrote the bishop of Oakland affirming my work and relationship to the province. He made clear that I was a Dominican "in good standing, with great respect" in the province. He said that although I had chosen a path for myself to develop a prophetic spirituality that was sure to "meet with resistance," still "we in the Province feel that it is a project worth our support and his earnest endeavor." In the letter he thanked the bishop for the support he had given me, and speaks of our "positive visit" in which he was impressed with my "cooperative and fraternal" spirit.

About six months after the theological commission submitted its report to Rome, the Vatican responded. This will not do, it said. Do another report. The finding that I was not in heresy did not fit the Vatican's opinions and purposes. On May 19, 1986, my provincial wrote a strong, 6-page defense of my work to the master general of the Dominican order. In it he said, among other things, that I was "in good standing within the Province" and that although I resided in Oakland, "there is no ambiguity" about my situation. He wrote of having conferred with the bishop of Oakland about me on at least two occasions and that "there was nothing in the Bishop's response which indicated concern on his part or scandal being given." He made the point that the bishop knew me and had heard me lecture on two occasions. Addressing himself to my theology, orthodoxy, and relationship to the magisterium, he insisted that the theological commission established by the previous provincial was reputable and not biased and that its conclusions "deserve great respect." Indeed, after serious reading of my works by three reputable and serious theologians, "there is no basis on which to say that there is something heretical" in my writings or that my theology is not in accord with the magisterium of the church. He then challenged the Congregation to put forward any theological issues they had with my work and made three points: there was no evidence to suggest my teaching was not orthodox and Catholic and that I was attempting to recover the mystical tradition of the church for many of our contemporaries; the Congregation read some of the comments of the theological commission out of context; and I had been "very cooperative" with my superiors and with the recommendations of the theological commission. He noted how he had visited with me the previous November and how I was "completely agreeable" to suggestions made that I submit my future writings to theological critique.

Again, I am moved—though somewhat puzzled—to reread my provincial's strong defense of my work and my relationship to the province. Moved, because it is nice to hear; puzzled, because a few years hence Don Goergen would lead those who achieved my expulsion from the order with the comment that I was *always* a problem in the Dominican community. Indeed, he wrote to Rome at that time that my relationship with the province had been "seriously conflictual for at least twenty years."[2]

My father died in the autumn of 1987 and we buried him on his birthday, November 5. I was the last of the family to say my good-byes, and shared what turned out to be his final lucid hour with him. I began by saying, "Dad, I bet you wish I had been an ordinary parish priest, don't you?" He squeezed my hand very tightly and said, with a firm voice, "Yes, I do." I replied, "Well, I could not have been the kind of priest I have been without the courage you and Mom taught me." We talked about many things—music (for he was tapping his fingers on his chest to the music on the radio), his and Mom's going out dressed up to dance together ("She couldn't sing, but boy could she dance," he remarked). It was a beautiful leave-taking. He was at peace. When, three days later, a nurse was preparing him for a trip to a nursing home for dying cancer patients, she turned to him and said, "I hear you are going to a beautiful place today." He replied, "Yes, I am," dropped his head, and died of a brain hemorrhage. It was a credible last line.

My father was a man of real integrity, who lived by the rules and saw those rules change dramatically in his lifetime but was saved in many ways by those same rules from his own demons of pain and hurt and anger as a child growing up in the Depression. He owed much of his integrity to his faith and to his religion. He was quite an exemplary Catholic. Among the best, I would say.

As hurtful as it is to lose a parent and a husband (we had celebrated my parents' fiftieth wedding anniversary the previous summer), most family members agreed that it was a blessing that he went as he did, not only because he did not have to linger and suffer physically but also because he did not have to endure the subsequent ecclesial battles in which I would be engaged. I was of course trying to undergo my own grieving and assist my mother in hers to the extent that that was possible at that time.

The Struggle Heats Up

But I also had Rome to deal with, for Ratzinger was breathing more heavily down my neck. My provincial and I agreed to keep communication lines open. And so a new chapter began in my life, that of dancing with the Vatican's Congregation for the Doctrine of the Faith. Aware that a struggle was ahead of us, I gathered a team of my most trusted advisers and together we discussed options and strategies. Documents from Cardinal Ratzinger had by now been passed on to me from the master general. I reproduce them below.

December 9, 1985

This congregation gratefully acknowledges receipt of your letter of last May 29, 1985 with which you transmitted a copy of the report elaborated by members of a theological commission. . . . The problems exposed not only render unacceptable any commendation of this author; they make questionable his very capacity to continue in such work. . . .
[signed] Joseph Cardinal Ratzinger

September 17, 1987

Dear Father General,
. . . Given the circumstances, then, this Congregation would be grateful if you would personally use your good offices to assure that Fr. Fox's present assignment as Director of the Institute for Creation Spirituality at Holy Names College, Oakland, CA, USA, be terminated and that he be instructed to cease from further dissemination of the central thesis of his book, *Original Blessing*, either in writing or in the form of speeches or workshops, etc. It appears also necessary that he disassociate himself from "wicca," the ideology of "Starhawk," a self-styled witch.
[signed] Joseph Cardinal Ratzinger

Included with the letter was a document about my *Original Blessing* book, calling it an altogether personal, gatuitous [*sic*] and subjective interpretation of Christian spirituality, of its theological foundations and of the history and thought of the spiritual writers he himself mentions. . . . His treatment of homosexuality (pp. 268–271) is neither inspired by the Scriptures, nor by the doctrine of the Church.

Regarding spirituality, he contrasts the traditional three ways (purgative, illuminative, unitive) with four (the positive, the negative, the creative and with several aspects which have to be a cause of concern [cf. pp. 220ff.] especially the figure of God as Mother, Child, and ourselves as mothers of God).

In short, the book has to be considered dangerous and deviant. It is not in touch with authentic Christian spirituality and so it is far from the doctrine of the Magisterium.

My provincial wrote a solid letter of response to this attack on April 26, 1988. In seven pages he dissected in detail the accusations against my work and answered them in depth. He points out that the commission's report "was quite thorough, indeed more thorough than the one-page summary provided by the Sacred Congregation itself." He defends my calling God "Mother" as being part of our tradition, and he says the notion that I deny original sin "is simply a misreading of *Original Blessing*." He cites Teilhard de Chardin's observation that "a certain pessimism, perhaps, encouraged by an exaggerated conception of the original fall, has led us to regard the world as decidedly and incorrigibly wicked." He also talks of my "complete cooperation" and how "there was never any question of his cooperative and fraternal spirit."

Another letter, dated April 29, 1988, was received from Cardinal Ratzinger. It spoke of "the ever-increasing urgence of this case" and asked the master general to act against me. One action I and my advisory team took was to call in a canon lawyer with considerable experience in Rome as well as in archdiocesan positions in the United States. He studied Ratzinger's letters, then paid me a visit. As we sat together in my living room, he laid out a scenario that was nearly identical to the one that would eventually come to pass. He said that it seemed pretty clear that Ratzinger was "out to get me" and would "stop at nothing" and that eventually, if nothing else worked, the Dominicans would give me an order I could not in conscience obey and then expel me in the name of my vow of obedience. I'll never forget his words: "You must remember that taking on the Vatican is like standing in front of a train. You cannot win; no one ever has."

Indeed, the Dominicans eventually did give me an order I could not obey. They ordered me to abort the work at ICCS and the magazine and the support community in California and go back to Chicago. But before that happened there would be several years of struggle.

We made some concessions to the master general that we hoped might slow the process down and diffuse the enmity of the Vatican. For example, I stepped down as director of ICCS and took on the title of "founding director." I also promised to submit my book manuscripts to two Dominican theologians for review before publishing. But that did not suffice. Now they wanted me to go silent for a year as well.

Silencing and a Creative Response

Going silent meant no teaching, lecturing, workshop leading, or preaching. It meant ceasing all my public work except quiet research behind the scenes.

My first response to this demand was negative. I felt it conceded too much; that it was a bad precedent to set, allowing the Vatican to silence thinkers; that it would encourage the fear that fascism always tries to rain on others. On the other hand, I didn't have many choices, unless I wanted a showdown then and there. The master general assured me my going silent would most likely accomplish all the Vatican wanted, and it would make his and the order's job of defending me much easier.

In addition, since I had never had a sabbatical in nineteen years of teaching, this would be my first sabbatical opportunity. I was feeling strangely public—as if I was some kind of object of embarrassment that the order and church had to hide in an attic or a musty basement. Yet this conflicted with my experiences of nineteen years of public ministry in which I had been openly welcomed by the recipients of my writing, teaching, and lecturing. The introvert in me wanted all the noise just to go away. A year off more or less promised that possibility.

I tried in these circumstances to listen to my own message from creation spirituality about the importance of the *Via Creativa*. I thought if there was ever a time for creativity in my life, this was it. I decided to fashion a creative response and cut a deal in regard to the timing of the silencing. If I went silent on December 15, then I would have completed a semester of teaching and that would seem best for the students at ICCS. Also, it would give me time to prepare a surprise for the Vatican. That surprise would be an Open Letter to the Cardinal Inquisitor of our day in which I would call to task both him and the church structures he represented for their sins of omission and their failure to teach a credible faith and spirituality. I would use the occasion to try to educate him, the Vatican, and the public about creation spirituality. I would also have a press conference in which I laid out my case to the public. Fr. Charles Curran had used this mode of education to considerable effect during his struggles with the Vatican while he was at Catholic University. Brazilian liberation theologian Fr. Leonardo Boff, also silenced by the Vatican, had commented that the silencing meant that millions more people got to hear about liberation theology. This seemed appropriately ironic to me: there might be some providential humor behind this whole scenario after all. In addition, I considered running an ad in the *New York Times* to bring to the attention of a broader public the abuses going on in my church.

I wrote the public letter and called it "Is the Catholic Church Today a Dysfunctional Family?" I used the research being done at that time by persons such as Anne Wilson Schaef and Diane Fasel on dysfunctional organizations and families. The letter had been typeset for our *Creation* magazine when lo and behold it appeared in its entirety as front-page copy in the *National Catholic Reporter*. Later the publisher of *NCR* told me that my letter evoked more mail—most of it favorable—than any other piece *NCR* had ever run. Apparently I was not the only one experiencing the psychological dysfunctions of the church. A Protestant student at the Graduate Theological Union in Berkeley told me that they studied the letter in their theology class and that, just by altering names, it applied perfectly to their own denominations as well. Another response came from Fr. Schillebeeckx, the Dominican theologian in Holland, who said that he read my letter a couple of times, laughing each time as he tried to imagine how Rome would respond to this. "Only an American would write so direct a letter," he remarked.

In the letter, I laid out some of the following points: Cardinal Ratzinger's congregation (CDF) "has not done either its intellectual homework *or* its inner work," since it has totally misrepresented my work. "I detect a kind of intellectual sloth in those who condemn without studying, and a spiritual sloth in those who accuse without feeling the oppression of others that is addressed in my and other works of liberation theology." I explained ten dimensions to a dysfunctional organization and applied them to the Catholic church at this time in history. Foremost among these is when addictive leaders ignore advice from pastoral bishops and others close to the people. Another is obsession with sex; I called the Vatican's obsession with sex and the misogyny that follows "a worldwide scandal which demonstrates a serious psychic imbalance." Other signs of dysfunction include illusions of grandiosity and power that come from persons reinstating a modern-day Inquisition; an illusion of control; appointing Opus Dei bishops; secretiveness; loss of memory and loss of the primary mission of the church; blaming all troubles on outside forces; isolating itself; a need to kill the future. I cite Hildegard of Bingen's warning to the papacy of her day: "O man, you who sit on the papal throne, you despise God when you don't hurl from yourself the evil but, even worse, embrace it and kiss it by silently tolerating corrupt men. The whole Earth is in confusion . . . and you, O Rome, are like one in the throes of death. . . . For you don't love the King's daughter, justice."

I also asked, "Is the Catholic Church reverting to fascism in our times?" Following Susan Sontag's definition of fascism as "institutionalized violence," I laid out some characteristics of the "creeping fascism" in the Catholic church—issues such as the silencing of thinkers; judgmentalism; scapegoating; the launching of the fascist society, Opus Dei; rewarding of authoritarian personalities. "Fascism is the ultimate expression of father dominance," I pointed out, citing a psychologist who has written on authoritarianism. I suggested, "Perhaps this is why your congregation cannot read straight or see straight or remember the past when I write of 'God as Mother.' Because fascism—father dominance—has no place for a Motherly God in it." I suggested that Ratzinger's attacks on American theologians are best explained by this analysis, for "if 'the Führer is always right,' which is what the authoritarian personality needs to believe, then healthy theological debates will always take a back seat to games of political power." I proposed Jesus' teaching as a way out of fascism—the way of compassion—and I pointed out that "it is patent hypocrisy for the church to call for justice in society when it is itself so mired in injustice" and that "a church that chooses to remain deaf is no longer healthy. It may even be already dead." I also predicted that silencing me would not destroy creation spirituality but in fact assist in its message being more widely known. "Good news can never be silenced." I also invited Cardinal Ratzinger to come to ICCS for a year to undergo some spiritual renewal. (He never sent in an application as far as I know.) I concluded that I would go silent as requested by my master general on December 15, 1988.[3]

It has always struck me that American readers of this letter love to talk about the church as dysfunctional (and one Franciscan priest has subsequently written an entire book on the subject), but they seldom pick up on the fascism. That is typical of our culture: we think psychologically but bristle at thinking politically. But to silence thinkers is both a psychological *and* a political act; as Leonardo Boff puts it so well, "physical torture has been abolished but psychological torture continues." This torture includes secret denunciations, no acknowledgment of explanations that are offered, insecurity behind the entire secret process—all this has led some theologians "to the dark night of lonely suffering, psychological worry, and even physical death."[4] As Boff points out, the rules employed by the Congregation for the Doctrine of the Faith "curtail a series of sacred human rights that are acknowledged even in manifestly atheistic societies." The process that proceeds is a "Kafkaesque" one in which "the accuser, the defender, the lawyer, and the judge are one and the same."[5] What Boff describes as "marginalization" in the local church is certainly my experience. For twenty years I lectured and led workshops at Catholic churches and religious education conventions. But because of the cloud of CDF censorship that hung over me from this moment on, most such invitations ceased, and when on occasion a particularly brave parish or Catholic university invited me to speak, there would be demonstrations of raucous right-wing fanatics that made the occasion unpleasant for everyone. Finally, I simply declined most invitations on Catholic premises. All this is part of the genuinely scary fascist attitude that the CDF encourages and even inflames.

My mother was a widow in her midseventies living in Boulder, Colorado, and I did not want her to learn of my silencing from the newspapers. Discreetly, I took aside my sister who lived near my mother and asked her, "Will Mom be able to take the news and can she keep a secret?" My sister replied, "She can take it but she can't keep a secret." That left me with a challenge. I had to come up with an oblique way of breaking the news to my mother, so I sat down with her and said, "Mom, how does it feel to be the mother of a somewhat controversial priest?"

She replied, "Oh, I walk out of sermons all the time."

I said, "What? When was the last time you walked out of a sermon?" (This form of ecclesial protest on my mother's part was a complete surprise to me.)

"Oh," she said, "I walked out on a sermon a few weeks before your father died. Your father and I had an agreement. If I could not in conscience endure a sermon, I walked out and waited in front of church until the mass was over and your father came out. Then we drove home in silence with no argument."

I was amazed, especially since she could only walk that year with the help of a walker because she had had hip trouble. I concluded that there would be no real problem for her when word of my silencing became public.

At Holy Names College we had an autograph party for my new book, *The Coming of the Cosmic Christ,* which had been published at the same time as my silencing. An enormous crowd of about nine hundred people packed themselves into the Skyroom there and were obviously offering moral support for my stand. The media were there also. During the question-and-answer period a large man with a long white beard strode up to the microphone, waved in the air a copy of the magazine containing my public letter, and said in a prophetic, sonorous voice, "Tell us, Dr. Fox, why this letter is not to be compared to that of Dr. Luther's Ninety-five Theses nailed on the church door." It was an amazing moment for me. I had never consciously made connections between what we were doing at ICCS and beyond and what Martin Luther had done. My reply was to diffuse the *personality* comparison as I pointed out that indeed our times were as tumultuous culture-wise *and therefore* religion-wise as those of Dr. Luther and we could expect some deep changes to occur in our religious loyalties and structures.

We decided to hold the press conference regarding my silencing at the Press Club in San Francisco to make access easy for the media but also to take the spotlight off the Oakland diocese. I had gone to the bishop of Oakland, who had always been friendly and cordial with me, to let him know what to expect. I said, "The issues at stake—women's rights and native peoples' rights and the recovery of mysticism in the church—these are all matters of conscience for me." I still chuckle at his response. He rose from his chair and shouted, "Conscience! Conscience! Don't ever use that word in front of me! Every time I hear that word someone is getting in trouble!" Several faculty members were at the press conference, which was introduced by the then editor of *Creation* magazine, David Gentry-Akin. I had worried for weeks about the press conference and was so nervous before it began that I inadvertently left my reading glasses in the car and had only my driving glasses with me. Thus I was just barely able to read my prepared statement to the press. Part of that statement follows:

> The Vatican seems incapable of understanding the spirit or the struggle of the Americas—of liberation theology in Latin America and of creation spirituality in the first world. Creation spirituality offers a liberation for "first world" or "overdeveloped" peoples. This movement liberates us from addictions because it regrounds us in our own Western mystical roots; it liberates us from sexism and dualism between body and spirit; it liberates us from boring worship because it resets worship in a cosmological context; it liberates us from the antagonism between science and religion by giving us back a cosmology which brings together science, mysticism, and art; it liberates us from the despair which plagues our youth the world over who are without hope because of the unemployment, militarism, and the lack of spiritual vision which adults offer them. Above all, creation spirituality can assist us in liberating Mother Earth from the horrendous attacks made on her by the anthropocentric civilization of the past three hundred years. As scientist Paul Ehrlich has remarked, looking at the crisis of the greenhouse effect, "scientific analysis points, curiously, toward the need for a quasi-religious transformation of contemporary cultures." Only a religious revival can turn things around and creation spirituality offers us that revival.

I believe that Cardinal Ratzinger's theological objections to my work are unbelievably thin. Now that I am going public about this investigation, persons can judge for themselves. For example, he complains that I refer to God as "Mother" in my *Original Blessing* book. Yet, the

Scriptures, the medieval mystics, and even Pope John Paul I all used motherly images for God. The inability of the Vatican to deal with God as Mother tells us more about the sin of patriarchy than it does about the Godhead. . . . The Congregation complains that I am a "fervent feminist." Jesus was a feminist; Meister Eckhart was a feminist. I do not understand how any follower of Jesus could be so deaf to the suffering of women in recent Western history that she or he would not be a feminist. . . .

I believe that power, rather than theology, is the real issue in this case. . . . The very act of silencing theologians instead of engaging them in dialogue is a sign of institutional violence. . . . In the bishops' document *Justice in the World,* published in 1971, we read that "the Church recognizes everyone's right to suitable freedom of expression and thought. This includes the right of everyone to be heard in a spirit of dialogue which preserves legitimate diversity within the Church." Speaking of my own experience, it is a fact that the Congregation has not only rejected the conclusions of the theological commission which investigated me, but has afforded me no direct communication, no true list of theological objections, in short, no "right to be heard in a spirit of dialogue.". . .

If I could have my way, I would recommend that the headlines for this event ought not to read "American Theologian Silenced" but rather, "Is the Catholic Church Going Deaf?" The news is not that one more theologian has been silenced but that the Vatican has grown deaf—deaf to the cries of Mother Earth, deaf to the cries of women, of native peoples and persons of color, of artists, of young persons, of the unemployed, of addicts, of the poor, and of the overprivileged who are so often spiritually poor. Creation spirituality responds to these cries in deep and effective ways. An institution that chooses to remain deaf in the midst of all this suffering is no longer healthy. It may even be already dead.

Meanwhile, the need for a spirituality which can heal Mother Earth and usher in an era of a global renaissance goes on. I am proud to be a part of that movement. I encourage those who have found a spiritual home in creation spirituality to continue to speak out from a place of "inner wealth," as Eckhart says. Let us be united in spirit with political prisoners the world over—as well as those who silence them. Let us pray for one another so that the fear that urges a few people to imprison others might melt in the face of the divine awe that shines on all of us—and yearns to shine through all of us.

It was interesting to me how prominently the issue of native rights played at the press conference. The Vatican had been trying to canonize Fr. Junípero Serra, a nineteenth-century Franciscan missionary in California who was so committed to colonialism in the name of Jesus that he was beating Indians fifty years *after* the governor of the state had forbidden it.[6] I had taken a stand in our magazine and elsewhere against such an abominable misuse of the canonization process. The first question at the press conference was from a Native American woman who asked, "Isn't it true that the reason the Vatican is attacking you is because of your strong stand on behalf of native peoples?" I replied that I could not speak for the Vatican but that the effort to canonize Serra was wrong. Starhawk was also an issue, and I simply said that I could not in conscience fire someone who was doing such a good job teaching. Nor could Holy Names College do so legally since it, unlike the Vatican, was committed to academic freedom.

We also launched a letter-writing campaign, and over five thousand people wrote letters to the Vatican on my behalf. The letters were powerful and poignant, and we sent five hundred of them to the Dominican master general. Needless to say, I was moved by the quality and quantity of support expressed in them and by the time and effort people had taken to express the meaning that creation spirituality and my work in it had brought to their lives. A few excerpts from the letters follow.

> It is no more possible to silence creation theology than it is for Cardinal Ratzinger to quell the Holy Spirit. I am reminded of the story in Luke 19 where Jesus is asked to rebuke his disciples and he answered, "I tell you, if these were silent, the very stones would cry out." Creation theology becomes a part of a person's whole being—it is too closely integrated into one's lifestyle to be silenced. (Judy from North Delta, British Columbia, Canada)

> No single book published in the thirty or so years since my ordination has had a greater impact on me. It has been a healing work in my life, enabling me to experience a deeper faith that is both intellectually honest, morally sound, and profoundly in touch with the biblical truths that are so central. (Robert from Kindston, New York)

> This work [*Original Blessing*] approached me as an intellectual equal and . . . gave me the tools and incentive to set about naming and educating and reworking my life and that of those around me. As a full-time wife, mother, and homemaker, I am now also involved with adult education, started a food cooperative, joined a sitting cooperative, and was

active from the inception of a local ecumenical effort (thirty-seven churches) to help the needy in our local area. (Nancy from Findlay, Ohio)

If the Roman Catholic church cannot stand the challenge from its own most creative, loyal, and faithful sons and daughters within the household of its own tradition, then you hardly want to waste your time engaging in ecumenical dialogue with those of us who are not of the Roman Catholic tradition. . . . Our task as Christian people is not to protect the institution we represent. It is to seek the truth of God. Matthew Fox has been a great blessing to my life and to the lives of many Episcopalians. (Bishop John S. Spong, Newark, New Jersey)

Geologist Thomas Berry wrote a beautiful article of support in which he offered his own prophetic wisdom.

What's being done at ICCS is too important to permit ourselves to be distracted either by fundamentalist iconoclasm or by bureaucratic procedures. Let's get on with the historical task assigned to ourselves and our generation: the task of establishing a religious sensitivity to the divine as communicated to us through the natural world. . . . Our Christian fate as well as the fate of the entire human community is inseparable from the fate of the earth. . . . [ICCS] is awakening Christian consciousness to its religious and moral responsibility for the fate of the earth.[7]

Long before the public troubles with the Vatican, I had felt support for the work we were doing from many quarters. One person, a Lutheran pastor in a Midwest city whose spiritual directors have been Native American shamans, sent me a unique gift—a pair of vulture feathers—with the following letter.

I want to give you this feather. It is a very special medicine feather from a vulture from New Mexico. Native peoples held vultures sacred because they fly and soar more beautifully than any bird, even the eagle—signs of the Spirit. In Egypt they were images of mother nature—death and rebirth as they re-cycled and fed upon death like the mother did. The Parsees placed their dead in towers so that vultures would consume them, bringing re-birth. In India vultures [are a] symbol of tutelary spirits—denoting spiritual counsel. I give you this vulture feather because your work is like the sacred vulture—you are taking what was dead and bringing forth through your body—transmuting—into new life and re-creation. You are a warrior of the heart.

I had never seen my work in that light before: taking what was dead in Christianity and recycling it, like a vulture. I was touched and honored to have my work remembered in this fashion, and I cherish the sacred feather to this day.

We videotaped the press conference so that our ICCS students could watch it that afternoon. After that the students, faculty, staff, Tristan, and I had a party. The students lifted me onto their shoulders and sang, then presented me with a poem signed by all of them and containing the following inscription: "Your prophetic life must continue / with love and support, ICCS Class, 1991/1992." The poem was from the sixteenth-century Sufi poet Mirabai (translation by Robert Bly). It is called "Why Mira Can't Go Back to Her Old House."[8]

> The colors of the Dark One have penetrated Mira's body;
>   all the other colors washed out.
> Making love with the Dark One and eating little, those are
>   my pearls and my carnelians.
> Meditation beads and the forehead streak, those are my
>   scarves and my rings.
> That's enough feminine wiles for me.
> My teacher taught me this.
> Approve me or disapprove me: I praise the Mountain
>   Energy
> night and day.
> I take the path that ecstatic human beings have taken for
>   centuries.
> I don't steal money, I don't hit anyone.
> What will you charge me with?
> I have felt the swaying of the elephant's shoulders;
> And now you want me to climb on a jackass?
> Try to be serious.

9

A Year of Silence—
1989–1990

The year of silence came on swiftly and when it finally arrived on December 15, 1988, I was ready for time off. The media attention was overwhelming and exhausting, and trying to balance all the interested parties—the master general in Rome, my provincial in Chicago, Holy Names College, the faculty and ICCS students, readers of my books and the magazine—was a full-time obligation. Now I had surely *earned* a sabbatical. Of course, when I call this a "sabbatical" I am being benign. The Vatican and the order, though silencing me and thus cutting off all income for a year, did not offer me any money to live on. Instead, I was fortunate to receive a grant from Laurance Rockefeller, who had supported the magazine and its staff for several years, and the money allowed me to live that year.

I decided to keep a journal during my year of silence. The first entry for that year was as follows:

December 17
My first Sunday as a silenced preacher. It is strange sitting through mass
as a layperson, even though I do this whenever I am free to do so. But this
time there is a deep difference. Knowing I cannot talk even if I want to.
For twenty-eight years I've been a "preacher" of the "Order of Preachers."
Now I join all those others whom this papacy has forbidden to preach—
women, laymen, all but the ordained. Francis of Assisi and his band
preached and were not ordained. Same with Hildegard of Bingen. Yes,
we live in fearsome times.

Hibernating in the Canadian Woods

My first action in my year of silence was to retreat to the woods of Canada near Toronto, where a woman offered me her home while she was in India on a study trip. For two weeks I lived silently and alone in that home amid the snow and cold of a Toronto winter. This deep hibernation time seemed to correspond to a poem by Tagore that one of my ICCS students had given me after our press conference party.

> No more noisy, loud words from me—
> such is my master's will. Henceforth I deal in whispers.
> The speech of my heart will be carried on
> in murmurings of a song.
> Men hasten to the King's market.
> All the buyers and sellers are there.
> But I have my untimely leave in the middle of the day,
> in the thick of work. . . .
> Full many an hour have I spent
> in the strife of the good and the evil,
> But now it is the pleasure of my playmate of the empty days
> to draw my heart on to him;
> and I know not why
> is this sudden call
> to what useless inconsequence![1]

December 27
Notes from a Hibernating Bear—

Am now in snow and woods in Canada. A cat asleep and purring on my lap. Why was I drawn to this style of "retreat" at this time? Perhaps as a "return to my origins"—it is Wisconsin-like with snow and temperatures in the thirties. The woods and earth under my feet speak to me of memories unforgettable but deep. Indians surely stalked these woods in the past as I did this morning—only with surer results. (I saw deer tracks but no deer. That encounter will happen another day when I am more grounded and ready for it.)

Also, it's a memory here of Third Lake [Illinois] where I lived and birthed and struggled. And walked daily in weather and terrain like this—sparse woods but real earth—with Tristan. How he would love these woods!

Another return I imagine is the Musical, Mystical Bear archetype. Bears hibernate during the winter months, and I am being asked to do the same by my order. After twenty years of public goings-on, I'm ready for a bit of hibernation. Winter and snow are good for hibernation. They seem to blanket all for a long, cold winter's sleep.

It snowed last night! How fortunate I am to have a fresh blanket of snow for my first foray into this forest that surrounds me. It would be easy to get lost amidst these stripped-down trees, but the snow furnished me with tracks

*for following my way home—just like Hansel and Gretel, or I should say un-
like those two who got lost in the woods. Something archetypal speaks to me
about "following my tracks back home." A spiritual tradition is a path, a
way, Christ is "the way." I have tried to retrack Western spirituality and follow the paths home again. I have had expert guides such as Chenu and
Ruether and Cognet to assist me. Strange, though, how my own church hierarchy is afraid of its own tracks! I am to hibernate their fears away. Good
luck to them!*

December 28
*Snow again. Wonderful! What is it about snow that awakens the mystical in
us? That all things become one again, as "in the beginning"? Snow reveals
the common is-ness of all things—the interconnectivity of things. For truly
snow does blanket all things equally—the ground and the tree limbs, the picnic bench and bird cages; even the car and the highways for a period remain
part of the oneness of all things. Maybe this is why a certain silence, a certain mystical silence, accompanies snow. All creatures are in silent awe once
again to experience their commonality and interconnectivity. Lessons of
compassion inherent in the snow blanket.*

December 29
*I have been watching Laurens Van der Post's three-part series on Carl Jung.
Striking was Jung's journey around the world to support his "collective unconscious" theory. It sounds more and more like my "deep river" and "deep
ecumenism" theory! (which in fact—like Jung's—is practice, not just theory).*

*Most striking was his saying that African was the key to it all—along with
Native American and Aboriginal. Remember how Picasso was influenced by
Native American and African as well. In my work on ritual and cosmology I
too have been deeply influenced by the native religions—they had a creation
spirituality and a "living cosmology." What gifts they have to give Western
religion for its own renewal! But time is running out.*

*Question: Should I keep this journal for my coming months of silence
and call it "Journal of a Gagged Theologian"? It allows me a chance to
speak in a more direct idiom than I have employed in the past. It also gives
me a "friend" or "life partner," one might say, albeit a somewhat imaginary
listener to hear my thoughts. I am feeling, with all the media attention, etc.,
these past months, a deeper than ever feeling of deep loneliness and lack of
intimacy. Is this the price for celibacy? I will write this journal as if I were
communicating with a very close friend.*

*Maybe my access to the media today and my skills in communicating have
to be balanced and nurtured not only by the enforced silence from the Vatican but by a much, much deeper silence—that I share with all widows and*

widowers, all lovers who have felt betrayed, all divorced people, all lonely young people, and so many lonely others in our society-without-community. It is hard being so companionless after all these years of adult living.

The trees and the earth, the snow and the sun, the cats in this house with me—we are companions too. I must learn to listen to their talk and to enter into their language.

Jung's comment in the movie last night—that the churches are emptying because the symbols no longer touch people and because the church has lost touch with its symbols—supports my deepest intuitions. ICCS is more and more trying to get the symbolic, i.e., mystical, tradition alive. And mother church—how incredible this is—is trying to abort us!

December 30
Tomorrow night begins a New Year.

I called the magazine office today and heard that the response continues to be heavy to our New York Times ad and other PR efforts. That new articles on us have appeared in Boston and Florida papers. And that there are more and more thoughtful letters from persons—many of them ministers apparently—who have taken time to study in depth the New York Times announcement. This is very good news, for I intended the announcement to be an educational moment, as we hoped all my response to Ratzinger would be. My favorite line in the ad was "healthy religion must stand up and be heard" amidst all this fundamentalism. I trust it is truly happening. Reading this book on Nazi Germany reinforces, as nothing else possibly could, my resolve to resist appeasement and stand up and be heard. Nineteen eighty-nine promises not to be dull . . . either!

December 31
Len Deighton's brilliant study of Nazism in Germany² is based on his conviction that Hitler was the choice of Germany's "middle class" and that this was a choice of resentment. Hitler the politician exploited the resentments of Germany's middle class, which had indeed suffered much from the First World War in terms of family destruction with its component abuse of the children; unemployment; inflation; insecurity; and perhaps above all, loss of soul as projected onto their Imperial State. All this is deeply telling, I believe, for American politics today. How much of our politics is a "politics of resentment"?

If Jack Kennedy was in some way a "great" president, it was because he appealed not to resentment but to our power.

Religiously, resentment is a by-product of fall/redemption ideology. One who knows she is an original blessing does not have a need to resent others but looks for ways of mutual healing, celebration, and shared passion, i.e., compassion. Those whose wounds are unattended will respond to resentment. Ask Hitler. Ask also these TV *evangelists whose messages of hate and enemies "out there" are so appealing to so many wounded people. Part of resentment is scapegoating.*

How can we educate people out of resentment? That question reveals issues of caring for the wounded child, of telling the good news of CCS [creation-centered spirituality]—*of original blessing, of our mysteriousness, our divinity, etc.*

Tonight is the New Year! May it be a year of lessening resentments and replacing them with struggles for justice. Maybe religions should examine themselves actually for whether they speak to resentment or to the healing of resentment.

For me this New Year promises to be something special. I do not know its outcome in any sense as to my status in the R.C. church and priesthood. I will have to "stay loose," as we used to say, or as Eckhart would say, "let go" and "sink eternally from letting go to letting go."

January 1
In front of me on the flight from Toronto to San Francisco is a young Vietnamese father cradling his new baby. There is great tenderness in this act. Tenderness. Our species is capable of great tenderness. How can we cultivate it more? Why not courses in tenderness? I can see it now: Tenderness 101; Tenderness 202.

People ask me why the New York Times *ad? And what about the cost? Legitimate questions these. My whole purpose in responding publicly to the event of my silencing is to educate, because silencing is a dangerous precedent that will intimidate Catholic thinkers for years to come if we allow it to go unresponded to. I wanted to take this last and unique opportunity of being silenced to educate about* CCS. *To put our story out about this wonderful tradition in spirituality to a whole new audience. To people who do not subscribe to* NCR *or* Creation *magazine or attend religious education workshops but who think, read, are critical, are concerned about directions our culture is and is not taking. People also who are decision makers in our various institutions. For the news of* CCS *has implications far beyond religious institutions alone as to parenting, relationships, education, politics, economics, psychology. Spirituality is not confined to religion (in fact it is often quite distant from it).*

Another level of education, though secondary to me, is to let the big boys in the Vatican know that Americans do not take the act of silencing or the unjust treatment of theologians lightly. We—unlike the Vatican—have had a Bill of Rights for some time now. By awakening the kind of folks who read the New York Times *to* CCS *and to the goings-on in today's Vatican, we are continuing our strategy of getting the Vatican to back off from trying to squelch the spirit of the church of the Americas as it did the spirit of the church of Holland.*

Happy to report, two weeks after the ad, indications from mail coming in are that a lot of intelligent and thoughtful readers are responding and wondering and desiring more information about CCS. *In addition, they are sending in donations and subscriptions to the mag—which answers the question of where the money came from. It was a risk—when David takes on Goliath, David risks. We risked the fact that enough money would come in to pay the $16,000 for the ad. This price is the bargain-basement price, called a "remnant ad," which means we gave it to the* Times *and could not specify our date for appearing. They slip it in if and when they have a cancellation or an open page. We had no guarantee that the ad would even run at all. It had to appear, obviously, before December 15. It did—December 13 in eastern editions and December 14 in national editions. We borrowed the money from next year's funds to pay for it.*

January 3
"Washing our hands like Pontius Pilate"—so speaks an Australian aboriginal poet whose poems I have been reading.[3] How true this is of the lack of moral courage evident in the Catholic church hierarchy in our time. Last night I heard that the cardinal of Chicago joined the homophobic forces of our society and church in condemning equal-rights laws for homosexual persons. Yet the people did speak out and the law passed in Chicago anyway.

It seems to me that for those who have eyes to see and ears to hear with, for those willing to read the signs of the times (Vatican II) instead of hide their heads in the sands of so-called tradition, Christianity is at the point of a radical awakening. As is the whole human race. The signs of the times tell us that it is time to respond to the injustices done women, homosexuals, earth, the young, artists, the poor, now before it is too late.

This response will take two ingredients that church authorities seem weak in: (1) faith, i.e., trust in the Spirit and its ability to create and re-create and make order of chaos, and (2) courage, i.e., a big heart that puts heart before power and control. The times do not allow anyone the luxury of waiting around for others to lead. All have leadership charisms to offer the community and ought to be invited to do so.

A paper I read today had a significant article on the olde gift of creation we have been taking for granted long enough—water. And how a shortage of water is soon to befall the Middle East, whose sole aquifer lies under the West Bank. So now we have the truth—the fight is over water rights as much as over ideological rhetoric. Creation is now the name of the struggle. It could also be—if we dare—the solution. For water is neither Jewish nor Islamic, Arabic nor Zionist. Water is. Its is-ness is holy indeed.

Can't scientists manufacture H_2O? We did it in laboratories in high school. Put your money there instead of in weapons, my brothers, and we could all live in peace. For living is a creative act!

A lesson about archetypes came home to me in a big way during the year of silencing. I learned that many people were deeply distraught by my silencing. Jewish people, especially, showed an empathy for my situation, and understandably so, since their voices were cut off for so many centuries of Christian history. At a party that Harper San Francisco gave for its authors in February, I was engaged in a rich conversation with a writer on Native American spirituality when a woman flew at me from across the room and practically leaped on me—I remember the moment well because we were standing by a balcony and I nearly went over it. She is a well-known scholar on the goddess and is Jewish, and the words she shouted were: "Matt Fox, you are a cultural hero." I was as surprised by the words as I was by the action, but in reflection I see the moment to be one more evidence that silencing someone brings up a lot of dark memories from our collective pool of experiences, especially for women and for Jewish people. She identified with what the church had done to me.

Vision Quest

One promise I had made for the year was to do a vision quest. A vision quest is a kind of retreat Native American–style in which one goes into the wilderness to hear one's call anew and to respond accordingly. For years people had come up to me after talks and asked, "Have you done a vision quest?" and my thought had always been the same: I have too many visions already; I don't need or want any more. But now it was different. I knew I needed some spiritual recharging. Since Native American prayer forms had always proved powerful for me in the past, I went north to the rainy woods in the foothills of the Cascade mountains outside Seattle to submit myself to a vision quest under the guidance of Buck Ghosthorse.

It began with fasting several days beforehand and preparing 150 prayer ties on a string that would mark the parameters of my prayer space. I remember thinking as I fashioned these prayer ties how ironic it was that I, who had practically flunked out of Boy Scouts because I couldn't learn the art of knot tying, was now so involved with many knots. It struck me too that the number 150 is also used in the rosary—150 beads. We would do a sweat lodge on Saturday morning, then be led to our respective places in the woods to stay alone there overnight fasting and praying. Just before I left for the woods,

Buck called me back and said, "Take this with you." It was a stick with an eagle feather on it. He told me to place it near such and such a flag in my prayer circle.

The story of my vision quest is told in my journal.

July 3

Home from the Vision Quest. What an experience it was! Twenty hours of heaven and six hours of hell.

Three women made the quest with me. I slept alone the night before in a tepee next to the sweat lodge. Such hospitality! They spread fresh fir boughs on the floor of the tepee, and there was a pit in the center where I had a fire. I've never slept that close to a fire before—I was able to throw wood on from the bed itself (a cot plus sleeping bag). The aroma of the boughs was something. Though it rained all night, I barely got wet—water runs down the poles into a trench dug around the tepee.

In the sweat lodge before their putting us "on the hill," something very striking occurred. Immediately, with the very first rock I looked at, I saw a mean, ugly, and menacing face glowing red and staring at me. I stared back and prayed into it, and the face gradually withered away into something benign.

Skye, a woman graduate of ICCS, befriended me with tea, a wool blanket from Guatemala, which I took to the Quest Site with me, matches, sage. And a womanly presence. Buck assigned her to be my "helper" during the quest. She took me to the site to set up my prayer ties, etc., and came to get me at the end and prayed for and with me.

I should point out that when I placed my prayer flags with the black (West) first, the red (North) second, etc., as instructed, I had the inspiration to say, "The black is Meister Eckhart"—Eckhart in black, tied with white string, looked like a Dominican preacher in his cappa. After all, he is the champion of the Via Negativa, *nothingness, God as "superessential Darkness" in the West. "The red is Mechthild of Magdeburg" (whose key symbol is fire)—when I said that, a bird started singing wildly in the forest. The yellow was Julian of Norwich (East)—and I must say that early on I saw a face on this flag that was present throughout the quest. It had on a bonnet like a fifteenth-century woman might wear. (Later, I saw two persons on the flag—one instructing the other—again medieval in their garb.) The color fit so well! Yellow (East, sunrise) seemed right for Julian, who saw that "all will be well"—blessing even in the midst of Black Death–ravaged England.*

The white (South) I called Francis of Assisi. Francis in white glowed most of the night from whatever meager light came into the forest. The blue, which stood for the Creator God, I called Thomas Aquinas—"Thomas the Creator" as G. K. Chesterton calls him. Blue seemed right for Aquinas, and I challenged him to help me with my book about him.

And the green—for the Earth Mother—was, of course, Hildegard of Bingen, famous for her "viriditas" or "greening power" images. One feature of Hildegard's green was that the stick was stubby and short—she was the closest to the earth of them all.

This pattern of Western, medieval, creation-centered mystics was present throughout the weekend. We had a "powwow" and I called on them as I called on the six directions. It felt wholly good and natural to do so, combining as we did Native American and Western mysticism.

At the site, in the woods, I first just was. I prayed to the six directions—as Buck told us to do every hour—and I looked into every direction I could. Then I sat down and when I did, I heard a "zap" kind of noise that scared me—like someone running into an electric fence—and I shouted "What's that?" or "What the hell was that?" It occurred to my right but out of my vision, a bit behind me. Actually, it occurred where Buck had told me to place a certain stick with an eagle feather on it—something he handed me "at the last minute" before "going on the hill." [The significance of this exchange will become clear later.]

I had come to the hill naive but openhearted and with an open mind. I had three "agenda items" with me, and then I was going to be open to whatever else transpired. I did not want to set so busy an agenda that I would in any way control things. After praying to all six directions (and six saints) and being with the space and its six directions, I began my first ritual. It was to be Thanksgiving. I went through a litany of names of persons who have blessed me in my life, beginning with my parents—I would name things they had done for me; grandparents; brothers and sisters and their families; mentors (Chenu!) and teachers; students; doctors; friends and co-workers; Indian teachers—Ed Savilla and Jose and Buck, for example; faculty members; administrators. It truly was a lengthy litany and I forgot a few, for whom I did another one later in the evening. I also thanked my enemies. I mentioned some by name and I danced this Thanks.

I burned a memento of someone who had hurt me deeply. The ashes were on the ground now. I blessed my forehead with them in the sign of the cross, "ashes to ashes and dust to dust." I moved on after asking for forgiveness and dancing a Kyrie Eleison for us both.

The third question I came with—interesting how the Four Paths are played out here, (1) Thanksgiving for blessing, (2) letting go and forgiveness, (3) creativity and transformation—was the following. What form should my leadership—for I have been given some by the events of my life—take? Where does creation-centered spirituality go from here?

I chanted and prayed and danced and kept the pipe in my hand, as instructed, at all times. Then I would sit on the log that was in my space of about four feet by six feet. The log contained a lot of mosquitoes, but it was good to be able to sit on it—though I could only look in one direction.

Two redemptions of Catholic piety came to me:

One is redeeming the rosary by way of a new (more ancient?) Hail Mary: "Holy Mary, mother of God, pray for us cocreators now and at the hour of our creativity."

I saw the Benediction of the "Blessed Sacrament" in a creation-centered form. Every creature is a Blessed Sacrament, including the galaxies, sun, earth, etc. The Divine Names litany applies to each creature as well as to the communion host. Why not devise a ritual that honors a different creature each day—like a host—for each is a Cosmic Christ and a Blessed Sacrament (cf. "original blessing")?

If I'm not mistaken, it was after this "theological reflection" that, as the sun began to set in the forest, the light show began. Light as light of Christ, Lumen gentium, light of the nations, became "lumen animalium" and "lumen creatuorum," light of creatures [light of animals]. It was then that I noticed the polar bear in the tree, i.e., a leaf the shape of a polar bear. I first noticed it in the leaves of a modest cluster of bushes—"Isn't that a polar bear?" I asked; and next to it is a bird—several of them; and all the leaves were lighting up. There was behind this bush a rocklike "grotto" that looked Celtic and lots of little people would be beside it. Behind this were tree trunks that became snakes and a chimpanzee on its knees.

As the woods were coming alive at dusk with this green, translucent garden of creatures, I saw at the back of the forest to the left an immense structure forming a kind of backdrop to the scene. It was like a castle or museum, and then I realized it was both. It was the Vatican, covered with moss, much as a deserted castle might be. It was "back there"—while all this action of life and light was taking place here, *in the foreground, in* our *forest. Every place I turned there were forms to be seen: leaves of animals, each one lit up and shining—deer, monkeys, a dinosaur, crocodiles, elephants, iguanas, birds, pandas, bears—also tree trunks took on such shapes and forms. In one tree, a deer appeared; there was also—was I seeing it right? Yes!—a Madonna, in fact Raphael's Madonna with a child on its lap. This Madonna was especially translucent and bright. Directly in line with the Mother Earth and Hildegard flag were two objects: ten feet away was a tree limb that became a snake, and twenty feet beyond that was a tree stump that became transformed into a goddess grotto like Druids or Cretan worshipers would have honored.*

Near to me was another tree stump that became—was I seeing it right? Yes, absolutely—a crèche, a manger. Joseph was there with his staff and the

animals and all. "Francis, get a load of this," I commented—since he is cred-
ited with inventing this object of veneration. How peaceful and, above all,
amazing this illuminated forest seemed, and how natural that Mary and Son
should be in a tree right alongside a deer and how on the other side there
would be a manger. I said, "My whole Cosmic Christ book is coming alive."
This is quite a show.

As the sun set, the only light was directly above me, at the tops of certain
tall trees. What did I see when I looked up? A ceiling where each opening to
the night sky was a face of an ancient mask such as Aztecs and Incas or the
people of the coastal regions (as Buck reminded me afterward) created. Some
were large, like on a battle shield, and some were more clearly mask-sized.

Then the space between the upper trees glowed and I realized I was in a
cathedral—these were stained glass. "So this is how medievals invented
stained glass," I said, "—by being in the forest at night." The cathedral was
aglow with all these creatures—who are spirits that Buck (and Hildegard
too!) calls angels and archangels, and this ceiling of amazing faces and these
towering windows also lit up between the trees. Yet, it was sacred. A good
place to be. I danced before the manger. The young Indian men came to the
other side of the hill and sang Indian chants for all us "questers," and they
sang some of my favorite ones from the Rosebud Sun Dance. After the
singers left, I realized how my heart had been touched so deeply by their
(surprise) visit. I was serenaded—by three men no less—in an ancient tongue
with an ancient song. How wonderful if in our neighborhoods we could do
that every night—bands of wandering singers singing us to sleep. Sacred
songs for sacred dreams. When they left, I heard songs from women, on the
hill perhaps and elsewhere. Someone sang "A Rose" (Bob Fox's favorite
song). Then I wanted to sing. I sang some Gregorian chant—first the Good
Friday piece with words altered, for example, "Aleph—Listen to the voice of
the poisoned water and weep for your children. Humanity, humanity, be
converted and love your Mother Earth." With slight changes to "soil," "air,"
etc. Then a Sanctus and Agnus Dei. Then I sang the Peter, Paul, and Mary
song that goes something like this:

> Jesus, he died on Calvary street.
> Nails in his feet.
> Mary, she rocked him, little baby to sleep.
> Still though he died like a tramp on the street.

I had with this song—so nonelitist and simple—a glimpse of why I was a
Christian. How could anyone object to this amazing story and fail to understand it—poor child, good man, killed like a tramp on the street. Why oh
why has Christianity made it all so complicated?

I saw a dark cross near my location and near the manger, and I danced a dance to the tune of one of those Indian dances (after the chanters had left). I made up words something like: "For the first time someone is dancing before the cross." Yes, we must dance before the cross, not just gaze at it.

Buck told me when we discussed this experience afterward that the lighted creatures were spirits of the creatures—all of whom had sometime before lived on the land—and they were showing their support for my work. "Sometimes leaders feel lonely," he said—a grand understatement indeed. "But now you know you are never alone."

The dance of green lighted figures lasted, it seemed, until the light was totally extinguished in the forest. The light-colored flags—Francis's white especially, but also Julian's yellow and Hildegard's rather chartreuse green—glowed for a long time. But then came immense, utter darkness. I could not see my feet even, or where my tobacco ties were—I thought I might have stepped on them in the dark as I stumbled around, singing, praying, sitting, shooing mosquitoes off my hands without killing them. I wrestled with my blanket, for it was cold and damp and my sore back was feeling it. The blanket allowed me to put my hands underneath it and thus avoid the mosquitoes. But it was clumsy holding that from the inside and also trying to hold the pipe. The rattle, which I used a lot when I wasn't burdened by the blanket, I let rest in the dark (besides, I couldn't see it anyway).

Now I understood Eckhart's "God is superessential darkness"; I was in it. I realized that a shadow is a positive thing. It moves and evolves with the setting of the sun and it changes shapes and forms—it is alive. Darkness is not just absence but a moving form that covers the earth every sixteen hours or so.

Also, an icon appeared that was distinctly African—two black figures standing together—framed, it seemed, as in an icon of the Madonna figure. They seemed to be two male adults. Trans-African, Druid-goddess, and Celtic were represented along with Christian and Native American. We were having all the fun in this enchanted forest and the Vatican structure, highly fortified and heavy with moss like an abandoned museum or fortress, was not close enough to the earth to join us. A theological thought occurred after the Thanksgiving ritual: is not all prayer of petition in reality a prayer of Thanksgiving? For we only petition on behalf of what we in some way cherish as blessing—but that is Thanksgiving, gratitude for the blessing. When we petition without thanks we are mere spiritual consumers.

For the three or four hours that the forest was completely dark and almost totally still—save for my mosquito companions—I would alternatively sit, stand, dance. But my legs were very tired from dancing (the ground was not at all smooth), and it was so dark I felt I might be trampling on prayer ties. *My throat was so sore from singing and from lack of water that I had to keep my singing out loud from then on to a minimum. I began to get very sleepy and repeated Jesus' words—"could you not keep watch with me" this night? I did manage, it seems, to stay awake; "keeping watch."*

Finally the light began to emerge—first the white flag of the South and Francis picked it up; then the yellow and the green flags. I was very happy to see the dawn. Then, to my surprise, the images reappeared, and new ones as well. The Madonna and Child were back, with the deer that looked up at them. Many clowns appeared—smiling, funny, and even goofy faces. "What is that up in the top of the tree? Is it he? Yes!" It was Ernie, the Sesame Street *character, smiling at me from on high. Misatola, Buck's dog, was there—no question it was he lit up in a green leaf.*

I asked some questions of the spirits. "Should Brian and I start a ritual center?" The reply was a figure, lit up in green leaves, of the ancient theater symbol—two masks, one of which was smiling. "What about a life of some intimacy for myself?" A beautiful sculpturelike leafy figure (Rodin-like) of a naked man "flying" through the air after another person. It was graceful and beautiful.

The mosquitoes ever since the sun came up were ferocious and aggressive. They, plus my tiredness and sore throat and thirst, were getting to me. I was eager to come "off the hill" and get grounded again in the sweat, for I was beginning to get somewhat concerned about all the images that kept appearing every place I looked. I seemed overwhelmed by it all. I actually ceased asking questions and ceased looking—preferring to shut my eyes or look at the ground. Waiting, waiting for deliverance—now I knew what redemption meant—being take off the hill.

But it didn't come and didn't come. Singers came and I was sure that deliverance would shortly follow. Not so.

My mood had changed from Via Positiva *and exhilaration to hardly praying at all—a kind of waiting-for-the-bus attitude. I was emptied. Spent. Exhausted. Tired. Desolate. Though the sun was on the rise, the dark night of the soul was taking over. I accused myself of not appreciating what a beautiful experience the night had offered. It seemed like I had no prayer left in me. I was not sure if I would ever have energy again. Instead of dancing, I paced in order to throw off the mosquitoes a bit.*

It was then that I noticed for the first time a peculiar and striking thing. A mask, made it seemed of leaves, partially burnt and torn, lay next to the feather stick Buck had given me. The mask lay three-quarters out of my ring of prayer and one-quarter inside, as if it had fallen there. It was ugly and sinister with big teeth. I stared at it. I was with it for some time. Then I looked around, and around three out of four sides of my prayer circle there were masks—all of them ugly, all of them burnt or partially split down the mid-dle. Most were on the side of the eagle stick, which was by the blue flag of Creator God, i.e., southwest, between Eckhart's and Francis's flags (near Aquinas's). The next largest number were between Francis and Julian, i.e., southeast. And just a few were outside the green flag or Hildegard . . . of the east and earth. There were none in the direction of northwest, i.e., between Mechthild and Eckhart. Interestingly, that was the direction I faced 95 per-cent of the time when I sat on the log, for it was the only way I could face while sitting on that log with any comfort (sitting the opposite way I would fall off). I take the first mask I saw to be the "zap" I heard when I first sat down in the woods. It is interesting that I first said to myself when I began, "That area behind my right shoulder is where trouble will come from if it comes."

Buck explained to me afterward that he and his elders felt I would be at-tacked by negative forces from the Vatican, and that is why I was given the special eagle-defense prayer stick. He told me the right place to put it, that is for sure!

I was amazed to see all these "fallen leaves" of menacing masks. I had not really felt any attacks during the night other than mosquitoes, tiredness, weariness, sore throat, and depression as the morning dragged on. I guess I was too busy praying to see the battle going on around me. As Buck says, "It shows we have defeated and can defeat these bad attacks." And that is so. Not one of those menacing masks got into the prayer circle.

Buck says that humans create evil forces out of their hatred, but that all of it can be defeated by prayer and courage. These evil forces prey on fear. How important! So much fear runs the world, that of fundamentalism for example. Only when fear lets the evil in does evil happen. Thus, the impor-tance of spirituality—to build the strength, the big heart (courage)—based on faith, i.e., trust, which is the opposite of fear—that combats evil success-fully.

This seems to have happened on the hill.

By the time the rescuers came—preceded by a beautiful song from a bird—I was silent, hurting but in some way strong, yet doubting about my ability to get through the day. Returning to the sweat lodge site, one noticed a lot of supportive people. But all I wanted was to be in the sweat. I was shivering with cold. My muscles were very sore from the damp night on the hill.

The sweat healed body, soul, and mind. Even my throat felt better. Fol-lowing that, I was allowed my first drink of water and my first chance to pee in twenty-five hours. Then came a meal. Did food ever taste so good? And some brief sharing of our experiences "on the hill."

One lesson learned—or reaffirmed: that spirituality is indeed about strength.

Pilgrimages

During my year of silence I did a lot of reading and considerable traveling, including trips to South America for the first time. I spent time with Leonardo Boff in Brazil and found him to be as deep and warm as he is strong and clear. I attended the twentieth anniversary of the base communities, a gathering of thousands of people near Rio de Janeiro where Boff spoke and I met his brother, Clodius Boff. I also met the bishop-poet of the Amazon Indians, Pedro Casadaliga, who came to the gathering with a quiver of arrows on his back, a symbol representing his people. Later I visited him in his diocese in the Amazon basin (the trip included a thirteen-hour bus ride standing up all the way). Over his bed was a charcoal drawing of him, sketched by a priest in his prison cell who was tortured to death shortly after finishing the drawing. On a wall of his house—which he shares with four other persons, men and women—are mementos or relics of persons working with him in the diocese who have been tortured and killed. Dozens of such relics. I was struck by a shoebox on top of a locker that served as the file cabinet for his episcopal papers, and I was especially struck by the prominence of art. "Art is everywhere," I wrote in my journal, from the simple refitting of a vacuous room into their cathedral, to the mementos of prisoners, to the Negro Mass that Pedro himself composed and recorded but which the Vatican forbade them to celebrate ever again. In the backyard is their chapel—a large tree with a bench underneath where they all gather to pray and reflect.

Why so much opposition to his ministry? Because Bishop Pedro and his people are standing up for justice and the rights of the endangered rain-forest Indians *and* the endangered rain forest. Taking a boat trip up the river, we received a fuller flavor of the jungle area. Its wildness and wisdom were everywhere apparent, from exotic birds and fishes to alligators and cranes and sandbars on which all sorts of animals beached alongside our canoes.

During the week we were in town there was a gathering of about eighty church workers, all of whom were both heroes and ordinary people. At one mass dedicated to "our martyred ones," everyone lit a candle and pronounced two names of persons they had known who had been tortured and killed defending the rain forest and its people. Afterward a participant told me that the hard part was limiting it to two names—he knew at least ten martyrs. A young Jesuit priest spoke to me about his life on an island with a rain-forest tribe whose special totem is the monkey—they pray with the monkeys, eat monkeys, include them in their ceremonies. He had learned their language and was thoroughly immersed in their way of life. But he had one problem: "I don't know what I'm doing there," he said. "I don't know what I have to give them."

"But what are they giving to you?" I asked.

Immediately he responded, "*La joie*. They experience more joy in a day than my people do in a month."

I also visited Dominican bishop Tomás Balduino, who works with the *campesinos* in Brazil and who is the bishop's representative on land-rights issues in Brazil. One of his helpers drove us in a jeep over the most rugged terrain I would ever expect to drive on this side of the moon—rocks jutting up from the invisible road everywhere—to an encampment where the poor lived in huts with mud floors and no basics whatsoever. A woman I met who looked about sixty-five turned out to be about thirty. These people's encampment is raided periodically by the landowners or their hired thugs just to intimidate them and to kill the young men in the village if they feel like it. Yet the dignity of the people was everywhere evident. They had built a school for their young people—education was all-important to them. And they kept their places clean and neat, even though pigs and chickens roamed freely through their dirt-floored homes. We spent several hours talking and laughing with them. Their hospitality was overwhelming, their willingness to share what meager gifts they had to share. As did so many did in Brazil, they begged us to "tell our story to your people."

In Brazil I experienced a church that knows what solidarity means. A church of martyrs whose blood today is flowing like blood once flowed in Rome for the faith. The faith of these saints in America today is that of people truly committed to one another and to justice for the poor and for creation itself. I remember especially three points that Leonardo Boff made in our conversation. First, he was learning English in order to study the new cosmology. "I've been writing about the mystery of the church for twenty years," he said, "but the mystery of the cosmos is where the true power lies. And this is being told us by scientists writing in English." Second, though I did not raise this subject, he did: "Don't voluntarily leave the Dominican order," he said. "Let them kick you out. It will be a moment of education for the people." And third, he said he would not go silent a second time, "for it is against human dignity." My sentiments exactly.

I was deeply moved by the courage and vision of the hierarchy I met. Cardinal Arns was the one who kept all the records on the civil-rights abuses and torture that the Brazilian military dictatorship was involved in for fourteen years. I was surprised to hear him say, "The future of the church is in ecumenism," because I had never envisioned South America as particularly an ecumenical place. Arns supported Leonardo Boff and the base-community movement to the hilt—he even went to Rome with Boff when he was subjected to an inquisition there, and I believe his pressure and intervention in Rome helped reduce Boff's "sentence" of silence from a year to a few months. The Vatican persecuted Arns by dividing up his diocese and putting him in charge not of the poor population, which was where his heart was, but of the rich sector of the city. In the end, not even Arns could withhold the tide of envy and right-wing pressure that eventually drove Boff first from his teaching position, next from his magazine editorship, and finally from the priesthood itself.

My trip to Brazil was moving and powerful, frustrating and emptying. Seeing mile after mile of the hovels and shantytowns in which so many people are trying to live and survive as one goes down the highway is sobering. Seeing the thousands of young people abandoned on the streets of Rio looking for means to survive—and realizing that in Latin America half the population is under fifteen years of age—all this was sobering in the extreme. Learning that 5 percent of the population is rich and 15 percent middle-class, and seeing bullet-ridden bodies in gutters along the highway, victims of crimes that I am told the police will never bother to investigate. Learning from these people that 70 percent of Catholics live in the third world and only 30 percent in the first world, and that 50 percent of the Catholics are in Latin America. Seeing these people stretch and breathe and wake up to their own power, especially the women, whom a cultural air of machismo has kept down for centuries. Seeing and breathing the pollution in the air and in the water, seeing the topsoil disappearing as well as the native populations, looking out from a small airplane on the rising plumes of smoke as the rain forests are burned down—all this is beyond sobering. The consciousness of the people puts North Americans to shame. When the Rio summit a few years later became an occasion for some northerners to realize for the first time the real ecological consciousness of the two-thirds of the world living in poverty, I was not at all surprised. Only embarrassed at my government's (Bush and company) hiding its head in the sand on these issues of survival that affect all of us and all of our children.

My final entry in my journal from that visit follows.

July 23

Has this trip been a Pilgrimage or Tourism? I think, pilgrimage, for at least two sound reasons. First, because we stayed in people's homes the entire trip, with only one restaurant meal (this two nights ago to relieve the amount of cooking our hosts have been doing for us). And, second, because I am seeking with my heart open. That is how I would define a pilgrim—seeking with one's heart open. A pilgrim seeks—looking for something. (I'm thinking of Thomas Merton's last journey to Asia.) I have been seeking—is this why the trip really began with my vision quest a week before we left the country? But what have I been seeking? I am not even sure of that. Connections? Solidarity? Concretizing of the suffering and the celebration of the earth and the

*peoples—all of us earth—in the "third world"? Creation of my own work
for the disadvantaged? Evidence of creation spirituality among the world's
poor? Challenges to us "first-world" people?*

*All this I have found—or has it found me once again?—and more. It is
the "more" that convinces me of the pilgrim nature of this trip. The pilgrim
needs the Sacred—which is always "more" in the sense of bigger than ourselves (transcendence not as "up" but as great). I find persons here—theologians, bishops, priests, campesinos, organizers and sisters, parents and
children—who dance with death every day, yet remain grounded. They are
big. Martyrdom has moved from Rome (surely the last religious martyrs
there were seventeen hundred years ago) to the New World. From their
blood a new church is indeed being born. It is a joy to be a part of it. Perhaps my "vocation" will be renewed in this context.*

I also made a trip to Nicaragua, where the American-sponsored war of
contras against the Sandinistas was still raging. The occasion was the tenth
anniversary of the Sandinista revolution, and Jerry Stookey, a committed Dominican from my province who had been living in Central America for several years, was our guide. We were privileged to attend an outdoor mass celebrating the tenth anniversary. The president of the country, Daniel Ortega,
was in the front row and singing all the songs at the mass—hardly the "atheistic Communist leader" that the North American press and politicians painted
him to be. It was telling that three bishops led the mass but not one of them
was Nicaraguan—they came from Mexico. The Vatican had so split the
church in Nicaragua that there were clearly two churches: the people's and
the pope's. Following the mass, the president went into the church and faced
a totally honest barrage of questions from ordinary people (all his cabinet members were there as well). I remember one woman complaining that women
were not represented well enough in his cabinet; another, that the elderly were
being ignored. Again, this totally ungerrymandered "town hall" with the
president of the country did not exactly jibe with my country's images of a
ruthless dictator. I had never experienced such democracy vis-à-vis my own
president back home.

Another high point was visiting Ernesto Cardenal, cultural minister of the
government and former student of Thomas Merton at Gethsemani Abbey.
(On leaving the abbey Cardenal had founded a colony for artists on an island
off the Nicaraguan coast, and Somoza had actually *bombed* the village. This
is the Somoza that the United States government supported for forty years.)
Cardenal spoke of his latest work, *El Cántico Cósmico,* a 600-page poem
telling the new creation story of the universe from the initial fireball through
to the Sandinista revolution. It had me vastly excited, and later we were able

to translate some pages of it in our magazine. (It now exists in English in its entirety.)⁴

Ernesto, a lively-eyed, white-bearded, young-souled revolutionary still, was a joy to be around. He led me into his library, which was also his bedroom, and showed me his newest interest: a telescope that he was just putting together. He was like a child eager to see the stars up close for the first time. In addition, he showed me his books, and there on the bookshelf were works by my mentors: Erich Jantsch's *Self-Organizing Universe* and Brian Swimme's *The Universe Is a Green Dragon,* Fritjof Capra and others. All of them living in the Bay Area. I was struck by how ironic it was that a man whose *second* language is English, who is from one of the poorest countries in our hemisphere, and whose country is at war found the time and interest and *passion* to read English-speaking scientists, to realize the momentous meaning that a new creation story has for us, and to write an epic poem about it. Where are the English-speaking poets? Why are they not writing about the new creation story? Have we no sense of cosmology left? And of the relation of cosmology to liberation? Enlightenment-trained leftists would complain that my work wasn't "social-justice oriented" enough—but here where the left had *done something,* has overthrown a perverse dictatorship of forty years' standing, they found the wisdom and the energy to announce the new creation story to the people.

Also moving was a visit to the Alphabet Museum, where a history was kept of the early years of the Sandinista government (before the American-led contra war began) when the government set literacy as one of its main goals. Their strategy was to send teenagers who read into hamlets and villages to teach reading to others, especially the older ones. Illiteracy dropped from 80 percent to 13 percent in that three-year period, and what is more, the young made sacrifices (several who lost their lives in the rugged areas were remembered in this museum), underwent a kind of rite of passage, served the greater community. The origins of that revolution had truly been filled with hope before it was all sidetracked by the war.

Two other experiences in Nicaragua stand out for me. One was a visit to an ecological museum that told of the destruction of topsoil and forests over the past twenty-five years in that land. Of course, American multinational fruit companies were largely responsible for that horrible loss—a loss that includes loss of animals and birds as well as soil for farming and that creates devastating floods and more soil erosion. This situation is repeated countless times in countries the world over, and the starvation and floods that await so many people from Bangladesh to India to Indonesia to Africa to Central America are in no way unrelated to the ripping off of forests and topsoil achieved by multinationals. I met with an American scientist and Methodist missionary in

Nicaragua, Howard Heiner, who had lived there for years gathering the sobering data he shared with me. Since 1950, 75 percent of Nicaragua's forests have been destroyed. From him I learned that today the bulk of the deforestation comes from cattle raising to feed the U.S. hamburger market and that banks, including the World Bank, were behind the destruction of much of the rain forest of Central America. He said, "The misery and the death which this [destruction] portends to me for the generations to come is frightening. . . . It really doesn't matter whether we espouse capitalism, communism, or some other 'ism'; humankind must face the fact that we are destroying the earth."[5]

Another learning moment was standing over the still-smoking volcano where President Somoza had helicoptered his political enemies and thrown them in to their deaths. I will never forget that place—and my complicity in it as an American citizen. Our government supported that cruel man and his family and henchmen for forty years—and then continued to support his bodyguards and political allies who made up the contra forces after his dismissal by the Sandinista revolution. And of course I will never forget the poor in their mud huts, who were being organized to run enterprises such as chicken cooperatives by good people, including some Catholic sisters. These sisters, however, could let no one know they were sisters—*not* because the poor would object but *because the cardinal, the pope's man in Nicaragua, would have them deported.* I brought this point up to Cardenal, saying, "You seem to have two churches here—that of the people and that of the pope," He laughed heartily. "It is that way everywhere," he said, "in Holland, in North America, everywhere. It's just that we are so poor that it is more visible here."

A month after returning home I wrote a few thoughts in my journal about what I called my "trip south."

Human rights—this is the issue in Latin America and in the church. We must emphasize the latter and struggle for its implementation. Otherwise, the church is in schism from the gospel.

The courage and beauty and faith of the people of Latin America, today's "church of the martyrs," is a sign of their spiritual leadership. We cannot just imitate them up north—we have to find our own path—but we can be in deep communion, support one another, and learn from one another.

Creation spirituality has much to offer, resonates deeply with their experience, traditions, and struggle. The struggle out of colonialism—five hundred years old, and now mostly North American colonialism—is also the struggle of women, blacks, Indians, the young the world over. And in our country. I feel my new book on Liberating First Worlders being born soon.

Within a year (1990) I wrote the book *Creation Spirituality: Liberating Gifts for the Peoples of the Earth.* The book is my thank-you to my brothers and sisters in the south and my expression of solidarity with them. I begin with a story from a Costa Rican I met who urged me to write about the liberation of North Americans, for, he said, we in the south have gone about as far as we can go in liberating ourselves. We are stuck until you northerners start doing your own liberation. The book was truly my response to my trips abroad during my silencing, especially my interaction with the liberation and base-community movements of South America. The essence of my approach was to underscore the *deep differences* between liberating North Americans and liberating South and Central Americans. Our historical, sociological, religious, economic, and political contexts were so different from those of the southern nations. (Is *context* another word for *culture?*) For years North Americans had been translating liberation theology from the south into English, but what had really altered up north? Why had liberation theology taken so little foothold in the north? Might it be that translations were not enough; that *we had to create our own base communities and our own liberation from our own particular demons?* And what are those demons that are unique to us? Try addiction first and foremost. We are the culture enmeshing ourselves in addictions of all kinds: drugs (U.S. citizens use 64 percent of the illicit drugs in the world though we make up only 4 percent of the global population), alcohol, shopping, sports, television, work, relationships, sex, religion—you name it, we know how to become addicted to it. And so our liberation must begin with an analysis of what our slavery is. And we must create our own version of base communities—which in fact we have been doing for some time without calling them that. For example, AA and its many successful spin-offs; hospice; womenchurch; men's groups; and so forth.

Though I emphasize the differences between our culture and those of the south, I also use the analysis of Leonardo Boff regarding the road to liberation and how that can be translated into our context at a level of understanding that is deeper than the lame rhetoric for which the north's self-isolating left wing so easily settles. I also discuss areas of similarity between the Americas and what a "spirituality of the Americas" might look like. Such common ground as wilderness; history of oppression; search for alternative education; wisdom of native peoples—all these characterize the American spiritual experience, north and south. Indeed the very interest in *spirituality* is a gift that could help move European religion–based churches to new levels of depth and life.

A few years later, when I was invited to Costa Rica and to a daylong seminar with theological instructors there, I was all the more moved by the reception that creation spirituality received among the poor and those working with the poor. Theologians in Costa Rica understand immediately (as do the Irish) the connection between liberation and cosmology. A similar awareness was evident among the fighters for human rights in the Philippines. When I taught there in the spring of 1995, I was deeply shocked by the level of ecological devastation and its relation to the colonizing of the indigenous peoples and everyone else—floods are occurring and temperatures are rising all over the islands because of the destruction of the forests. Brazilian liberation theologian Leonardo Boff also addresses this issue in his recent book, *Ecology and Liberation*, a book that demonstrates a deep alliance between liberation theology and creation spirituality.

During my year of silence I also took a trip to Holland. I wanted to seek the Dutch Dominicans' advice on how to deal with Rome and the order. I found in them what I had experienced in Paris with Fr. Chenu years before: a sense of the importance of ideas and social justice and the humor and humane camaraderie that links all of them. A kind of beautiful déjà vu descended on me of what it meant to be a Dominican. It was most refreshing. And it inspired me to fight all the harder to stay in the order. When I first walked up the steps of their large priory, the Albertinum, in Nijmegen, I was met by a retired though very lively biblical scholar whose first words were, through a deep smile, "Original blessing. Yes, you are an original blessing!" He had actually read my book! And understood it. And appreciated it. I was touched to meet Dominicans who wanted to discuss seriously my ideas as a theologian. Their solidarity was real and contagious, and I owe deep thanks to the provincial, Fr. Piet Struik, and his assistant provincials, Wim Nielen and Karl Derksen (whom I knew from the Trier movement twenty years earlier). They were resourceful and real, and they even offered me what they called "religious asylum" in Holland. Though a tempting offer, it would have meant giving up my work in California because my provincial would not allow this to happen unless I left the United States permanently (later he withdrew even that option and said he wouldn't allow it under any circumstances).

A few years later in a conversation with Fr. Schillebeeckx, who is now retired from teaching, I was moved when he told me he is now writing about creation theology as well. He had begun his career teaching in the late forties on creation and was going to make it a full circle and return to that subject.

Another memorable moment for me during this year was my stopping by Marshfield, Massachusetts, where the ocean had kept me in the order nineteen years earlier. I asked the ocean for a dream that night to help guide my way—something I very seldom do—and a special dream did indeed emerge. It was that same ocean, I was on that same beach, and it was nighttime. A silver moon shone from a silver sky on the all-silver ocean. And out of the ocean there emerged Adrienne Rich in a silver wet suit. She said nothing but she pointed at her knee. It was a very transcendent dream, still, quiet, and totally bathed in silver. Clarissa Pinkola Estés says that silver represents an archaeological layer in the old wild feminine and the color bespeaks the spirit world and the moon.[6] The knee represents prayer (*genou*—which rhymes with Chenu—is the French word for "knee," and from it we get the word *genuflection*). In addition, the knee connects us to the earth, pulls us *down,* and is also part of our *flexibility.* Flexibility was one of the lessons this same sea had instructed me in years ago. Adrienne Rich, of course, is one of the premier feminist poets and thinkers of our day and certainly one of the most important poets in my life. Emerging from the sea as she did, she represented the Magna Mater, the great mother of the sea, the return to our origins in *la mère, la mer* (mother, sea). Sophia, lady wisdom, also seemed to be speaking in the dream. The beauty of the dream and its simple message seemed to be encouraging me not to abandon my work in bringing the feminine and the mystical back to religion and culture. The dream healed.

Two other trips awaited me. One was to the south of France to visit the twelfth-century church at Vézelay and other goddess shrines. I had always been moved by Chartres and Reims cathedrals and others like them dedicated to the goddess, that is, to Mary, in the twelfth century. I learned on this trip that the twelfth-century French carved and hauled more stone than did the Egyptians to build their pyramids! On the way to Vézelay we stopped at Reims, Laon, Noyon, and Amiens. At Laon precedence in the cathedral is given to the *ox*en without whom the stones would not have been dragged to town and up the hill to build the temple—a fine example of nonanthropocentrism here, to put numerous statues of *ox*en on the top of the front twin towers of the cathedral. At Vézelay, Bernard preached the Second Crusade and Thomas à Becket and Joan of Arc visited. There is where Mary Magdalene's remains are supposedly interred. Vézelay was so much more primitive in every way than these more consciously constructed cathedrals that it held its own power and its own reminders of that goddess energy that swept France and indeed much of Europe in the twelfth century. It had everything to do with what Chenu meant when he said the renaissance of that century "was the only one that succeeded" in the West. It was people-centered, earth-based, carried by peasants and freed serfs, by women and the young. It included the green man as well as the mother goddess. And it gave us the invention of universities and cities, new styles of living in community, and a new theology and a new marriage of theology and science. It eventually resulted in the Franciscan and Dominican orders. But seeing and feeling the earth-based energy of these temples while hiking up their craggy precipices was a special experience for me.

When we continued on to Italy to visit Florence and Assisi and then Rome, I took the goddess experience of France with me. Standing in the large sixteenth-century piazza at St. Peter's at the Vatican, I said out loud to myself, "I am not a Roman Catholic so much as a twelfth-century French Catholic." It was Chartres that kept me in the church; not Rome. It was the goddess, not the inquisitors fighting to keep their version of "God" enthroned on high, legitimizing their clerical privileges and lifestyle. It was panentheism and the entire mystical tradition of our saints, not theism and its tradition of crusades, pogroms, witch burnings, gay burnings, and inquisitions.

April 1—Rome

The ruins of the pre-Christian Empire are everywhere, shouting at you from every lone brick. But then there are also the ruins of the Christian era. Two churches per block seems to be the rule. Yet how many are used today other than as museums to relocate the past? And of these churches, how many depict any architectural truth other than triumphalism and egoism and defensiveness?

It hardly matters, perhaps. For the era has surely ended, that of "all roads leading to Rome" and of Roman hegemony in spiritual leadership—today's martyrs are not Christian scapegoats thrown to the lions in the Coliseum but other kinds of scapegoats—ministers, women, homosexuals, third-world peoples—thrown to the lions of our church and society. One does not regret the past, yet it is important not to live in it or wallow in it. Or to relive it as if life and creation and God do not expect new and fresh and daring things of us today. Our spiritual centers will be, not the place of ecclesial bureaucracies, but where the new cosmology is being articulated and celebrated. Hopefully, a global network of such spiritual centers will bear rich fruit.

The Vatican

Marble, marble everywhere. No ounce of nature from the piazza through to the high altar. All is cold marble. All is man-over-nature. Concrete and marble, marble and concrete. Our inheritance from the sixteenth-century Renaissance. Man-over-nature. Man the measure of man. The future of the church does not lie here—in marble.

The future of the church lies in the flesh, in the fur, in the spirit, in the heart. A totally different church-center awaits us. Where heart meets heart, where hearts expand, where body (heart's home) meets body (soul's home too) awakening spirit.

One unexpected result of the visit has been the letting go of anxieties I may have had should Ratzinger call me to Rome. I understand better the worldview in which he sits and over which he presides. It is ridiculous and dead, but it obviously feeds a need in him. His world is one of the "grandeur that was Greece and the glory that was Rome." It is of marble and of museums and of ruins.

My work on the other hand is more subtle than that—trying to discover the Spirit in historical events, bodily events, the signs of our times, the movements of our times—and to connect this with our heritage, tradition, past and future. America is a great place to be engaging in this connection-making. It is important that we feel our Roman and French and European roots for all their glory, grandeur, and weaknesses. Yet we must also forge anew and especially with third-world peoples and with the Crucified One, Mother Earth. Marble makes for good, man-made laws that seem endurable eternally: "The pope is ruler of the universe" wrote a theologian at the time St. Peter's came to be. But our work today is with people and especially the imagination, hope, and fears of the young. And with the cosmos. How rare to find birds or animals, for example, represented there—yet in a twelfth-century cathedral it's impossible not to!

Santa Maria Maggiore
Ceiling is gold from America. St. John Lateran—ceiling is gold from Peru. So it goes. The plundering of the "New World" to serve the European appetites. How it continues! How the lesson has been learned by North American secular institutions—now engaged in similar plundering of . . . rain forests, land. When will it stop? How many Native Americans were made slaves so European churches could boast of their riches? Today the plundering persists vis-à-vis American money and the sacking of theological ideas.

We met one of the world's truly unhappy priests as our guide in the catacombs of St. Sabastian. He kept putting down "the pagans" as he calls them, and even said that Hindus, Native Americans, and other pagans worshiped the swastika—making no distinction between Hitler's swastika and the ancient symbols. So righteous was he that one wonders where all these anti-pagan Christians were during the heyday of Mussolini's and Franco's and Hitler's fascism. His theology was as appalling as his history, but above all it was his persecution complex, his wounded-child-as-killer-adult, and his utter unhappiness that came through so loud and clear to all visitors. A genuine scandal. A sad case. How often is it repeated in today's clergy? What can liberate them from this system? . . .

Have the catacombs and the three hundred years of persecution in Rome and the subsequent overthrow of this state of affairs rendered the Roman church ever so eager for Augustine's theology of church as Kingdom and of dualism and of emphasis on Fall and Redemption versus creation? It would appear so. A certain necrophilia is in the air where too much emphasis on catacombs overthrows a grasp of faith and creation. Asceticism and a flight to the desert was one response to a too successful Christian empire. Today

different responses are in order. Study must be reunderstood as a basic asce-
sis or spiritual practice (Dominic and Aquinas grasped this). Having plun-
dered America's gold and imprisoned or wiped out her native populations,
now they want to canonize Fr. Junípero Serra, who set up the most effective
of all systems to accomplish the decimation of native populations. Why? Is it
one last effort to assert their power? The Roman Empire versus the Ameri-
can Indian? Whatever the intention, hidden or unhidden, the whole thing is
a deep disgrace and is shameful to the core. When will the European coloniz-
ing of America and the papal colonizing of America cease?

The final leg of this journey was a gift I prepared for my own soul. I had never been to Greece and my heart was especially set on visiting the island of Crete, the land where the goddess culture had not been totally obliterated. Would there be messages there for my own soul as it hungered for more than patriarchy could give me?

I was not disappointed. On Crete, with its blue, blue sea and its tiny white Orthodox chapels that house a sense of religious mystery still, and above all with the Temple and Knossos and the local museum filled with statuaries from the time of the goddess religion, I felt a deep kinship. Food for my soul. How startled I was to stand before six-thousand-year-old statuettes of a woman priestess leading a circle dance of worshipers—"just like ICCS," I re-marked. We were involved in something very ancient, very real. We were part of a great remembering. It must not be allowed to fail; it must not be snuffed out still another time by patriarchy's fears and power games. At Crete I think I made deeper resolves to keep ICCS going no matter what the opposition.

April 5—Crete!
The night voyage was memorable for its simplicity and beauty. When I woke
up to the arrival of Crete out our port-side window, that was very moving.
Visited the powerful and rich site of Knossos, the oldest ruling palace in
Western civilization. Most elaborate and impressive, especially when juxta-
posed with the excellent archaeological museum in Icartharus. The role of
women in the Minoan civilization in particular stands out. First, the queen's
rooms in the palace, so ample and beautifully laid out on a par with the
king's rooms. Then, the important role that the priestess played, as is clear
from frescoes of ceremonies wherein men and women bring offerings and
dance with musical instruments to the priestess.

I also visited Delphi and found this ancient place of the goddess and oracle to be a very moving setting. One can appreciate what the rugged journey to the top of the mountain meant to pilgrims of old. Of course the layers of subsequent ideologies and inhabitants of the mountain were also clear to see. A journal entry follows.

April 8—Athens Airport
Delphi was deeply moving. Yet the remnant of the goddess times is the stone of Sybil or Chair of Sybil—a huge rock on which the original Sybil prophesied. The temple to Athena at the bottom of the hill (below Apollo's and the gymnasium) also celebrated the goddess. (I just learned this morning that the Parthenon was itself constructed on a former temple to the goddess.) All this is living proof—as if more were needed—of the success the masculine religion had in displacing and in many cases dismantling the feminine religion. Though both epochs boast their power and gifts as well as their sins of excesses, what we yearn for today is a combination of the best the feminine can give us and the best the masculine can give us. And let us leave aside the sinful dimensions of both.

Delphi was deeply impressive—the road to Thebes is so striking with the rich valley of agriculture all around it. It was not made easy, this spiritual journey or pilgrimage to the "navel of the earth." The mountain roads even today present their challenge to the voyager—imagine how it must have been twenty-five hundred years ago! Yet they came. The leaders and politicians, the youth and the aged—for some spiritual insight, for help in discernment, for refreshment. The Greeks were not a secularized people. Nor are they today, judging from the number of churches, all well kept up, and the casual encounters I have had with Greeks in cities and countryside while here.

"Navel of the earth"—how much that sounds like "cathedra," throne, center of the universe from which twelfth-century cathedrals to Mary derive their power. And like Israel's temple, "center of the universe." Clearly a cosmology was at work among the Greek peoples. As among early Christians and twelfth-century Christians. Can we retrieve a cosmology? That is the question, the spiritual and moral question of our time. For if we don't, drugs and despair, addictions and denial will continue to overtake us, and the best of our youth—those rebelling against boredom and despair—will all end up in jail.

The aspect of my trip to Greece that most surprised me was the Parthenon. I had expected the flat hill overlooking Athens to be quite secularized and museumlike, but in fact I felt spiritual energy at that site that pleasantly surprised me.

These were some of the pilgrimages I took during my year of silence. As one friend said to me recently, "You were silent but you were not still." I was gathering nourishment for the next round of struggle. I would need all I could get. The travel, plus the broad amount of reading I was able to undertake that year, allowed me to gather nourishment like a squirrel gathers nuts before winter arrives; or a bear eats heartily before hibernation.

Lessons Learned

In the eleventh month of my twelve months of silence, I received a letter from a woman who said, "I was a Catholic and left the church over its treatment of women. Then I read your work and felt there was some room for me in the church and returned to it. Now, when they silenced you, I felt they were silencing me all over again, for I have always felt, as a woman, silenced in the Catholic church. I was so upset by this experience that it has taken me these eleven months just to be able to write you a letter of support." Again, a lesson in the archetypal feelings behind human beings silencing other human beings.

My last week of silence I spent alone with Tristan at Bodega Bay buried in Thomas Aquinas's Latin tomes, specifically his commentary on Isaiah. On the very eve of the end of my silencing, I was studying his commentary on Isaiah 62, which says, "Do not keep silent in Zion." Aquinas's comment on this text follows.

> Take note of the saying in Isaiah, "On account of Sion I will not be silent." The saints are not silent—first, because of their burning desire, as Jeremiah says (20): "And the word of the Lord was shut up in my heart, like a seething fire." Second, on account of evident truth, as Acts says (4): "For we cannot speak of the things we do not see." Third, because of required duty, as in 1 Cor. (9): "Necessity lies upon me: for woe is me if I do not preach the good news." Fourth, because of an expected reward, as in Galatians (6.9): "Let us not be deficient in doing good; for if we do not give up, we shall have our harvest at the proper time."[7]

Surely this passage played some role in my later refusal to allow my work to be permanently silenced by leaving Oakland. The next morning Tristan and I rose early to walk on the dunes before heading back to Oakland, where a "coming out" party awaited me. Something unique happened as we walked up the steep sand dunes at the bay as the sun was rising. Just as I reached the top, a bird came swooping down at exactly my eye level. Then another. Then a third. Three blessings: eye to eye with the wild birds. That was nourishment for the journey that awaited us.

10

Expulsion—
1993

When the year of silence was up, I received no notice from the master general that I was free to speak again. It was strange. I spoke to my provincial, who said just to start talking again, so I did so.

Ending Silence

I first came out of silence in January 1990 at a five-day summer program in Melbourne, Australia. In America, my first public speech was in Chicago at a Call to Action gathering of about two thousand people in February 1990. Call to Action is a group of Catholics committed to change within their church. There was a palpable electricity in the air. Before I was introduced, they played one of my favorite pieces, from Bernstein's *Mass:* "Go and lock up your bold men and hold men in tow, / you can stifle all adventure for a century or so, / smother hope before it's risen, watch it wizen like a gourd, / but you cannot imprison the word of the Lord." Then Sister Teresita Weind, an African American sister who was a real leader in the Chicago church, introduced me in the most moving fashion: she invited all participants to join her in a hymn of liberation from her own people.

> Oh, freedom! Oh, freedom! Oh, freedom over me!
> An' befo' I'd be a slave, I'll be buried in my grave,
> An' go home to my Lord an' be free.

It was the most powerful introduction I have ever felt. When it came my turn to speak, my opening lines caused quite a sensation. Many people failed to hear the rest of my talk but seem to remember the opening lines to this day. I said simply, "As I was saying fourteen months ago, . . . when I was so rudely interrupted . . ." These words had come to me in a dream—in fact, the dream had awakened me at the time. I had gone silent; I had played the game. But I was not going to water down the message that had gotten me in trouble in the first place. And I had resolved—even before I met Leonardo Boff, who urged the same strategy—that I would never go silent a second time.

Following my year of silence there was a greater and greater interest in creation spirituality and the work we were doing. *Rolling Stone* ran an interview, which I heard some time afterward upset some American Dominicans. Road trips brought me to audiences that were larger and more varied both at home and abroad. One very rich experience was visiting a Jewish spiritual community in New York State and dialoguing for several days with the Jewish theologian Arthur Waskow, who, along with Rabbi Zalman Schachter, is doing excellent work in what they call "Jewish renewal" and what I would call resurrecting the creation-centered mystical tradition of Judaism. The prayer and circle dancing were deep and passionate all week long, and our time together culminated in our concelebrating a mass dedicated to Lady Wisdom. A sixty-five-year-old Jewish man cried afterward, saying it was a "healing event of a lifetime." I was also moved and healed and pleased to meet and pray with Rabbi Schachter.

One surprise that week was a visitor from Israel who was a scholar on Martin Buber. As I sat listening to him talk of Buber, tears started to well up in my soul. I was experiencing memories of and gratitude to Buber, who had helped water my mysticism when I was only twenty-two years old—*and then for all the Jewish guides of my life:* Rabbi Heschel, Adrienne Rich, Karl Marx, Sigmund Freud, Otto Rank, Marc Chagall, Leonard Bernstein, Albert Einstein, Starhawk. Where would my soul be—where would any of our souls be—without these prophets and mystics? And, of course, Jesus Christ, Isaiah, Jeremiah, and more.

But my tears were also tears of grief and sorrow for the great loss. The unconscionable anti-Semitism and split of Christianity from its mother religion; the horrible pogroms and the Holocaust; and the *deadening of the Christian soul to the extent that it ignores or attacks these spiritual figures.* And, without knowing it, I was probably also weeping for the loss of Jewish and creation-centered mysticism in the church and its obvious preference for Hellenistic, dualistic, fall/redemption religion. Might creation spirituality actually help to bridge the two worlds, as a Swiss Jewish scholar had told me it could years ago when I was lecturing in Berkeley? And what about the fanatical Jewish settlers and others who were making enemies of Palestinians—how to heal those wounded hearts and souls? Tears happen at so many levels of the psyche.

The Train Comes Again

For the many years that the Vatican had been attacking me, I had worked in total cooperation with my provincial and his stated wishes. I compromised on many issues—not only going silent for a year but stepping down as program director at ICCS, submitting my manuscripts for review, contributing to an issue of *Listening* magazine that it turned out was stacked against me, attending meetings in Chicago that were gerrymandered against me, and more. I attended meeting after meeting with the provincial council members in Chicago and with the provincial when he visited Oakland. On one visit, he met with my faculty and emerged apparently deeply moved and impressed and promised to communicate his feelings to the council.

All this proved to no avail. I was given an ultimatum to return to Chicago or be expelled from the Dominican order. I wrote letters galore and submitted documents of all kinds, offering every manner of compromise except one: I could not in conscience abandon the work at ICCS and with the magazine and with the community of scholars and activists that was recovering the creation-spiritual tradition with me. I offered to return to provincial houses three months out of the year, but I needed to continue the work in California the rest of the year. To quit my work in Oakland would be allowing myself to be silenced *a second time*—and this time for good. My conscience would not allow this. Though my efforts at compromise were of no avail, at least the record will show that I did all I could short of betraying my conscience. (It is interesting that a Dominican friend asked our vicar provincial, "If you were in Matt Fox's shoes, would you quit Oakland to return to Chicago?" and his answer was "No.") The Dutch Dominicans offered to mediate, and they offered me what they called "religious asylum," but both offers were turned down by my provincial. Individual Dominicans also went to bat for me, imploring the provincial on my behalf. I am grateful to them, for they each paid a price, some being transferred suddenly from their homes or places of work.

Part of my resistance to the Vatican's effort to abort ICCS is revealed in a journal entry I made about my need to stay in Oakland even before I was pressured to make a decision.

September 7, 1992
A five-hour meeting yesterday to brainstorm about new directions for the Creation *magazine. It was a very grounded meeting and very valuable. Rich ideas, much passion, healthy criticism about magazines of the past. Once again I'm confirmed about how it is that the people I am working with here in Oakland—at ICCS and at* Creation—*these, plus the students of ICCS, are*

my primary community. I say this in the shadow of my provincial's tele-
phone conversation last week, where it sounds like his and the master gen-
eral's "strategy" is to order me back to the Midwest. And why?

Do they know the power of the ideas and work my faculty and fellow
workers are involved in here? It is all appeasement. To appease the fanatic
right wing in the Vatican and in the United States, the "liberals" would
break up my "radical" work. So much for liberalism. I have never trusted it,
nor have I ever called myself one. Beginning with the bear book, I named my
stance as "radical," meaning root. From that I have not wavered. I cannot
and will not abort ICCS or the magazine by leaving Oakland for no reason
except political appeasement. "Actio in distans repugnans est," said the an-
cients. How could I possibly do my work on the magazine, etc., from Chi-
cago when my co-workers are in California? I moved out here purposefully
because science, creativity, and culture are bubbling here. For that same rea-
son I must stay here.

About the time of the Call to Action event, my provincial's attitude changed
drastically. After years of support and fraternal communication, there was
now coldness and hard-line demands. The train was coming back at me a second time, and there were fewer and fewer buffers between me and the train.
When my provincial told me that I was "not worth defending any longer," I
understood the price that the province had paid by defending me. But I
pleaded with him "not to do Cardinal Ratzinger's dirty work for him. Let me
handle it alone, but don't make the Dominicans take the heat." I cited for him
the scenario that the canon lawyer had presented to me: that Ratzinger would
get the order to expel me for refusing an order I could not in conscience obey.
I genuinely hoped that the order would not get damaged as the train came in
for its second run.

Unfortunately, and for reasons that have never been made clear to me, the
order chose otherwise than to defend its theologian.[1] To me it was never primarily a personal matter, and it still is not today. It was a political issue, and
so it was a question of whether the order would stand by its theologians. My
provincial admitted as much in an interview with the *New York Times* in
March 1993, when he said that "the whole Church moved to the right" but I
did not. Up to the end—and especially after the election of Timothy Radcliffe
as master general in 1992—I believed that the order would not cave in to
Rome's demands. I felt that if any order would stand up to this papacy it
would be the Dominicans. I was wrong.

I went to Europe to lecture and to visit with Dutch Dominicans in the summer of 1992. While in Paris, I wrote the following entry in my journal:

July 1, 1992
A reawareness that Paris is my mother. My intellectual and artistic and theo-
logical/spiritual mother. Here I began to come of age, connecting my thoughts
and experience to that of my ancestors—the morphic field?—"morphic fields
as history and collective memory." Here I walked the streets, consciously
and unconsciously, with Albert and Aquinas and Eckhart—with my Domini-
can ancestors (no matter what decision the current Dominicans make re-
garding me). Here I began the articulation of what prayer is and is not; of
how mysticism and prophecy connect; of art as the missing link between
spirituality and politics, education and spiritual education, being alive and
being dead.

Here in Paris I met Chenu and I met Cognet and I met the artist in me
again after all those rational years of study (though the lived Dominican
life—the praxis—included much that was beyond the rational, such as chant-
ing, celibacy, community, friendship). Here, in those years, I became a mother
myself, recognizing that "I was happiest writing" and was therefore a writer.
Fifteen books later, I cannot deny the fact, or the "mothering" of ICCS or FCS.

There is a certain return to the Source, a back to beginnings, a filling out
of the circle, in this particular trip at this particular synchronistic moment
when the Dominicans are deciding my fate and future direction eight thou-
sand miles away in the Americas and in the most polluted city in the world.
[The Dominican General Chapter was meeting in Mexico City.] *Here, in the*
bosom of my second mother, Paris, I want to make a resolution comparable
to that which I made here some twenty-one years ago (21 = come-of-age
time! A second rite of passage): that the work of creation spirituality toward
launching the Environmental Revolution and the Renaissance it will give
birth to must not lose its steam. It must go forward with whatever energy I
can lend it regarding European work, ICCS, books, talks, or whatever.

As I wrote that entry, my fate had already been decided in Rome, although
I did not know it. On August 8, 1992, I was stunned to receive a letter from
the master general dated June 30 (his last day in office) in which he informed
me that he had sent my papers for dismissal from the order to the Congregation of Religious. What stunned me was that I could have no recourse to him
now because he had since left office and the notification of the act arrived six
weeks after the deed was done! And why did he delay my reception of the letter for six weeks except that then the chapter of the order, meeting in Mexico
City, would not be able to debate the issue?

Earlier that year, hearing that the master general was coming to America, I
had written him asking for a meeting to discuss my situation. He wrote back

and said he would not meet with me unless I returned to Chicago. I wrote again and told him that my return to Chicago was the topic I needed to discuss with him. He never answered that letter. Nor did he ever write a word of response to the thirty-page letter that I had sent him in January 1992 as a formal defense of my work as a Dominican. I cannot help but contrast this deliberate lack of communication with the way the superior general of the Jesuits dealt with Fr. Bill Callahan of the Quixote Center in Washington, D.C., who, under Roman pressure, was expelled from the Jesuit order. At least Bill and his superior general had two lengthy conversations in person. We Dominicans had always claimed that we were the democratic order and the Jesuits were the military order. Our claim to democracy rings rather hollow in my ears after my experience. One would think that a brother who had been in apparent good standing in the order for thirty-four years as I had might at least be allowed to meet with the master general for a last conversation. Such was not to be my fate, however.

In November I received a letter of support from Leonardo Boff of Petrópolis, Brazil, that was dated October 24, 1992. He wrote:

> My dear confrere Matthew,
>
> The Divine is bigger than the Church and human rights are more important than ecclesiastical discipline. Don't let them take away your liberty and your creative capacities. Jesus conquered liberty by shedding his blood and therefore we shouldn't let authority take it away. For this same reason, if they take away vital space, protest. Have the courage to follow new paths even if it means giving up the ministerial and clerical priesthood for the lay priesthood of Jesus.
>
> Remember that we live only once and life should be lived with passion, joy, and creativity. The clerical Church is closer to the palaces of the Caesars than the boat of Peter.
>
> You can count on my support,
> L. Boff

Dismissal

The ending arrived with no warning on March 3, 1993. It was a surprise because the Dutch had pretty much convinced me that the new master general, the Englishman Timothy Radcliffe, was sympathetic to rights in the church and the order, and when I had met the man in England, when he was still a provincial, I had felt him to be open and supportive. If he made efforts on my behalf it was too late, for the previous master general had sealed my fate.

I was at my computer working on my next book, *The Reinvention of Work,* when I received the official letter by express mail from my provincial informing me that I was out of the order. As so often happens in my life, there was deep synchronicity here, for in the book I was talking about the need to reinvent work as a spiritual imperative in our time. The order to which I had belonged since I was nineteen years old, and under whose tutelage I was raised in a Dominican parish since I was one year old, was informing me that it was time to reinvent my work. Rome had spoken.

When I told the ICCS students and faculty of my dismissal, the response was mixed. Some expressed a kind of relief, as for example in the following poem written by our artist in residence, M. C. Richards:

Silence!
SILENCE!
    demanded the Pope.
Silence! echoed
    the judges
Silence! pleaded
    the teachers
Silence murmured
    the clergy
and still the UPROAR
    continued . . .
Of the free and
    passionate spirit.

FOR MATT FOX, EQUINOX, 1993,
BRAVO!

Other associates found themselves in considerable anguish, and in processing these feelings we found that the archetype Expulsion had triggered many deep experiences in these people's memories. For example, one person told how her family had publicly disowned her when she graduated from college years ago because of her anti-Vietnam protests; another told of being fired from her job after many years of faithful service; others—especially Roman Catholics—were concerned because they had found in creation spirituality a way to redeem their own faith roots and were now feeling that they too were being condemned by the church and the Dominican order. One of the ICCS students wrote me a letter about the event. Included was the following paragraph.

You see, it's not just you . . . it's the brave, passionate, justice-oriented troublemaker in all of us that was expelled. We feel this act on the part of the Vatican and the order to be deeply symbolic of our own struggles in this world . . . as women, as blacks, as gays, as Native Americans, as oddballs and rabble-rousers. It brings up a deep fear of what is in store for those of us who dare to oppose the system . . . a deep fear and a deep resolve to continue. Many of us have moved from anger, to fear, to deep commitment . . . to action. But it is a frightening day when we get such a powerful symbol from the dominating system. We are all subject to the same violence. (Shana Weber)

Aquinas and Others in Solidarity

One of the great gifts given me by the universe at this time was the friendship of Fr. Bede Griffiths, the English Benedictine monk who fifty years previously had gone to India and set up an ashram there for Christians in a Hindu cultural context. I had tremendous respect for him, his work, and his writings, and now he was in the Bay Area telling me that the future of monasticism was with laypeople and the future of his work was in California and very likely at ICCS. He offered to read my 600-page manuscript on Thomas Aquinas (it seems reading the *Summa* as a young man played a considerable role in his conversion to Christianity) and to improve on my translations from the Latin, rendering them in the Queen's English so to speak. He actually read the text twice and wrote an afterword to it. He blessed ICCS with its newest faculty member, Russill Paul, a superb musician who had been Fr. Bede's student at the ashram for seven years and who brought the power of Sanskrit chant and Eastern wisdom to the institute. Bede's humor and wisdom were equally welcome. He once said, "Don't worry about the Vatican. It will all come tumbling down overnight someday, just like the Berlin Wall."

For years, and especially during my year of silence, I was working on my book on Thomas Aquinas called *Sheer Joy: Conversations with Thomas Aquinas on Creation Spirituality*. In it I interact with Aquinas's writings, including many that had never been translated into English before, especially his commentaries on Scripture and his greatest mystical work, done when he was twenty-six years old, his *Commentary on Denys the Areopogyte*. During that final year, as things were heating up for me at the Vatican and in Chicago, I would hunker down at my computer with Thomas Aquinas (whose presence I often felt behind me in the room). I had an image of missiles flying over my head while I was paying attention to the task at hand: getting his deeply ecumenical and ecological mysticism out into the world again. I was holding to the naive assumption that surely the Dominican order would be so pleased to have a new and contemporary rendering of their own brother Aquinas that they would be buttressed to defend a theologian so engaged. There was much in his thought and life that encouraged me deeply: his work with science, for example, and his cosmological mysticism, and that he was condemned three times before he was canonized a saint. And, of course, his strong stance on the primacy of conscience, as when he writes:

> One ought to obey God more than human beings.
> Conscience binds more than the precept of a superior.
> It is a grievous matter for anyone to yield to another what ought to be one's own.[2]

I could feel his support during this struggle. There is no question in my mind that working on Aquinas as my Dominican life came to a denouement was a kind of therapy for me. Here I was going back to the primary influence on me in my years of Dominican training, and not only making peace with him but getting excited anew by finding riches that had never been presented to me. I chose to interview him rather than just to translate his heavily scholastic and therefore quite inaccessible manner of presentation. There was gratitude but also irony in the gift of the *Conversations* I was leaving behind for my Dominican brethren. Somehow, the older I get, the more I trust irony. (It is said that "where consciousness is partial, irony is inevitable.")

One thing I loved about working on Aquinas was the deep sense of cosmology in which he swims. For example, his teaching that "one indissoluble connection consists in all things" and "all are joined together in a common bond of friendship with all nature."[3] And that "the most excellent thing in the universe is the universe itself."[4] A former Dominican who was known in the order as Brother Antoninus, but who is better known in poetic circles as William Everson, wrote me the following letter on reading my Aquinas book.

> Your great book on Aquinas came in the wake of your difficulties with the Dominican order, leaving me uncertain as to how to best reach out to you at this time of trial, finally deciding to await the moment the brethren can carry you back in on their shoulders!
>
> The book bears its own challenge. Your Introduction is the finest thing on Aquinas I ever read. It picks him up from where Piper and Chenu left him at midcentury, and lifts him bodily through the paradigm shift into the new millennium. I made a stab at it with my foreword to Victor White's reprint of *God and the Unconscious*, but lacked the erudition to bring it off. But you really rise to the occasion. Seizing the Master by scapular and capuce you haul him point by point through the fundamental issues of our day, providing in your questions the freshness which seven hundred years had stifled in his diction. It is an incredible feat.
>
> The final thing I want to commend in your accomplishment is your spirituality. This comes through in the eagerness with which you pose

your questions. May God sustain you in this moment of triumph in your vocation.

The letter was dated "on the Feast of Saint Antoninus," May 10, 1993. I will always be grateful to Bill, who died one year later of Parkinson's disease, for his stalwart support and encouragement over the years. I first met him as a young Dominican in Dubuque, Iowa, when he came and spoke to us of the mystery of the Mississippi and its valleys. He was the first truly contemplative Dominican I felt I had ever encountered. It was a blessing that our paths crossed often when I moved to California and was able to visit his "Kingfisher Flat" rather regularly.

In contrast to this kind of solidarity from poets, I have to say that certain Catholic liberal theologians let me down and contributed to my marginalization. The only explanation I have for this comes from Fr. Albert Nolan, a Dominican and liberation theologian from South Africa, who said to me: "North Americans know nothing about solidarity."

My favorite teaching in all of Thomas Aquinas, something that caught my eye very early in my Dominican training, was his teaching on one virtue in particular (*virtue* in Latin means "power"; being virtuous is about being in touch with one's own power, one's own strength; about being empowered and acting out of that power). That was his teaching on *magnanimity*. In Latin this word means "great soul." The opposite is *pusillanimity* or cowardice, being puny-souled. Here are some of Aquinas's teachings on magnanimity.

Magnanimity is the expansion of the soul to great things.

It is characteristic of magnanimous people to be more solicitous about the truth than about the opinions of others.

It is a mark of magnanimous people to speak and work openly. . . . That people hide what they do and say arises from the fear of others.

Magnanimous people deliberately determine to forget injuries they have suffered.

Magnanimity is part of the virtue of courage or fortitude.

Magnanimity strengthens a person to take on good tasks.[5]

All my life I have admired courage, or what Aquinas more fully elaborates as magnanimity. That is one thing that so attracted me in reading about Abraham Lincoln as a child—his perseverance and courage in the midst of so much travail and misunderstanding and opposition. I am certain too that that is one of the deep attractions I had to persons I read about who underwent the Holocaust—the courage it took to do so. Surely in my own lifetime there have been heroic examples of courage as well, many of which have caught my attention. I think of Gandhi, Martin Luther King, Jr., Tom Dooley, Dorothy

Day, Daniel Berrigan, Robert Kennedy, Pope John XXIII, Père Chenu, and those struggling for their rights in Central and South America. But the American Dominicans were not up to a great deal of magnanimity or courage; nor were the American bishops. I had thought that the obvious sign of the times, namely the Vatican's international policy to silence thinkers to whom the people of God were listening and to substitute Opus Dei control mentalities in the place of theology, would give the Dominicans the spine and motivation to resist. That, plus the negative publicity that might result and that the motto of the Dominicans was "Truth." But it was not to be the case.

Thus my deepest response to my dismissal—which a friend and faculty member said I ought to consider "a release and not a dismissal"—was one of sorrow and disappointment. What has hurt me the deepest through this ordeal has been disappointment in persons I have known for years. It is sad to discover that people we thought we could trust can disappoint so profoundly. Or to see conscience yielding to political pressure and inventing rationalizations. But rejection is not the end of the world, for there are always new friends to make.

New Friends

In 1992, part of our strategy was to launch a second letter-writing campaign. We asked people to write Rome to request that I be allowed to remain a Dominican. Over five thousand people responded with letters that were often powerful and moving. It was this kind of support, plus my own conviction in the work of creation spirituality and the essential timeliness of its message for renewal of spirituality, that kept me going and even happy (for the most part) during the struggle. Not just individuals but groups wrote letters to Rome supporting our cause. Among these groups were entire communities of Catholic sisters as well as priests and monks and others. Protestant parishes and some Greek Orthodox believers and rabbis also took up the cause. This kind of support was very gratifying. It demonstrated to me what I had felt throughout my years of writing and lecturing; namely, that the issues of our time were as much cultural as spiritual, as much spiritual as cultural, and that many people of varied backgrounds and professions were as eager to learn about creation spirituality as I had been. Among the letters that supported our work were the following:

From Rabbi Zalman Schachter-Shalomi:

Dear Master General Byrne:
    I write on behalf of Father Matthew Fox. I deeply understand the issues connected with obedience. I also know that the warrant for obedience is rooted in the existential covenant of a soul with her G-d. The

riskier the path a soul takes to answer her G-d's call the more it needs the help of the beloved community. Matthew has more than one community to which he is bound by love, and making him choose will, without doubt, make him give up the order.

I write to you with fraternal concern and beg you not to make him have to face that choice. The invisible community he has come to serve is the whole planet, its healing and renewal. He is the current voice of Vatican II. He makes it possible for RCs as well as other Bible-rooted religionists to be loyal to their traditions *and* the emergent spirit. I am certain that as there is an abyss between St. Dominic and Tomás Torquemada so is there an abyss between Fox and Ratzinger.

Pushing him out will rob you of the glory that will be yours in fifty years from now when Creation Theology will have become the central doctrine of the faithful. . . .

I would gladly continue this plea in person and at greater length. We Jews are dealing with some of these issues in our own domain. This is why I am involved in Jewish Renewal. . . .

From a person named Jamey:

Dear Matt:

My mind tells me to ask you to do what your heart tells you to do. Maybe you've outgrown the mold that originally formed you. Maybe you are trying to fit new wine into old wineskins.

I do know that I don't feel right about writing to Rome or Chicago. Why beg them to reconsider? You know who you are. They don't. In your case, I've asked myself, What would Jesus do? I can't see Jesus writing letters to Rome.

From a person named Betty:

You and John XXIII are the only reasons I am still a Catholic.

But every time I learn of another silencing, and now your recall, I want to weep. That authoritarian strain is straining the patience of hundreds of us—especially the females among us.

My faith is no longer dependent on the Roman Catholic Church for its strengthening; the Curia are destroying it. Instead, it is kept strong by the knowledge that only love is important, no matter where it is found. There seems very little of it to be found among authorities in our Church.

From a person named Joyce to the master general:

A personal story: In 1976, *Time* magazine ran an article about a Catholic Church in trouble. It focused on the huge drop-out rate among Catholics in America—how the Church was not meeting our needs.

That article changed my life, because someone at long last acknowledged my pain. It attuned me to the deep spiritual wounding and abandonment I had experienced since childhood. My Mother Church was simply not "there" for me—not there on women's issues, the Earth's issues, and on issues of spiritual expansion. . . . Then I found Matt Fox—at last a priest who had "discovered fire." Could my dream come true? The mysticism, ritual, and beauty of Catholicism (my *heritage*) in a spirituality that honors Earth and makes room for "spiritual over-achievers" who think none of it matters unless it translates into practical, earthy, day-to-day acts of love?. . .

It's too late, Father. The Word is out, and the Fire is spreading. The consummate freedom lies in waking up humanity to the inner fire of our own spirituality. This is the only freedom and highest law—and the only way we can truly know God.

From a United Church of Christ minister to the master general:

Matthew Fox has given us hope in view of the environmental crisis, has renewed our interest in the Catholic mystical tradition, and has given us a truly Catholic (universal) perspective of Christianity in general.

Please give careful consideration to how this issue is handled—not only will Catholics be affected by your decision, but many Christians of other traditions as well as many non-Christians who have seen hope in his message.

From Jean, a former religious who had left the church because of its abuses of authority:

It was creation spirituality that called me back—so much so that I am now enrolled in a Roman Catholic seminary—the Washington Theological Union. It was creation spirituality that made me aware of a mystical tradition that I longed and hungered for but did not experience in the convent or in the Catholic Church until recent years. . . . If Matt is called to work in creation spirituality, expelling him from the Dominican Order will not suppress this—it will only cause it to spread. One only has to look at history—Meister Eckhart, Galileo, Joan of Arc, Thomas Aquinas. What happened when authorities tried to suppress that dangerous radical, Jesus Christ?

I was going to ask you not to expel Matt from the Dominican Order, but I find myself paradoxically wishing that you would because if this is authentic, if this is truth, your action will cause creation spirituality to flourish all the more.

Judy from Louisville, Kentucky:

I hope you too have read his works. . . . I encourage you to read and reflect on Acts 5:33–39 in Scripture . . . "in the present case, I tell you, keep away from these men and let them alone; because if this plan or this undertaking is of human origin, it will fail; but if it is of God, you will not be able to overthrow them—in that case you may even be found fighting against God!"

Julie from State College, Pennsylvania:

I am a retired young-people's teacher and worker with young children of alcoholics. My whole life, it seems to me, has been a rather chaotic spiritual quest to find a way of fitting together what I know in my heart, what I studied as a Biblical History major in college, and what I have learned about life in my sixty-eight years. Matthew Fox has, for the first time in my life, offered me a creative, fresh, and at the same time thoroughly studied way in which to make inner and outer sense of the Holy Spirit, Jesus' life, justice making, and the mystery and wonder of life. Also, I am a recovering alcoholic. Matthew's vision deeply augments and sanctifies the work of the founders of Alcoholics Anonymous, which makes it all the more meaningful to me.

From the executive director of HospiceCare, Inc.:

I was delighted when Matthew Fox was invited to give the final plenary speech at the National Hospice Organization's annual conference last November in Seattle. His topic, "Passion and Compassion," was a thought-provoking, inspirational, and deeply moving message to thousands of hospice workers who heard his speech. He told us to value the work that we do, even in the midst of suffering; he told us to hold to the essence of our mission of respecting individual life. He told us to pay attention to our pain as well as our joy.

There are now approximately seventeen hundred hospices in the nation. His message went to each of us and I think it was no accident that he was called upon to give us this final send-off at the end of the conference. . . . As a hospice worker, I am deeply indebted to Father Fox and his mission of creation spirituality.

From a youth minister in the Catholic church in Massachusetts:

What has impressed me about Fox is that he has never held himself up as a guru of Creation Spirituality. If anything, he emphatically made it clear at one conference that he was saying nothing new; just giving us the message of the mystics spoken centuries ago. His presence and work at ICCS in Oakland is needed.

The people in this country are yearning for authentic leadership, begging for change that puts aside singular self-interest for the greater common good. We write letters, we call politicians in the hope that we are heard. I, for one, am frustrated. Are we ever really heard? And I wonder will you hear my cry on behalf of Matthew Fox, which is really not for him but for all who need his presence so that the vital work of social justice and Creation Spirituality will continue.

From Jerry in Portland, Oregon:

Whenever I return to my hometown now I notice a decided lack of people of my age group in our church. . . . It's a church for the young (dependent) and the old (afraid of their mortality).

I know this because *I have returned to the church*. Matt opened my eyes to a new way of perceiving Catholicism that is not morbid in its focus. Creation spirituality is much more in line with my own feelings and beliefs and it has allowed me to accept the religion I was raised in. . . . I wonder about the goals of a church that would silence members of its community who are making such a difference and having such a positive effect. I hope you reconsider.

In Holland, the council of the Dutch province expressed its "shame and disappointment" at the "disgrace" of my dismissal in a statement that decried the lack of response to its efforts to mediate and the reduction of my commitment "to an internal disciplinary matter." They ask why "our order rids itself of a brother, who, for over thirty years, has been committed to the priorities of the Order, formulated by the General Chapter of Quezon City 1977, *with* heart *and* soul *and* reason, and who explicitly dwells at the margins, described by the General Chapter of Avila 1986."

With support like this, who need worry about enemies or even persons who disappoint? These are the people I had committed myself to serving years ago when I began my work. They understood what I was about and what it meant to them. I am grateful for our mutual support and for the time so many of them took to support the struggle.

In the spring of 1993 I found myself teaching a two-week class at Schumacher College in the rolling green hills near Devon, England. Satish Kumar—a Jain monk in India for nine years who escaped and walked a peace walk from India to Moscow to Paris to London—is editor of the Schumacher magazine, *Resurgence*, and director of Schumacher College. He said to me, "Your Dominican brothers must love you a lot *unconsciously* because they have done so much to spread your work by expelling you." That put a different spin on things! I participated in a conference at nearby Dartington and wrote the following in my journal:

How interesting that I'm in a conference with Satish, who escaped the Jain monks after nine years; with husband-and-wife teachers who left the Buddhist community after many years. And me, expelled from the Dominicans. Gaia is calling us all to let go; travel more lightly; salvage what wisdom we can from our religious forms . . . and move on. So be it. The Spirit has spoken. Here I am. Do with me what you will.

At Christmas that year, I reflected on being a non-Dominican for the first time since my senior year of high school in 1958. And in a real sense, since I was raised in a Dominican parish, it would be the first non-Dominican Christmas *of my life!*

Christmas—1993
I attended Christmas midnight mass with a friend who is Hindu (though very interested in Christianity, and Catholicism for that matter) and who had never been to a mass in his life. Then at 11:00 A.M. I took my mother to Christmas mass in another parish.

Both services had earnest and hardworking choirs that led us in Christmas carols. Both churches were decked out nicely with boughs and poinsettias—a bit of nature in the church—for the Christmas mood.

The Scripture readings of both services were dynamite—all about angels and glory and Sophia-wisdom (John 1 was the gospel at the morning service) and cosmology. Shepherds, wisdom, angels, doxa, Shekinah, "princes of peace." I could hear the trumpets sounding and New Creation being born. Such archetypes to play with; such wonders to behold in the divine puer, the mystic child in every soul yearning to be born anew at this dark season of our souls, of our solstice time and of our species at this time in evolutionary history. The people were eager at both services, which were well attended.

BUT, oh, the preaching. Not one of the pastors preaching had anything to say about the meaning of Christmas today. One read his sermon, which was all platitudes about "ideals becoming real" and words like "peace" and "joy" thrown around that had no grounding in a single chakra of our body or souls. That sermon gets a D.

The other was totally extemporaneous as much as I could tell. No message about the good news—only repeating the term. He gets a C-. Horrible! Seven hundred and fifty years after Dominic founded the Order of Preachers and the preaching still stinks. . . .

On Christmas Day one of my brothers tells us his children in their twenties are adrift as regards religious values and their Christianity. No wonder! Church representatives have nothing to say even on Christmas.

The decadence is complete at the institutional level. The institution is irredeemable in its current form.

Base communities will resurrect its deeper meaning. So too will those who, while they preach, take time to turn these truths over in their hearts— contemplative time.

What a treasure the church is sitting on! What deep meaning lies in the good news of shepherds and angels cavorting on a winter night. How deeply an awakening is needed in the churches.

Nonetheless, I am moved by the liturgy, the music and the Scripture readings and the Eucharist, and what strikes me most deeply is the immense cosmology *inherent in the Christmas story. How cosmological our ancestors were! Christmas is truly a* new creation story. *What a challenge to connect this to the other creation story we are receiving today. And to stand back for the fireworks that will come!*

I cannot say I regret my own story. Perhaps it was all inevitable. I, like many of my generation, had taken Pope John XXIII's *aggiornamento* and vision of a New Pentecost to heart, was destined to pay a price for trying to live it out. Though the train did indeed run over me, I still had my life, and other options awaited me.

PART FOUR

QUESTIONS FOR OUR RELIGIOUS FUTURE

11

The End of the Roman Catholic Era?

In 1948 the German theologian Paul Tillich published a provocative essay entitled "The End of the Protestant Era." In that essay he argued that those cultural and social forces with which Protestantism had allied itself—the Enlightenment and capitalism and bourgeois humanism, as well as economic and spiritual individualism—had evolved in such a way that Protestantism as we know it was not going to survive. "The Protestant era is finished, after nearly all the historical conditions upon which it rested have been taken away from it," he declared.[1] A whole new expression of Protestantism was needed. Tillich also observed that mass community movements such as socialism, fascism, and Roman Catholicism would speak more to the average person than would Protestantism, since the latter was basically a professorial approach to religion.

> The minister's gown of today is the professor's gown of the Middle Ages, symbolizing the fact that the theological faculties as the interpreters of the Bible became the ultimate authority in the Protestant churches. But professors are intellectual authorities—i.e., authorities by virtue of skill in logical and scientific argument. This sort of authority is the exact opposite of the kind that is sought by the disintegrated masses, whose disintegration is to some extent an echo of the endless arguments and counter arguments among their leaders.[2]

This critique appears not only insightful but even prophetic in light of today's successful fundamentalist religious movements (which are also antiprofessorial). Tillich felt that the "new Protestantism" had to involve itself much more deeply in symbols, metaphors, rituals, and other dimensions for which Roman Catholicism was famous. "Bishops, priests, and monarchs have a sacramental authority which cannot be taken away by arguments and which is independent of the intellectual and moral qualities of its carriers."[3] But while the Protestant era was finished, the *Protestant principle* was still very much required. The Protestant principle is "the principle of prophetic protest against every power which claims divine character for itself—whether it be church or state, party or leader."[4]

Roman Catholicism in Decline

The question now looms large: Is the end of the Roman Catholic era also upon us? The cultural forces that made Roman Catholicism attractive in the modern era are melting away, and the Roman Catholic church seems to be disintegrating even as the modern era is disappearing. How ironic it is that the Vatican—such a Johnny-come-lately to the modern era (after all, it condemned Galileo in 1633 for bringing it about and only removed this condemnation in 1979)—is willing today to die with that era and to bring down with it eighteen hundred years of its own history. I am speaking of course of the sacramental system and other traditions in the Western church.

One of the principles of the modern era was that there is *one center to the universe*. The alliance of the modern era and the papacy might be said to have begun in the anthropocentric sixteenth century when a theologian declared, "The pope is ruler of the universe." In this theology the pope replaces the cosmic ruler and displaces the goddess who sits on the throne at the center of the universe. One can see why such a *modern* interpretation of the papacy would resist women's rights and power and ordination at all costs. Part of the modern era has been patriarchy's assertion over nature (the pope rules the universe) and over women (dare the Catholic church allow altar girls?).

How being the center of the religious universe appealed to any weak egos in the Vatican's employ! A statement from the pope, a visit from the pope, an election of a pope—all this fed the desire for one leader to which the modern era pointed. The Vatican as we know it is an institution of the modern era: consider its preoccupation, beginning with Vatican I, with the "infallibility" of the pope; consider its preoccupation with corralling all *teaching* power, its calling itself the exclusive "magisterium" or teacher (St. Thomas Aquinas in the thirteenth century never called the Vatican the magisterium; rather, he refers to all theologians as the magisterium); consider its preoccupation with appointing all bishops and cardinals everywhere and these only after litmus tests proving the candidate's politically correct misogyny; consider its preoccupation with being sole canonizer of saints—and its obvious politicization of that process in such recent instances as the efforts to canonize the founder of Opus Dei, Fr. Serra, Queen Isabella, and similar figures. All this is *modern* in its mentality.

The physics of the postmodern era displaces the mentality of "unity as one." The new story is that the universe is omnicentric—there is no one center of the universe. There are many centers, depending on the beauty and depth and light of each place in the universe. It is now time for base communities, not papal palaces. As Fr. Schillebeeckx put it to me in a private conversation, "Only base communities hold any hope" for the future of the church. But base communities can be anywhere. There can be many centers.

Second Vatican Council as Deconstructive but Not Reconstructive

Since Tillich's essay was published, the Roman Catholic church underwent its own reformation under the inspiration of Pope John XXIII. The Second Vatican Council did much to draw attention to religion's struggles in today's global culture. The media beamed some of its color and pageantry into our living rooms. In many ways the Vatican Council played a postmodern role; that is, it deconstructed much of Catholicism as people knew it: its strict laws of fasting and abstinence from meat on Fridays; mandatory religious habits for Catholic sisters; lack of religious liberty; mass in Latin; hostility to other religions, be they Protestant, Jewish, Hindu, or whatever; a "withdrawal from the world" kind of spirituality. There are those liberal Catholics—mostly in their fifties—who today still harken back (a bit nostalgically one wonders?) to the days of the Vatican Council as "the good old days" and yearn to see its more radical documents put into effect. But these people miss the point that Fr. Chenu, wily observer of history that he was, points out. "Vatican II is obsolete now. It was, in essence, prophetic; therefore, it brought about its own obsolescence." It worked its way out of a job. Now the Holy Spirit has to make things happen at different levels and in different ways in the church and beyond it.

Something altogether different has happened since Vatican II. With the election of John Paul II, an election that was rushed through following the untimely death of Pope John Paul I after only one month in office, a concerted effort has taken place at the highest echelons of the Roman Catholic church to undo the work of the Vatican Council. Instead of reconstruction we have had restoration. One of the ringleaders of this effort is Cardinal Ratzinger of the Congregation for the Doctrine of the Faith who has said, "I want a smaller church." That is exactly what he is getting. When the present pope was elected, 63 percent of Dutch Catholics were practicing. Indeed, when I visited Holland in 1969 as a student in Paris, I found the energy and vitality at the Sunday parish masses unbelievable. Music was diverse, ranging from African American spirituals (with Dutch words overlaid) to Gregorian chants to a "Beatles mass" with snare drums. This respect for diversity was manifest everywhere among both young and old. But the present papacy appointed bishops who were sure to squelch anything creative. As a result, 12 percent of Dutch Catholics are practicing their religion today. Other Dutch Catholics call themselves "the other face of the church" and, while refusing to leave the church, are doing it their way, including concelebrating mass with women.

What has happened in Holland is a microcosm of what has happened in most Western countries, where the present papacy's deliberate efforts to erase the memory of Vatican II have met with opposition of various kinds and, the most telling of all responses, with people voting with their feet. To cite one local example, the diocese of San Francisco has just closed twelve parish churches. Why? Twenty years ago 164,000 Catholics were attending mass on Sunday; today, the number is 42,000. A 75 percent drop in twenty years. As one observer has put it, "This is a mismanaged corporation—they are selling off their assets instead of asking: 'Why doesn't anyone want to buy the product we are offering?'" In France today, 4 percent of Catholics are practicing; in Cardinal Ratzinger's Germany, 7 percent; in America the drop is precipitous as well. I meet far more wounded or recovering Catholics than practicing ones. Indeed, one New York priest who attended ICCS a few years ago told of putting a classified ad in the *New York Times* inviting any "wounded Catholics" to come to church on a Tuesday night to talk about it. He was expecting about thirty-five people. Four hundred showed up—far more than attend Sunday mass. What is peculiar is that the papacy is so embedded in its ideological commitments that it is proud of its downsizing of the church. Rather than change, it wishes to die and abort new life wherever it shows itself—in women's movements, in gay and lesbian liberation, in third-world base communities, in native peoples' recovery of their stolen religious consciousness, in married priests, even in its own sacramental system, which it is effectively destroying by denying the priesthood to a diverse lot of persons. How strange that a papacy so against fetal abortion thinks nothing of aborting life wherever else it appears.

We might say that the Vatican Council *deconstructed* Catholicism's liturgy and, in theory, its system of operating. However, it failed in *reconstructing* either, and the result is that new forms of worship and of church polity are nonexistent. Artists have not been flocking to assist the renewal of worship that is so desperately needed. It cannot happen in a *system* that is more committed to control than to fostering emergence.

If we can talk of a "Roman Catholic era" it was surely short-lived, essentially from the late fifties to the seventies. Some of its high points were

—the election of their first Catholic president, John F. Kennedy;
—the compassion of Dr. Tom Dooley, who volunteered to be a doctor among

the poor in Laos and who became the model for Kennedy's Peace Corps. Randy Shilts's recent book on gays in the military, *Conduct Unbecoming*, reveals that Dooley, who died on the day Kennedy was inaugurated, was dishonorably discharged for being gay;

— the beauty of John XXIII, his encyclical on *Pacem in Terris,* and his calling of the Second Vatican Council;

— the deliberations of that body over a four-year period;

— two decent presidential candidates, Eugene McCarthy and Robert Kennedy;

—substantive theological thinkers such as Karl Rahner, Edward Schillebeeckx, Johannes Metz, and others;

— Pope Paul VI's visit to the United Nations and to India and the Holy Land and his encyclical on *Populorum Progressio;*

— the awakening of the South American church to its own empowerment and its source as a boon to democratic forces of liberation in Latin America;

— its development of liberation theology and base communities as new forms of doing theology and of doing church in both praxis and theory;

— the emergence, especially in America, of feminist theologians and women church leaders;

— the struggle of religious orders to renew themselves according to the charism of their founders;

—ecumenical rapprochement among churches and among Christians, Jews, and others;

— the awakening of the Catholic Native American movement and the appointment of its first Indian bishops;

— the appointment by Archbishop Jadot, the apostolic delegate to the United States, of some quality persons as bishops in America in the 1970s;

— the resistance movement as represented by people such as Daniel and Phillip Berrigan, Molly Rush, Daniel Ellsberg, and other Catholics willing to go to jail rather than acquiesce to government orders;

— the accomplishment in the Catholic educational system of being able to offer a truly alternative educational experience to inner-city youth;

— the establishment of ICCS and the unusual spread of creation spirituality materials. (The numerous translations of my books into German, for example, is very unusual. Previously, American theology was translated from the German; very rarely did it occur the other way around. I was told a few years ago by a German theologian that "German theology is dead" and "creation spirituality may be the theology of the future.")

Above all, on a cultural level, there was the confluence of television and the papacy. The papacy is made for television. Television yearns to zero in on just one personality—if that personality dwells in an operatic castle, wears colorful outfits that in terms of gender are outrageous, travels a lot and gets PR advice to kiss the ground on arriving, what a wonderful TV shot this will be! The papacy as entertainment. But this connection will probably not endure, for television quickly tires of itself. Thus the papal affair with television has already worn thin, and of course this divorce is related to other, more shadowy matters with which the papacy has been involved in the past few decades. While the present pope loves to travel and those running things in the Vatican also love for him to travel, some unsavory events are going on there in his absence (and presence).

For example, for several years a particular Archbishop Marcincus, an American from Chicago who had been the papal financier, was actually hiding out from the Italian courts and police in the Vatican because he was wanted for questioning about his financial dealings. The pope's other financial adviser was found hanging from a bridge in London. Pope John Paul I not only died suddenly and suspiciously but so did his closest adviser, the cardinal of Florence, six months later. An investigator who examined the pope's death over a three-year period and wrote a detailed study on it concluded not only that it was murder but that it had to be an "inside" job; that is, some churchmen were involved in the murder. A cardinal from Colombia who has been implicated in the drug trade has been "elevated" to a post in the Vatican and is operating with impunity there. (Journalist Penny Lernoux, who lived in Colombia for over twenty years, told me that she had evidence of the cardinal's involvement with the drug trade and that she received a phone call from his secretary saying, "We know the exact time your daughter leaves for school and comes home from school." It was then that Penny Lernoux and her family left Colombia.)

The disastrous encyclical on birth control, *Humanae Vitae,* put out by Pope Paul VI against the advice of the board of advisers, set up to explore the subject (a board that actually included some married couples), was a warning of how far the church had sunk into a pseudoprophetic role as guardian of sexual matters. This encyclical, more than any other document, has been the rallying cry and orthodox litmus test for the right wing in the church. The church condemned homosexuals in a document entitled "Some Considerations Concerning the Response to Legislative Proposals on the Non-Discrimination of Homosexual Persons" released to the public in July 1992. That document, as bitter in its tone as it was biting in its lack of compassion, has contributed its weight to the increase in violent attacks on homosexuals that is taking place around the world in this time of AIDS. When I read that document, which I had to do because I was asked to speak on it to a Dignity group in San Francisco, my stomach turned over. I asked myself, What am I feeling? and my response was horror: Whoever wrote this document wants gays and lesbians in concentration camps. Then I realized the author was Cardinal Ratzinger and that is exactly what his parents' generation did in Germany—put homosexuals along with Jews into concentration camps. I researched his story more fully and found that he had been in the Nazi army from the age of sixteen to twenty-one. A formative period for any young man, especially one of his somewhat-sensitive temperament. The wounded child as killer adult who plays over the tapes of his youth. Now I understood my opponent more fully.

I once asked Penny Lernoux, "Is the problem in the Vatican Cardinal Ratzinger? If he were to go, would the Vatican be healthy again?"

"Ratzinger is only the front man," she told me. "The entire Vatican is filled with people like him, mostly Germans. A German mafia. It would make no difference now if he stayed or left."

Catholicism: Its Bright Side

If we are truly talking about an "end of an era," it is appropriate to list some of the *good things* I and others have experienced from the Roman Catholic church. I can thank the church for the following:

—the mystics
—Mary, our own Christian goddess and bearer of cosmology (Have you ever heard the amazing images of the Marian litany where she is called "star of the sea" and "pillar of ivory" and "mystical rose"? I never knew what these images *meant*; they were too deep in the right brain for meaning's sake. They were just sensual and rich and full of ancient connections to be made.)
—the twelfth century
—Chartres Cathedral
—the mass
—Gregorian chant
—an aesthetic sense
—tactical ecstasies for prayer such as fasting, abstinence, and so on
—tradition: old; older (medieval); oldest (New Testament, Old Testament)
—Thomas Aquinas and a medieval tradition that cared about science
—John XXIII and the thrust for ecumenism
—Vatican II while it lasted
—people we call saints, and some we don't (see chapter 13 for more on this)
—religious and monastic orders (when they were healthy)
—rites of passage in these orders
—an intellectual tradition, and study as a yoga or spiritual discipline
—spiritual disciplines
—the word *spirituality*

—some strong women (especially Benedictines)
—base communities
—liberation theology
—value of artists in Latin cultures
—immigrants in the United States and the educating of them
—supporting the unions when they supported the poor
—ethnic glue when it was most needed
—a tradition of hermitage
—the quest for holiness

Catholicism: Its Shadow Side

Now it is only fair to list the shadow side of Roman Catholicism as well, those things from which a great number of Catholics are in recovery:

—clericalism
—ignoring of its creation spirituality tradition and mystics in seminary training in the order
—closing of churches without asking why no one wants to come to mass today
—pedophilia and its cover-up
—rigor mortis
—fascism
—sexual morality as taught by the hierarchy
—inquisition yesterday and today, and the fear it spreads[5]
—infallibility
—papalmania and cult of personality
—links with the CIA, and the National Security Council under Reagan, in destroying peace movements, liberation movements, base communities, and liberation theologies[6]
—hypocrisy
—homophobia
—power!
—sexism
—fear
—sins of the spirit ignored while sins of the flesh are preached
—ignorance of its own mystical-prophetic tradition
—lack of curiosity
—resentment
—envy
—witch burnings
—complacency
—Vatican as a modern power base, not postmodern

—condemnations

—lack of accountability

—silliness on birth control, and consequent ignoring of global population crisis

—silly opposition to condoms, a position that can result in death by AIDS

—anthropocentrism: pride, arrogance

—treatment of native peoples and their religions

—colonialism and its sins

—sectarianism/tribalism/lack of "catholic" spirit

—anti-Semitism

—inability and unwillingness to stop its radical right fringe

—Opus Dei (the secretive spiritual lay order embraced by Franco and other fascists of this century)[7]

—bad people in high places: Torquemada, Cody, Ratzinger, and others

—Pius IX's Syllabus of Errors

—inability to admit past errors

—bad popes[8]

Sexuality

Before the pope came to Denver in the summer of 1993 to speak to young people, a fifteen-year-old San Franciscan who was planning to attend was interviewed about his enthusiasm for the event. He was asked what he thought of the pope's condemnation of condoms. "That's dumb," he said, expressing bewilderment at this news that the Vatican outlaws condoms even in an age of AIDS. "That could kill people." It is gratifying to learn that the next generation is so much smarter than the guardians of ecclesial power. Truth will prevail. The Catholic hierarchy is still committed to carrying on Augustine's sexual neurosis—no sex without babies to legitimize it. When will they ever shake it? I remember giving a day's workshop in San Diego for Catholic diocesan workers years ago, and I made a facetious remark about how a rabbi had told me that we Christians ought to let go of the Ten Commandments, which were given to Jews at a certain period in their history, and ought to teach "those two commandments Jesus taught you." I remarked to the audience, "Of course, we Catholics know those two commandments are the sixth and ninth. Our bishops come out of the woodwork every time a moral issue arises that has to do with sex." The crowd laughed uninterrupted for ten whole minutes. During the lunch break I asked one of the participants, "Why was the laughter so prolonged?" The answer I received was this: The bishop of the diocese does nothing about the real issues, for example, urban Indians who are suffering so much. But one week he took out a *full page ad* in the secular paper. Why? To protest a nude beach!

Years ago I read a poem written early in this century by a Celtic poet. I regret that I have not been able to find it or its author, but I believe the title was "Pater Noster." The image, though, I will never forget: the Catholic church as a great ship that for nineteen centuries made its way through the great sea amidst storm and hurricane and danger, surviving all the while. Then—in the twentieth century—it crashed upon a rock, splintered, and sank. The name of the rock was Sex.

Just as European spirituality lost its wilderness on the outside, it also lost touch with the spiritual wilderness on the inside. Frederick Turner's *Beyond Geography*, a history of the Americas from the time Columbus landed from the point of view of Native Americans, is subtitled "Western Spirit Against the Wilderness." His thesis is that European Christianity had so repressed sensuality and sexuality—the inner wilderness—by the time it came to the shores of the "New World" that it committed genocide on the peoples here because of this pent-up lust and rage. Seeing "savages" at home in the "wilderness" was just too much for it to take. Surely they needed *our* redemption and *our* religion? And if they did not see its value, we would force it on them. Turner called his work "an essay in the history of spirituality," and it is that: a critique of the price indigenous peoples paid when the church lost the sense of the sacred wilderness, including the wilderness of the second or sexual chakra.

On my trip to Florence during my year of silence I made the following journal entry.

Wednesday, March 29, 1989—Florence. Capital of the Italian Renaissance. Here, in the release of erotic mysticism, lies the energy of centering as a spiritual discipline and of renaissance, i.e., new birth. Here lies the initiative— moral, spiritual, and physical—for awakening our souls, our youth, our institutions—to letting go and re-creating.

How do we experience erotic mysticism? I was made love to this morning on waking by the birds singing and the cool breeze tickling me. The sun makes love if we enter its sphere willingly and receptively. And color and music and fresh air and beauty of all kinds, not least of which is that which humans—cocreators—also birth. Isn't this the essence of creation spirituality? That creation loves us lavishly and makes love to us—ravishing us, even when no one else has or can do so? We need to safeguard creation in order to safeguard our lover. (Cf. Hildegard of Bingen on this erotic gift from creation.) I, as lonely man, wounded celibate, need to make room more and more for this lovemaking in my being. It strengthens me for the struggle for earth justice. A garden will help to do this, I am sure.

A journal entry on May 27, 1989, follows up on the same theme of sexuality and the church.

May 27

Hearing the stories of married couples and the pain they are under because of the church's teachings on sexuality has one wanting to scream.

Our sexuality is proof that we cannot control nature. It pulsates through us, creating through us, cocreating with us, whether we like it or not. The other day I heard a mother of three teenage boys relate a story of overhearing two of them argue about who has the most pubic hair!

Cf. Jesus on "one hair of your head is numbered."

So much humanness in our sexuality that we seldom pay attention to. How it binds us together, men with boys and men with men and women with girls and women with women even before it binds us together, man and woman (or man-man, woman-woman, as the case may be). Sexuality therefore is one of the ways we are truly catholic, i.e., universal and together. The church can no longer afford to see sexuality as a problem. Our sexuality surely links us to creation as well in all its power, fecundity, future, and past. All our inheritance is sexually transmitted by chromosomes, DNA, and "luck."

When the risen Christ says "Peace to you," he surely includes being at peace with our sexuality. A homophobic or pornographic or sexist society is not "at peace" with its sexuality. Or with creation itself.

Roman Catholicism's tradition of celibacy is not all negative. Unfortunately, it has become a requirement for the priesthood, whereas it ought to be an option (as it was for many centuries). My own experience with celibacy is that there is a place for it but it must be optional, not required; and it is better understood as an art form that elders should be teaching all the young people rather than a lifelong vow. Following are some lessons I learned from practicing celibacy over the years that I practiced it:

— Go inside
— Question everything
— Let go
— Be empty
— Be strong
— Be naive
— Wonder
— Learn to wait
— Laugh—even at your sexuality
— Be nonjudgmental
— Be open
— Enter the darkness
— Wrestle with the demons of loneliness

—Cherish solitude
—Learn to convert loneliness to aloneness or solitude
—Learn to receive
—Entertain contemplation
—Love silence
—Share solidarity with those who suffer from loneliness, sexual oppression, or abuse: be a feminist
—Do physical exercise and keep yourself in shape
—Be creative

Lessons I've learned from letting go of celibacy include:

—fun
—giving and receiving
—play
—energy
—hope
—body-soul-spirit continuum
—the presence of God in nature—our own human nature
—incarnation: Sophia made flesh
—cosmic mysticism enhanced
—lovemaking as art as meditation
—how sexuality takes one through all four paths of creation spirituality
—how celibacy should be an art form elders teach the young rather that a vow for a few
—responsibility

Deconstructing the Papacy

Deeper than all the scandals in the present papacy is the *unspoken faith-crisis* that looms there. Faith is about trust—but the present Vatican, at the end of the modern era, trusts no one. It does not trust women; or married priests; or homosexual persons; or indeed, sexual persons; or theologians; or its priests; or Protestants; or Anglicans; or anyone outside the tight circle of its male celibate (or claiming-to-be-celibate) club. Most serious of all, it does not trust the Holy Spirit. The cause of this lack of trust is one of the sins of the spirit that never gets talked about enough. I am speaking of the *sin of fear*. For a sin it is; as Aquinas put it, "those who are wrapped up in fear are so involved in their own passion that they cannot notice the suffering of others." The real sin of the present Vatican is its shutting its eyes and doors to the immense suffering in the church and beyond. Otto Rank reflects on what he calls the *decadent fear of extinction,* which "is self-created by man, who becomes afraid of his own power-ideology, which he has set up against the forces of nature in himself."[9] Thus anthropocentrism creates its own demons.

The opposite of fear is *trust,* and *trust* is the biblical word for *faith.* Therefore a fear crisis is a faith crisis, a crisis that exists today in the highest echelons of some of our religious structures. In a church that claims to preach belief in resurrection and the overcoming of the fear of death that comes with that belief, the present hierarchy, committed as it is to control, is clearly a hierarchy of unbelievers.

Numerous Catholic European theologians are saying privately today that the Vatican is in schism. But if the Vatican is in schism, should not Catholics who recognize this *do* something about it—other than get depressed and watch their energy and that of others be sapped from them? Soviet writer Yevgeny Alexandrovich Yevtushenko published an essay during the glasnost period of Russia's liberation in which he criticized his fellow citizens for practicing an excess of *priterpelost* (servile patience). He writes:

> There is patience and tolerance worthy of respect—the patience of a woman suffering in labor, the patience of real creators at work, the patience of people under torture who will not name their friends. But there is also useless, humiliating patience. How can we respect ourselves if we allow such disrespect for ourselves every day?. . .
>
> Let's be honest and admit that it was not only the ruling clique that was guilty [during Stalin's reign of terror], but the people as well, who allowed the clique to do whatever it wanted. Permitting crimes is a form of participating in them, and historically, we are used to permitting them. That is *priterpelost.* It is time to stop blaming everything on the bureaucracy. If we put up with it, then we deserve it.[10]

I believe these words should challenge the heart and conscience of every Roman Catholic. The inquisitions and crusades and witch burnings and gay burnings and colonialism and religious wars in Jesus' name and in the church's name over the centuries cannot all be blamed on the Roman bureaucracy. The people who shut their eyes to it or who hide in the comfort of their private parish pew asking not to be disturbed or told the truth are part of the problem. "If we put up with it, then we deserve it."

When Harvey Cox and I sat down to talk in Oakland a few years ago, he told me the following story. He and other Protestant theologians he knew had been invigorated, encouraged, energized by the ecumenical spirit and other spirits let loose by Pope John XXIII and the Second Vatican Council in the sixties. But today, under the present pope, he found himself—and he was not alone in this—depressed. "Just like the rest of us," I volunteered. This story demonstrates how the papacy is no longer a Roman Catholic prerogative; its debasement is everybody's business. In the short run, the present papacy depresses most thinking people; but in the long run, it is doing us all a tremendous service. It is freeing us from our conscious or unconscious dependencies on the papacy. A Jungian analyst friend of mine tells me that he is convinced that the number-one addiction is addiction to our parents—that this addiction lies behind all others. Since "pope" means "papa," isn't it time that we got over all temptations to carry on parental addictions and simply let go of that relationship, to the extent that it is codependent?

I once met a Polish woman from Kraków at one of my lectures who told me the following story. She and others danced in the streets on hearing of the election of Cardinal Wojtyla to the papacy. They rejoiced for three reasons, in the following order. First, they knew how authoritarian and sexist he was, for he was their bishop, and they rejoiced because they were getting rid of him. Second, they knew that in his new position he would no doubt raise considerable funds for Solidarity. Third, he would be the first Polish pope.

Another irony is this. The present pope, though he represents the end of the modern era of the papacy, is in fact being used by the Holy Spirit to usher in the postmodern era of Christianity. He has demythologized and deconstructed the papacy more in his 14 years as pope than Protestants were able to do in 450 years of trying! It is an accomplishment of historic proportions. The papacy will never be the same again. It has been denuded of its egoism and pretensions. Now the church can begin anew in earnest at the grassroots level, and interdenominationally so. Deep ecumenism can now happen, now that this pope has leveled the playing field, stripped the Vatican garden of all its foliage, made nude the sins of papal power.

For middle-aged Catholics it has been a culture shock first to live through John XXIII's good humor and peasant honesty and then the goings-on in the present Vatican. But our generation should remind itself that John XXIII was an aberration. In the papacy's nineteen-hundred-year history, how many papal saints have there been? Most of the popes have been rather dull people, and a goodly number have been scoundrels of the first order. Indeed, during my year of silence, one task I set myself was to learn more about the bad popes and about the Inquisition and witch-burning times than I had been taught at a Catholic college or theology schools. It has been my experience that few Catholics are ever educated about the Inquisition or about the bad popes of the past. Only at the close of the nineteenth century did Pope Leo XIII begin to open the Vatican archives to "tell the truth" of papal history (lessons that the present papacy might deeply regret, as for example the recent finding by Yale historian John Boswell that the premodern church had liturgical rites for same-sex unions for many centuries, and that some of these rites are preserved in the Vatican library).[11] Here are some lessons I learned from my reading on the subject:

1. "Many Roman pontiffs were heretics" (a quote not from a radical Protestant but from Pope Adrian VI in 1523). The fallibility of popes is far

more obvious than any rare infallibility. Even the powerful Pope Innocent III said, "I can be judged by the church for a sin concerning matters of faith," and Innocent IV said, "Of course a pope can err in matters of faith. Therefore, no one ought to say, 'I believe that because the Pope believes it, but because the Church believes it.' If he follows the Church he will not err."[12]

2. Pope Gregory VII set up an entire school of forgers and inserted these forgeries into canon law. When Gratian wrote the Code of Canon Law in the mid-twelfth century, of the 324 passages he quotes from popes of the first four centuries, only eleven are authentic quotes! "Against a thousand-year-old tradition, [Gregory VII] made all bishops take a personal oath of loyalty to him. From now on, they were bishops 'by favour of the Apostolic See.'"[13] On being made pope, this man drew up a list of his powers. Among them were the following:

The pope can be judged by no one on earth.

The Roman church has never erred, nor can it err until the end of time.

The pope alone can depose bishops.

He can dethrone emperors and kings and absolve their subjects from allegiance.

All princes are obliged to kiss his feet.

A rightly elected pope is, without question, a saint, made so by the merits of Peter.[14]

The last point, especially, stretches one's faith when one considers the facts about many of the popes' lives. For example, Alexander VI, in the fifteenth century, had a stable of mistresses, a litter of illegitimate children, and a habit of murdering cardinals for their money. He fathered a son who became pope and whose son also became pope. His grandson was such a libertine that women pilgrims were warned not to go to Rome lest they be raped by the pope. As the conservative magazine *The Catholic World* put it in reviewing E. R. Chamberlin's honest and balanced book *The Bad Popes*, "Seven different popes, each of whom precipitated a crisis in the Church . . . stole, plundered, gambled, fornicated, killed." Pope Boniface VIII sent armies into Florence to destroy its fledging democracy in the fourteenth century, exiling such defenders of democracy as Dante.

3. Power overtook popes time and again. In the southern French province of Languedoc, in the town of Béziers, Innocent III in the thirteenth century killed twelve thousand Christians for heresy in one afternoon—more than any Roman emperor did in his entire reign. In 1232 Pope Gregory IX published the bull establishing the Inquisition, and in the next year he restricted inquisitors to members of the mendicant orders, of which, sad to say, the Dominicans held special place. The principle was established that "heretics have

no rights," and in one day, May 29, 1239, Dominican Robert le Bougre put to the stake 180 people from the town of Champagne, including their bishop. The inquisitors operated "arbitrarily and in total secrecy," and torture was readily used.[15] The papal guide for inquisitors, *The Black Book,* spoke thus: "Bodily torture has ever been found the most salutary and efficient means of leading to spiritual repentance. Therefore, the choice of the most befitting mode of torture is left to the Judge of the Inquisition, who determines according to the age, the sex, and the constitution of the party."[16] Since inquisitors were paid from the proceeds of confiscation, they "never lost a single case." We have not a single record of an acquittal. Only in the nineteenth century was the Inquisition disbanded by the papacy. Of eighty popes from the thirteenth century on, "not one of them disapproved of the theology and apparatus of Inquisition. . . . The mystery is: how could popes continue in this practical heresy for generation after generation?"[17]

4. On July 17, 1555, Pope Paul IV produced a bull that was a landmark in the history of anti-Semitism. Persecution of Jews was part of the Constantinian (Christian) empire from the fourth century onward, but in Paul IV's bull they were deemed to be slaves by nature and confined in the papal states to a particular area, that is, to a *ghetto.* Only one synagogue per city was allowed; all their books including the Talmud were burned; they were forbidden to engage in most types of work. "The impact of Paul's Bull was immediate. Within days, there was a ghetto in Venice, another in Bologna called the Inferno."[18] Only in 1870, when Italian troops took Rome, were Jews given their freedom by a royal decree—a freedom that "the papacy had denied them for over fifteen hundred years. The last ghetto in Europe was dismantled."[19] Four centuries after Paul IV's bull, a man named Adolf Hitler would tell a Roman Catholic bishop that he was only doing to the Jews what the church had done for centuries. (Hitler, along with Goebbels, was a Roman Catholic, and neither was ever excommunicated.) Are the Nuremberg laws of 1935 that different from the decrees of Innocent III and Paul IV? "When the Nazis named the Jewish living-spaces 'ghettos,' they were aiming expressly to give their policies continuity with that of the popes and a species of respectability."[20] History has recorded the loud silence of Pope Pius XII about the treatment of the Jews in the Second World War, as well as the Vatican's role in smuggling many former Nazis to safe havens in South America.

One can see from this brief reflection on the history of the papacy that the system lends itself to deep corruption. Catholics—especially American Catholics—have to get over their denial and face the truth. The solution is not to "wait" for the next pope, crossing one's fingers and hoping that he will be a "good man." The issue is the structure, not the personality. The papacy was not as central to the church in the past as the modern era has made it. And now that we are moving into a postmodern era, it will become even less important. The present pope has now leveled the playing field for a third millennium of Christianity wherein the bishop of Rome will play a modest but possibly useful role. The Holy Spirit, whose sense of humor far exceeds the Vatican's, is seeing to that.

People ask, "But shouldn't we stay in the church and fight?" It seems to me that *some* will have such a vocation—and it is an honorable one. I myself stayed and fought for over ten years. The analogy I used was that of Rosa Parks, who refused to go to the back of the bus. "We are the bus too," I declared. "We will not leave voluntarily." So I did not leave; and I did fight. But I was expelled from the bus. Let those who feel called to stay on the bus and fight carry on the fight. But this ought not to constitute more than 10 percent of the effort of the people of God. Let 10 percent stay and fight the church authorities—let us all support these generous warriors, who can be said to represent our collective *tithe* to the church. But let the other 90 percent, the rest of us, get on with the task of tomorrow and let go of the sins of yesteryear.

Didn't Jesus say, "Let the dead bury the dead"? We must get on with living. With spirituality and the Spirit's work. And the Spirit is interested in the new. God, says Eckhart, is always "in the beginning." What tasks are we beginning? What gifts are we preparing to leave behind for your children's children? What contribution are we making to the much-needed Environmental Revolution? What new forms for a living, truthful, vulnerable, compassion-bringing church? In short, are we involved in *ecclesiogenesis* (church birthing) or aren't we? One cannot birth church or indeed anything new at all if one is *addicted to old forms, old fights, old, dead ideologies*. This is why I am stretching my boundaries of "catholic" and moving beyond this current *Roman* version of Catholicism. I am impressed by a statement of Meinrad Craighead: "I don't have to deny my roots to know that I've grown beyond them."

The End of Two Eras

We should not be surprised, lost, or depressed because the "Roman Catholic era" as we have known it and lived it in the sixties and seventies is rapidly coming to an end. The historical conditions on which it rested are fast melting away. Like Tillich, who says the Protestant *principle* ought not come to an end, but ought to take on new form, I think it can be said that the *Catholic principle* ought not come to an end but ought to take on new form. What is the "Catholic principle"?

It is decidedly *not* about popes or infallibility or sex as such. The Catholic principle, as I have experienced it, is about *cosmology, mysticism, and wisdom*. To me what is authentic in the word *catholicism* does not apply to religion or church as such but to an attitude toward life that is universal, that is, cosmological.

The Catholic principle is our *Yes* to life just as the Protestant principle is our *No* to life's enemies, all that claims to be Life that falls short of it. Indeed, if we put these two together, a Protestant principle and a Catholic one, we are talking about a reconstruction of Western Christianity. We are also talking about what constitutes a deep spirituality, namely, our mystical *and* prophetic responses to life. This would move us from religion to spirituality. A postmodern era gives us permission to do just that: take what is worth saving from the burning building of Western ecclesial history and forge a simpler, more radical spiritual effort for the next millennium. A faith that has more in common with Jesus of Nazareth's teaching of compassion and with the Cosmic Christ's teaching of divinity everywhere in the universe.

If it is true that we are living through the end of the Protestant era *and* the end of the Roman Catholic era, then surely we are required to take the *best* of the Protestant principle and the *best* of the Catholic principle and leave the rest behind. We must get on with the task of reconstructing Christianity. There is no time to waste if we are to bring about an Environmental Revolution within seventeen years, as Lester Brown of the Worldwatch Institute cautions we must. Regarding religion's future, I made the following journal entry on August 2, 1993.

The gap between religion and spirituality is growing ever wider and deeper. Of that I have no doubt. Religion seems to have less and less to do with Spirit, courage, joy, youthfulness, love, or compassion. And more and more people see this and recognize it. Is it at all possible to bridge that chasm and renew religion by renewing worship and offering spiritual praxis? Will all persons who attempt this get expelled as troublemakers?

Whatever our religious tradition, I think all of us need to heed the warning of Rabbi Heschel: "Religion has always suffered from the tendency to become an end in itself, to seclude the holy, to become parochial, self-indulgent, self-seeking; as if the task were not to ennoble human nature but to enhance the power and beauty of its institutions or to enlarge the body of doctrines."[21]

Somehow I find it easy, in reading wisdom like this, to see Jesus' spirituality coming alive again.

12

A Postdenominational Priest
Standing Outside the Rusty Gate

Howard Thurman has written of a "soul-searching conflict of loyalty" that occurs in our lives. I certainly went through that kind of soul-searching in my move from the church of my ancestors to the Episcopal church.

Outside the Rusty Gate

In February 1994 I had a dream that moved me to tears (something that happens rarely in my dreams), and I recorded it:

Ash Wednesday, February 16, 1994
Dream last night (I cried in the dream)—I'm at an old gate, outdoors, made of iron. It is like a cemetery gate and I hear the statement (have I been teaching it?): "Everyone is here for a purpose. God has a role for everyone."

And then I hear a question: "Has my role been to make creation spirituality known?" With that I cry because of the simplicity of it and the clarity of it and (I think) because it says something about my life and its many choices, including the recent one to become Episcopalian and the Vatican's choice to dump me. And also because it suggests that maybe my life and life work have had some meaning after all.

In reflecting on this dream, I suspect that being "outside the old gate" means being outside the church as I have known it and also outside the modern culture. Both of these structures are getting very old—indeed the gate is a *cemetery* gate, thus a dying church and a dying modern structure. There is grief work to do—ashes to bless ourselves with—as we want to give them a decent burial. Yet my vocation remains alive—I am here *for a purpose* and there is continuity in my work, that of making creation spirituality known. Indeed, *all* our vocations are alive. That is why we are still outside the cemetery gate and not within. Ash Wednesday is a prelude to Easter Day. The gate is an iron gate and it is rusting. This speaks to me of the modern age, which is industrial and whose metaphor in the nineteenth century was the iron horse, that engine that spanned the continent but destroyed the buffalo and the indigenous peoples' way of life and so much more. Now that era is a cemetery, a rust belt, and we are asked to let the dead bury the dead and move on. The key to our moving on from the modern era will be our heart work—the grief *and* the joy that come from doing the true work for which we are here.

I recognized the iron gate in the dream as being the gates that surround the Luxembourg Garden in Paris, located midway between the Latin Quarter and the Catho. The order and the institutional church rejected what I had learned beginning in my Paris days. The fact that I am expelled from the garden has obvious archetypal meanings; yet the garden is no longer a garden but a cemetery; and the gate is no longer beautiful and polished but is rusting. All this speaks to me of death and rebirth; of letting go and moving on; of grief work and—with the words that accompanied the dream—hope for the future. For my existence in the garden was for the same purpose as my existence beyond the garden. I am no longer protected by the *cloister* and the garden it represented, as in my novitiate days. But the vocation continues. The tears were of grief—for all that might have been (what if the Dominicans, instead of turning on me, had sent another brother out to work with me?). But the tears were essentially tears of joy and relief and beauty. For they did not flow because the gates were closed; they flowed at the moment when the voice said, "Your vocation has been to make creation spirituality known." Joy is deeper than sorrow. In spite of the expulsion, my vocation continues. Inside or outside, my vocation goes on. Everyone's does.

Modern Era Yielding to the Postmodern in Religion

When I was dismissed by the Vatican, the first thing I did was sit down and meditate. In my meditation it came to me that the Vatican had made me *a postdenominational priest in a postdenominational era.*

What is postdenominationalism? What does it mean to be a postdenominational priest? I see postdenominationalism as postmodernism playing itself out in the religious sphere. A young artist from England said to me one day, "We are the generation that will understand your work." When I asked why, he responded, "Because creation spirituality is *postmodern.*" That got me scurrying to study the movement known as postmodernism. In the process I have learned that one helpful way for me to understand my journey is to grasp the difference between modern and postmodern times.

The modern era began with the invention of the printing press in the fifteenth century and extended to the invention of the electronic media in the 1960s. My generation has straddled the two eras. The modern era was characterized by anthropocentrism and cultural elitism—it was the time when Europeans sailed around the globe, encountered indigenous peoples everywhere, and overcame them with military might and colonial control. The modern era dismissed other cultures as inferior because they were not book oriented and text oriented. Indeed, it elevated textual truths to the sum of all truths, as when Descartes declared that the soul was in the head and that truth was "clear and distinct ideas." The modern era was patriarchal with a vengeance, and it ignored the body and the heart and the passions as sources of truth. It also dismissed the wisdom of beings other than the human (other beings have no souls, according to Descartes). Beholden to a physics of piecemealness, it honored parts more than the whole. In contrast, postmodernism is pluralistic and honors the wisdom of premodern peoples; it honors the whole body, not equating truth exclusively with patriarchal headiness; it looks for the *whole,* that is, for cosmology. As the physicist David Bohm puts it, "I am proposing a postmodern physics which begins with the whole."[1] In many ways my work in creation spirituality has been postmodern—to be *creation-centered* is to be cosmologically centered. Creation is about the whole. And to speak of spirituality is to speak of *our experiences of the whole.* Mysticism is nothing if it is not an experience of the whole. Awe is not piecemeal; it connects to all things.

Postdenominationalism is about pluralism and ecumenism in religion. It is about stretching our piecemeal religious boundaries and *setting aside our boxes* to the extent that they are neither challenging us nor nourishing us deeply anymore, or to the extent that they are interfering with the pressing earth issues of our time. Denominationalism mirrors the physics of the modern era, when we were taught a parts mentality and that atoms are rugged individualists that never interpenetrate. In the name of denominationalism we have, over the centuries, fought wars, tortured people and whole towns, excommunicated one another, hated one another, competed against one another, banished one another to hell for eternity, and more or less managed to miss the point of what Jesus of Nazareth was teaching: such behavior characteristics as compassion, justice making, loving your enemies, telling the truth. How many of our denominational differences today are no more than "the narcissism of minor differences," to use Freud's phrase? It is hoped that a postdenominational era will improve our efforts to live out the message of Jesus.

To me postdenominationalism means that denominations pale in comparison to nature, creation, and creation in peril. How can human beings come to the aid of creation? How can denominations come to the aid of creation? Consider how the ecumenical movement in this century among Protestants, Catholics, and Jews was born in the death camps of the Second World War. In the face of death, denominationalism wanes. So today, earth itself has become a kind of death camp. As Lester Brown puts it, "Every species on the planet is in a state of decline." In so dire a state of emergency, the question is clear: What can religion do about this? Lapsing into denominational flag-waving and moat-deepening and wall-thickening and orthodox-litmus-testing is the opposite of what we need. Postdenominational means that denominations come second (or third . . . or last) and that other values come first. The richness of worship; the courage of spiritual warriors who will struggle for social justice and ecojustice. In short, holiness, which I will discuss in the final chapter.

Becoming Anglican as a Postdenominational Move

Does being postdenominational mean belonging to no denomination at all? I believe in the Protestant principle of prophecy and protest, *and* I believe in the Catholic principle of mysticism.

I think postdenominational means to belong to one *and* many. In my last summer as a Dominican I did back-to-back workshops with Unitarian ministers and Unity church members. Following the Unitarian workshop a woman stood up in the back of the room and said, "You are one of us. Why don't you join us?" Following the Unity workshop a man said, "You are one of us." What was the universe telling me? Before I heard that my dismissal papers had been forwarded from the master general to the Congregation of Religious in the Vatican, I had written the following in my journal:

[Summer, 1993]
While grateful to all the offers for refuge and ecclesial homes proffered to me already by all my brothers and sisters in other Christian denominations, I believe my path at this time is to say yes to all and yes to none. What does that mean?

It means, I believe, that the times call for me to stand up as an ecumenical priest. (Is that not the real meaning of "Catholic," i.e., ecumenical or universal?) Thus I shall continue to pray and celebrate ritual with all those who care to pray and celebrate with me. Together, Anglican and Methodist, UCC and Unitarian, Unity and Lutheran, Native American and Jewish, Roman Catholic and other Catholic, we shall recommit ourselves to the pressing task today to provide new and ancient forms for our traditions of worship. I offer my services to those who desire them. This is so that the earth might be renewed, the people awakened, justice come alive and real, and compassion birthed. The Environmental Revolution calls us all, and Deep Ecumenism is a contribution religion can make to that revolution.

Now, instead of a vow of poverty, I make a renewed commitment to living a
    sustainable lifestyle and encouraging others to do so.
Now, instead of a vow of obedience, I make a renewed commitment to reinvigorating democracy and small communities.

*Now, instead of a vow of celibacy, I make a renewed commitment to rever-
ence in all my relationships, and if I'm blessed with a primary relationship,
especially there.*

*We need renewable religion today, and "intermediate rituals" analogous to
"intermediate technologies." Sustainable and nonpolluting spirituality.
Simple living spirit-wise. Maybe this is behind the Spirit's work in remov-
ing Leonardo Boff, Bill Callahan, and other American priest-theologians
from active priesthood. Maybe this is why the bureaucratic and hierarchical models of religion are fast being supplemented by base communities
and intermediate ritual experiences.*

When I was dismissed from the Dominican order I felt that three options
presented themselves to me, as I have previously mentioned:

1. hide under a rock (the Vatican's choice)
2. do what Fr. Leonardo Boff did: seek laicization
3. make a lateral move to another tradition in the Christian church

For me, and my culture, I felt the third option to be the most creative
choice. I consulted only one Roman Catholic clergyperson on making this decision and he was a liberation theologian and elder Dominican, Fr. Albert
Nolan of South Africa. He had been elected head of the Dominican order several years earlier but had turned the job down—the first time in its 750-year
history that anyone had!—which says something of the wisdom of the man.

He told me that the Vatican's intention was to isolate me, that I should do
whatever it takes to stay within a larger community. The Episcopal decision
made all the sense in the world. This very much confirmed my own convictions, and at the same time it reminded me of a statement of Cardinal Arns in
Brazil that "the future of the church is in ecumenism." In retrospect, I return
to a statement of Père Chenu: "I'm all for dialogue with non-Catholics, non-
Christians, atheists. The theology of today and tomorrow must make itself
into a dialogue with those who think they are unable to believe." All my
work in creation spirituality can be understood as an effort to get those who
think themselves unable to believe to at least experience, and trust again. And
true belief—as opposed to the mechanical reiteration of dogmas—arises exactly from that juncture of experience and trust. "For God is at home—it is
we who have gone out for a walk," as Meister Eckhart put it. The Source of
all sources (including the Source of all healthy belief) is at home with us.
"Emmanuel," God-with-us.

With this lateral move on my part, I am practicing what I preach. The future does not lie with denominations but with base communities. Those very
theological arguments that kept so many Protestants and Catholics literally
at one another's throats for the past four centuries are passé. No one cares

anymore. Can you name any twenty-some-year-old who can tell you the difference between a Methodist and a Presbyterian, an Anglican and a Roman Catholic? Denominationalism is no longer an issue. And that is a good thing, for denominational*ism,* like rac*ism* and sex*ism* and adult*ism,* has to be held accountable for its many sins over the centuries. Today, though, we can admit that we are living in a postdenominational time. While traditions and local roots matter, these are all traditions spelled with a small *t.* They are relative; they are human-made (though often spirit-inspired in the past); they are socially constructed realities; they can be mined for their wisdom; and let go of.

On the night before the press conference in which the Episcopal bishop of California, William Swing, and I were to announce my switch to the Episcopal church and my reasons for it, I had a dream that seemed significant. The operative line in it was clear and lucid. It was from the gospel. "Shake the dust from your feet." This was Jesus' advice when he spoke about entering a house and wishing "peace upon it" and not getting peace in return. This pretty much summarized my struggle with the Roman Catholic church at this time in history. By going public with the Episcopal bishop, I was indeed shaking dust from my feet. Now the work could go on—not outside the church tradition or community, but very much within it. Yet in a more modest corner of that tradition. Speaking of modesty, my heart leapt during the press conference when Bishop Swing made the point in response to a question that "the Episcopal church does not exist to make other people Episcopalians." I look forward to the day when a pope will make a similar statement. We will all breathe more deeply on that day. But I cannot wait around for that to happen. There is too much work to be done and too little time to get it accomplished.

On April 23, 1994, I preached my first sermon as an Episcopalian in Grace Cathedral at the eleven o'clock Sunday mass. I began my sermon as follows:

> This past week I received a letter from a retired seventy-four-year-old Anglican priest in New York. He said: "Rome's loss is our gain. You have jumped the sinking ship of the Vatican for the leaky rowboat of the Episcopal church.". . .
>
> The funny thing about being told that I've jumped from a sinking ship to a leaky rowboat is that I actually feel like I'm on very firm, dry ground. Earthquake prone—but dry. And that what I want to do is to go deeper into the cellar, into the kiva, into the underground, into the lower chakras of the cathedral, into the basement of this cathedral, for example, where the young school students sweat in the gymnasium, and to go there with young adults who are artists and ritual makers and can help resurrect and restore our traditions of worship.

Following the mass a woman came up to me and said, "I'm Roman Catholic and I disagreed with your decision. But I've read your books and felt I should come to hear you speak. During the mass I was hit right here"—she pointed to her heart—"first by a woman celebrating mass and second by your talk. Now I get it. You have to speak—you have so much we have to hear and your church won't let you speak."

Ecumenism and Postdenominationalism

Ecumenism is postmodern and may even be another word for postdenominational. Worship is becoming more and more ecumenical. Shortly before I flew to Sheffield, England, to experience the special Anglican mass there, I did a weekend workshop in a large Presbyterian church in the inner city of Pittsburgh. They do wonderful work at that church in so many ways, but when I spoke about my upcoming hopes of experiencing renewed liturgy in Sheffield, the pastor himself said to me, "Come back and tell us what you have learned. Our liturgy needs such a boost of new ideas and new forms." When I looked at their worship service I realized it paralleled exactly the form of the mass in Roman Catholicism and the Episcopal church. "Yes, since the Second Vatican Council we have all shared the same basic rite," he reminded me.

Recently I met with a friend who has been ordained in the United Church of Canada for only six months. He told me that he is already feeling the pinch of being responsible for a liturgy that lacks energy. All this tells me that worship is already ecumenical—it is ecumenically boring, and the reason is the same in each denomination: it is not a matter of lack of goodwill on the part of ministers and priests, nor lack of work; it is a matter of our being saddled with forms from the modern era that prevent prayer from happening.

A postdenominational era will be eager to learn from premodern religions instead of proselytizing to them. I have learned so much spirituality from premodern religions. I remember being ushered into a classroom of sixth-grade Maori youngsters on my first visit to New Zealand in 1987. First the girls, then the boys sang welcoming songs in their ancient tongue. I was overwhelmed by the power of the songs and the power of these youngsters as they sang them. There would be no suicides in this group, I said to myself, thinking of the sad number of suicides that hit Native Americans at the same age. These people had managed to preserve enough of their culture in spite of the white colonialists that their souls were still strong and their song was strong medicine.

Eddie Kneebone, an Australian aboriginal, spoke to a roomful of artists that creation spirituality people had gathered in Melbourne, Australia, and showed us his painting. It was his—contemporary—but it was also very ancient: it depicted the life of the soul, the life of a person from conception through childhood, adolescence, adulthood, and death—which returned to conception again. He explained how in his culture one doesn't hang a picture on a wall; instead it is placed on the floor and all sit around it, as you would around a campfire. Since everyone has a different topography from which to relate, everyone has a different story to tell about the picture.

To speak of these ancient traditions as being preliterate does not do them justice. "Oral traditions" are not just "preliterate." (How would Catholics like to be called "pre-Protestant"?) Oral traditions are *oral*; that means they are sung from the depth of the very first chakra. That is their deep power and their deep gift to a culture such as ours that has invested all its power in the upper chakras. Oral traditions still have the lower-chakra power to *get us down*. This is sure to have a lot to do with the recovery of holiness in our time. Clarissa Pinkola Estés's book *Women Who Run with the Wolves,* wherein she exegetes ancient stories from her own multiple ancestral traditions, offers a superb example of the power and the wisdom of oral traditions. Robert Bly provides a parallel service in his exegesis of *Iron John,* an ancient myth from his Nordic ancestors. Again, the wisdom from the oral traditions.

In many respects I have been living a postdenominational priesthood for many years. The majority of my invitations to speak in recent years have not been in Roman Catholic settings but in churches of other denominations: Episcopal, Unity, Methodist, United Church of Christ, Unitarian, Presbyterian, and others. Indeed, the very last workshop I did as a Dominican was at All Saints Episcopal Church in Pasadena, California. It was a powerful experience, as many art-as-meditation leaders led groups of various kinds on Friday and Saturday. It was the following Monday that I received notification of my dismissal from the order. Once, at a Common Boundary conference near Washington, D.C., when I finished a daylong workshop on liberating the Cosmic Christ in all of us, a man with a long white beard came up and kissed me on the cheek. "I am a rabbi in New York City," he said, "and I feel closer to you than to most of my fellow rabbis." I remember my last year teaching at Barat College when a middle-aged Jewish woman who had taken several of my courses approached me and said, "You are a good rabbi." And I remember the toothless old Indian man following a presentation I gave in New Mexico who said, "During your talk my ancestors came and sat on my shoulders and said: 'Listen to this man, he is one of us.'" And the Filipina Catholic sister who was raised by a family that practiced both Catholicism and the ancestral religion and who wrote that she finds in creation spirituality "what was ours in the past. The European Christianity that was brought to us had put aside our own way of worshiping God and we have been left alienated from our own tradition." Her desire now is "to recover our creation-centered spirituality and also to undergo the process of grieving for what I and my people have lost." So many people I have encountered from so-called third-world nations express similar sentiments on learning of creation spirituality.

Postdenominationalism recognizes the closeness we feel to one another when we are all engaged—no matter what our denomination—in the search for mysticism and the struggle for justice. Mysticism and prophecy are much, much larger than denominations. To know that is to be postdenominational. It may or may not mean we are still part of denominations, but the fact is that it is difficult to live without one. Communities and traditions are important—provided we write "tradition" always with a small *t*. We are indeed living in an age in which, as Walter Anderson puts it, "whenever we describe ourselves, we should add 'etc.'"[2] This "age of the fading boundaries" applies to our religious and denominational boundaries as well as to other boundaries. Does this help explain my experience of being a postdenominational priest and of embracing the Anglican tradition of Catholicism? Ought I, now that I am a Roman Catholic priest *and* an Anglican priest, just sign "etc." after my name?

Recovering Christians outnumber practicing Christians in the world today. Because so many people have been wounded by the church, we all need to apply Alice Miller's work on the wounded child to our various church experiences. Just as I alluded in chapter 9 to my horrible experience with a priest guide in the Roman catacombs and the need for the church to heal its child wounded at the time of the Roman persecutions, so too the church needs to pay attention to the wounds it received earlier in the synagogue. As Rosemary Ruether has pointed out in *Faith and Fratricide,* anti-Semitism began very early in the church. It is present in the Gospels. But there it is present as a child hurt by its parent—not as a parent hurting children. The latter is what happened when the church took over the empire; one finds in St. Augustine, for example, references such as "those lustful Jews" and other anti-Semitic statements. Christianity will never grow up to its adult stature until and unless it heals its *wounded Roman* and its *wounded Jewish* child. And when it does this it will finally let go of aspirations to Roman imperialism (including, one could pray, its very names of "pontifex maximus") on the one hand; and, on the other, what seems to go with all empire building in the West from Augustine to Bossuet to Hitler to Jerry Falwell—its anti-Semitism and abuse of Jews as scapegoats. Then, being rid of anti-Semitism, it might begin to learn what I have had the privilege of learning over the years: the deep, deep gifts that Jewish theology has to give to Christianity.

Indeed, if I were shipwrecked on an island and able to read only one theologian, I would choose the works of Rabbi Abraham Joshua Heschel. When I read him I feel I am the closest to the mind and heart of Jesus. After all, Judaism *is* the morphic field, the collective memory, the ancient matrix that not only nourished Jesus but the entire early Christian community, including the writers of the Gospels and Epistles of the Christian Bible. It amazes me to this day how deeply the dualistic teachings of an Augustine, for example, can penetrate the Christian religion while the holistic teachings of Jesus pass almost unnoticed.

Ecumenism with Judaism is part of the postdenominational mind-set that can reinvigorate our species with spirituality. To this we should add ecumenism with Islam as well. And especially the Sufi mystical tradition, which is so rich in spiritual practices of dervish dances and other forms of healthy meditation. Is it mere coincidence that what Chenu called "the greatest renaissance in the West"—that of the twelfth century—occurred under the impetus of the Islamic intellectual tradition that swept into Europe at that time?

Ecumenism with Buddhism and Taoism and Hinduism—in other words, East meeting West with its wisdom—is also important to a postdenominational and postmodern awakening. This is happening but usually on a personal scale, as individual Westerners go to Eastern meditation centers for their spiritual praxis. But I sometimes get frightened by what academia does to this interaction, reducing it so often to studying foreign languages and going over ancient texts. I would like to see more spiritual praxis and therefore "deep ecumenism" in the coming together of East and West. But, of course, if Western academicians are themselves not in touch with their own spiritual practice or that of the Western tradition, then connections that matter are hard to come by. The Dalai Lama recently put forth his own view on deep ecumenism when he said, "There are now no grounds for making distinctions between East and West. What we need now is a melting of minds, a coming together. Human compassion is the most important factor—not ethnic divisions, racial divisions, religious divisions."[3]

A few years ago when I was doing a workshop in Malibu, I was put up for the night in a beautiful home with a Buddha altar and statue. The Buddha and I spent the night alone together in that house, and I woke up with an insight that I shared with the retreatants that morning: namely, that Buddha lived a full life into his eighties and died a natural death. He knew midlife crisis and he knew serenity. Jesus, on the other hand, was a prophetic, angry, even impetuous Jew, and he was killed before his time when he was about thirty-three. What does this mean? Judaism and Christianity have a life force about them, a prophetic imperative, that is essential; but Buddhism has a serenity and a sense of longevity that the West can use. My conclusion? We need both. Buddhism needs the West and the West needs Buddhism.

Postdenominationalism also means that denominations are far less important for spirituality today than are our *professions*. It is at work more than at church that the real moral—and immoral—decisions are being rendered about the health of our planet, our bodies, our children, our very souls. Work is the adult arena for spiritual decision making, whether we are talking about the waste our species spews into the earth, or the violence and titillating sex that dominates our television programming, or the inane political issues that get raised to fever pitch in order to drown out the real issues. It is *in our work,* as I argue in my book on *Reinventing Work,* that the moral issues of our lives play out. And, as I conclude in that study, it is in our work that spirituality itself will be redeemed. As the Bhagavad Gita teaches, "They all find perfection who find joy in their work."[4] The bringing of spirituality back to our work worlds will amount to a revolution in work, and it will also allow us to pay more attention to the great amount of inner work that needs doing in our time. In paying attention to this, we will find that *unemployment is not only unacceptable but unnecessary.* There is work for everyone, so long as we include inner work as integral to our definitions of work—something the industrial era failed to do.

Postdenominationalism recognizes that our church affiliations, as dear as they are or might have once been to us, are themselves more often than not *socially constructed realities.* The concept of socially constructed realities helps us to understand denominations—their limits *and* their grace. Our ancestors created expressions of their faith that today we call tradition. Awareness of this does not strip them of all their power. Nor does it mean that their differences do not count; only that idolatry of these differences and temptations to narcissism about them ought not to prevail. What I call "ethnic religion" is the lowest form of all religions, and in many instances it is at that first, collective level of religion that we fight our wars and battles. Northern Ireland of the past twenty-two years seems a case in point. There religion is the outward excuse for a struggle involving class, jobs, political decision-making power. Fear rules and religion takes the brunt of it. To recognize our denominational expressions as socially constructed realities is to allow ourselves to move beyond them. Or, if we choose to stay, to stay with a kind of denominational humility. Charles Jencks believes that part of any postmodern movement is a practice of "double-coding," which is the "strategy of affirming and denying the existing power structures at the same time."[5]

Postdenominationalism, then, allows us to get over our superiority complexes when it comes to religion. To let them go. It means taking what we can believe in in conscience and moving beyond.

Protesting Catholicism *and* Protestantism

In my own case I can now say the following: I am now, officially as of January 1994, a Protestant (Episcopal) Christian. What does this mean to me? It means I honor the principle of protest, of saying no, of prophecy therefore. When it comes to religion, this is what I protest: I know Catholicism rather well, having lived it out quite faithfully for fifty-four years, thirty-four of those in a religious order, twenty-six of those as a priest, twenty-one of those as a theologian (thirty-one years of theological studies). What I protest I have listed in chapter 11 as shadow factors in Catholicism signaling the end of an era. I protest those parts of the tradition—the tendency toward fascism, the preoccupation with sexuality as a problem instead of a spiritual mystery, the sexism, the loss of its mystical tradition.

But I also protest things within Protestantism, including the following:

1. its lack of premodern roots—indeed its conscious and deliberate ignorance of the medieval church with its great accomplishments in spirituality and theology and art

2. its silly notions of predestination and biblicalism, as if the Bible didn't come through the believing community

3. its preoccupation with texts, as if the "word of God" is words from human books and not every creature of God

4. its being stuck in the modern era

5. its headiness and patriarchal roots and banishment of the goddess

6. its boring worship, based as it is on words, words, and more words

7. its swallowing hook, line, and sinker the Enlightenment and capitalism

8. its lack of a universal outlook, that is, its acquiescence to nation-state ideologies

9. its fragmentation resulting in a papal-control compulsion at the local level

10. its lack of mysticism

11. its seminary system that owes more to Descartes and Kant than to Jesus and our tradition of mystics/prophets

12. its substitution of sweetness and kindness and "fellowship" for prophecy and anger, moral outrage and healthy love

13. its Eurocentrism

And so, I am clearly neither Catholic nor Protestant—or, if you wish, I am both Catholic and Protestant. I hope I bear within me the cosmic mystic of Catholicism and the protesting prophet of Protestantism. But to do this today, we must both draw from these two traditions *and move beyond them.* Who can predict what spiritual energy might arise and flow again were we to apply spiritual lessons of "letting go" to religion itself and were we to succeed in washing away religious imperialism and the competition that goes with it? Postdenominationalism is a kind of appeal to nonelitism in religion. The symbols and metaphors and rituals of a healthy religion will rise to the surface, and it is these, rather than denominations themselves, that will save our souls. Charles Jencks describes postmodernism's task as one that ought to "challenge monolithic elitism, to bridge the gaps that divide high and low cultures, elite and mass, specialist and non-professional, or most generally put—one discourse and interpretative community from another. . . ."[6] Is this not all activity that postdenominational religion would be about as well? A bridging of the gap between high and low cultures (might we say religious sects), specialists and professionals, one community from another?

Why Priesthood?

But what about being a "postdenominational *priest*"? Why do we need priests? Walt Whitman had his answer to this question a century ago:

There will soon be no more priests: their work is done.
They may wait awhile, perhaps a generation or two, dropping off by degrees.
A superior breed shall take their place;
The gangs of kosmos and prophets en masse shall take their place.
A new order shall arise and they shall be the priests of man,
And every man shall be his own priest.
The churches built under their umbrage shall be the churches of men and women.
Through the divinity of themselves shall the kosmos, and the new breed of poets,
Be interpreters of men and women, and of all events and things.
They shall find their inspiration in real objects today, symptoms of the past and future.[7]

Rabbi Heschel had his opinion on the priesthood as well. He wrote: "The great dream of Judaism is not to raise priests, but a people of priests; to consecrate all men [*sic*], not only some men."[8] One wonders if this was not Jesus' aim as well, where "all men" meant "all women and men." M. D. Chenu used to insist that the New Testament priesthood was not about "cult" but about prophecy. Priests were to be prophetic. Thomas Merton also wrote about a radical revision of priesthood:

I think the whole thing needs to be changed, the whole idea of the priesthood needs to be changed. I think we need to develop a whole new style of worship in which there is no need for one hierarchical person to have a big central place, a form of worship in which everyone is involved.[9]

I agree with Fr. Bede Griffith and the study by James D. G. Dunn that he recommended so highly (*Unity and Diversity in the New Testament*) that the priesthood was not part of the early church. It was a second-century invention.

And yet that still gives it an eighteen-hundred-year, if somewhat checkered, history. So there is some use to the priesthood, some power there. Yet the Quakers and others who have managed to transcend the priesthood offer some eschatological hope that we too will before long outgrow the priesthood as we know it in its clerical representations. I do believe, however, that human communities require leadership from among them, and that notion of spiritual leadership will not disappear. Granted that its abuse has been at times offensive *even to religion,* saying nothing of spirituality.

In my own case, I stay in the priesthood because I feel that, at this crossroads time in religious and planetary history, something useful might still be forged from that tradition. Especially if a new generation, one that is genuinely committed to a postmodern worldview and the value it puts on nonelitism, can reinvent the priesthood, making of it a source of authentic spiritual renewal and leadership. With women just recently entering the priestly traditions of the West, there is considerable hope that new forms and interpretations and training methods may be implemented to reinvent the priesthood.

In my own case, I felt that since I had been ordained twenty-seven years previously, and since no decent rationale was given me for abandoning that leadership role that I believed I had discharged honorably over the years, I might as well stick it out to see what the next chapter would unfold. For me it is not at all a matter of clinging to the priesthood. The reader will recall that I "left the priesthood" before I was even ordained when I chose to go to the hermitage under threat from my provincial of not being ordained thereby. Thus I have all my priestly life been very little burdened by the office (I was helped in this by being primarily an educator and not a parish priest). But when the Sheffield group told me that I could actually assist their movement by remaining in the priesthood and becoming an Anglican to boot, I felt it was some good use to which I could put the holy oils.

As a certain farewell to my Roman Catholic history and as a courtesy to the man, I wrote the Roman Catholic bishop of Oakland on April 6, 1994, when I made my leave. In the letter I thanked him for his "quiet support" and concluded with the following paragraph:

> This decision has not been easy. But I believe that issues of ecological justice, native peoples' and women's rights, and reaching the young by way of new forms of worship are of sufficient merit that some of us, caught '"between times," just have to make some uncomfortable moves. I do not feel I am leaving the Roman Catholic church but am rather embracing another expression of catholicism. I believe that the Vatican has made me a postdenominational priest in a postdenominational era, and I am responding to that reality.

Eight months later I received a personal response from the bishop in which he talked of his confusion and concern.

As I was making my move formally into the Episcopal church I received a phone call from Deborah Koons, the fiancée of Grateful Dead guitarist Jerry Garcia. It happened that just that month Jerry and I were featured in the same magazine, and on reading his interview I said to a friend, "This guy is a creation-centered philosopher if ever there was one." Deborah told me that they were planning their wedding and wanted me to be the officiating priest. I asked her how she knew of me and learned that they had been discussing my theology, especially that of *Original Blessing*. "Well," I said, "you have to understand that I'm not on very good terms with the Vatican these days." "Oh!" she replied, "an outlaw priest for an outlaw wedding!"

We were able to secure the support of the Episcopal church to hold a very private wedding in an intimate chapel in Marin County. Though I am not a great fan or frequenter of weddings, I have to say that I have never seen a more loving couple than Deborah and Jerry were that day. At the wedding I spoke on elements of a postmodern marriage, including the imperative not to bore each other (if we live in a cosmology, we will not be boring); on the need to see marriage as a creative act—a verb and not a noun—requiring the same daily effort at creativity as our art does; and on the importance of fun.

When I visited them at their home months later, I was touched by the utter child in Jerry—his enthusiasm for a new telescope he was setting up that afternoon, his relish at showing me the computer on which he painted and the work he was doing on an illustrated book of his childhood. Yet he was a philosopher in his own right and loved to talk theology.

I was honored that Jerry and Deborah continued to support me in my transition. They were in the last row of Grace Cathedral the Sunday morning I delivered my first homily as an Episcopalian; they were in attendance at my formal reception ceremony as an Episcopal priest; and they were present for the Planetary Mass in the basement of the cathedral. As Jerry put it to me on the day of my reception, "Religion is important to society. It has to be reinvented. We can't get along without it."

One and a half years later, Jerry died peacefully in his sleep at a rehabilitation center. Again I was asked to officiate as a priest, this time at his funeral. Synchronicity abounded at the service, beginning with the irony that it was held at St. Stephen's parish in Tiburon, and one of the Grateful Dead's earliest songs was called "St. Stephen." Deborah's strength was manifest in the heartfelt talk she delivered at the service about her and Jerry's love and relationship. Numerous other examples of wisdom arose from the friends and associates of Jerry, including a hastily written and passionately presented eulogy from the lyricist of the group, Robert Hunter, who delivered his gift like a bard of old. I made the point in my eulogy that Otto Rank describes three ways of healing in a society: therapy that heals one-to-one; art that heals small groups; and religious prophecy that heals the masses. The response to Jerry's work with the Grateful Dead demonstrated that theirs was a healing work both of art and of religious prophecy. It healed the masses. Its appeal was spiritual and mystical but also prophetic—it interfered with a culture that lacked joy and effective ritual. Jerry was a wounded healer, wounded by seeing his father drown in front of him when he was four years old and wounded by much in life. But his wounds contained his power, and he turned them to compassion for many. I learned from my brief but rich association with the Grateful Dead inner circle that I was one of many who felt indebted to Jerry for his brilliance and friendship. Knowing him was another gift of living in California. Before the service I was anxious, aware of how diverse the mourners would be in terms of religious affiliation and alienation, artists, special fans, and others. But during the service—as so often happens to me—peace settled in as the spirit of the group raised us all to heights of healthy grieving and remembering and laughter. At the last minute of the service, an inspiration came to me to invite the mourners to give Jerry one last standing ovation—this not just for his music but for his life. The applause was prolonged and deep, and I knew I had once more been blessed to assist some real people at real prayer.

Planetary Mass

On Reformation Sunday, the last Sunday of October 1994, a wonderful event happened. In the basement of Grace Cathedral we hosted the first Planetary Mass in America. The posse was the priest and the posse consisted of thirty-six dedicated young people from the Nine O'clock Service (NOS) of Sheffield, England, who came to America for eight days to set up the service and put it on. I preached at that mass; the Gospel text was from John 1, which talks of the "Word" of God as the light through which "all things came to be." I spoke of all the things our century has done with light, beginning with a young scientist in his twenties named Albert Einstein saying, "All I want to do my whole life is to study light."

> In the twentieth century we have lassoed light in all new ways. The military harnessed light for its purposes: Dresden; Hiroshima; Nagasaki; MX missiles; napalm in Vietnam. The entertainment and news industries lassoed light for their purposes, first in black and white and then in color; business lassoed light in forms of computers, CD ROMS, fiber optics, for its purposes.
>
> The question we ask at the end of this century is the following: Can we lasso light so that the Sacred can more fully reveal itself to us? So

that the "Word can become flesh," that is to say, "light," living and dancing in our midst?

I spoke of the meaning of Reformation Sunday, the Reformation representing not only a response to corruption in the dominant church establishment but also the religious response to the emerging modern era, an era opened up by the technological breakthrough we call the invention of the printing press. The printing press democratized the Bible, making it available to laypersons and others. It caused a religious revolution that was only partially successful in renewing religion. Why the failures?

> The biggest mistake in religion in the modern era has been to confuse "the word of God" with human words or textual words in a book. If "the word was in the beginning," then clearly the WORD is bigger than human words or textual words. It preceded all words by about fourteen billion years!
>
> The creation-centered mystic Meister Eckhart said in the fourteenth century that "every creature is a word of God and a book about God." This carries us far beyond the overly anthropocentric idea of the Bible alone as the "word of God," a modern notion that emerged because of our fascination with texts at the invention of the printing press.

But now—with the emergence of the postmodern era, we can get it right. Because we have overemphasized "words" in religion, we have lacked a language for the mystical. Now we may have such a language—light itself—dancing, moving, living light. Physicist David Bohm says that matter is "frozen light." If matter is frozen light, then Spirit may be "melted, thawed, warmed up, and flowing light," and "flesh" is both! Our postmodern times were ushered in by another invention, that of electronic media, electronic music, light dancing, the harnessing of light. We have been gifted with a new language, a language for microcosm/macrocosm; for connecting to the universe again; past and future; for moving beyond anthropocentrism; a language that awakens awe and mysticism, heart and soul and body and, hopefully, body politic. Is the lassoing of light in our time not a special opportunity for a new generation to reinvent the "Word" that is with God and had been in the divine presence playing since the beginning of the world?

What were my feelings about the event of the Planetary Mass? As I sat on the floor amid hundreds of other worshipers, many of them young street people, I was deeply moved. Indeed, I was filled with joy and I am still, three weeks after the event, as I attempt to process my experience.

One thought awakened in me was this: Western culture has been running for two centuries on René Descartes's egoistic and heady statement: "I think, therefore I am." More recently, American consumer culture has altered this philosophy in its own unique way to: "I buy, therefore I am; I consume, therefore I exist." But as I participated in the Planetary Mass I sensed that a new philosophical era was opening up. Its shibboleth would be: "We celebrate, therefore we are." And of course, it is founded on a deeper truth: "We are, therefore we celebrate."

One thing I have learned from knowing the NOS community of Sheffield is that the alternative to capitalism does not have to be communism. It can be community. A community gets much more done and at a far cheaper price than does bureaucratic capitalism or bureaucratic communism or the modern state. For one thing, community allows giveaway to happen. These thirty-six people who came ten thousand miles for nine days of intense work to set up, put on, and take down the wonderful sacred space they created for the Planetary Mass did so for nothing. A lot of labor went into this effort and a lot of gift giving. It was truly a spiritual giveaway. Finances were handled by asking donors for contributions behind the scenes—not by asking anyone present at the mass. That makes for a much purer gift than is often the case.

In rediscovering the giveaway, the community was also rediscovering the authentic meaning of *sacrifice*. The idea of sacrifice has, I think, been severely tainted during the patriarchal era; it has been presented in an almost sado-masochistic setting in which, verbally or nonverbally, the message is: you are to sacrifice for me. But it is time to redeem that word *sacrifice,* which, after all, clearly includes the word *sacred* in it. Is anything sacred without sacrifice? Surely there is no love without sacrifice. Love inspires sacrifice and requires it, whether we are speaking of parental love or partnered love or love of friendship or love of art, work, environment, and so on. Sacrifice may just be another word for gift giving. There was a plethora of gift giving at this mass, ranging from the four Sufi dancers who twirled in the four directions of the room throughout the mass, to the singers and the rappers who gave their gifts with abundance; from the mixers and deejays with caps on backward, to the wild young man dancing madly under the strobe lights; from the designers of the mass to the leaders of it. All sacrificed (many took a week off from their jobs to come and work on the mass in San Francisco). This was evident. It helped to make the occasion special and spiritual and pure. A night of deep prayer.

I suspect it was this prayer dimension that most filled me with joy and is the reason I said to myself during the mass, "I could do this every night of the week." I joined the Dominican order thirty-six years ago in order to pray, to explore more deeply my relationship with the divine. I stayed in the order many years for that reason and to lead others in real and effective prayer. Yet, sad to tell, some of the dullest, most rote and dead liturgical experiences I have had in recent years have been at gatherings of Dominicans.

This was not the case at the Planetary Mass in the basement of Grace Cathedral. There was beauty going on wherever I looked. It was like being in a forest, where every direction displayed beauty and something interesting to behold. This included not only the singers, dancers, and rappers but also the projections on large video screens, on television sets, on a huge globe suspended over the beautiful altars (one a sun altar, the second a crescent-moon altar). On the screens were hummingbirds hovering, galaxies spinning, flowers opening, human beings marching, protesting, embracing, and polluting (sin was present and indeed renamed for us at the mass). Life was there in all its panoply of forces, good and not so good, human and more than human.

It was the opposite of dull, the opposite of boring. There was wonder everywhere—as in the cosmos itself. And beauty. Indeed, here microcosm and macrocosm came together magically. And why shouldn't they? Why shouldn't there be wonder and beauty everywhere when we worship? How has it come to pass that our civilization has practically managed to close down ritual and render it boring, especially in church? It need not be so. This mass was *interesting,* and to be interesting means to be about what goes on *inter esse,* between beings. It was that kind of experience—a cosmological one, wherein the relationships between things is named and celebrated and nothing is left out, especially not the Source of all things. Indeed, it was to thank that Source of all things that we gathered to pray at all.

A major feature of the Planetary Mass is that it is designed and executed not by theologians with Ph.D.'s in liturgical niceties but by a team of artists. That is why it works as ritual and as aesthetics. (That plus the fact that it has a solid, creation-spiritual theology to underpin it and give it depth and scope, including a connection to our ancestral mystical tradition.) What is art? What is the work of artists? A young artist, a painter who in fact attended the mass, wrote me recently about his vocation: "I think I've come to know that I paint in order to arrive at the point of surprise, to learn of myself."

The painter—literally—goes to the edge. In this case, of the canvas. Every artist goes to the edge. Is that what creativity is—"going to the edge"? To the horizon? To the frontiers? Or as Rank phrases it, to the *Beyond?* And why? To be surprised, first. And second, to surprise. And what is surprise? It's part of awe and curiosity and wisdom and fun and celebration and, therefore, compassion. It's also part of cosmology, for if cosmology is a study of the whole, the whole must include the edge and the surprise and the unborn of things, even the unexpected *between* things (thus, our word *interesting*).

But surprise is also transcendence. "Transcendence" comes from *transcendere*, to *climb across*. We all want to climb across new portals, be ushered into new rooms and vistas where our hearts and souls can experience awe anew and fall in love again. Artists assist us in this crossing over, this climbing over. The word *climbing* implies a certain arduousness to the task of following the artist's lead. Art is not itself the new vista; it is (merely) the door to the new perception. Like Jesus speaking of the kingdom—"do not look here or there"—it is *among you*. Art tells us what is deeply among us—*not* by its objectifying of some object but by its release of our powers of hearing, seeing, feeling, knowing anew. ("The blind shall see and the deaf shall hear and the lame shall walk.") In a new place and space. Art is a threshold experience. Artists carry us over the threshold—and leave us there. The rest is up to us.

This is reconstructive postmodern art. Spirituality is at its core. The invitation to *climb across,* to transcend. I had the feeling at the Planetary Mass that many people had come for transcendence—and that they indeed underwent a transcendent experience. In fact, that was the feedback I received that night and since. Following are some responses that I picked up from the mass.

From a woman Episcopal priest: "When I dance, I dance hard and when I pray, I pray hard, but no one had invited me before to dance *and* pray hard at the same time. It was dynamite. I want to spend the rest of my life working with these young people."

From a middle-aged woman: "This morning I went to church, sat in the pew, and prayed very hard. I felt good; this much of my soul was affected." Here she put her thumb and middle finger together to make an egg about two inches in diameter. "But tonight, tonight *all* of me was affected" (and here she threw her arms up into the air).

From a twenty-three-year-old street person and writer: "I would come to this mass every Sunday. It was fabulous."

From a twenty-some-year-old woman who is a secretary at a major publishing firm: "I have never been to a church in my life or to a rave. But ever since the mass three days ago, something has been vibrating in my mind. I have never felt like this before."

From a middle-aged woman theologian: "All my life I have read the mystics and I have never had the experience that Julian of Norwich writes about, that is, of seeing the cosmos in the hazel nut and Jesus in the hazel night. Until tonight. At the consecration, when the universe was born on the video screens at the same time, I truly got it. It entered my heart: the Cosmic Christ is in us and we are all in the Cosmic Christ."

From a twenty-seven-year-old artist: "I was moved by the mass and liked it a lot. But every day since, a new level of vibrations has been going off inside of me. Its effect keeps growing on me."

From a fifty-some-year-old executive: "The last time I went to communion was in the 1940s when I was nine years old. I took communion tonight. It was so moving."

I think the Planetary Mass represents a new, postmodern stage in human development. Postmodern worship has arrived. Asking the artists and the young to lead us in celebration is just common sense. It is a return of the repressed, for in the modern era neither artists nor youth nor mystics were asked to lead us in anything.

Implications abound in the renewal of ritual for the future of politics in America. For example, in the 1994 congressional elections, 62 percent of registered American voters did not even bother to vote. (Since fewer than 69 percent of Americans are registered voters, this means that the Republicans who won the election did so by capturing about 15 percent of the adult American citizens' votes.) The future of American politics may lie less with either party than with those efforts that can awaken the disenfranchised to fuller citizenship. This includes the 62 percent of the registered voters who did not vote as well as the 31 percent who have not even registered. Otto Rank warned fifty years ago that you don't cure an ailing democracy with more democracy. You must step out of that structure to awaken what is missing in it. It seems to me that renewed rituals may furnish a cure for our ailing political life. It holds such potential because it is grassroots; because it is led by those who know alienation, and by those who have the most at stake, namely the young, if our civilization continues on a path of self-destruction; and because its outcome is to awaken energy and hope. Thus, creativity can happen again.

A community in Leeds, England, called REM sponsors an alternative Mass on a regular basis that includes visual media such as computers, video, and slides along with music. The music includes a voice-over about creation theology and has a strong beat that is quite premodern or indigenous in its flavor. A Leeds group called Synergy sent me their album, which includes elements of techno, dub, rave, house, and ambient music to dance to. I used this tape in three workshops recently, one in Boston, another in Orlando, and a third at Esalen near Big Sur in California. The response was very strong. After the workshop in Boston, one woman in her early forties told me that in the middle of the dance she started to cry because she thought of her ten-year-old son who cannot stand going to church. Being Episcopalian herself, she was very concerned about his religious future. "Then, in the middle of the dance, I realized that here is a language my son will be able to pray in." Thus, her tears. Tears of joy.

At Esalen, a large man in his mid-forties approached me after we danced to this CD and celebrated a simple Eucharist: "I was raised Catholic and was deeply wounded by Christianity and left it years ago," he told me. "This was the first experience I have ever had of God in worship." Then he started to cry on my shoulder.

What we have here is a revolution. A nonviolent revolution. The return of celebration. This revolution will not be stopped. It is what the left lacks to the extent that it ignores the sense of the sacred. And, because healthy worship awakens a critical moral and ecological ethic that leads to action, it is also what the right lacks. Thomas Aquinas warns of the courage that true worship takes when he puts worship in the same category as prophetic justice making: "Magnanimous people put themselves in all kinds of danger for great things, for instance, the common welfare, justice, divine worship, and so forth."[10]

Worship ought to be the energy source from which a people heals itself and lets go and starts over. A space where a new politics as well as a new economics and a new art can begin. And a new priesthood. New and ancient ways to midwife transcendence. This postmodern worship makes all this possible and even fun.

Orthopraxis

I believe that the renewal of forms of worship represents an exercise in *orthopraxis*. Orthopraxis is more important today than orthodoxy. Part of belief today is the conviction that we must walk our talk, that what we *do* is the only authentic measure of what we claim to believe. In the nineteenth century John Henry Newman wrote a book called *Essay on the Development of Christian Doctrine* in which he underscored his reasons for leaving the Anglican fold for the Roman Catholic tradition. Newman's work needs to be supplemented today. Instead of debating the development of *doctrine,* it is time to implement *the development of polity.* Polity, which Webster's dictionary defines as "the form of government of a religious denomination," is about orthopraxis more than orthodoxy. Ours is a time, as liberation theologians insist, for paying more attention to orthopraxis. How can the church preach justice to others if it remains sexist or clericalist or racist or colonialist itself? Orthodoxy holds the danger of being idolatrous, especially when it comes at the expense of orthopraxis.

I sense that Newman's passion as a young theologian for the church standing up to the state was an authentic prophetic cry about the lack of orthopraxis in the Anglicanism of his day. His search for a period in church history in which he saw orthopraxis more appropriately displayed was commendable.

While it is possible that John Newman and I have passed like trains in the night—he to Rome and I to Canterbury—there may be another way to look at our differences: that were he living in the latter half of our century, he too would have seen what I have come to see—that Rome is not on the right track for orthopraxis and that the Second Vatican Council, while it contributed to a healthy development of doctrine, has proved to be a failure at the level of development of praxis. It did not clean the Vatican house out; in fact, with the advent of computers and fax machines and instantaneous electronic communications, those who control the Vatican now wield more power than ever before in Rome's history. An openness is necessary to provide a more fluid and flowing avenue in which the Holy Spirit might operate. And this, after all, is the purpose of *ecclesia* in the first place, is it not? To be a space where the Spirit can move freely? Celebrate openly? And struggle justly?

We must make room for honoring local roots and local decision making. When we make room for development, we make space for evolution. This sense of space better fits the physics and cosmology of our times and the practical level of church organization, structure, and decision making. Thus it has the capacity to lead us in a postmodern era. A diverse decision-making apparatus needs to be in place for polity to evolve. Lay participation and decision making are a requisite.

What is lacking in Newman's preoccupation with fourth-century ecclesial history is a concern about the polity *of the earliest church*. I believe that it is there, in the respect for the diversity of local churches that we should look in a postmodern era. (Is diversity not a prerequisite for development?) The Christian churches before the imperial ambitions of first Constantinople and then Rome took over church polity respected diversity. Would that Newman had been as passionate about emulating the first-century church as he was about emulating the fourth-century church. (The polity of the Celtic church, so sadly dismembered by southern European Christianity beginning with the Synod of Whitby, was much looser and more closely mirrored the early church.)

Most Christians recite the Nicene Creed, which speaks of the Church being "one, holy, catholic, and apostolic." The meaning of what constitutes *oneness* or *unity* is at issue among them. Oneness cannot be enforced from above or outside. The cosmology of the postmodern era, a cosmology that teaches us that *there is no one center of the universe but that the universe is omnicentric,* can teach us healthy oneness again. If the universe is omnicentric, then no one space or place (Rome or other) holds the reins on all issues of polity. Rather, issues of unity and diversity need to be honored locally where they arise. This model of church has much in common with base communities of Latin America. It may be a less efficient model in the short run than that of Rome, but it allows more room for the Spirit to express itself.

A certain *humility* is needed by church itself. A humility not unlike that of any individual who sincerely sets about a search for truth, Spirit, and the God of both. A search that is never ending and that is sure to be intensified as we move into a third millennium of Christianity in the context of ecological destruction, youth despair, population explosion, deep ecumenism, and Christians often being minorities around the world. More than ever, we need to listen to the Spirit who speaks through all avenues of church and society and try our best to discern our process of development from there. Newman's solution was too simplistic. The Protestant and Anglican reformation got some things right. The church does need ongoing criticism of a prophetic kind. Forms in which the church chooses to organize itself are and always have been subject to development and evolution, just like the rest of God's creation. Socially constructed realities are part of the human condition, as sociologist Walter Truett Anderson insists. The modern (as distinct from postmodern) effort of the Roman church today to be the center of the religious universe is doomed to failure, for it presumes a physics that is already passé. A genuine *development of polity,* one that mirrors some lessons learned from democratic institutions of the West, is a development to be welcomed.

Newman himself writes in the *Apologia Pro Vita Sua* about the "awful, never-ending duel" between authority and private judgment and how "it is necessary for the very life of religion, viewed in its large operations and its history, that the warfare should be incessantly carried on."[11] But there are multiple ways to carry on this "warfare," and it need not always be *one* authority versus *one* individual. Rather, blocs and groups and teams can support and healthily challenge one another. Newman maintains that "Catholic Christendom is no simple exhibition of religious absolutism" and that concerning infallibility, "both its subject-matter and its articles in the subject-matter, are fixed" with respect to "what the apostles held before us."[12] But when it comes to issues like birth control and celibacy in the twentieth-century Roman Catholic church, issues of polity have been elevated to a position of preeminence if not downright obsession that is nowhere mirrored in the Gospel times of the early church.

"The unity of the Catholic Church is very near to my heart, only I do not see any prospect of it in our time," wrote Newman.[13] Is it any nearer in our time? Surely the efforts among Anglicans and Protestant bodies indicate some hope, as did the efforts by Pope John XXIII and Pope Paul VI. But I would say that the biggest obstacle to unity is Rome's disregard orthopraxis when it refuses to allow polity to evolve and develop.

Bishop Swing, the Episcopal bishop of California, is one of those leaders who will allow and even encourage jumps to take place even in religion. This is evident in his genuine support of the NOS community and its efforts to jump-start our liturgical tradition so that it includes postmodern language and symbols. He demonstrated his commitment when he invited the NOS community to San Francisco, and in an article entitled "Let 'em Rave for God's Sake" that he wrote for the Episcopalian newspaper. In the article he defended the Planetary Mass against people upset by rumors they had heard about it.

> In 1994 there will be a minimum of 2,600 regular worship services in our Diocese and one Rave Mass, on October 30. We aren't recklessly abandoning our liturgical tradition. We are simply making a little room for young adults to offer their culture and music and lives to God. A recent survey of 50 young adults joining the United States Navy showed that 48 of the 50 had no religious affiliation and that 42 out of the 50 had never stepped foot inside a church. This, more than questionable decorum, is the scandal before us. . . .
>
> It is clear that a lot of hostility is pent up around Fox and the Rave Mass. One person just called to say that she didn't want "that trash" around Grace Cathedral. She meant the young adults who might come to share in the Eucharist. Well, I'm committed to "that trash." In fifteen years I have never received a phone call or letter berating this Church for its almost total spiritual neglect and abandonment of young adults. But when we take one step to respond to the youth, we suddenly are seen as dealing in trash. So be it. I am personally proud to be associated with a deep compassion for our ecology, with its respect for water, air, earth and young people as gifts from God and thus having abiding worth. Let 'em Rave, for God's sake.[14]

This kind of defense of orthopraxis is what will make a difference in ecclesial and religious history. It is a pity it is so rare in our time. I am blessed to have found it in the Episcopal leadership in California as well as in dioceses of northern England.

My Reception as an Episcopal Priest

After five months of tutorial with a retired Episcopalian professor of church history, I was to be accepted as a priest in the Episcopal church on December 3, 1994. The night before, I made the following entry in my journal.

December 2, 1994
The eve of my "second ordination." I remember my first and the deep experience of the "Litany of Saints," the experience of communion with a brotherhood that went before me in the ministry. I wonder what awaits

me tomorrow. I am pleased that at least the brotherhood is a sisterhood as well.

I received a gift on my phone answering machine. A friend in New York spoke words of enthusiasm and support that nearly moved me to tears. "The Vatican tried to kill you," he said, "but your choice to join the Episcopal church is a rising from the ashes."

I think of Bishop Swing's statement when we first discussed my switch. "All I want to do is give you a place where you can continue your work." Amen. Thank you, Bishop Swing! Thanks to all of the Anglican tradition who are welcoming me.

The event included myself and a Roman Catholic priest from India being received and concelebrating mass with the bishop and a newly ordained deacon. It was low-key and appropriate. Supporting me were new Anglican friends as well as a former Dominican, now an Anglican rector in New York, whom I knew back in my days of study in Dubuque. I felt a new beginning under way.

13

What Will Belief and Holiness Mean
in a Postmodern Era?

What will we believe in a postmodern era? I was once interviewed by a television commentator in Holland who took me aside afterward and said, "I don't understand you Americans. You talk as if we can still experience God."

I believe that finding God—the Divine, the Spirit, the Great Mystery—is still possible; that divinity and grace are eager to find us. And I believe that holiness happens. Other beliefs I hold to be important in a postmodern era I will try to name in this chapter, for they constitute my testimony or *confessions* and so they seem an appropriate way to end this story.

Finding God

Most of my conscious life I have had a desire to pursue the experience of God. That is why Fr. Clancy's sermon in our first novitiate retreat still carries weight for me: Teresa of Ávila ran away to the convent because, she said, "I want to know God." This is what brought me to the Dominicans, and ironically, what I discovered there and beyond is primarily what got me expelled from the Dominicans. It has also propelled me into other explorations.

In my desire to experience God I have been alternately surprised, amused, bemused, wounded, overjoyed, emptied, disappointed, misunderstood, and blessed.

I have had the good fortune to be able to try to instruct others in what was my primary passion: the experience of God. This I have had opportunity to do in my writing, teaching, workshops, and retreats, in preaching and in leading worship and many other kinds of prayer, in hiring and showcasing artists and ritual leaders and scientists who are leaders and "priests" in their own right. I have tasted the Divine in nature, in solitude, in loneliness, in intimacy, in community, in friendship, in music, in grief, in liturgy, in meditation, in the cinema, in (most especially) study and writing, in work and lecturing, in listening to others' stories, in silence, in cities, on farms, in South America and North America, in Europe and Australia and Asia, in allies and in enemies. I could never say that I have been thwarted in my quest to experience the Divine.

I have sought God as a Catholic and a Christian, as a Dominican, as a Roman Catholic priest, as a theologian. Now I continue the pursuit. I do it by throwing my lot in with the upcoming generation and in particular those committed to the making of good work through birthing postmodern forms for traditional Western worship. I am becoming an Episcopal priest to contribute to this movement. Where will it all lead us? If I knew the answer to that question, I would risk boredom. Predictability is the least-known quality of the spiritual journey as I have known it. Curiosity and wonder and a willingness to fail seem much more valuable virtues for those on spiritual paths. One can only hope that these communities stay true to their calling at this critical time in earth and religious history. And one hopes too that the God/Goddess we seek is still seeking us. That would mean that grace still abounds, or as my father put it years ago, citing Jesus to me when I was a teenager and we discussed my becoming a priest, "You have not chosen me but I have chosen you."

Letting Go of Images of God

As a pilgrim traveler—journeying in common, I believe, with many others of my generation—I have found that a lot depended on the God we were looking for and the gods we were willing to let go. As Meister Eckhart put it, "I pray God to rid me of God." The God of fascism and control, of Peeping Tomism and retribution, of dualism and patriarchal violence, of order and so-called unity forced from the outside has no appeal for me. Perhaps I am talking about the God of modernity that holds no interest for me. Perhaps I am talking about deconstructing and reconstructing our images of God.

To find God we must let go of God. Then God will find us with new breakthroughs of grace and divine experience. The death-of-God issue that played so prominently in our theologies of the late sixties was less a death of divinity than a death of our old images of divinity. Now we must begin to reimagine from experience, learning to trust our experiences of awe, wonder, darkness, nothingness, creativity, compassion, justice, celebration. I can now see the four paths of creation spirituality as the medicine for a society whose God is dead. It is true that the spirit that gave birth to purgation, illumination, and union is dead or ought to be; but the spirit of wonder, nothingness, creativity, and transformation has barely emerged. A time like ours—a transition time—is a time for old images of God to be buried and new ones to emerge.

Images of God for the Future

I look for a different kind of deity from that of the modern era in the coming century: a God of justice, of beauty, of celebration, of creativity, of truth, of wonder, of mystery, of nature, of humor, of earth and earthiness. A God of flesh. A God of Jesus, of Buddha, of Buffalo Woman, of Gandhi and Martin Luther King, Jr., of Malcolm X and of Mother Jones, of Howard Thurman and of Chief Seattle, of Albert Einstein and of Otto Rank; a God of the many artists who wake us up, of the *anawim* (those without a voice), of the forgotten ones, of earth, of animals, of supernovas and galaxies, of imagination and of music, of time and of space, of light and of darkness; a God who is author of both passion and compassion—in short, a God of *Life.* I think this is the God I have pursued for some time, as "a radical response to *Life.*" This is also the God of the Goddess times. As feminist archaeologist Marija Gimbutas puts it, the essence of that era was the "celebration of life." It is also the God of Jesus, who, as Dietrich Bonhoeffer wrote from his cell, "does not call us to a new religion but to life." Being the God of Jesus, it must also be the God of the Jewish tradition at its best: "Just to be is a blessing, just to live is holy," as Rabbi Heschel reminds us. Life is the goal of the living. The French playwright Antonin Artaud saw our situation this way: "It is good that from time to time cataclysms occur that compel us to return to nature, i.e., to rediscover life."[1] Surely a spiritual search in our day—the day of the ultimate cataclysm of nature itself—will be a search that compels us "to return to nature . . . to rediscover life." Life—"God is Life, *per se* Life," Thomas Aquinas wrote seven centuries ago.

If this is the God we seek in our experience, then holiness is about living; it is about living life as blessing and passing it on as such. Spirituality is about *coming alive.* Religion can so readily complicate these matters. We need spirituality to simplify religion. The poet William Everson celebrates this yearning for the God of Life when he says that the mystic

> grapples God on earth, God in the sea, God in the sky. He smells him out in bed. At the Table of the Lord he eats divinity, devours God's flesh. He is insatiable, because the food that feeds him incites him in his hunger. Hunger is his need and his need is unstaunchable. Reason may balk, but imagination knows no end. . . . He relinquishes possession in order to be trapped, in order to be possessed.[2]

These images of God-seeking are those of passionate panentheism indeed. I believe that today a saint must be hungry as Everson sees it, for the God-flesh, for tasting the divine being, not just talking *about* the divine. A communion-hunter, a spiritual warrior stalking the Source behind the Source. Ecstasy is the essential God-experience, though I emphasize that there are blue and green ecstasies as well as red and orange ones. Cool and hot ecstasies. But it is the union that makes the God-experience tasteable. Rabbi Heschel makes explicit the point that asceticism does not lead to prophetic spirituality when he writes, "The source of evil is not in passion, in the throbbing heart, but rather in hardness of heart, in callousness and insensitivity. . . . It is to the imagination and the passions that the prophets speak, rather than aiming at the cold approbation of the mind."[3] Asceticism has reigned in the modern period as a synonym for spirituality. Creation spirituality rejects its hegemony. For, as Heschel warns us, asceticism does not produce prophets.

Robert Bly points out that Pan was the Greek god "whose name means 'everything,' and which, by indirection, suggests nature itself." I have learned that the Vatican is so afraid of nature that any theology with *pan* in it—even the thoroughly orthodox theology of panentheism—is dismissed out of hand. Why? Because anthropocentrism cannot deal with the "all," the "everything," with "cosmology" or "nature itself." Bly also reminds us that

> Pan had hairy legs, which, one could say, belonged to the very same goat that Esau loved so much, and which the Church later slandered by giving the legs to Satan.
>
> The ascetic attitudes, or the popular longing to repress the libido, which grew so strong at the end of the pagan era, joined in Roman culture with fears of the libertine emphases of the Great Mother to form an antisexual front.[4]

This "antisexual front" reveals some of the enemies Dionysus has. The fundamentalists stand to judge him, and so do the guardians of the culture's institutions. Apollo represents the god of light and consciousness, reason and commerce and rationality. In contrast, Dionysus welcomes the irrational and spontaneous, the creative and the sensual. Apollo fears Dionysus, but both are integral to what it means to be human. Religion (and its kept, ascetic spirituality) prefers Apollo while spirituality (at least creation spirituality) prefers Dionysus.

It is clear that I have been developing in my fashion a more Dionysian kind of path to holiness. My book on ecstasy as God-experience, *Whee! We, wee All the Way Home,* is evidence of that, as is my desire in the bear book to define prayer understood as a radical response to *Life.* A commitment to Life, per se Life, is a Dionysian kind of commitment. It will not sit well with the fundamentalists or the guardians of the cultural status quo. And it has not. Everson warns of the political sins that result from locking up the Dionysian spirit—sins that still haunt the American soul.

The annihilation of the American Indian, the enslavement of the African Negro, the hysterical atom-bombing of the Orientals, persist as a terrible fear and a compulsive guilt in the American unconscious. The solution, after a thorough examination of conscience, true contrition followed by a heart-felt confession, would call for the incorporation of genuine ecstatic and mystical needs in the interplay of the collective psyche.

But even this may only bait the return of the Apollonian forces, for the Apollonian, "in his civilized fear, calls ecstasy Satanic, and stands ready to strike again."[5]

The Thirst for Holiness

Rabbi Heschel says that "holiness is the most precious word in religion."[6] Indeed, a new era like our postmodern one *cries out* for new meanings of holiness and new ways to get there. As Frederick Turner puts it bluntly: "Twentieth-century culture is full of an angst, an unsatisfied and inexplicable yearning, which we can now identify as a thirst for things like *glory, sanctity, conscience, and heroism,* which were forbidden to us by the doctrines of existentialism."[7] We have repressed greatness, and in its place we suffer great longing. In place of stories about holiness, we have substituted drugs: "As the doctrines of materialism triumphed first among intellectuals, then among the population at large, so did the use of opium, cocaine, mescalin, and cannabis." But drugs cannot do our transcendence for us—they "destroy the tension and the hunger and thus the process of transformation."[8]

Terms such as *holiness, sanctity,* and *saints* all correspond to the third article of faith that Luther named but that so few Protestants even got around to talking about—that of our "sanctification" or "divinization." This lack of development of a theology of holiness is a principle reason Protestantism verges on the soporific. It so easily becomes flat and bland and boring; and Catholicism, to the extent that it ingests the Protestant principle in itself and fails to develop its own *catholic* principle, renders itself equally flat and bland and boring. Protestantism, to the extent that it only protests, has little to offer of a positive nature (other than "positive thinking")—little challenge to adventure beyond the status quo that culture offers us. Such a religion, whether appearing in Protestant or Roman Catholic guise, has no sense of *extreme.* Sainthood is about *extremes* and the holiness that that entails. Another way of putting this is that in modern Western religion, wildness and wilderness are tamed, excluded, fenced in, domesticated. When religion becomes domesticated, it worries the individual soul about its redemption in the next life—but it has little or no adventure to offer the soul in this one. Then, of course, it is set up for becoming a *kept religion,* one that hangs around just to legitimize social institutions and the status quo. And the big issues become: Shall we allow a public prayer at a school graduation? Who will marry us? Who will bury my loved one? Who will baptize my baby? Little or nothing is made of the development of consciousness and the means to do that—via meditation practices and healthy encounters with great mystics, for example. In short, religion takes over and spirituality dies.

Poet Bill Everson testifies to the reality of sanctity and extremes when he writes about the vocation of the poet: "It is in the order of imagination, the order of poetry, that the possible exceeds itself, is sanctified in excess. In the extremes of imagination the poet and the saint concur."[9] Sanctity has to do with imagination and with excess. This "pushing of the envelope" seems like a necessary task in a movement from the modern to the postmodern. Again, it is not altogether jettisoning the envelopes we have inherited; but it *is* pushing them, reinterpreting them, reinventing them. Somehow, this effort is a great one; it takes some greatness. Thus, it is the making of heroes or saints. It calls forth our greatness, our magnanimity. Ours is a time—the postmodern era is a time—for greatness and saint-making that is very close to soul-making and has nothing in common with ecclesial political efforts to canonize dead people provided the money is there to get the job done in style.

Holiness is everybody's business. And the way we define it is everybody's business. That is to say, the meaning of holiness lies at the substratum, the very basement, of our collective definition of community, of why we are here together and what sacrifices we are willing to make for a future generation. I think that is the *single greatest difference* between fundamentalism and creation spirituality: our definitions of holiness.

Further Signs of Holiness

Looking at my own story, I can see that my life has been a search of holiness. I received one definition of holiness in religious life and it worked for a while. It had something to do with following certain rules laid down by my religious order that would help me develop my soul. Jesuit theologian Karl Rahner wrote about holiness in an article I read as a seminary student:

> In spite of every objective word, it is the Saints who sustain the
> Church. . . . [God] has said that his Church will always be the holy
> Church, the Church of Saints. And *this* holiness, the glowing heart,
> selfless dedication, the heroic throwing away of life, the divine impa-
> tience, the dark night of mystical suffering, the smiling love for a poor
> brother—all these glories of the Church are no less important, no less

constitutive of her reality than the infallible truth of the divine word and the objective holiness of the sacraments. In fact, all these "objective" realities are in the last analysis only there for the purpose of bringing into and maintaining in being the subjectivity of happily loving hearts.[10]

I found other definitions of holiness through my work and lived experience: that of justice and mysticism and its culmination point, "compassion." As the psalmist says, "Compassion is where peace and justice kiss." The question in a time like ours is not, Do we strive for holiness? but, What does holiness mean at this time in history? Many of the examples Rahner gives do not touch me today as being examples of holiness. The question today is not, Is holiness a good thing? (Of course it is—it's about greatness, magnanimity, and not wasting our lives in trivia.) But, in a time of our moving from one worldview to another, we can get confused messages about holiness and its meaning. For example, was Pius XII with his aristocratic demeanor and his ascetic visage an image for us of what holiness is? He was awfully silent about the Holocaust and never even excommunicated Hitler. What about the definition of holiness from the Opus Dei, the right-wing secret society that the papacy of John Paul II is so fond of? Is Jerry Falwell holy? Or Jimmy Swaggart?

What about diverse images of holiness? We have to know something about holiness if we are to have much chance of arriving there. What then might holiness mean in a postmodern context? I propose seven signs of holiness in our times:

1. *Courage or Magnanimity.* For me holiness has everything to do with *courage*. No courage equates with no holiness. It takes courage to be; to create; to fail; to fight; to trust; to let go; to stand up and stand by; to get up and try again; to face beauty toe to toe; to experience awe, wonder, darkness, diversity in all its forms. It takes courage to be oneself, to be truthful and "live beyond the psychology of one's day," to make one's way on new terrain without sanctions and a lot of outside support, to rely on one's inner strength. Thomas Aquinas says, "Saints have a heart full of justice,"[11] and the first act of the saint is the work of justice, which takes the strength of divine power. How can there be anything great without an enlarged heart and soul? "God is delighted to see your soul enlarge," Meister Eckhart says. One can understand why. Nothing great can get done—or be resisted—without courage. Years ago, in the midseventies, I visited St. Dominic's tomb in Bologna and while there one word kept going through my mind as if it were in the air: courage. He had the courage to invent a new form of spiritual praxis and religious life. I felt that if he were living today he would be on the side of all

those daring to give birth to new forms of education and community and spirituality.

2. *Lack of bitterness.* Aquinas says that bitterness comes from keeping anger in a long time. A lack of bitterness means that persons have done something real and creative with their anger—they have not allowed it to fester or build up into expressions of passive-aggressive behavior. They do not become violent or attacking. One learns to be emptied of anger and resists making a cosmology of anger and of cynicism. A saint has learned not to keep anger in. (The modern era produced untold minions of passive-aggressive Christians because they kept their anger in. This also creates a preoccupation with gore, suffering, and death.) The letting go that is part of releasing anger nourishes a sense of humor that oversees all.

3. *Curiosity!* According to Thomas Aquinas, healthy curiosity is a pathway to wisdom. Its opposite, a self-satisfaction with the answers *and the very questions we possess,* marks the pathway to folly. This seems to parallel Rabbi Heschel's teaching that "learning is not for life; learning is life." Holiness has to do with always learning, always being young enough to ask questions, to seek new answers, to wonder at new angles of things (is every question not a newly discovered angle?). There are those among us who seem satisfied with just one angle on things—a ninety-degree angle that makes for square boxes and square thinking. But there are at least eighty-nine other angles! Wouldn't it be a shame to die without examining them too?

I recently had a conversation with a twenty-nine-year-old Indian man who had lived in a Christian ashram in India for seven years. He observed among Indian Christians what I have seen among American Dominicans: *a lack of intellectual curiosity or spiritual curiosity.* A kind of passive complacency with what is—even when that "what" lacks depth and vigor and passion and compassion. This way is the way to acedia, laziness, cynicism, tiredness, and a refusal to begin new things. It is life without passion. It lacks holiness.

What is lack of curiosity? *Complacency.* Lack of desire to seek God and learn new things about God. A child is curious as a baby; the negative senex, the professionally depressed, are not. Curiosity and wonder are closely allied: no curiosity—no aliveness. No spirit.

4. *Unbored and unboring!* If our lives are boring or we are compulsively making up for boredom by addicted recreation, work, or business, then we need to become more imbued with the cosmological. We can grow bigger hearts, bigger souls, bigger imaginations, bigger senses of humor, bigger tasks. So much of our work and institutional living during the mechanistic or industrial era has trivialized our lives and those of the young that we are in danger of settling for this trivialization. But holiness in my experience has to

do with what is interesting. I do not find holy people to be boring people. They get in trouble; they disturb. They question. They grow. The are *alive.* Prophets are many things, but boring they are not.

5. *Prophetic.* A saint today must be engaged in some way in raising consciousness or educating or struggling to make justice happen in the midst of so much injustice. A spiritual warrior assisting the birth of the environmental revolution—that is the work of prophetic "interfering" that needs doing today. A mystic who is not a prophet is a false mystic. Mystical energy is meant to be put to the task of liberating one another, of freeing the prisoner and bringing sight to the blind, of healing the sick and energizing the depressed of soul. But we should think of holiness more in terms of *prophetic communities* at work in solidarity with one another and less in terms of saintly individuals.

6. *Creativity or being at the edge between order and chaos.* The French taught me a phrase twenty-five years ago that has often recurred in times of doubt: that of "living *sur la marge,*" on the margin. Holy people I have known have always lived on the margin. Is this what the Christ of John's Gospel means when he talks of being *in but not of* one's culture? Without living on the margin there is no genuine creativity; nothing really new is allowed to penetrate our beings or our lifestyles. Architect Charles Jencks, in his most recent book, *The Architecture of the Jumping Universe,* talks about the importance—even for the universe itself—of being on the margin. The high point of creativity lies

> "on the edge between order and chaos." This boundary condition,
> more simply put "the edge of chaos," is now understood to be the place
> of maximum complexity and computability, the only place where life
> and mind can emerge. . . . Everything in nature and culture is pushed
> toward this creative edge by evolutionary pressures, by natural selection
> and internal dynamics.[12]

It is here at the edge that "jumps" take place both in nature's evolution and in human imagination and morality. Holy people live at the edge. A willingness to take risks is built into that choice. Again, courage is called on. Holy people are ready to jump. And their prophetic side is ready to bring organizations along, jumping to new levels of depth and simplicity.

7. *Community.* The modern age was characterized by isolation and loneliness, but the postmodern age will rediscover the power of community and kinship with all beings, all of us contributing to a common cause. Base communities, more than ecclesial bureaucracies, hold the future to spirituality. The formation of ritual-making base communities may well be in order today. By employing the current "urban language" of rap and rave, these communities

may draw many participants. Today's global scene requires a global language, and a global network of youth cultures is primed for this kind of movement. This moment is a historic opportunity.

Rave culture was originally a group "religious" ecstatic experience that welcomed all ages and classes. Zap Club in Brighton Beach was such a place. An ecospiritual vision, not unlike that of creation spirituality, imbues the rave culture. Spirituality is very important there. When rave goes to church, worship can preserve the best part of the rave culture: its power to create a spiritual community. At the same time, rave can bring alive what is dormant in worship by bringing the body and cosmology to worship and by bringing an ecological ethic alive. Such ingredients would reinvigorate church and synagogue communities. The rave culture's shadow side, the presence of drugs, can be displaced by the ecstasy of worship. (A recent study concludes that the drug Ecstasy, which is the drug of choice in rave clubs, damages the brain and causes chronic depression.)[13] These base communities can be "in the tradition but not part of the institution" of religion. A worship community serves the young by giving them a *source of identity*. Such an identity is key to answering their problems, problems of alienation and despair, of addiction and failed relationships, of drugs and alcohol and compulsive behavior.

The effort at community is an effort in building a living organism. People will not join because of the music and dancing—though these do constitute the proper language for the people—but because the community offers a *sign of hope*. That, plus being part of something useful and visionary—creating common worship—draws people in. The worship inspires community to happen. One's first ritual is a starting point for a new vision of hope and possibility. People join because of the healing, the community, the vision for justice.

Saints I Have Known of a Postmodern Kind

Another way to define holiness is to look at examples and models. Perhaps this is one reason our postmodern world is so keen on stories: it is looking, searching, grasping for possible myths and role models who, in Walter Anderson's words, "show what a mature and morally responsible person is like." We are looking for saints after whom we can pattern our behavior and our choices. We look for elders and mentors.

One problem we run into is the love-hate relationship with heroes in our culture, and the media's habit of first putting them on a pedestal and then shooting them down. This process of elevating heroes and heroines (in our anthropocentric way we call them "stars") and then reveling in their downfall shows signs of serious pathological behavior and projection. We seem incapable of simply loving people and not putting them on pedestals. (The O. J. Simpson adulation and that of our other "stars" of athletics and entertainment are examples of this projection.) The psychologist Otto Rank warns against projecting one's own greatness onto others and the damage this can do to our own need to live life fully and not vicariously.

Perhaps I can begin with holy persons I have known directly or indirectly. Among religious leaders, I have been inspired by Dorothy Day; Rabbi Abraham Joshua Heschel; John XXIII; Thomas Merton; Thic Nhat Hanh; M. D. Chenu, Howard Thurman. Among writers, I have been moved by Adrienne Rich; Wendell Berry; Audre Lorde; Rainer Maria Rilke; Walt Whitman; Martin Buber. Among cultural activists, I have been impressed by Martin Luther King, Jr.; Mahatma Gandhi; Sojourner Truth; Chico Mendez; Nelson Mandela; Václav Havel; Gloria Steinem; Ralph Nader; Saul Alinsky; Cesar Chavez; Mother Jones; E. F. Schumacher; Tom Dooley; and more. Among scientists, I have been moved by Albert Einstein; Thomas Berry; Brian Swimme; Rupert Sheldrake; Beverly Rubick; and more. From the past, I have gotten to know Hildegard of Bingen; Meister Eckhart; Thomas Aquinas; Teresa of Ávila; John of the Cross; Henry Adams; Otto Rank; and others. Among martyrs there are Oscar Romero and the numerous martyrs of Central and South America and the Philippines in our generation—including the four church-women raped and murdered in El Salvador and the six Jesuits and the two women who worked with them killed there; and Sister Dianna Ortiz, tortured in Guatemala—all these are saints by any traditional definition. The church of martyrs has moved from ancient Rome to present-day Central and South America and the Philippines and elsewhere. It is remarkable how many martyrs and saints our generation has witnessed.

Directly, I have been blessed to know some contemporary saints. None of them was pious; none was overly religious; none would have pleased the guardians of the status quo. But all demonstrated remarkable evidence of courage, lack of bitterness, healthy curiosity, nonboredom, prophecy, and living at the edge. Each was a unique personality in his or her own right. Each accomplished significant gifts for others. And yet they were all diverse. None was an imitator. Let me name a few.

Fr. Bede Griffiths, a Benedictine monk who moved to India fifty years ago and set up an ashram there in the Hindu style but for Christian monks and nuns. He wrote several books, and he underwent the letting go of his Western ways to take on the wisdom of Eastern ways. He endured attacks not only from conservative Christians but also from conservative Hindus. But he was revered for the authentic spiritual pilgrim that he was, a prophet paving the way for a more pluralistic and deeply ecumenical religion, one based on spiritual experience and not on empire building. He used to say, "Look at your hand. Consider the world religions as the fingers. Now if we look at only their visible elements, they look very distinct and independent. But follow the fingers to the palm and you see they all share their depths in common." A fine image of deep ecumenism, to which he dedicated his life.

Ken Feit, a spiritual fool, who got himself educated in fooldom through attending clown school and sitting at the feet of Indian and African storytellers. He traveled around the world sharing his "Fool's Mass" and "silent haikus" and many other spiritual wake-up experiences to get people to see the world paradoxically again. "My work is to make the ordinary extraordinary and the extraordinary ordinary," he would say. He made a special effort to teach others the way of holy foolery and ritual making and storytelling.

Bob Fox, a street priest in Harlem for over twenty-five years, who sought out the liberation of his people by way of creativity. Empower the people to create and they will liberate themselves, he felt. He sponsored "the thing in the spring" in Harlem in 1967, wherein forty artists joined street people for the summer, and all kinds of possibilities and energy and empowerment became released. He sponsored the return of middle-class persons to the inner city to work on rehabilitating housing and above all on rehabilitating hope.

The women saints I have known and who have been my teachers in so many ways are for the most part still living, so I dare not mention them by name just yet. (I don't want to jinx their spirit work.) I do remember Zuita Giordani, however, a Corsican rebel I knew in Paris who struggled with the poor and for the poor wherever she was. She would do things like invite the homeless in the métro station to come home with her, where she would give them her only bed and care for them. And I think of Marjorie Tuite, O.P., who waged battles for the oppressed of South and Central America when it was not politically correct to do so. And journalist Penny Lernoux, whose writings on banks and religion in South America were so revealing and carefully researched.

Where would my life be had I not rubbed shoulders with these and many other people of courage and prophecy? I have known artists who are saints and married couples who are saints; scientists who are saints and businesspeople who are saints; unemployed who are saints and politicians who are saints; homosexuals who are saints and heterosexuals who are saints. We have been blessed to share time and space with many saints in our generation. I am reminded of the biblical use of the term *saint* in the Book of Acts. That it applies to *each of us*. All who are attempting to imitate the Christ in their lives merit the title of "saint." Some do it more fully than others and are willing to let go of more to get the job done.

I believe that every person is called to be a saint in his or her unique way. The greatest sadness in life is to see people who, often due to circumstances beyond their control such as failures in family, religious, economic, or educational systems, cannot live to their full potential.

Of course, in speaking of saints I have known, I must also include Tristan and all the non-two-legged creatures, the animals and birds, the trees and forests, the waterfalls and rivers, the stars and galaxies who are displaying their beauty and their grace. Saints are everywhere. I also had an experience with the saintliness of bears—as I am sure many did—on seeing the movie *The Bear.* I felt on leaving the theater that I was blessed and honored to be sharing a planet with such a marvelous creature. My friend Jose Hobday, with whom I attended the movie, had a discussion afterward about "why bears exist," and my answer was simply "to be bear." They are *so good* at it. Therein lies their holiness. In their excellence.

What Holds Us Back?

Theologically, I see two big obstacles holding us back from recovering our passion for holiness. The first is the elitism that the modern era associates with saintliness. A postmodern hagiography will let go of that elitism by offering us an invitation *and means* for developing our mystical and prophetic gifts.

The second big obstacle is the presumption that *grace is scarce.* In an anthropocentric worldview, grace is *indeed scarce.* When human beings cut themselves off from the cosmos and other creatures, they set themselves up for a shortage of grace. I remember being asked by a group of Jewish women at a conference one day, "What is grace? We have been asking our rabbi this question for twenty years and have not been satisfied with the answer." I proposed that grace was the *unconditional love* of the universe for us and of the universe's maker for us, and their faces lit up. It made me wonder whether we have been teaching of late that grace is rare—when in fact it is everywhere. If we succumb to a theology of the scarcity of grace, are we not condemning ourselves to addictions, especially the addictions of overachievers? Do we not also condemn ourselves to a lifetime of therapy—are not our trips to therapists often a kind of pilgrimage in search of grace? A graced listener, a graced presence, a graced caring, a graceful soul, a graceful heart? But if "nature is grace," as Eckhart taught, then grace is close and everyday, as near as our return to nature—including our own deepest human natures. Then we become instruments of grace to one another—and grace moves around more freely, becomes less rare. As we realize that grace is more abundant than we have been taught in the modern era, we will become a more graceful species. But we have to know *where to look for it.*

What is it I believe in? What do I confess? I believe in being. The holiness of it; the surprise of it; the divinity and glory of it; the gratuity of it. "Being is God," said Eckhart. Yes! This is what binds all people and all creation together—the gratuity of the gift of being. For the being I am speaking about is graced being. We need to heal the damaging split between nature and grace, a split that affects our attitudes toward our bodies and sexuality as much as toward food, land, air, forests, water, animals, plants, and birds. I see the ecological crisis as a nature/grace crisis writ large. Earth itself is paying the price for a damaged attitude in the human soul.

A great wound exists in Western religious consciousness, a wound that was created in the fourth century when Saint Augustine of Hippo separated nature from grace. This is a very un-Jewish thing to do, separating nature from grace; but Augustine was in fact quite anti-Semitic, among other things. When religion separates nature from grace, then it becomes *afraid of nature* and it resorts to coercion to control nature. Fundamentalism and religious fascism occur as control mechanisms to hold nature in (including our own human nature).

So too does ecological destruction occur, because if nature is not sacred *in itself,* then human beings can simply *use it* and *destroy it* as they will. Which is what we have been doing to forests and soil and water and land.

When nature is separated from grace, awe is lost! Anthropocentric awe replaces nature's awe. Titillation, sensationalism, drugs, sports, shopping—the latest fashion, and additional addictions usurp the place of authentic awe.

In addition, when religion separates grace from nature, grace becomes more and more *scarce.* There is a feeling of leakage of grace going on everywhere. Inertia results. Acedia. No energy to begin new things. Cynicism, nihilism, pessimism follow in its wake. Depression follows because without grace there is no creativity, and without creativity, pessimism, despair, and depression take over. For creativity IS grace. An ideology develops that there is only so much grace to go around—a trickle-down theory of grace develops. And only a few—the governing elect (i.e., the ordained ones)—control this ever-so-rare grace. The rest of us must get on our knees in acts of submission to this *"dispensing"* (their word: "the dispensing of grace") and this priesthood.

Such a perversion of the meaning of priesthood! The priesthood, if it should be allowed to exist at all, is a midwife to grace. The priesthood is to let grace out; let it flow; help heal those blockages, what our ancestors called the "sins of the spirit," that impede grace. Blockages that experiences of abuse, wounds, bitterness, anger, addictions create in us.

The church, then, is not the only dispenser of grace. Nature is too. In fact, Meister Eckhart, who tried as all creation theologians have to heal the rupture of nature and grace that Augustine created for us, said, "Nature *is* grace." This is evident in the gospel parable of the good shepherd in which the listeners were assured that sheep and shepherd, animal and human being, creatures and Creator, can have an I-Thou relationship. This is a deep ecological metaphor about grace and nature, about earth systems loving us and us them.

Community is another source of grace. In community we are meant to grace one another; to be sources of grace; healers by way of grace.

Yes, grace is abundant, not scarce. We gather in ritual to remind one another of the grace flowing elsewhere in our lives—our work, our relationships, our experiences with nature, our universe. All is holy; or nothing is holy. For everything is connected.

I believe that our species, so enmeshed in its collective dark night of the soul today, is involved in a colossal grace crisis. A grace crisis and a praise crisis. Without grace we have nothing to praise. Without praise we have nothing to enlarge our hearts and souls. We have no way of dealing with our suffering, grief, and pain.

What Do I Believe? Ten Principles of Creation Spirituality

I believe that creation spirituality can help us with our grace and nature split and with our praise crisis. What I believe about creation spirituality I can summarize in the following ten principles:

1. Everyone is a mystic (i.e., born full of wonder and capable of recovering it at any age—of not taking the awe and wonder of existence for granted).

2. Everyone is a prophet, that is, a "mystic in action" (Hocking) who is called to "interfere" (Heschel) with what interrupts authentic life.

3. The universe is basically a blessing, that is, something we experience as good. (Rabbi Zalman Schachter says, "There is more good than evil in the world but not by much.") Indeed, creation is an Original Blessing.

4. Human beings have to dig and work at finding their deep self, their true self, their spirit-self. If we do not, we live superficially out of fear or greed or addiction or someone else's expectations of us. That salvation is best understood as "preserving the good" (Aquinas).

5. The journey that marks that digging can be named as a fourfold journey. I believe that the four paths of creation spirituality derive from a Jewish and biblical spirituality like that of Jesus.

   a. *Via Positiva:* delight, awe, wonder, revelry
   b. *Via Negativa:* darkness, silence, suffering, letting go
   c. *Via Creativa:* birthing, creativity
   d. *Via Transformativa:* compassion, justice, healing, celebration.

6. Everyone is an artist in some way, and art as meditation is a primary form of prayer for releasing our images and empowering us and the community.

7. We can and do relate to the universe as a whole since we are microcosm of that macrocosm, and this relationship "intoxicates" us.

8. We are all sons and daughters of God; therefore we have divine blood in our veins, the divine breath in our lungs; and the basic work of God is compassion.

9. Divinity is as much Mother as Father, as much Child as Parent, as much Godhead (mystery) as God (history), as much beyond all being as in all things.

10. We experience the Divine in all things and all things are in the Divine (panentheism), and this mystical intuition supplants theism (and its child, atheism) as an appropriate way to name our relation to the Divine.

Learned Beliefs

I believe in the artist and the scientist and the mystical tradition joining hands and bringing about a renaissance, a rebirth of civilization based on a spiritual initiative.

I believe in diversity and its power to create.

I believe that even God is diverse and that no one (and certainly no institution) controls the Spirit.

I believe that we cannot live deeply without forgiveness, which is a special act of letting go that is not about altruism but is about psychic survival itself.

I believe that the shadow and enemies are part of life's teachers.

I believe in the power of *ideas* to liberate, support, heal, build understanding and insight, and feed healthy imagination. And I believe that the alternative view of ideas, namely, anti-intellectualism, creates frenzy and appeals to the worst side of human nature—titillation, distraction, separateness, sensationalism.

I believe that Gaia is not inert and passive, as the modern age taught us, but is actively involved in interfering with her own demise, and that she is doing this by waking people up from their illusions and feelings of disempowerment. I believe that she is especially waking up the young to be leaders in celebration and the compassion that follows from that.

I believe that culture and spirituality are all mixed up together. From language to art to weather to geography to topology to politics to economics, spirit is nothing if it does not penetrate all. But culture is *not* the same as life—a healthy culture mediates life; an unhealthy one does not and must be interfered with.

I believe that prayer is our radical response to life, a response with two "root" (or radical) directions to it: mysticism—our Yes to life in all its mystery and glory and grandeur and pain; and prophecy—our No to injustice and all that interferes with life.

I believe in the wisdom found in *all* world religions and in the spiritual power found in such prayer forms as sweat lodges and vision quests and chanting. The Spirit *is not labeled* Christian or Muslim or Jewish or Buddhist. The Spirit blows through us all, wherever it wills. Just like the wind.

I believe that the so-called first world needs liberation badly, but because its historical, economic, political, and religious *context* is utterly different from that of third-world nations, its method of liberation must also differ. I believe that the third world has waited long enough for the first world to start liberating itself and that until this liberation happens in the northern countries, the scandal of the ever-growing gap between rich and poor will continue to increase. The principal victims of this lack of balance will be the young, the indigenous peoples, women, and earth systems.

I believe that the first world ought to begin its liberation by addressing its enslavement to addictions, which, as Anne Wilson Schaef observes, are always to an *external reference*. For this reason mysticism holds the key to liberation, because it is to an *inner reference,* to the image of the Divine in us.

I believe that it is no coincidence that the century in which Christianity inherited an empire was also the century in which Augustine filled us with guilt for our sexuality and our bodies. The second chakra (our sexuality) is necessary for other chakras to come alive—especially the third, fourth, and fifth (our moral outrage and empowerment, our heart, and our throat chakras). Thus the sensual and the prophetic go together; they need each other. The Song of Songs was correct in celebrating this same mystery as a redemption of the Garden of Eden and as an integral dimension to celebrating Sabbath, celebrating the gift that creation is.

I believe that the operative word for Christian and biblical spirituality is *not* "contemplation" (the word never once fell from Jesus' lips, for it is not a Jewish concept), but *compassion*. In compassion, "peace and justice kiss" (psalm) and in compassion, as Jesus taught, we imitate God (Luke 6:36); thus our divinity comes forward. In compassion, social justice and mysticism come together and we learn to cease climbing Jacob's ladder and to get on with dancing Sara's circle—we mirror the sacred hoop or the holy macrocosm in our microcosmic dances.

I believe that the quest for the historical Jesus *and* the Greek councils of the fourth century distort the experience of Jesus as the Christ to the extent that they ignore the cosmology of the Scriptures and the cosmic wisdom or Cosmic Christ tradition. I believe that recovering this tradition speaks loudly to issues of our day such as the environmental crisis, for it is about experiencing all beings as sacred, all beings as Christ.

I believe that a viable spirituality must speak to us about *work,* especially at this critical moment in earth history when the Industrial Revolution is winding down and so much unemployment and bad employment and addictive employment haunts the human race. And that the Environmental Revolution, along with spirituality and cosmology, can help us reinvent work. And that a spirituality of work will constitute a theology of sacrament. And that renewed ritual is one of the biggest breakthroughs in *good work,* for it is how the community heals and celebrates. And that work *on the human heart* is the work that earth and future generations are most asking of us today.

I believe that every doctrine worthy of our consideration has to speak to us of *cosmic* truths. For example, the Christian belief in the Pascal Mystery of the life, death, and resurrection of Jesus needs to apply to the life, death, and resurrection of all cosmic entities. The same is true of the Eucharist, the belief that all things get eaten in this universe, even divinity itself.

I believe that all religions of the world should band together to pressure all governments to declare the year 2000 a Jubilee Year, which according to biblical teaching means the forgiveness of all financial debts. This would allow all peoples of the world five years to sit down and reimagine an economic system—one that takes into account the plight of the earth and its species, the source of all real wealth, and the possibilities of the poor countries to reinvent their economies without the debts that strangle them and thus truly enter the much-heralded marketplace. (The World Bank, begun fifty years ago to accomplish on a world scale what the Marshall Plan would accomplish in Western Europe, has been a manifest failure.) With this great act of collective imagination, new relationships would be forged among all persons of the world and all economies and all species. We would enter the next millennium with some real hope for our children because, as someone once declared, *all* people are created equal and born with inalienable rights to life, liberty, and the pursuit of happiness.

The Future

Divinity and the universe seem deeply biased in favor of the future. Both celebrate emergence. Call it: Resurrection. Call it: New Life or New Creation. Call it: Evolution or Creativity. I believe in the future and the possibilities for hope and new leadership. That is why I remain a priest in this transition time when we must work to make the posse the priest.

The young require a sense of the future—indeed we all require this: possibilities for the future. Hope is always about a possible future. For too long we in the West have been looking backward when we hear the term *history.* But history is about what is emerging and *can* emerge as well as what has already emerged. In practical terms, this underscores for me the importance of paying attention to the wisdom of the young—their pain and their talents and their vision.

Today the median age on the planet is seventeen years. What does the future hold for the half of humanity that is under seventeen? How can we who are far older than seventeen assist their coming of age? The world requires today *a preferential option for the young.* A preferential option for the young is not about patronizing the young or forcing them into boxes or institutions that are no longer working—even for the older ones. It is about *letting the young lead*—not without elders, but with elders who are still young at heart and young in spirit. Celebration and healing are at the heart of the work that awaits us. Holiness demands paying attention to the young. Hope can happen, provided possibilities are both tangible and visible. It must, one might say, be made flesh and incarnated in deeds and dreams, in institutions and practices. The young have a role to play in leading us to deeper and more appropriate meanings of holiness, for they have the new language of computers and digital and electronic media at their fingertips—the language of the postmodern era.

I eagerly look forward to seeing what communities of committed young persons can accomplish in making creation spirituality come alive in our postmodern institutions and practices. Of course, trial and error will be the order of the day, but the work will continue. As of this writing, the NOS community, which has inspired so many, is experiencing an upheaval. A number of women there have accused priest Chris Brain of abuse of authority going back twelve years. The church is investigating the charges and the community is struggling to heal itself. I believe that their work will continue in one form or another. After all, the need for ritual that speaks a new language is not going away.

Yes, deconstructing and reconstructing forms of western worship—rather than throwing them out on the one hand or clinging blindly to moribund forms on the other—offers hope and promise to our times. In early December 1995 there was a gathering in York, England, of all those persons involved in alternative worship in northern England, including a bishop.

Back in the United States, sixty people met in downtown Oakland, determined to get a Cosmic Mass up and running in America. These meetings coincided with my first anniversary as an Episcopal priest, January 1995.

In the fall of 1995 a painful chapter unfolded at ICCS. Unbeknownst to me, our acting director met with the college administration to alter the structure of ICCS. I only learned about this plan weeks later. After five hours of intense meetings with the director, the academic dean, and the president, it was the dean who finally said, "it is time to institutionalize ICCS." To me that would be like drying water. The moment she uttered those words I knew we had outlived our welcome at Holy Names College.

I went into considerable darkness during the semester as I wrestled with what to do. Finally, after painful searching, an answer came: We would leave home. In 1996, ICCS will be nineteen year old. It has had a wonderful run, but perhaps it is time to let it go in its present form; we should leave academia as it is currently constituted and create something more bold and more focused as the millennium approaches. What, I wondered, would that be?

I envision a university in Creation Spirituality, the first postmodern university, modeled on the medieval university for its simplicity and direct link between students and faculty. We will keep our books open and our costs low. The Ritual Center will be housed at the university both to protect the community of artists and to inspire the learning process with a sense of cosmology and celebration. After all, the word *university* originally meant a place to find your place in the universe. We will leave the hills of Oakland and move down into the flats where working people live. We will be a small university, a kind of prototype, to demonstrate how we might all redesign education to be lighter and leaner. I am inspired by this new vision and even as I finish the writing of this book I am busy looking at possible sites for the university in downtown Oakland. Maybe, by establishing a university of Creation Spirituality, we will be offering medicine to a society that has, in Gregory Bateson's words, been "rotting its mind from a slowly deteriorating religion and education." A university of Creation Spirituality will be addressing both of these issues.

I will leave Holy Names College grateful for its support during these sometimes turbulent years and proud of what we accomplished together. I am, of course, also disappointed in its recent efforts to control the work of ICCS and, as I see it, control the spirit at work through ICCS.

I should also lend a warning to my readers: Beware of writing a book called *The Reinvention of Work*. Since I wrote that book I have had to reinvent my work as a priest and now my work as an educator. Life would be easier if no one had ever advised me to practice what I preach!

For some time I have been cognizant of W. B. Yeats's observation that theologians are persons "striking terror into the hearts of children and being ignominious in the eyes of lovers." Creation spirituality, I believe, does not strike terror in children or bring about ignominy to lovers. In fact, it honors both. I like it that way. I believe in creation's ecstasies. I have tried to develop a model of education that honors the child in the adult, and I hope we can resurrect worship on the same working principle. I like pianist Arthur Rubinstein's philosophy of life as he articulated it in his autobiography: "I have noticed through experience and through my own observation that Providence, Nature, God, or what I would call the Power of Creation seems to favor human beings who accept and love life unconditionally."[14]

To love life unconditionally is to respond radically to life. It is to honor life as spirit, spirit as life. This is the spirituality that I too have tried to live out and to teach to others. Whatever the results, I am grateful for the opportunities I have been granted by my parents and family, by the Dominican order and the Catholic church, by my enemies and my friends, all of whom blessed me without spoiling me. The journey has been hard—tougher and lonelier than I would have predicted, more rugged than I would have chosen were the scenario mine to paint. And immensely different. But it has not been boring. Not for a minute. And I anticipate that what is to come will be even less boring.

NOTES

Introduction

1. Karl Rahner and Herbert Vorgrimler, *Theological Dictionary* (New York: Herder & Herder, 1965), 93.
2. Cited in Matthew Fox, *Sheer Joy: Conversations with Thomas Aquinas on Creation Spirituality* (San Francisco: HarperSanFrancisco, 1992), 247.
3. Mary Catherine Bateson, *Composing a Life* (New York: Plume, 1990), 16.

Chapter 1

1. Personal correspondence, October 28, 1993.

Chapter 2

1. Robert Bly, *Iron John* (New York: Addison-Wesley, 1990), 127f.
2. Bly, *Iron John*, 130, 132.
3. Brendan Doyle, *Meditations with Julian of Norwich* (Santa Fe: Bear & Co., 1983), 95.
4. Doyle, *Meditations with Julian of Norwich*, 97.
5. Cited in Bly, *Iron John*, 130.
6. *Listening*, (fall 1965): 2.
7. *Listening*, (spring 1966): 150–161.
8. *Listening*, (fall 1966): 170f.
9. *Listening*, (winter 1966): 3f.
10. *Listening*, (winter 1966): 4.
11. Karl Rahner, *The Theology of the Spiritual Life*, vol. 3 of *Theological Investigations* (Baltimore: Helicon Press, 1967), 310.
12. Karl Rahner, *Theology of the Spiritual Life*, 316.
13. Matthew Fox, "The Prayer of Jesus in the New Testament and Its Significance for a Contemporary Theology of Prayer" (master's thesis, Aquinas Institute of Theology, 1967), 128f.

14. Fox, "Prayer of Jesus," 130f.
15. Personal correspondence, January 23, 1967.

Chapter 3

1. David Halberstam, *The Fifties* (New York: Villard Books, 1993), xi.

Chapter 4

1. Class notes, January 11, 1968.
2. Marie-Dominique Chenu interview: "We've Got to Get Rid of the Magic," (interviewed by Bob Reilly), *U.S. Catholic,* December 1981, 22.
3. Gary Wills, "The '60s: Tornado of Wrath," *Newsweek,* January 3, 1994, 41.
4. Working paper presented by the International Dominican Conference at Trier, Germany, 1 n. 2.
5. Working paper, 3 n. 5a.
6. Working paper, 4 n. 5d.
7. Working paper, 4 n. 6.
8. "An Open Letter to the Provincial," December 19, 1968.
9. Cited in Matthew Fox, *Religion USA: An Inquiry into Religion and Culture by Way of* Time *Magazine* (Dubuque: Listening Press, 1971), 53.
10. Fox, *Religion USA,* 8.
11. Fox, *Religion USA,* 416.
12. Fox, *Religion USA,* 431.
13. Fox, *Religion USA,* 431 n.
14. *Listening,* (spring 1968): 107, 112.
15. *Listening,* (spring 1968): 113f.
16. Ernest Hemingway, *A Moveable Feast* (New York: Charles Scribner's Sons, 1964), iii.
17. Wills, "The '60s," p. 41.

Chapter 5

1. Wills, "The '60s," 40.
2. T. S. Eliot, "Portrait of a Lady," *Collected Poems 1909–1962* (New York: Harcourt Brace Jovanovich, 1963), 21.
3. Clarissa Pinkola Estés, *Women Who Run with the Wolves* (New York: Ballantine, 1992), 351–356.
4. Matthew Fox, *On Becoming a Musical, Mystical Bear: Spirituality American Style* (New York: Paulist Press, 1972), 141.

5. Matthew Fox, *Whee! We, wee All the Way Home: A Guide to Sensual, Prophetic Spirituality* (1976; reprint, Santa Fe: Bear & Co., 1981), xxif.

6. Fox, *Musical, Mystical Bear,* xii.

7. Matthew Fox, "NCCD Papers: Religious Education and Spirituality," *The Living Light* (summer 1975): 171.

8. Fox, "NCCD Papers," 169.

9. Fox, "NCCD Papers," 171f.

10. Fox, "NCCD Papers," 195.

11. Matthew Fox, *Breakthrough: Meister Eckhart's Creation Spirituality in New Translation* (New York: Doubleday, 1980), 441.

12. Matthew Fox, *A Spirituality Named Compassion* (1979; reprint, San Francisco: HarperSanFrancisco, 1990), 168.

13. Fox, *Spirituality Named Compassion,* 140.

14. Fox, *Spirituality Named Compassion,* 104.

Chapter 6

1. Louis Cognet, *Introduction aux mystiques rheno-flamands* (Paris: Desclée, 1968), 47, 92.

2. Fox, *Breakthrough,* 472.

Chapter 7

1. William Everson, *Archetype West: The Pacific Coast as a Literary Region* (Berkeley: Oyez, 1976), 7.

2. Everson, *Archetype West,* 19.

3. Everson, *Archetype West,* 49.

4. Everson, *Archetype West,* 51f.

5. Everson, *Archetype West,* 53.

6. Everson, *Archetype West,* 18.

7. Everson, *Archetype West,* 58.

8. Everson, *Archetype West,* 57f.

9. Everson, *Archetype West,* 8.

10. Edward Schillebeeckx, *Christ* (New York: Seabury, 1980), 530.

11. Joseph Campbell with Bill Moyers, *The Power of Myth* (New York: Doubleday, 1988), 22.

12. Jaroslav Pelikan, *Jesus Through the Centuries* (New Haven, CT: Yale University Press, 1985), 1982.

13. John Dominic Crossan, *The Historical Jesus: The Life of a Mediterranean Jewish Peasant* (San Francisco: HarperSanFrancisco, 1991), 421f.

14. Robert Van de Weyer, *Celtic Fire* (London: Darton, Longman and Todd, 1990), 92.

15. Rainer Maria Rilke, *The Selected Poetry of Rainer Maria Rilke,* trans. and ed. Stephen Mitchell (New York: Vintage Books, 1984), 87.

Chapter 8

1. Introduction to "Report of the Theological Commission Appointed by the Very Rev. Damian C. Fandal, O.P., Provincial," 9.
2. "Background Materials for the Discussion with Matthew Fox, O.P.," 9.
3. The letter appeared in its entirety in *Creation Spirituality* (November-December 1988): 23–37.
4. Leonardo Boff, *Church: Charism and Power* (New York: Crossroad, 1985), 37.
5. Boff, *Church,* 38.
6. See Daniel Fogel, *Junipero Serra, the Vatican, and Enslavement Theology* (San Francisco: ISM Press, 1988).
7. Thomas Berry, "Let's Get On with the Work," *Creation Spirituality* (January-February 1989): 15, 16.
8. Robert Bly, *News of the Universe* (San Francisco: Sierra Club Books, 1980), 277.

Chapter 9

1. Rabindranath Tagore, *Gitanjali, Song #89* (New York: Macmillan, 1930), 82.
2. Len Deighton, *Winter: A Novel of a Berlin Family* (New York: Ballantine, 1987).
3. Kath Walker, "Dark Unmarried Mothers," *My People* (Brisbane: Jacaranda Press, 1970), 8.
4. Ernesto Cardenal, *Cosmic Canticle,* trans. John Lyons (Willimantic, CT: Curbstone Press, 1993).
5. Howard Heiner, "Restoring the Land," *Creation Spirituality* (March-April 1990): 21.
6. Estés, *Women Who Run with the Wolves,* 405.
7. Fox, *Sheer Joy,* 280f.

Chapter 10

1. One of the false accusations against me was that I had come out west entirely on my own without the permission of my Dominican superiors, but that is simply not true. My vicar provincial David Hynous wrote the chancellor of the diocese of Oakland requesting faculties and, after relaying some of my history, he stated that "Father Fox has the approval of his superiors to make whatever arrangements are necessary for the establishment of his Institute at Holy Names College."

[Personal correspondence from David M. Hynous, O.P., Vicar Provincial for Personnel to Rev. George E. Crespin, Chancellor, Diocese of Oakland, September 16, 1983.] When years later I showed this letter to a member of the western province he went visibly ashen and said, "I never knew such a document existed." But neither he nor any of the rumor-spreaders ever asked me or spoke to me. All this makes me remember my experience years earlier when every faculty member of GTU was represented at my public lecture on compassion *except* the Dominicans.

2. Fox, *Sheer Joy,* 474, 476, 477.

3. Fox, *Sheer Joy,* 90f.

4. Fox, *Sheer Joy,* 28.

5. Fox, *Sheer Joy,* 350–352.

Chapter 11

1. Paul Tillich, *The Protestant Era* (Chicago: University of Chicago Press, 1948), 286.

2. Tillich, *The Protestant Era,* 227.

3. Tillich, *The Protestant Era,* 227.

4. Tillich, *The Protestant Era,* 230.

5. See Henry Kamen, *Inquisition and Society in Spain* (Bloomington: Indiana University Press, 1985); Jeremy Cohen, *The Friars and the Jews: The Evolution of Medieval Anti-Judaism* (Ithaca, NY: Cornell University Press, 1982).

6. See Carl Bernstein, "The Holy Alliance," *Time* (February 24, 1992): 28–35; Martin A. Lee, "Their Will Be Done," *Mother Jones* (June 1983): 21–27; Penny Lernoux, *People of God: The Struggle for World Catholicism* (New York: Viking Press, 1989).

7. See Michael Walsh, *Opus Dei: An Investigation into the Secret Society Struggling for Power within the Roman Catholic Church* (San Francisco: HarperSanFrancisco, 1992); Don Lattin, "Opus Dei's Roots in Francisco Franco's Spain," *San Francisco Examiner,* June 1, 1986, A16.

8. See E. R. Chamberlin, *The Bad Popes* (New York: Signet, 1969).

9. Otto Rank, *Beyond Psychology* (New York: Dover, 1941), 262.

10. Yevgeny Alexandrovich Yevtushenko, "We Humiliate Ourselves," *Time,* June 27, 1988, 30.

11. See John Boswell, *Same-Sex Unions in Premodern Europe* (New York: Villard Books, 1994).

12. Cited in Peter de Rosa, *Vicars of Christ: The Dark Side of the Papacy* (New York: Crown Publishers, 1988), 204.

13. de Rosa, *Vicars of Christ*, 60–62.

14. de Rosa, *Vicars of Christ*, 58.

15. de Rosa, *Vicars of Christ*, 163f.

16. Cited in de Rosa, *Vicars of Christ*, 164.

17. de Rosa, *Vicars of Christ*, 176.

18. de Rosa, *Vicars of Christ*, 193.

19. de Rosa, *Vicars of Christ*, 195.

20. de Rosa, *Vicars of Christ*, 196.

21. Abraham Joshua Heschel, *God in Search of Man* (New York: Harper Torchbooks, 1955), 414.

Chapter 12

1. David Bohm, "Postmodern Science and a Postmodern World," *The Post-Modern Reader,* ed. Charles Jencks (New York: St. Martin's Press, 1992), 390.

2. Walter Truett Anderson, *Reality Isn't What It Used to Be* (San Francisco: HarperSanFrancisco, 1990), 257.

3. Don Lattin, "Dalai Lama Tells Truth-Seekers to Beware," *San Francisco Chronicle*, April 21, 1994, A18.

4. *The Bhagavad Gita,* trans. Juan Mascaro (Middlesex, England: Penguin Books, 1962), 119.

5. Bohm, "Postmodern Science," 13.

6. Bohm, "Postmodern Science," 13.

7. Walt Whitman, cited in William Everson, "Introduction to Leaves of Grass," *American Bard* (Santa Cruz: Lime Kiln Press, 1981), 33.

8. Heschel, *God in Search of Man,* 419.

9. Thomas Merton, *The Springs of Contemplation* (New York: Farrar, Straus & Giroux, 1992).

10. Fox, *Sheer Joy,* 351.

11. John Henry Cardinal Newman, *Apologia Pro Vita Sua* (New York: Norton, 1968), 193, 194.

12. Newman, *Apologia,* 194f.

13. Newman, *Apologia,* 149.

14. Bishop William Swing, "Let 'em Rave, for God's Sake," *Pacific Church News,* July 1994, 2.

Chapter 13

1. Antonin Artaud, *The Theater and Its Double,* trans. Mary Caroline Richards (New York: Grove Weidenfeld, 1958), 10.

2. Cited in Lee Bartlett, ed., *Earth Poetry: Selected Essays and Interviews of William Everson* (Berkeley: Oyez, 1980), 18.

3. Abraham Joshua Heschel, *The Prophets* (New York: Harper & Row, 1962), 258.

4. Bly, *Iron John,* 247.

5. Bartlett, *Earth Poetry,* 22.

6. Heschel, *God in Search of Man,* 245.

7. Frederick Turner, "Escape from Modernism," *Sacred Interconnections,* ed. David Griffith (Albany, NY: State University of New York Press, 1990), 157. Italics mine.

8. Turner, "Escape from Modernism," 157.

9. Bartlett, *Earth Poetry,* 17.

10. Rahner, *Theology of the Spiritual Life,* 311.

11. Fox, *Sheer Joy,* 419.

12. Charles Jencks, *The Architecture of the Jumping Universe* (London: Academy, 1995), 40, 41.

13. "Rave Drug Could Damage Brain," *San Francisco Chronicle,* August 15, 1995, A7. The study was published in the August issue of *The Journal of Neuroscience* and was supported by the National Institute of Drug Abuse. The drug may have long-term harmful effects on appetite, sleep, mood, impulsiveness, and other functions.

14. Arthur Rubenstein, *My Young Years* (New York: Popular Library, 1973), 488.

Grateful acknowledgment is made to the following for permission to reprint copyrighted material:

To Darton, Longman and Todd, Ltd. and Doubleday Dell Publishing Group, Inc. for excerpts from *Celtic Fire* by Robert van de Weyer. Copyright © 1990. Used by permission of Doubleday, a division of Bantam Doubleday Dell Publishing Group, Inc.

To Faber and Faber Limited and Harcourt Brace & Co. for an excerpt from "Portrait of a Lady" in *Collected Poems 1909–1962* by T. S. Eliot. Copyright © 1936 by Harcourt Brace & Co. Copyright © 1964, 1963 by T. S. Eliot, reprinted by permission of the publisher.

To Farrar, Straus & Giroux, Inc. for an excerpt from *The School of Charity: The Letters of Thomas Merton on Religious Renewal and Spiritual Direction,* selected and edited by Brother Patrick Hart. Copyright © 1990 by the Merton Legacy Trust. Reprinted by permission of Farrar, Straus & Giroux, Inc.

To Simon & Schuster for excerpts from "Song #89" of *Gitanjali* by Rabindranath Tagore. Reprinted by permission of Simon & Schuster from *Gitanjali* by Rabindranath Tagore (New York: Collier, 1971).

To Sierra Club Books for the poem "Mirabai," version by Robert Bly from *News of the Universe* by Robert Bly. Copyright © 1980 by Robert Bly. Reprinted by permission of Sierra Club Books.

To The William Everson Estate for an excerpt from a letter by William Everson, dated May 10, 1993. Reprinted by permission of the William Everson Estate.

To M. C. Richards for permission to cite her poem "Silence!" All rights reserved to the author.

To Melidoma Some for permission to cite from his letter.

To Shana Weber for permission to cite from her letter.